1 9 8 9 — 1 9 9 0

AMERICAN DEFENSE

D·E·F·E·N·S·E

A N N U A L

WITH~~~

Edited by
Joseph Kruzel

Mershon Center
The Ohio State University

Lexington Books
D.C. Heath and Company/Lexington, Massachusetts/Toronto

1989–90 *AMERICAN DEFENSE ANNUAL*
Photo Credits

The cover art for Chapter 2 is the Battle of Granson from the Schodoler Chronicles, Kantonsbibliothek, Aarau, Switzerland. The photo in Chapter 3 is provided by Wide World Photos. The interior photo in Chapter 4 is provided by the Department of the Air Force. The photos in Chapter 6 are courtesy of the Department of the Navy. The Department of the Army provided the cover photos in Chapter 7 and Chapter 8, and the photo for the book cover. The pictures in the collage in Chapter 9 are provided by the various services and the Department of Defense. The artwork in Chapter 11 was inspired by similar works in the Army Times and was recreated, with the permission of the Army Times, by Thomas Slayton. The Army Times also provided the cover photo in Chapter 5 and the interior photo in Chapter 7. General Dynamics graciously provided the cover photo in Chapter 12. The remaining photos are courtesy of the Department of Defense.

The Library of Congress has cataloged this serial title as follows:

American defense annual. — 1985–1986–   — Lexington, Mass.: Lexington Books, c1985–
    v.;28 cm.
    Annual.
    Sponsored by the Mershon Center at Ohio State University.
    ISSN 0882-1038 = American defense annual.

    1. United States—Defenses—Yearbooks.   I. Mershon Center for Education in National Security.
II. Title: American defense.
UA23.A1A47   355′.033073—dc19   85-646241   AACR 2   MARC-S

Library of Congress [8511]

Published simultaneously in Canada
Printed in the United States of America
Casebound International Standard Book Number: 0-669-21118-4
Paperbound International Standard Book Number: 0-669-21119-2
Library of Congress Catalog Card Number 85-646241

The paper used in this publication meets the minimum requirements of American National Standard for Information Sciences—Permanence of Paper for Printed Library Materials, ANSI Z39.48-1984. ∞™

Year and number of this printing:

89 90 91 92 10 9 8 7 6 5 4 3 2 1

Contents

Illustrations

Figures

Photographs

Chapter Art

Tables

Preface and Acknowledgments

his is the fifth edition of the *American Defense Annual*. All of us associated with the series are gratified to see that a critical review of contemporary U.S. security policy has found a secure niche in the defense literature. The *Annual* has been adopted as a textbook by scores of colleges and universities and has found a growing readership among defense professionals and attentive nonexperts who want to know more about the issues facing the United States in a changing strategic environment.

The *American Defense Annual* is quite deliberately a critique of defense policy, an exploration of alternatives to the prevailing wisdom. No useful purpose would be served by restating and applauding the defense rationale of the incumbent administration. In any case, such a justification is already provided by the *Annual Report* of the secretary of defense, a document designed to sell the defense budget. Free of such constraint, the *American Defense Annual* is able to raise questions about the assumptions underlying U.S. defense policy and the manner of implementing American security objectives. No reader will agree with everything presented in this book but everyone should find much of value. I hope that these chapters stimulate public awareness and informed debate of the vital issues in contemporary U.S. security policy.

Given my additional administrative responsibilities this year, preparation of this volume of the *American Defense Annual* fell heavily on Mark Wayda and Don Lair, invaluable colleagues whose title of research assistant belies their critical role in every aspect of this enterprise. They edited and reviewed all the chapters, prepared the appendixes, located the photographs, developed the graphics, and generally managed the flow of drafts, correspondence, and other material that eventually yielded this finished product. Our colleagues at the Mershon Center, many of whom have detailed knowledge of security issues and broad experience in the U.S. defense community, critiqued these chapters in draft form and made many useful comments and suggestions.

The inventive and patient staff of Telcomp Graphic Designs is responsible for the overall layout that contributes so much to the readability of the *Annual*. We also gratefully acknowledge the assistance of the Department of Defense and the individual military services for providing many of the photographs used in the *Annual*.

Our publisher, Lexington Books, continues to show extraordinary flexibility and exemplary forbearance in helping to devise a production schedule permitting the *Annual* to appear in timely fashion.

Finally, I am pleased to acknowledge our continuing debt to the John D. and Catherine T. MacArthur Foundation, whose generous grant has made possible publication of this edition of the *American Defense Annual*.

Glossary and Abbreviations

AAW Antiair warfare.

ABM Antiballistic missile.

ABM Treaty This 1972 treaty between the United States and the Soviet Union culminated SALT I. Amended by a 1974 protocol, the treaty limits ballistic missile defense systems in each country to one site with 100 ABM launchers and missiles. The treaty also restricts the location and number of phased-array radar systems to be deployed and the development of new ABM systems at the flight testing stage and beyond. The United States does not deploy an ABM system as allowed under the treaty, but doubts about future compliance have arisen because of the U.S. Strategic Defense Initiative, the Soviet construction of a new phased-array radar system at Krasnoyarsk, and U.S. improvements in its own early warning radar net.

ACM Advanced cruise missile.

AFAP Atomic Field Artillery Projectile.

ARG Amphibious ready group.

ASAT (antisatellite) Any system that attempts to render enemy satellites inoperable.

ASW (antisubmarine warfare) Any operations conducted with the intent of destroying or denying the adversary effective use of its submarines.

ATA Advanced tactical aircraft.

ATB (advanced technology bomber) Also known as the B–2 Stealth bomber, this aircraft is the planned penetrating bomber of the 1990s. Plans call for approximately 130 aircraft with an initial operational capability in 1991 or 1992. The initial rollout and public display of the aircraft occurred in November 1988. The aircraft is being built by Northrop Corporation.

ATBM   Antitactical ballistic missile.

ATF   Advanced tactical fighter.

AVF   All-volunteer force.

BBBG   Battleship battle group.

Budget authority   For the Pentagon the amount Congress authorizes it to spend, or become contractually obligated to spend, each fiscal year.

Budget outlays   For the Pentagon, the expenditures made in any fiscal year.

C^{3}I (command, control, communications, and intelligence)   The coordinating functions of a military headquarters, either at a battlefield or a national strategic level.

Carter Doctrine   The declaration, by President Carter in the State of the Union Address of January 1980, that the protection of Southwest Asia and the Persian Gulf was in the vital interest of the United States. He requested that the Rapid Deployment Force (now CENTCOM) be created to protect these interests.

CAS   Close air support.

CFE (Conventional Forces in Europe talks)   Previously known as the Conventional Stability Talks (CST), they were renamed in early 1989.

CBO   Congressional Budget Office.

CENTAG   Central Army Group.

CENTCOM   Central Command.

CIC (Combat information center)   The area of a warship dedicated to the collection and coordination of information vital to the performance of the ship in battle.

CINCs (Commanders-in-Chief)   Unified and specified commanders.

Conventional weapons   All instruments of war except nuclear weapons, biological weapons, and most chemical weapons. Incendiary and riot-control chemical weapons are considered conventional weapons.

Counterforce   A term of nuclear strategy that denotes the targeting of enemy military forces, both nuclear and conventional, rather than industrial and population centers. Counterforce targets include strategic C^{3}I operations.

Countervalue   A strategic concept that entails the targeting of civilian population and industrial centers, with the goal of disrupting or destroying the social structure of the enemy state. Countervalue strategy is the foundation of mutual assured destruction.

CRAF   Civil reserve air fleet.

Crisis stability   A condition in which even during the most intense political confrontation there is no incentive for a state to launch an attack because enough of its opponent's military forces will survive to inflict unacceptable damage on the initiator.

Cruise missile A guided missile that maintains a constant velocity once launched and does not leave the atmosphere. A cruise missile is capable of delivering both conventional and nuclear warheads. The first cruise missiles were the V-1 rockets used by Nazi Germany late in World War II.

CTB Comprehensive Test Ban.

CVBG Carrier battle group.

DACOWITS Department of Defense Advisory Committee on Women in the Services.

DCA (dual capable aircraft) Aircraft that are designed to carry either conventional or nuclear payloads.

DD Destroyer.

DDG Guided-missile destroyer.

DOD Department of Defense.

Dual Track Decision The decision made at a meeting of NATO foreign and defense ministers on December 12, 1979, that approved the deployment of 108 PERSHING II and 464 ground-launched cruise missiles in Europe under American control. The ministers also called for arms control negotiations between the United States and the Soviet Union that could limit or even prevent this deployment.

EUCOM European Command.

EMP (electromagnetic pulse) A pulse of radio frequency energy resulting from asymmetric ionization of the atmosphere after a nuclear explosion. A high-altitude nuclear blast can blanket a large area of the earth's surface, severely damaging unprotected electrical equipment.

ERIS Exoatmospheric reentry vehicle interception system.

Fiscal year A term used to define the accounting cycle of an organizational budget. For the U.S. government, the fiscal year runs from October 1 to September 30. Thus, FY 1989 runs from October 1, 1989 to September 30, 1990.

Flexible response A strategic concept that gained prominence during the Kennedy administration. The strategy entails developing a military force structure capable of responding to varying types and degrees of crisis or confrontation. Originally a response to the Eisenhower administration's apparent reliance on massive retaliation.

FOFA (follow-on forces attack) A NATO doctrine developed under the supervision of General Bernard Rogers, SACEUR, for possible use in Central Europe. FOFA emphasizes deep air strikes against enemy second-echelon forces.

FYDP (Five-Year Defense Plan) The five-year budget requirements projection established yearly by the Defense Department. The FYDP is a planning document, not binding on either the Defense Department or Congress, because funding is appropriated on a yearly basis.

GAO (General Accounting Office) An independent nonpolitical agency in the legislative branch of the U.S. federal government. Its responsibilities include legal, accounting, auditing, and claims settlement functions within the federal government and as assigned by Congress. It also recommends ways to make government operations more effective and efficient.

Gates Commission   A commission established by President Nixon and headed by former Secretary of Defense Thomas S. Gates. The commission's report in 1970 called for the draft to be replaced by an all-volunteer force that would rely on market inducements to attract recruits.

GLCM (ground-launched cruise missile)   See *cruise missile*.

GWEN   Ground wave emergency network.

Hard target   A site constructed to withstand the blast and associated effects of a nuclear attack and likely to be protected against a chemical, biological, or radiological attack. Most often used to denote an ICBM missile site.

HASC   House Armed Services Committee.

ICBM (intercontinental ballistic missile)   A ballistic missile with a range capability from about 3,000 to 8,000 nautical miles.

INF (intermediate nuclear forces)   Forces with a range capability greater than tactical nuclear weapons and less than intercontinental nuclear forces. INF includes intermediate-range ballistic missiles, medium-range ballistic missiles, ground-launched cruise missiles, and medium-range bombers.

INF Treaty   An agreement between the United States and the Soviet Union that entered into force in June 1988, it calls for the elimination of U.S. Pershing II missiles and ground-launched cruise missiles stationed in Europe and the elimination of Soviet intermediate-range forces from all theaters. It has been hailed as the first agreement to eliminate an entire class of nuclear weapons.

IRBM (intermediate-range ballistic missiles)   A ballistic missile with a range capability from about 1,500 to 3,000 nautical miles.

JCS   Joint Chiefs of Staff.

JTFME   Joint Task Force Middle East.

LCAC   Landing craft air cushioned.

LIC   Low-intensity conflict.

LID   Light infantry division.

Long-range bomber aircraft   A bomber designed for a tactical operating radius over 2,500 nautical miles at design gross weight and bomb load.

LRINF   Long-range intermediate-range nuclear forces.

LTBT (Limited Test Ban Treaty)   A 1963 agreement by the United States, Great Britain, and the Soviet Union that prohibits nuclear weapons tests in the atmosphere, in outer space, and underwater. The treaty is considered a hallmark event in nuclear arms control.

MAB   Marine amphibious brigade.

MAC   Military Airlift Command.

MAD   See *mutually assured destruction*.

MAF   Marine amphibious force.

MAG   Marine air group.

MAGTF   Marine air-ground task force.

Maritime strategy   The U.S. Navy's strategic policy emphasizing broad-based offensive actions in the event of sustained war against the Soviet Union. There are three prominent themes: aggressive protection of sea-lines of communication, especially the North Atlantic route that would be used in carrying supplies to NATO forces; a large-scale sea and air campaign in the Pacific to divert Soviet resources and to attack Soviet vital interests; and a great emphasis on the quick and effective nullification of the Soviet submarine threat through an intensive ASW campaign. The Navy's maritime strategy also places great emphasis on interservice tactics and operations and the adept use of the Marine Corps' mobile projection forces.

MAU   Marine amphibious unit.

MBFR (Mutual and Balanced Force Reductions)   Now-cancelled negotiations in Vienna, which began in 1973, with the goal of reducing NATO and Warsaw Pact conventional forces in Central Europe. MBFR negotiations stalemated on two issues. The first was the question of counting the existing troops. The United States claimed Warsaw Pact forces outnumbered NATO forces by approximately 300,000 men, while the Soviet Union claimed that the two sides had roughly equivalent numbers of troops in Central Europe. In 1986 the United States gave up its insistence that the numbers issue be settled before the talks moved on, but Soviet obstinacy on verification issues continued the stalemate.

MC 14/2 (Military Committee 14/2)   The NATO decision document, approved in 1956, by which the alliance formally adopted the strategy of massive retaliation. This strategy relied heavily on the use of nuclear weapons for the defense of western Europe.

MC 14/3 (Military Committee 14/3)   The NATO decision document, approved in 1967, by which the alliance formally adopted the strategy of flexible response. This strategy called for the NATO nations to confront the Warsaw Pact with a range of capabilities, including stronger conventional forces, tactical nuclear weapons, and American strategic nuclear weapons, thus allowing a variety of responses to Soviet aggression against Western Europe.

Megatonnage   The explosive yield of a nuclear weapon in terms of millions of tons of TNT equivalents.

Midgetman   A mobile, single-warhead missile, weighing approximately 37,000 pounds, proposed as the complement to the MX missile in the land-based portion of the U.S. strategic triad. The Midgetman is in the testing stage.

MILSTAR (military strategic and tactical relay system)   A network of satellites designed to provide a communications link between the national command authority and the military forces during a nuclear war.

Minuteman   A three-stage solid propellant ballistic missile that serves as the foundation of the ICBM portion of the U.S. strategic triad. The Minuteman II is a single-warhead missile; the Minuteman III is equipped with three MIRVed warheads.

MIRV (multiple independently-targetable reentry vehicle)   A reentry vehicle carried by a delivery system that can place one or more reentry vehicles over each of several targets.

MLRS (multiple launcher rocket system)   Part of the Emerging Technologies

Initiative, the MLRS is a self-propelled artillery piece that can ripplefire twelve rockets in less than a minute, at targets up to 30 to 60 kilometers away.

Mutual assured destruction (MAD)   A declaratory U.S. nuclear strategic doctrine initiated during the tenure of Defense Secretary Robert S. McNamara that remained prevalent during the 1960s and 1970s. The fundamental premise is that each side in a bilateral nuclear relationship retain a second-strike capability that could devastate the industrial and population centers of the enemy should that enemy initiate a nuclear first strike. The prelaunch nuclear standoff would then create a situation of mutual deterrence.

MX (also known as the Peacekeeper missile)   Most recent addition to the ICBM portion of the U.S. strategic triad. The MX weighs 190,000 pounds, carries ten warheads plus decoys, and has a range of over 8,100 miles. The MX is highly accurate, with a Circular Error Probable (CEP) of approximately 165 yards.

NASA   National Aeronautics and Space Administration.

NATO   North Atlantic Treaty Organization.

NCA   National Command Authority.

NDU   National Defense University.

NORTHAG   Northern Army Group.

NSC   National Security Council.

Nuclear Risk Reduction Centers   On September 15, 1987, U.S. Secretary of State George Schultz and Soviet Foreign Minister Eduard Shevardnadze signed an agreement establishing these facilities in Moscow and Washington. The centers are staffed by personnel from the host country and serve as transmission and receiving points for notifications and exchanges of information to prevent nuclear war by miscalculation, accident, or misunderstanding.

O&M   Operations and maintenance.

O&S   Operations and support.

OMB   Office of Management and Budget.

OSD   Office of the Secretary of Defense.

Packard Commission (President's Blue Ribbon Commission on Defense Management)   A bipartisan commission established by President Reagan on June 17, 1985, to review Pentagon procurement practices. David Packard, an industrialist and former deputy secretary of defense, headed the commission. The major proposal was the centralization of all Defense Department procurement responsibilities under the authority of a new under secretary of defense for acquisition, a step the president ordered the Defense Department to begin to implement on April 2, 1986.

PACOM   Pacific Command.

PAL (permissive action link)   The lock placed on American nuclear weapons to prevent their unauthorized use. Early generation PALs consisted of simple physical impediments to access, specifically designed for shortrange systems in the European theater. Later generation PALs are electronic locks requiring special numerical codes and featuring limited try options. All U.S. nuclear weapons, except those controlled by the Navy, are equipped with PALs.

PGM (precision-guided munition)   Popularly known as "smart bombs." Electronically programmed and controlled weapons that can accurately hit a moving or stationary target.

POMCUS   Prepositioned overseas material configured in unit sets.

PPBS   Planning, programming, and budgeting system.

Presidential Directive 59 (PD-59)   The National Security Council decision document that modified official U.S. nuclear strategy. It was signed by President Carter in July 1980 and called for a countervailing strategy that would allow limited nuclear options in case of a limited Soviet attack.

Projection forces   Military units capable of rapid and sustained deployment, with the ability to wage low-intensity conflict. The Marines, forces of the Central Command, special operations forces in any of the services, airlift and sealift forces, or any combination of these constitute U.S. projection forces.

ROTC   Reserve Officer Training Corps.

RV   Reentry vehicle.

SAC   Strategic Air Command.

SACEUR   Supreme Allied Commander Europe.

SAG   Surface Action Group.

SALT I (Strategic Arms Limitations Talks I)   The SALT I agreements, signed by President Richard Nixon and Soviet leader Leonid Brezhnev in 1972, include the ABM Treaty (see *ABM Treaty*) and an Interim Agreement limiting offensive nuclear forces up to 1977. The 1977 deadline was extended while the follow-on SALT II negotiations continued.

SALT II   Continuation of strategic arms negotiations resulting in a 1979 accord never ratified by the U.S. Senate. During the Carter administration, verification problems, the "discovery" of a Soviet brigade in Cuba, and the Soviet invasion of Afghanistan stalled SALT II ratification, but the United States and the Soviet Union continued formal compliance with what President Reagan termed a "fatally flawed" treaty until 1986. In 1986 Reagan announced that because of Soviet violations of SALT II, he no longer felt compelled to continue U.S. compliance. In an effort to meet the challenge of MIRVing that SALT I did not address, SALT II constraints included a limit of 2,400 strategic nuclear vehicles (to be reduced to 2,250 after ratification), 1,320 of which could be MIRVed. Other constraints effectively limited the number of warheads on each missile to the greatest number tested up to the signing date, with any new ICBM limited to a maximum of ten. Additionally, only one new ICBM model could be introduced to each side's arsenal, and to increase verification procedures telemetry encryption was to be limited during missile tests.

SASC   Senate Armed Services Committee.

Scowcroft Commission   In early 1983 President Reagan ordered formation of a commission to investigate the future of the U.S. strategic triad. Lieutenant General Brent Scowcroft, national security adviser during the Ford administration, headed

A M E R I C A N   D E F E N S E   A N N U A L   1 9 8 9 – 1 9 9 0

the commission in its effort to discover whether a "window of vulnerability" existed for U.S. strategic nuclear forces. The commission did find that the ICBM portion of the strategic triad was vulnerable and suggested a broad range of pragmatic designs to make land-based missiles more survivable and more stabilizing, including development of the mobile Small Intercontinental Ballistic Missile (SICBM) in concert with the deployment of 100 MX missiles and a renewed emphasis on arms control efforts.

SDI   Strategic Defense Initiative.

SEAL   Navy sea-air-land special forces teams.

SIOP (single integrated operational plan)   The U.S. contingency plan for strategic retaliatory strikes in the event of a nuclear war. Targets, timing, tactics, and force requirements are considered for a variety of responses. The SIOP is prepared by the Joint Strategic Target Planning Staff located at SAC headquarters.

SLBM   Submarine-launched ballistic missile.

SLCM (sea-launched cruise missile)   See *cruise missile.*

SLOC(s)   Sea line(s) of communication.

SOF   Special operations forces.

SOLIC   Special operations and low-intensity conflict.

SOPAG   Special Operations Policy Advisory Group.

SOSUS   Sound surveillance system.

Specified Command   A command that is normally composed of forces from a single service. The Strategic Air Command is an example.

SSBN   A nuclear-powered ballistic missile-carrying submarine.

SSN   An attack submarine.

START (Strategic Arms Reductions Talks)   The acronym introduced by President Reagan for his version of arms control talks, which emphasized the need for militarily significant reductions. The START negotiations began in June 1982.

Theater   The geographical area outside the continental United States for which a commander of a unified or specified command has been assigned military responsibilities. In the *American Defense Annual,* the term has been narrowed to a focus on forces outside the strategic nuclear triad and not involved in purely naval exercises.

TLAM (Tomahawk land attack missile)   See *SLCM.* This is another designation for the conventionally-armed version of the Tomahawk SLCM.

TLAM/N   Designation for nuclear-armed Tomahawk SLCM.

Triad   The foundation of U.S. nuclear deterrence policy, the triad consists of the U.S. Navy's ballistic missile submarine force and the U.S. Air Force's ICBM and strategic bomber forces. The underlying principle of the U.S. triad remains the assured second-strike capability of at least one of the three strategic forces following an enemy nuclear attack.

Trident II   Latest U.S. SLBM, also called the D-5, it combines the survivability of the submarine basing mode with the accuracy and throwweight of ICBMs, making it the first hard-target capable submarine-based ballistic missile.

TTBT (Threshold Test Ban Treaty)   A 1974 agreement between the United States and the Soviet Union that prohibits underground nuclear tests above 150 kilotons. The treaty has not been ratified by the U.S. Senate, but both parties are obligated under international law to fulfill the treaty's stipulations. Recently the United States has proposed improved verification procedures for the TTBT because of concern that the Soviet Union has violated the 150 kiloton threshold.

UMT   Universal military training.

Unified command   A command in which the commander has at his disposal the forces of two or more services usually within a geographic area. The Pacific Command is an example.

USD/A   Under secretary of defense for acquisition.

USSOCOM   U.S. Special Operations Command.

USTRANSCOM   U.S. Transportation Command.

VLS   Vertical launch system.

V/STOL   Vertical and/or short take-off and landing.

War Powers Act   Passed in 1973, this act requires that the president consult with Congress before committing military forces to actual or imminent hostilities and that he formally inform Congress within forty-eight hours of their introduction. Congress must then approve or disapprove of the deployment within sixty days, although this period can be stretched to ninety days if the president certifies that the safety of the troops requires it.

Wing   An Air Force unit composed of one primary mission group and the necessary supporting organizations.

Zero Option   The Reagan administration's original negotiating position in the INF talks was offered by Ronald Reagan in a November 1981 speech. It called for the elimination of all intermediate-range nuclear missiles from the Soviet and American arsenals and formed the basis for the INF Treaty.

Chapter 1

Perspectives

Joseph Kruzel

Military-to-Military Talks

In the nuclear age Clemenceau's comment about war being too important to be left to the generals can be turned on its head: when there is no clear dividing line between political and military issues, peace is also too important to be left to the diplomats. Military adversaries ought to talk to each other. There is a shared culture, a common vernacular, and a professional bond that can make military-to-military communication less formal and sometimes more productive than diplomatic dialogue. Some candid and useful conversations in the strategic arms control process have taken place between the military members of the U.S. and Soviet delegations.

It was encouraging to see in the late 1980s the beginning of an institutionalized and open-ended channel of communication that ended four decades of little direct contact between the U.S. and Soviet defense communities. (Defense Secretary Harold Brown met Defense Minister Dmitri Ustinov and Marshal Nikolai Ogarkov during the 1979 Carter-Brezhnev summit, but the dialogue did not continue during the Weinberger years at the Pentagon.)

During the December 1987 Reagan-Gorbachev summit, the chairman of the Joint Chiefs of Staff, Admiral William Crowe, gave Marshal Sergei Akhromeyev a tour of the Pentagon, including an unprecedented visit to the National Military Command Center, a place few U.S. civilians have ever seen. In March 1988 Secretary of Defense Frank Carlucci conferred in Switzerland with his Soviet counterpart, Defense Minister Dmitri Yazov, a meeting that produced no breakthrough but did, according to the participants, establish a "bridge of communication." In July Admiral Crowe again hosted Marshal Akhromeyev, this time for a week-long tour of U.S. military installations and selected tourist sites, including a stop at a Cherokee Indian reservation. Despite some resistance from the State Department, Crowe was ultimately authorized to enter substantive discussions with Akhromeyev. The week ended with a meeting at the Council on Foreign Relations at which Akhromeyev was interrogated for ninety minutes by scions of the U.S. establishment.

In a more modest but also encouraging venture, the U.S. Army announced in early 1989 that it was beginning an exchange of cadets between West Point and a military academy in the Soviet Union.[1] Ten to twelve cadets from each side, all with a working knowledge of the other country's language, will exchange visits that will last about two weeks. News of this program came as a great surprise to many service academy graduates who can remember when the idea of exchanges between West Point, Annapolis, and the Air Force Academy seemed a daring innovation.

Open-ended discussions at the top of the chain of command are not likely to produce formal agreements, and bull sessions among cadets will not end the arms race, but such conversations will give each side an opportunity to present its objectives, defend its philosophy, and raise questions about the programs and policies of the other country. The United States should do all it can to encourage such dialogue; it has much to gain from the practice and little to lose. In democratic societies defense budgets, posture statements, and five-year plans are published and vigorously debated, but totalitarian governments afford few opportunities for outsiders to see their policy- and budget-making process at work. Any chance to probe the Soviets on policy, doctrine,

and force decisions will increase U.S. understanding of an otherwise opaque process. The result will be a better appreciation of the military confrontation and the respective concerns of the two parties. Routine talks among military people may well reduce the risk of accidents, incidents, and unintended provocations. They may even lead to the establishment of informal confidence-building measures, a useful step.

The Military Base Structure

The year 1988 will be remembered as the one in which Congress finally devised a way to close unneeded domestic military bases. In October Congress passed a law directing the secretary of defense to set up a committee of outside experts—business and environmental leaders, retired lawmakers, defense analysts, and retired officers—to recommend a list of bases to be closed. If Congress agreed to forward the list to the president and the president concurred, the law mandated that the recommendations automatically take effect. Neither the president nor Congress could make changes to the list. Congress could reject the whole package but not haggle over individual bases.

The process was followed to the letter. The commission was established, toiled away in secret, and eventually produced a list recommending the closing or severe curtailing of activities at eleven major military bases and eighty other installations around the country. Congress approved the package; the president supported it; and the closings were scheduled to begin in 1990, thirteen years after the last U.S. military base was closed.

The commission considered a number of criteria, including the ease of relocating the missions assigned to the base, the local economic and environmental impact of closure, and the physical condition of the base. The panel's report emphasized that military value was the primary consideration in determining which bases to close, but members were also constrained by the requirement to show that the cost of closing an installation could be recouped within six years.[2] This obligation, contained in the panel's charter, had the paradoxical effect of retaining some facilities whose closure could have resulted in great long-run savings but would also have entailed significant one-time costs in shutting down. The best example of such a facility was Fort Monroe, Virginia, routinely cited in articles about unnecessary bases but kept off the final list because the costs of removing old shells and other waste could not have been recouped within the required span of six years.[3]

Congressman Dick Armey (R–Texas), the author of the base closing bill, claimed before the final list was produced that the closings could save $2 billion to $5 billion a year, but the commission estimated that the various terminations and realignments would actually save less than $700 million a year—about two-tenths of 1 percent of the annual defense budget, or slightly more than the projected cost of one B-2 bomber. This is a modest sum only by comparison; in an era of fiscal austerity, any defense savings is good news. The base closings also held the hope of improving interservice cooperation by forcing the individual services to consolidate their separate functions.

Although improvements in efficiency are always welcome, the U.S. domestic military base structure should not be determined by narrow calculations of economic costs and benefits. Military bases serve other needs and yield additional benefits that cannot be easily measured simply in terms of military efficiency and dollars pumped into local economies. Military posts give civilians a familiarity with their military, as well as some sense of a return on their substantial investment in defense. How many Americans, in the course of an average week, ever see a serviceman in uniform? West Germany is host to a quarter-million U.S. GIs; its citizens are far more likely than most Americans to encounter U.S. soldiers.

With over 3,000 individual military facilities scattered across the United States, some bases obviously needed to be closed. A number of them existed only as the result of congressional pressure that made closing politically untouchable. Many had outlived their original purpose and were no longer able to perform a useful role. Fort Douglas, Utah, reduced to 119 acres in Salt Lake City, was too small to accommodate any significant military function. While closing facilities that are increasingly hemmed in by

---

Not all pro-military support is gratitude for the dollars that military installations bring to the civilian economy. There is an intrinsic relationship between a military presence and support for the military.

---

commercial development may make economic and military sense, it also serves to increase the physical and psychic isolation of the U.S. military from civilian society. Few U.S. bases are near big cities. As the population becomes more urbanized, the military finds itself increasingly confined to the hinterlands. Dollars are saved and military efficiency may be improved, but the unintended and enduring consequence is that fewer Americans will have any regular and direct contact with the men and women sworn to defend them.

Defense facilities should be spread around the United States. They provide civilian support jobs and a stream of money spent in the local area that is virtually immune to fluctuations in the national economy, but not all promilitary support is gratitude for the dollars that military installations bring to the civilian economy. There is an intrinsic relationship between a military presence and support for the military.

Most Americans think the country pays too much for defense, but most Americans do not know anyone in the military. Most can readily cite examples of fraud, waste, and abuse in the military—the infamous $100 hammers and $600 toilet seats—but few know dedicated servicemen and women who work long hours at hard jobs in the service of their country.

Before the base closings were announced, legislators from the Northeast and Midwest had feared that their bases would be particularly hard hit and urged the commission to consider existing "regional inequities" in its decisions. Their worst fear did not materialize; Rust Belt states were not singled out for special treatment (see figure 1-1). Nonetheless, the base closings did marginally increase existing regional inequities in favor of the South. Overall, southern states realized a net gain of over 1,000 new jobs as a result of positions transferred from closed installations in other regions.[4] According to the Pentagon, about one-third of the military's major installations are located in the

Figure 1-1. Facilities Targeted for Closure or Realignment.

⭕ Army

1. Umatilla Army Depot, for realignment
2. Presidio of San Francisco, to close
3. Hamilton Army Airfield, to close
4. Fort Douglas, to close
5. Pueblo Army Depot, for realignment
6. Navajo Depot Activity, to close
7. Fort Wingate, to close
8. Kapalama Military Reservation Phase III, to close
9. Fort Des Moines, to close in part
10. Nike Kansas City 30, to close
11. Fort Sheridan, to close
12. New Orleans Military Ocean Terminal, to close
13. Pontiac Storage Facility, to close
14. Jefferson Proving Ground, to close
15. Lexington Depot, to close
16. Coosa River Annex, to close
17. Alabama Ammunition Plant, to close
18. Army Material Technology Laboratory, to close
19. Tacony Warehouse, to close
20. Fort Dix, to semi-active status
21. Nike Philadelphia 41/43, to close
22. Former Nike Site Aberdeen, to close
23. Fort Meade, to close in part
24. Fort Holabird, to close in part
25. Cameron Station, to close
26. Cape St. George, to close

An additional 52 stand-alone housing installations in 13 states, to close.

◻ Navy

1. Naval Station Puget Sound, to close
2. Naval Station San Francisco, not to be constructed
3. Naval Station Galveston, to close
4. Naval Station Lake Charles, to close
5. Naval Station New York, to close
6. Naval Hospital Philadelphia, to close

◇ Air Force

1. Mather AFB, to close
2. George AFB, to close
3. Norton AFB, to close
4. Chanute AFB, to close
5. Pease AFB, to close

△ Other facilities

1. Salton Sea Test Base, to close
2. Bennett Army National Guard Facility, to close
3. Indiana Army Ammunition Plant, to close in part
4. Army Reserve Center Gaithersburg, to close
5. Defense Mapping Agency, to close
6. Naval Reserve Center, to close

Source: Data from DOD Summary of the Report of the Commission on Base Realignment and Closure.

South, along with more than 40 percent of the Department of Defense's (DOD) military and civilian work force. With retirement pay included, over half of the country's military payroll goes to residents of the South.

There are practical and historical reasons for this favoritism. Good weather makes the South a favored location for pilot training and military maneuvers, and the South has traditionally provided a congenial social environment for the military. The long tenure of southerners in key positions on Capitol Hill also ensured that the region was treated well in the allocation of military resources. Congressman Mendel Rivers, long-time chairman of the House Armed Services Committee, left his native Charleston and surrounding areas well fortified with military facilities when he retired; Senate Armed Services Committee chairman Richard Russell made certain that Georgia was not overlooked in the awarding of facilities and weapons contracts, a supervisory responsibility now discharged with equal acumen by his great-nephew, Senator Sam Nunn.

There is no sinister intent in any of this, but such regional disparities do have disturbing sociological and philosophical implications. Since the advent of the All-Volunteer Force, the U.S. military has become an increasingly unrepresentative body. The military services have struggled over the years to offer equal opportunity to females and to make the composition of the officers corps more reflective of the racial composition of society at large. But there is a sharp regional disparity in accessions to the military that attracts much less attention, and it is almost certainly a consequence of the maldistribution of military bases around the United States.

When most local communities and their elected representatives raised a predictable cry of outrage over base closures, Pentagon officials were quick to point out that base

'THIS WOULDN'T BE HAPPENING IF WE WERE A SAVINGS AND LOAN.'

closings do not have to be an economic disaster. Many communities have benefited from converting bases to industrial parks or commercial airports. Larson Air Force Base, Washington, provided 38 civilian jobs before it closed in 1966; it now supports over 800 workers in a pilot training center, an aircraft testing site, a community college, a housing development, a municipal airport and an industrial park.[5] At least one base closing was greeted with great local enthusiasm. The conversion of Pease Air Force Base, New Hampshire, to a regional airport will provide much-needed relief to Boston's congested Logan Airport and spur regional economic development. A Pentagon study released with the base closing report found that among the 100 base closings between 1961 and 1986, 93,000 civilian jobs were lost, but 138,000 new ones were created.

In a remarkable "additional view" appended to the report, former senator Thomas Eagleton felt moved to criticize the Navy for lack of cooperation in the base closing exercise. "The Air Force ultimately gave its cooperation. The Army begrudgingly gave its reluctant cooperation. The Navy stonewalled and got away with it. Intransigence paid off," Eagleton wrote. "When the new secretary of defense looks to further base closings . . . he should most certainly start with the Navy."[6]

The base closing initiative may also be remembered as the signal achievement of Frank Carlucci's fourteen-month tenure as secretary of defense. Without Carlucci's support, the idea would never have moved forward.

Defense Policy in the Bush Administration

There was little doubt that the defense establishment left by outgoing President Ronald Reagan was far better equipped and trained than the force he inherited. The great Reagan buildup was needed and did leave its mark. Ironically, however, the old charge of the late 1970s—that the United States was fielding a "hollow Army" and other deficient fighting units—was heard again in the late 1980s. The major challenge facing the Bush administration was how to fund the procurements begun during the Reagan years without crippling training, maintenance, and improvements in military personnel built up during the 1980s.

The public face of the issue was money: What happened to the $2 trillion of the great Reagan buildup? How much of the Pentagon's requested $1.7 trillion over the next five years would actually be funded? But the more fundamental question was the enduring political-military one of scaling military forces to political objectives. The perennial question of how much is enough depends on foreign policy objectives, perceived threats, and appropriate military forces to deter those threats and to prevail if deterrence fails. The late 1980s presented the most difficult time in the entire postwar era to try to shape a consensus on such questions.

The Air Force proudly rolled out a prototype of the $600-million-a-copy B-2 bomber just as negotiators grappled with the few issues standing in the way of a START (Strategic Arms Reduction Talks) agreement that would mandate significant cuts in strategic nuclear forces. The North Atlantic Treaty Organization (NATO) began work on an ambitious program of modernization just as it made final moves to sit down with the Eastern bloc to discuss conventional arms reductions in Europe. Low-intensity conflict seemed the one constant on the geostrategic map, but after years of furtive and inconclusive wrangling about military involvement in Latin America, the United States seemed further away than ever from a coherent national policy on this question.

President Bush vowed to continue the Reagan defense program, but keeping the nation's defense strong while improving education and the environment and not raising taxes seemed a feat possible only through the voodoo economics Bush so vigorously criticized in the 1980 presidential campaign. Even if the money were available, the American people by the end of the 1980s seemed to have lost their enthusiasm for high defense spending. Other issues, such as drugs, had moved up on the public agenda, and in foreign policy, the primary issue was the perceived decline in American economic power. A series of nationwide bipartisan surveys conducted on a rotating basis by a Republican polling firm, a Democratic firm, and a politically neutral firm, the Americans Talk Security project revealed some astonishing findings about attitudes.[8] More than half of those surveyed (56 percent) believed that economic competitors like Japan posed a greater threat to U.S. national security than did military adversaries like the Soviet Union. Nearly half (44 percent) believed that drug trafficking was an "extremely serious" threat to U.S. national security. It was also one that the American military was distinctly reluctant to engage in a military way.

In one of his last writings as a private citizen, General Brent Scowcroft estimated that $300 billion would have to be cut from DOD budget plans for fiscal years 1990–1994 assuming that Congress approved modest budget increases. With flat military budgets, the amount to be cut would be even greater, perhaps $400 billion. The most that the Pentagon could hope for, barring some drastic turn in U.S.-Soviet relations, was that defense spending would increase enough to offset inflation. And indeed the first Bush defense budget called for a freeze on defense spending in the first year, to be followed by modest growth beyond inflation over the next three years. To many, even that proposal seemed overly optimistic.

Brent Scowcroft

George Bush selected one of the many capable men in American public life as his national security adviser. Brent Scowcroft brought an impeccable background to the job, including prior service as Gerald Ford's national security adviser from 1975 to 1977. Scowcroft possesses an extraordinary combination of personal attributes. He is at once the ultimate self-effacing insider who ensures that all sides get a fair hearing, yet he is also a forceful intellect, not reluctant to put forward his own views even when they conflict with prevailing wisdom. As a private citizen Scowcroft wrote several stinging critiques of Reagan administration defense decisions, and his misgivings on the Strategic Defense Initiative were well known and of great concern to conservatives. He is an unabashed supporter of the 1972 Anti-Ballistic Missile Treaty and a realist about the lean years ahead for defense spending. He faced his most challenging assignment in attempting to convince the president and his other defense advisers that their ambitious plans for defense must be measured against the strategic and fiscal realities of the times.

One of President Bush's first bureaucratic initiatives was the establishment of two government panels dealing with national security issues under the chairmanship of General Scowcroft and Scowcroft's deputy, Robert Gates, a Soviet specialist from the Central Intelligence Agency. Representatives of the State and Defense departments were to serve on these two committees as subordinate members. The new arrangement appeared to raise the status of the National Security Council (NSC) staff and offered the possibility that Scowcroft would play a more visible and central role in the security policy-making machinery than had been expected, and it raised the prospect of a structurally preordained clash with Secretary of State James Baker.[7]

Since the creation of the NSC structure, rivalry between the NSC adviser and the secretary of state has been more the rule than the exception. In his earlier tour Scowcroft got along with his mentor, Secretary of State Henry Kissinger, and by all accounts General Colin Powell had a cordial relationship with Secretary George Shultz. But these two successful advisers generally maintained a low profile and on all issues of public diplomacy deferred to the appropriate cabinet secretary. At the start of the Bush administration it seemed unlikely that Secretary Baker would be comfortable in a subordinate capacity within the national security apparatus, although the laggardly pace with which he filled critical positions within the State Department led some to wonder whether his interest might be more engaged by domestic and economic issues than by foreign policy.

Keeping the nation's defense strong while improving education and the environment and not raising taxes seemed a feat only possible through the voodoo economics Mr. Bush so vigorously criticized in the 1980 presidential campaign.

The Tower Affair

The extended controversy surrounding John Tower's nomination as secretary of defense could hardly have come at a less opportune time for U.S. defense policy. The first months of any new administration provide a critical opportunity for new direction, evaluation, review, and housecleaning. No large bureaucracy should be left without leadership for long, certainly not a defense establishment that needs to come to grips with a shrinking budget.

The Tower nomination went down to defeat in a bitter partisan wrangle, with the final vote almost a straight party line roll call. But concerns about Tower predated his formal nomination, and the lengthy investigation by the Federal Bureau of Investigation that delayed President Bush's announcement of Tower as his choice for defense secretary suggested legitimate nonpartisan misgivings about his fitness for the position that in security terms is the most important in government.

In the end Tower was undone by concerns about alcohol and "womanizing," but a focus on these two vices eclipsed more substantive concerns about the would-be secretary's attitude toward defense management and reform. As chairman of the Senate Armed Services Committee, Tower had been the chief congressional advocate of the Reagan administration's unprioritized military buildup; his enthusiasm then was at least partly responsible for the problems that would have engaged his attention as secretary. More troubling was his brief but lucrative sojourn as a defense consultant, one of the

Figure 1-2. World Conflicts, 1988 ——————————————————————

Haiti
Anti-government demonstrations continue throughout the first half of 1988. A June 20 coup by General Henri Namphy removes the civilian leadership. The Tontons Macoute, a paramilitary force that operated under the Duvalier dictatorship, re-emerges and begins reprisals against critics of the Namphy government, attacking churches and brutally killing parishioners. On September 17 the military coups again, expelling Namphy.

El Salvador
Rebel activity sparks combat between government forces and rebels in the northern part of the country in September. More than eighty rebels and soldiers are killed.

Nicaragua
U.S. funding for the contras remains uncertain throughout most of 1988. Sandinista forces launch a massive offensive against rebel bases, sending more than 7,000 troops into Honduras beginning March 16. Within a week, Sandinista and contra leaders agree to a cease-fire.

Panama
Demonstrations against the rule of General Noriega continue throughout the year with troops repeatedly being sent out to restore order. In May Noriega reneges on a deal to leave Panama in exchange for the U.S. dropping several drug trafficking charges against him. All talks between Panama and the U.S. are then suspended.

Armenia/Azerbaijan
Unrest mounts throughout the year as Armenians and Azerbaijanis protest for independence. Armenian demands for the return of the Armenian enclave Nagorno-Karabakh which was incorporated into Azerbaijan in 1923, erupt in violence in February, resulting in thirty-two deaths.

Persian Gulf
The U.S. frigate *Samuel B. Roberts* strikes a mine April 14 severely damaging the ship. U.S. ships shell two Iranian oil platforms in response. Iranian gunboats attempt to return fire; six are sunk. On July 3, the USS *Vincennes* shoots down an Iranian airliner, killing 290 people.

Lebanon
U.S. Marine Lieutenant Colonel William Higgins, attached to the U.N. observer group, is abducted on February 17. In October a terrorist car bomb attack kills eight Israeli soldiers in southern Lebanon, and a series of retaliatory Israeli air strikes and battles between Lebanese militia and Lebanese Moslem guerrillas leave dozens dead and wounded.

Israel ——————
Israeli security forces and Moslem settlers battle in the West Bank throughout 1988.

Burundi
Long-standing inter-tribal hatred boils over as the minority Tutsi tribe lashes out against the majority Hutu tribe. By summer's end more than 20,000 Hutus had been killed and over 50,000 had fled the country. The massive influx of refugees in Rwanda strained the social and political system there and led the United Nations to seek funds to care for the refugees.

Ethiopia
The civil war continues throughout the year with both the government and the rebel leaders refusing to allow the delivery of relief supplies.

Angola/Namibia/South Africa
Conflict widens and rages through most of the year while negotiations for a peaceful settlement continue. An agreement is signed in December requiring the withdrawal of Cuban and South African troops and the independence of Namibia. Racial violence continues unabated in South Africa.

Iran-Iraq
The war escalates as both sides use short-range ballistic missles in an all out war on cities and charges are levelled that Iran used chemical weapons against Iraqi positions. By year's end, U.N. Secretary General Peres de Cuellar orchestrates a cease-fire.

Afghanistan
The Soviet Union agrees in April to withdraw all troops by February 15, 1989. One half are withdrawn on schedule by August 15. The withdrawal is suspended in November as the Soviets charge *mujahideen* rebels with escalating their attacks on retreating Soviet troops and Afghan urban areas. Hundreds die in stepped up Soviet missile and bomber attacks on rebel positions.

South Korea
Student protests for reunification and a reduced American presence explode in August, taking advantage of the media concentration on the Summer Olympics in Seoul. Security forces battle students daily.

Burma
Months of strikes, demonstrations, and riots disrupt virtually all government activities. Dictatorial ruler Ne Win resigns in July. A military group, said to be supporters of Win, take power in a September coup. Violence continues throughout the year.

Philippines
The New People's Army continues to pressure the Aquino government.

Cambodia
Vietnamese troops continue to occupy Cambodia. Cambodian troops loyal to Hun Sen work throughout the year to deny the Khmer Rouge any territorial gain. By year's end, Vietnam begins consideration of a complete withdrawal of its troops.

Pakistan
Saboteurs destroy the aircraft carrying President Mohammad Zia ul-Haq. Zia, a number of high-ranking military officers, the U.S. ambassador to Pakistan, and the chief of the U.S. military mission are killed.

Maldives
150 Sri Lankans attempt to overthrow the government of the Maldives in early November. After several days of fierce battles between the attackers and loyal government troops that resulted in the death of several dozen people, the government reestablished control.

Sri Lanka
Hostilities between Tamil separatists and the majority Sinhalese continue throughout 1988, with more than 20,000 Indian troops assuming peacekeeping duties in Sri Lanka. By year's end, the ethnic conflict was six years old and had claimed over 12,000 lives.

more brazen examples of the revolving door in the history of the military-industrial-congressional complex.

For what sort of advice did major defense contractors pay John Tower a million dollars? Certainly not for technical expertise, which Tower made no claim to have, or for lobbying "in the usual sense," as Tower himself put it. The payment was obviously for entrée and influence—plainly put, for the right to trade on the name and reputation of the former senator and possibly future secretary of defense. For people concerned about ethics in public life and eager to restore the concept of selfless public service, this was the most dispiriting aspect of the Tower affair: that after a long and influential career of public service and with the obvious hope of serving again in high office, a person would see nothing wrong with auctioning his reputation for private gain. "I firmly believe," Tower said during his confirmation hearing, "that the first vital step to broadening our national consensus on defense is to wring the last drop of waste and mismanagement out of the way we buy our weapons." Six-figure retainers to consultants for "enlightened guesswork" were evidently not part of Senator Tower's conception of waste and mismanagement.

The broader question posed by the Tower nomination was the requisite combination of qualities needed in a secretary of defense. Certainly a defense secretary could use the friendship and support of the president, qualities Tower had in abundance, but beyond that, what mix of business, political, and substantive defense policy skills would make an ideal Pentagon chief? President Bush declared cryptically that he wanted John Tower in the Pentagon for the same reason that Richard Nixon was able to go to China. Presumably the president meant that the chief Capitol Hill advocate of the Reagan buildup would be just as well equipped and politically positioned to reduce the budget and rationalize the weapons procurement process as the inveterate anticommunist president had been to make an opening to China. The reformed-poacher-as-game-warden theory of defense management has appeal, but the risks of recidivism are as obvious as the putative benefits of giving the job to someone who knows all the tricks. In any case, management of defense is only one dimension of the post.

An ideal secretary of defense would be compatible with the president in personality as well as ideas. He (or she) would have the savvy and know-how to get along with Congress and the independent political stature necessary to stand up to special congressional interests. He must also be equipped to do battle with the military services. James Forrestal once said, "The peacetime mission of the armed services is to destroy the secretary of defense."[9] To be prepared for such combat, the secretary should have military experience or other credentials that would earn the respect of the military and allow the civilian boss to assert himself over service parochialism.

A good secretary should also be a skilled manager, with business experience that would help bring rationality and efficiency to the weapons procurement process. But managerial skill, so highly valued a quality in the aftermath of Pentagon procurement scandals, may not be the most important attribute. Robert McNamara was a manager, and so was Louis Johnson, yet those secretaries' managerial skills and analytical techniques counted for little on the battlefields of Vietnam and Korea.[10]

Secretary of Defense Richard B. Cheney lacked military experience, but as a congressman he had served on the House Intelligence Committee and thus came to the Pentagon with some background on substantive security issues. Given his experience as White House chief of staff for President Gerald Ford, his long-standing friendship with National Security Adviser Brent Scowcroft, and his years as a respected leader of the House of Representatives, Cheney invited comparison with Melvin Laird, a veteran congressman himself before moving to the Pentagon and widely regarded as one of the most effective secretaries of defense.

Roles, Missions, and Competitive Strategies

The concept of competitive strategies promised to be a lightning rod for interservice debates over roles and missions in an environment dominated by a stagnant or even shrinking defense budget. The basic concept behind competitive strategies is as old as warfare itself: maximize your comparative defense advantage by capitalizing on your own strengths and exploiting the enemy's weaknesses. In U.S.-Soviet terms, this means that the United States should not match the Soviets weapon for weapon but use U.S. advantages, largely in technology, to negate the Soviet bloc's quantitative preponderance in weapons and manpower. In other words, the United States should "hit 'em where they ain't," or, as some supporters have put it, "fight smart, not rich."

One of the lamentable legacies of the Reagan era was the tendency to let the military services themselves set spending priorities. . . . Any integration of roles and missions was fortuitous, not deliberate.

Under its current label, the idea of competitive strategies has been rattling around in the Pentagon since the early 1970s when Andrew Marshall of the Office of Net Assessment began using it, but the idea did not catch on within the defense bureaucracy until the mid-1980s. Having captured President Bush's attention during the 1988 campaign, competitive strategies promised to be a major operating principle of U.S. defense policy in the Bush years despite rearguard actions by some in the military.

The problem was likely to come in translating the theory of competitive strategies into specifics: what new weapons to buy, which operating principles to adopt, and what tactics to develop. Any student of bureaucratic politics could predict trouble from ideas that threaten the military services' organizational essence, that which the dominant group within each service perceives that service's job to be. Air Force generals are instinctively drawn to concepts that suggest the need for new airplanes and repelled by those that suggest other solutions to military problems; the Army has a similar institutionalized affection for mechanized combat; the Navy feels the same way about surface combat ships.

Competitive strategies troubles the military for two reasons. It may provide the justification for new technologies like remotely piloted vehicles at the expense of more traditional service-preferred weapons, and it could provide an analytical tool allowing civilians to reassert dominance over the weapons procurement process, just as systems analysis and cost-effectiveness permitted Robert McNamara to do in the early 1960s.

One of the lamentable legacies of the Reagan era was the tendency to let the military services themselves set spending priorities. This led to acquisition decisions determined by the often conflicting goals of the individual services. Any integration of roles and missions was fortuitous, not deliberate. One area for the Bush administration to review is service roles and missions, particularly the question of which service gets the crucial battlefield mission of close air support.

The Air Force has that responsibility, although it has never liked the mission any more than it cared for the aircraft it was forced to accept to perform the mission. The A-10 was hardly a combat pilot's dream. Ugly and slow, the aircraft was rumored to be easily outrun by the Soviet tanks it was designed to search out and destroy. By 1989 the A-10s had been moved to the reserves, and the Air Force was busily lobbying for a new close air support aircraft. Its choice was the A-16, a new version of the F-16 supersonic fighter far better designed for air superiority than for direct support of ground forces. The Air Force's insistence on the A-16 as the solution to the close air support problem confirmed for many the service's unshakable lack of interest in the mission. Some analysts suggested that it was time to give the close air support mission to the Army—along with the funds necessary to get the job done.

In service terms the Army has been consistently shortchanged for years. It is the service with the least effective political constituency and could have the most to lose from competitive strategies and a new look at roles and missions. More than any other service, its future depends on a manpower-intensive force posture and a commitment to European defense. Questions about both are likely to be raised in the 1990s. Competitive strategies suggests a tendency to exploit America's technological advantage rather than compete on numbers of troops. Analysts looking for cost-effective substitutions of technology for troops will instantly be drawn to the Army's 750,000 soldiers.

Guard and Reserve Forces

In chapter 8 James Lacy offers an extensive discussion of National Guard and Reserve forces, and as 1989 began the issue of who controls the National Guard remained very much in the air. In October 1988 a federal court of appeals ordered Governor Michael Dukakis to permit the Massachusetts Guard to train in Honduras; two months later another court told Governor Rudy Perpich of Minnesota that he could refuse to send his troops to Central America. At the end of 1988 the Pentagon asked the Justice Department to challenge the appeals court ruling.

If the National Guard is to be truly national and effective, it must be responsive to federal authorities. In the nineteenth century, state Guards were essentially militia forces provisioned and maintained by the states, and it made sense to hold them accountable to state governments. Since the early days of this century, the federal government has provided the equipment and paid the wages of the state Guards. They are vital forces for local emergencies and should always be on call by the state governors for duty in such actions. But to imagine that fifty different individuals act as sovereign warlords with private armies is preposterous.

Guard and Reserve forces are good and can be better, as Lacy asserts, and they may also be a cost-saving device in a time of defense austerity. But no one should want to spend money on a military force that is unresponsive to national needs as determined by the federal government. At a time when defense dollars are in short supply, Washington cannot afford to pay and train soldiers who may or may not be available for duty, depending on the degree of support of the local governor. The Supreme Court should issue a definitive ruling upholding the 1986 Montgomery amendment clearly asserting the federal government's prerogative on this issue.

Conclusion

The international environment facing President George Bush as he entered office was relatively calm on the surface but potentially as unsettled as any other facing an American president since Harry Truman. In Europe there was growing uneasiness over U.S. military leadership, continued wrangling over burden sharing, a reluctance to support plans for nuclear modernization, great enthusiasm for the charisma and security initiatives of Mikhail Gorbachev, and moves to increase economic and military cooperation among the European member states of NATO, perhaps even moving to a genuine "second pillar" within NATO. In the Pacific, U.S. military planners faced a growing Soviet military presence as well as continued uncertainty about the terms and conditions of the U.S. military presence in Japan, the Philippines, and Korea. In Latin America, continued doubt about the future of regimes in Nicaragua and El Salvador, and in the Middle East the Palestinian *intifadah* and Iranian fanaticism continued to threaten the stability of U.S. allies and other U.S. interests in the region.

In 1987 the popularity of Paul Kennedy's book, *The Rise and Fall of the Great Powers,* suggested a U.S. public eager to entertain the notion of an America in decline and to look for appropriate behavior in the experience of other nations that had undergone similar decline. Quite apart from its intellectual merits, the book's popular appeal was difficult to explain in the last years of the Reagan buildup, which by virtually unanimous acclaim had restored American military vigor. Kennedy's message seemed more appropriate to the Carter years than to Reagan. In any event, by the first year of the Bush administration, the American people seemed to have shaken off their malaise. There was less sense of imminent military decline but at the same time growing skepticism about the relevance of military power to the problems likely to confront the United States in the future. The influx of drugs and illegal immigrants into the United States seemed to many people serious threats to the nation's security, yet these were problems the U.S. military was incapable of or at least unwilling to combat. American military power did nothing to redress the trade and budget deficits; indeed, correctly or not, high defense spending was held by many people to be a large part of the deficit problem that loomed as perhaps the gravest threat to U.S. national security.

George Bush entered office with great public and institutional support. He had an extraordinary approval rating and considerable backing among Washington insiders. He seemed to have a better chance of restoring bipartisanship to American security policy than any other chief executive since John F. Kennedy. Bush is not an ideologue and harbors no grand visions of world order. The world is unlikely to see a "Bush doctrine." But whether President Bush was the right person to shape an appropriate American response to the new international environment was very much an open question.

Chapter 2

Toward the Postnuclear Era: The Decline of Extended Deterrence

Edward N. Luttwak

W hat is loosely labeled "extended deterrence" actually describes a twofold extension of strategic nuclear deterrence beyond self-protection against nuclear attack, whereby what is to be protected is one or many foreign political communities and the attack to be averted may be nonnuclear or nuclear.

In reaffirming their willingness to employ nuclear weapons even against a purely nonnuclear attack, if they deem it necessary to avoid defeat,[1] the United States and its North Atlantic Treaty Organization (NATO) allies are relying on "twice-extended" deterrence—in addition to their own nonnuclear forces, considered insufficient for the task—to offset the broad and costly Soviet efforts to raise troops and equip forces.[2] That is the most demanding role that can be imposed on nuclear capabilities, in physical terms to some extent but mainly in regard to the plausibility of their threatened use.[3] Whatever doubts may be entertained about the credibility of nuclear use in other circumstances, those doubts must be all the greater if it is on behalf of others that the use of nuclear weapons is threatened and if the provocation of prior nuclear attack is absent.

What is the present status of twice-extended deterrence? In any particular case, it is obviously the who-whom that matters; but more generally it depends on the role of nuclear weapons within overall military balances, a role that has been in decline for decades.

The Logic of Conflict

No manifestation of the paradoxical logic of conflict is more commonly understood than the self-defeating progress of military innovations.[4] Civilian artifacts and endeavors exist in more or less competitive settings and in due course may be displaced by other artifacts and endeavors in some way more desirable; but the agency of decline is the greater attraction of competitive approaches, not the consequence of success itself. That is true only of military innovations, which elicit negating, not merely competitive, reactions in proportion to their actual, perceived, or anticipated success.

When a weapon of novel conception appears, its eventual decline toward insignificance as a determinant in the overall military balance is the net result of two contradictory processes, each of them many sided. Qualitative improvement of the new weapon by design advancement and perfected manufacture; its broader availability by production increases; and its fuller exploitation by organizational as well as tactical, operational, and perhaps strategic adaptation all increase the potential capabilities of the new weapon, to enhance the advantage of its possession, other things being equal.

But other things cannot be equal in the realm of conflict. The greater the one-sided advantage that possession of the new weapon could confer, the stronger will be the intensity of the adversary's reaction to resist it by technical countermeasures; circumvent it by new tactics, operational methods, or even higher-level strategies; and oppose it most directly by competitive acquisition.

It is the interaction of both processes that yields the characteristic pattern of rising importance, culmination, and decline for new weapons—a parabola that may contain a sequence of lesser interactions. The negating reactions will themselves be subject to the same paradoxical logic of conflict: the more they are successful, the greater will be the efforts to modify the weapon so as to evade countermeasures, outflank circumvention, and outperform prior equivalents already in hostile hands. And then there will be further countermeasures, more circumvention, and the enhancement of the competing enemy weapons, usually of the same conception but by adversaries. In addition, and quite separately, the science[5] contained in the new weapon may also evolve to yield magnified capabilities, setting off a further sequence of reactions.

Eventually the overall military balance will therefore tend to revert to its prior condition. By then yesterday's new weapon may finally be reduced to futility and universally abandoned, or, on the contrary, it may have become firmly established within the institutional structure of the armed forces. In either case its possession will no longer be a source of one-sided advantage.

New weapons easily produced and easily accommodated within military organizations will normally offer only the briefest advantage, with their decline swift, universal, and caused by emulation alone. The breech-loading rifle, for example, had a powerful impact on the overall Prusso-Hapsburg tactical balance in 1866 when only the Prussian army had the new weapon in the form of the needle gun, while the Hapsburg army had not developed tactics to circumvent its fire. By 1870 that particular innovation, centuries in the making, had already declined to insignificance in the Franco-Prussian tactical balance because both armies were equipped with breech-loading rifles (and neither side had developed circumventing tactics, as the respective battlefield massacres showed). In other settings, especially colonial ones, mere possession of the breech-loading rifle was decisive well into the twentieth century, but among the major powers the new weapon's impact on the outcome of battles was already nil by 1914 because all sides had their versions.

In the case of weapons that are more demanding in material and/or human resources, countermeasures may loom larger than emulation for prolonged periods. For example, when countries of unequal development engage in combat, one side tends to have much more air power[6] than the other, often to the point of a clear supremacy.[7]

Given the potential of air power, notably its twin capabilities of penetration to reach far beyond the frontage to attack high-value targets in depth and of concentration to mass firepower in time and space in a way quite impossible for ground forces, air power should be decisive in operational-level military balances[8] when present in sharply unequal amounts. But precisely because its potential capabilities are so great, air power has evoked an intense countermeasure effort, in the form of varied antiaircraft forces, less demanding in means or human abilities than direct emulation would be.

By intercepting some aircraft but mainly by imposing virtual attrition,[9] antiaircraft forces can reduce the actual (countermeasured) capabilities of air power to a mere

---

New weapons easily produced and easily accommodated within military organizations will normally offer only the briefest advantage, with their decline swift, universal, and caused by emulation alone.

---

fraction of its potential, especially when combined with tactical-level circumvention (dispersal, camouflage) and strategic-level circumvention by the resort to guerrilla modes of warfare. In retrospect, the impact of air power on theater balances is a typical history of rising capabilities (1914–1940), culmination (1944–1945), and decline.

When a new invention of war encounters organizational resistance, delaying its full impact on military balances, a longer period of gestation is thereby allowed for all negating reactions. That tends to cut short the culminating phase once full exploitation of the new weapon is finally achieved.

That has been true most notably of the battle tank because the British trench-crossing tactical device of 1915 did not evolve into the key weapon of German operational maneuver until twenty years had passed,[10] and the success of that tank-centered organizational innovation was not finally proved until five years later.

When the operational application of German tank forces to spearhead deep-penetration offensives dramatically disturbed the overall Franco-German theater balance in 1940 and then the German-Soviet theater balance until 1942, it was quite natural that the negating reactions should have been intense. But their exceptional rapidity and most varied scope were due to the accumulation of thought-out solutions, nurtured during the long years of gestation, and ready for immediate application, once the tank's success released resources for the purpose.

Countermeasures, beyond the ordinary field guns in low elevation of 1915, came immediately and took the form of an expanding torrent of conventional, low-pressure, reduced-caliber, and recoilless antitank guns, variously towed, motorized, armored, or mounted in aircraft; hand-held rockets and later small guided missiles, both armed with hollow charges; and mines, hard barriers, and obstacles.

Circumvention has been manifest at every level of warfare: tactically, by the exploitation of antitank islands[11] and nontrafficable terrain as bases for attack as well as for refuge; operationally, by the deployment of yielding elastic defenses that deny any rigid front to be pierced or by defenses in depth inherently resilient to narrow armored penetrations; and at the strategic level most broadly, ranging from guerrilla methods that deny any substantive targets that armor can smash, to the circumvention of all ground combat, by the resort to strategic air bombardment and naval blockade.

Emulation by the major powers was prompt after 1940, with the rapid British, Soviet, and U.S. imitation of the German Panzer division concept of self-contained battle groups spearheaded by tanks; and if these imitations lacked in quality, they more than made up for that in quantity (though because of its demands in skills and resources, emulation could not become universal even long after 1945; until this day, the number of genuine tank powers is under thirty).

The combined result of countermeasures, circumvention, and emulation has been to diminish greatly the impact of the operationalized battle tank (i.e., of armored formations) on military balances almost everywhere, even as armored forces have proliferated and now dominate the structure of modern armies. In other words, except in rare cases, the possession of armored formations can no longer be decisive as it was in 1940, when the innovation was well developed but still largely unresisted, and its decline had yet to begin.

The Advent of Nuclear Weapons

At the dawn of the nuclear era, it was widely believed that the unprecedented magnitude of the new weapon's destructive effect would exempt the fission bomb from the normal parabola of introduction, rising capabilities, culmination, and decline. While his analysis was characteristically more acute, that was the suggestion implied by Bernard Brodie's term *absolute weapon*.[12]

One connotation of *absolute* was that no other weapon more powerful than the fission bomb could possibly be invented—an assumption overturned within six years. Another implication, of later date and greater longevity, was that the new weapons would become the central instruments of warfare for the possessing powers, dominating the structure of their armed forces to the point of reducing armies, navies, and air forces to little more than custodians for nuclear weapons and their vehicles.

In other words, the absolute weapon was expected to transform military balances absolutely because the ability to field troops, maintain navies, or sustain air forces would no longer be of any real importance as compared to relative abilities in the manufacture, deployment, delivery, and targeting of nuclear weapons, thereby drastically altering power rankings worldwide. Thus high-technology nuclear Belgiums might dominate nonnuclear Prussias, and more immediately in 1946, a demobilized United States would not be left disarmed before Stalin's armies.

No military invention was more truly revolutionary than the fission bomb, yet there was no prolonged delay between invention and full application, let alone the two decades and more that passed for the tank, a far more prosaic invention. By a mere accident of chronology, a complete theory for its uses in peace and war had already been developed when the fission bomb so unexpectedly appeared on the scene. That was the strategic air power concept, as variously formulated by the Italian Giulio Douhet, the American Billy Mitchell, and the future Lord Trenchard, founder of the Royal Air Force, whose very independence implied a claim of independent effectiveness.[13] According to this theory in all its varied formulations, the air bombardment not of military forces in the theater of war but of the industries that sustained them in the homeland rear (that is, strategic bombardment) would entirely displace all other forms of warfare.

Specifically, because of the presumed rapidity of its effect, it was argued that air bombardment would decide the outcome of wars long before naval struggles of supply and blockade—the essence of naval warfare—could have any perceptible effect. Even if oil, rubber, vanadium, and other goods could reach their destinations quite unimpeded, that would count for nothing if the relevant factories had been destroyed. If they were not destroyed while those of the blockading side were, the latter would lose the war anyway, regardless of how successful its blockade might have been in the fullness of time, after the exhaustion of stocks. Besides, even bomber forces trained and equipped to attack industrial targets on land could always be diverted to sink enemy fleets in short order, if that were deemed at all worthwhile given the futility of fleets.

More important, in the wake of the massacres of trench warfare, was the claimed ability of air bombardment to outpace and wholly substitute the slow and bloody attrition of ground warfare by cutting off the flow of essential supplies to the front. Without ammunition there could be no offensive barrages or defensive curtains of machine gun fire, and without oil there could be no armored warfare either.

As Douhet explained clearly, strategic bombardment would leap over the outer perimeter of war frontages and reach into the depths of the enemy homeland, to attack its strength at the source.[14] That, he argued, was a far more efficient use of combat power than in any form of warfare at the front because the targets would be concentrated factories rather than dispersed forces, civilian buildings inherently vulnerable rather than fortifications, dugouts and trenches, and above all because it could be aimed at selected high-value targets rather than tracts of countryside containing scattered enemy equipment and even more thinly distributed individual soldiers.

Not integral to the theory, indeed only loosely associated with it, was the further claim that air bombardment could win wars even more directly by terrorizing the enemy's civilian population into demanding immediate peace at any price. In parallel with Douhet's argument, it was held that if the brutalities of war were translated from remote fighting fronts to the central stage of the major cities, from well-drilled troops to undisciplined urban masses, from fortifications and trenches to fragile civilian housing in the crowded urban landscape, the popular will to persevere in war would quickly be broken, leading to immediate demands for peace at any price and revolt if they were denied. Especially after the bombing of Guernica on April 27, 1937, by the Kondor air legion flying in support of the Spanish Nationalist cause, this notion gained widespread credence. In a close anticipation of future nuclear fears, many came to believe that another world war would inevitably begin with the mass bombardment of capital cities, when "gas-filled" bombs would promptly kill civilians by the million.

By 1945 the strategic air power theory had been totally refuted. Its twin technical errors were a gross underestimate of the effort required to deliver each ton of bombs onto worthwhile targets and an equally gross overestimate of the physical destruction that would result. The air power theorists had not realized that only a small part of the bombers acquired could be operational at any one time; that not all operational bombers sent on a mission would duly reach the assigned target zone; that only some of the bombs dropped within that zone would actually hit something worth destroying; and that not all bombs would explode. Cumulatively these separate detractions resulted in a wide gap between the theoretical bombardment capacity of any given inventory of aircraft and the actual tonnage of bombs that could be dropped on target in a given span of time. The overestimate of the destruction that a given tonnage of bombs on target would actually inflict was greater still. It turned out that more was needed to destroy a single plant beyond repair than had been thought sufficient to wreck entire industrial towns. Both technical errors were correctable given much larger bomber forces than had been envisaged, requiring a far larger industrial effort than anyone had anticipated, and with enough air crews exposed in protracted air campaigns to entail human losses on a great scale.[15]

The theory, however, also contained an error of strategy that could not be corrected. In a classic example of linear logic, as always, doomed to fail in the paradoxical realm of conflict, the entire sequence from the inception of bombardment to the enemy's surrender had ignored the effects of adversary reactions other than reciprocal bombardment.

The failure to allow for direct countermeasures, that is, active air defenses, was almost excusable until the advent of radar, but the theory also ignored the ability of civil society to circumvent the air attack. In the face of superior firepower, dispersal and fortification are normal reactions, and just as tactical bombardment would evoke them at the front, strategic bombardment evoked them in the rear. Thus the air attack was met by the decentralization of production, with separate component manufacture coming together in multiple assembly plants, selective fortification, and even the transfer of high-priority plants to underground sites.

Even more important than damage avoidance was the application to civilian industry of the characteristically military practices of damage control and reconstitution. For navies, damage control is the great hidden capability, often overlooked in facile comparisons of numbers, weapons, and tonnages but quite critical in determining the final results of battle encounters. It turned out that exactly the same damage control procedures could also protect factories: the secondary training of workers in firefighting and rescue, planned redundancy in providing essential equipment, and the quick triage of wrecked installations to focus remedies on those still repairable.

Similarly armies rely on reconstitution to keep their forces in the field by the inflow of trained replacements and new equipment, the refitting of used equipment, and the medical recovery, rest, and recuperation of the wounded and exhausted. Again, under bombardment, civilian industry adopted the typical practices of reconstitution: the accelerated training of apprentices (retarded in peacetime by union rules) to accumulate skilled workers in excess of current needs; the stockpiling of longlead components as production reserves; the acquisition of extra tooling and minor machinery, kept off-site until the moment of need; and the preparation of shadow plants operated on single shifts until needed for full production if main plants were damaged. These local measures were accompanied by the nationwide response of centrally allocated raw materials, compulsory labor, and the general adoption of output planning.

Civil society also outmaneuvered the intended political effect of bombardment. When civilian populations were directly attacked as if they were military personnel, the outcome was their militarization, not irresistible demands for peace at any price. In lieu of soldiers, many civilians were uniformed and disciplined just like soldiers, as air raid wardens, volunteer firemen, rescue workers, and auxiliary police; in lieu of trenches, fortifications, and dugouts, blast and splinter walls were built in front of doorways, windows were heavily taped, and air raid shelters of all kinds were provided, ranging from slit trenches in parks to veritable fortresses; and in lieu of a drilled military obedience, there was social pressure manipulated by state propaganda to ensure that the bombing would arouse energizing anger rather than induce demands for surrender. In

Germany, Japan, and the Soviet Union, moreover, the political police could outterrorize bombardment by swiftly punishing any active sign of defeatism.

So successful were the reactions evoked by bombardment that strategic bombardment was even counterproductive to some extent: civilian societies, far more resilient than had been anticipated, actually became better logistic bases for war because the bombing swept away dispensable retail outlets, service undertakings, and traditional crafts, releasing manpower for military industries and the armed forces.

When the fission bomb exploded on the scene in 1945, it seemed to revalidate in full the strategic bombardment theory that the war just ended had wholly refuted.

The Rise of Nuclear Weapons

When the fission bomb exploded on the scene in 1945, it seemed to revalidate in full the strategic bombardment theory that the war just ended had wholly refuted. Because a single fission bomb of the Hiroshima type could inflict as much damage as all the nonnuclear bombs of a 1,000-bomber raid,[16] the wide gap between the inventory potential of bomber forces and their actual operational capabilities was no longer of any consequence: one bomber on target was sufficient for any fairsized town, and a handful would devastate a city. For the same reason, inaccuracy in detail—the major cause of the wide divergence between anticipated and actual damage levels—became inconsequential. The circumvention of the impact of bombing on industry by damage control and reconstitution could no longer be effective. True, dispersal could still be a valid remedy for any single plant, but the assured vulnerability of the key infrastructures that could not be moved at all or at least not dispersed without colossal inefficiencies (dams, power plants, refineries) would largely nullify the benefits of such dispersal as might be feasible.

Nor could the militarization of civil society provide an antidote to the political impact of bombardment as it did before because no amount of propaganda, social pressure, or police control could resist the terror of instantaneous mass destruction and insidious radiation. As for the direct countermeasure of air defenses, even the highest attrition rates achievable could not have a significant impact on nuclear bombardment.[17]

It therefore seemed that with the fission bomb, strategic air power could finally have that monopoly of warfare that had been claimed so prematurely. Because their supply would be interrupted almost immediately, it would be futile to maintain armies, navies, or air forces—except for bombers armed with nuclear weapons, fighters of long endurance to escort them, and antiaircraft forces themselves maintained mostly for morale reasons, and to serve as the basis for the exploitation of any technical breakthrough in interception that might be accomplished in the future. Fission bombs, moreover, could readily destroy ground forces at all concentrated, sink capital ships at will, and render tactical air forces entirely useless by destroying their bases with ease. The absolute weapon, it seemed, would absolutely displace all other military forces, exactly as strategic air bombardment was to have done.

With war thus equated to swift mass destruction, peace would acquire an unprecedented attraction, it was thought. Actually the potential uses of the fission bomb in warfare were considered from the start to be less important than its ability to dissuade war altogether. It was the definitive certainty of its mass destruction that would, by precluding any hope of cheap victories, prevent war. Once again there was a direct precedent: because its anticipated effects on cities had been so grossly exaggerated before 1939, the strategic air power theory had also held out the promise of a terror-induced peace.

The Unusual Causes of Decline

We now know that the fission bomb and its even more destructive fusion successor did not succeed in monopolizing the preparation of warfare, thus making armies, navies, and nonstrategic air forces obsolete. And instead of dominating the composition of overall military balances between the possessing powers, nuclear weapons have a role of only discrete importance, and that too is diminishing.

Once again the paradoxical logic of conflict prevailed over military innovation, even one entirely unprecedented in its magnitude. But, again in perfect accordance with the logic, the importance of nuclear weapons within overall balances did attain a culminating phase before its decline started. This occurred within a well-defined period, so much so that we could even date the culminating point, to trace the characteristic parabola from 1945 to an apogee circa 1957, with the ensuing decline accelerating during the 1960s and continuing to this day.

Without attempting to prove the phenomenon by such means—not that it requires proof, being all too evident in the vast array of nonnuclear forces—it is interesting to consider the allocation of U.S. defense expenditures as between the forces classified as strategic and the general purpose forces. The former category includes all long-range nuclear forces with their ancillaries (bombers, and tankers, ballistic missiles both land based and submarine launched, and others), as well as North American air defenses; in other words, it is essentially nuclear. The general-purpose category comprises all U.S. Army forces (central defense overheads and research and development, for example, are included in neither category); all U.S. Navy forces except for ballistic missile submarines and their ancillaries; all Marine forces; and the tactical forces of the U.S. Air Force. Because the last include a great variety of nuclear weapons, usually in the form of warhead alternatives,[18] the general-purpose forces are hardly nonnuclear; but their very existence implies preparation for warfare on continental fronts, at sea, and in theater air campaigns where nuclear ordnance might play no role at all, as opposed to all-nuclear strategic bombardment. Thus the relative claim of general-purpose and strategic forces within total defense expenditures can still serve as an indicator, admittedly oblique and one-sided as well as systematically minimizing,[19] of the weight of nuclear weapons in the overall U.S.-Soviet military balance. It is interesting nonetheless, if only because it does suggest the chronology of the rise, culmination, and decline of nuclear weapons.

The significance of the numbers in table 2–1 is compounded by the varying nuclear

Table 2-1. Department of Defense Total Obligational Authority (by Program, Current Billions)

	Combat Forces			
Fiscal Year	Strategic (1)	General Purpose (2)	Force Ratio*	Comments
1950	2.468	5.093	48	Embryonic nuclear period
1955	6.990	13.321	52	Lingering Korea effect
1957	**11.182**	**12.995**	**86**	**Nuclear peak year**
1960	10.297	12.799	80	Denuclearization begins
1970	6.928	27.651	25	Full Vietnam effect
1980	10.992	52.307	21	Denuclearization advances
1984	26.053	100.493	26	Renuclearization underway
1985	27.682	120.584	22	Denuclearization resumes
1987	21.100	114.900	18	Denuclearization continues

*Strategic forces expenditures as a percentage of general purpose forces expenditures
SOURCE: Department of Defense data.

content of the general-purpose forces, which was near zero in 1950, reached a peak in the 1957–1960 period, and has been declining ever since.

While their parabola of rise, culmination, and decline has been quite ordinary, in the case of nuclear weapons the causes of decline have been unusual, and the entire process has been very slow for an age otherwise so fast. Moreover, when the original fission bomb, deliverable by larger piston-engined aircraft, was followed by other types of nuclear weapons both much more powerful and also much handier and deliverable by an entire panoply of means from artillery to ballistic missiles, the decline was reversed for a while, before resuming again.

Countermeasures have had an unusually slight role in the decline of nuclear weapons. In the case of most vectors, active defenses have not even been attempted because it has always seemed hard to achieve 50 percent effectiveness levels, 90 percent-plus levels have usually been regarded as virtually unattainable, and yet even 95 percent levels are doomed to insufficiency when the weapons that would still leak through are nuclear.

The Soviet Union did launch a huge air-defense effort soon after 1945, continuing over the decades to add radars and control centers, as well as jet fighters and, later, surface-to-air missiles, to the vast numbers of antiaircraft guns already in place by the end of the war. Obviously these air defenses could serve useful purposes even while totally failing to protect the Soviet Union from nuclear bombardment, notably by imposing resort to the latter; but while they made bombers much more expensive than they would otherwise have been,[20] they could never reduce the damage that nuclear bombardment could inflict. Equally, Soviet passive defenses (such as shelters) and evacuation provisions, extraordinarily elaborate as they are, have not been the cause of the decline of nuclear weapons.

Emulation—the too obvious cause of decline—has been important no doubt, but it can be argued that its importance is easily overstated, obscuring causes actually more decisive. What happened and failed to happen between 1945 and September 1949, when only the United States had the bomb,[21] offers a first oblique view of the question. Those were the formative years of the postwar order in Europe, when the East-West divide still with us was set and frozen. The impact of the fission bomb upon the balance of power should then have been at its peak, yet the United States did not use the threat of atomic bombardment to prevent the enclosure of the Soviet zone of Germany, Poland, Czechoslovakia, Hungary, Romania, and Bulgaria within the Soviet empire under a classic form of indirect rule, by client parties rather than the client princes of old. Nor did the United States attempt to use its monopoly over the fission bomb to ensure its own continued monopoly.

In retrospect, it is clear that the immediacy of wartime solidarity, the widespread recognition of the far greater sacrifice inflicted by the war on the Soviet Union, and the natural relaxation of effort in the wake of victory, along with the anesthetizing belief that the atomic monopoly would last for decades, were all part of the political reality that precluded any purposeful diplomatic exploitation of the new weapon. U.S. public opinion would turn decisively after 1950, but it would not have accepted a frankly adversarial and even bellicose policy in the immediate postwar years.

But there was a more fundamental reason for the failure to make more of the atomic monopoly: the destructive efficacy of the fission bomb exceeded the culminating point of utility. It was too powerful to be powerful.[22] The result was manifest in the degree to which use of the new weapon was inhibited, which in turn defined the scope for strategic-level circumvention. Faced with a weapon so powerful as to inhibit its possessors from using it, the entire effect of the weapon could be neutralized by adversaries who might do many damaging things but no single thing sufficiently provocative to overcome the inhibition. It was thus that Soviet strategic circumvention reduced the role of the American fission bomb upon the overall European balance of power between 1945 and 1948.

Instead of relying on direct and overt commands to establish client regimes in Eastern Europe—a species of political brutality that might have evoked some American response[23]—Stalin's government relied on the invisible workings of subversion. Personal duress secretly applied by Communist-controlled police and their Soviet supervisors on the leaders of majority political parties induced them to accept the formation of coalition governments in which the local Communist parties participated, usually with the police portfolio. In the next stage, coalition leaders were terrorized into excluding and banning center-right peasant parties, and then center parties, and then center-left parties. These salami tactics came to an end when the remaining non-Communist leaders dissolved their own parties, leaving the local Communist party in sole control. The potential dissuasion of the American fission bomb monopoly was never directly challenged; instead it was comfortably circumvented by the Soviet avoidance of any inhibition-releasing provocations.

Circumvention was to grow and diversify greatly from these beginnings, as first the Soviet Union and then the United States resorted to every variety of subversion and every form of indirect violence, from covert political action by intermediaries to outright third-party warfare. By these means, the monopoly of warfare that nuclear weapons were to have was both bypassed and restricted, and their role in determining the balance of power correspondingly diminished.

What the possessing powers have done to each other, the nonpossessing powers have done to all of them. Chinese, North Koreans and Vietnamese fought U.S. troops in the field without suffering nuclear punishment—and any notion that it was a peculiarly American lack of resolve that allowed it is disabused by such varied examples as the impunity of Argentina in the Falklands vis-à-vis the British "independent" deterrent,[24] and the complete Soviet nuclear inhibition in all its Afghan travails, not in regard to mere guerrillas impossible to target but to a steadfast Pakistan, which for year after year inflicted a bloody price on the occupation by way of interposed Afghans.

Circumvention could only grow when the fission bomb, itself too destructive for use in any war over peripheral interests, was succeeded by the fusion bomb capable of detonations a thousand times more powerful and more. Actually fusion bombs (or more accurately fission-triggered thermonuclear bombs) are of variable yield, and along with the smallest all-fission devices, they could have formed the basis of "domesticated" nuclear arsenals, composed not of inhibited megaton-range weapons[25] but rather of subkiloton weapons for use on the battlefield exactly as nonnuclear weapons, only far

---

The monopoly of warfare that nuclear weapons were to have was both bypassed and restricted, and their role in determining the balance of power correspondingly diminished.

---

more efficient. From a technical point of view, the (linear) logic of fielding all-nuclear armed forces that would be very small and very cheap, yet very powerful with their freely usable ultra-low-yield weapons, could easily seem compelling. But strategy allows no such one-sided solutions; any attempt to extract advantage from the smallest nuclear weapons would evoke the natural response of slightly larger weapons, and so on.

There was no domestication. Instead the fusion bomb appeared as a weapon that overshot the culminating maximum of military usability by an even greater extent than its fission predecessor.

This time, moreover, emulation was much more rapid, with the first American test at the end of 1952 and the first Soviet test in 1953. If emulation had been the crucial factor, a sharp decline in the role of nuclear weapons should have ensued in a situation in which both sides would be symmetrically inhibited by their too-powerful fusion weapons and thus obliged to protect their interests—except immunity from nuclear attack itself—by all other means, including nonnuclear forces.

But this did not happen. Instead, in what can only seem in retrospect as a triumph of statecraft, the Eisenhower administration claimed an asymmetrical advantage for the United States from 1954, under the so-called policy of massive retaliation,[26] which stated that nuclear weapons might be used to contend with aggression both direct and indirect, both nuclear and nonnuclear.

Stressing and exploiting the defensive stance of the United States and its allies, which placed the onus of war initiation squarely on the Soviet Union (or China), and taking full advantage of the apparent willingness of the American public to sanction the use of fusion bombs to defend even peripheral interests (in the wake of the bitter experience of the Korean War), the new policy relied greatly on nuclear weapons while discounting the importance of nonnuclear forces within the overall military balance (in which the United States was in a position of comparative disadvantage).

Had the Eisenhower administration acted in strict accordance with its own declared policy, the U.S. Army, Navy, Marine Corps, and the tactical parts of the Air Force would have been virtually disbanded after 1954 or at least drastically reduced. This did not happen, but the general-purpose forces were reduced in size and armed with a proliferating panoply of nonstrategic nuclear weapons of all kinds to offset the loss of (nonnuclear) combat capability. As a result, the parsimonious Eisenhower administration did achieve large savings in its defense expenditures: measured in constant (1986) dollars, these declined quite dramatically, from $309.5 billion at the peak of the Korean rearmament in fiscal year (FY) 1952 (mostly not war expenditures), to $176.5 billion in FY 1954, with the total remaining below $200 billion until 1962, after the advent of the Kennedy administration.[27] Those were the savings of all-around nuclearization, which substituted for larger, better-equipped, and better-stocked conventional force, savings that would soon be sacrificed to denuclearization.

One risk, duly noted at the time, was that the new policy was mere bluff, that it did not reflect a principled and, if need be, suicidal determination to use nuclear weapons, notably against peripheral aggression; if so, the bluff could be called, and the United States would suffer a catastrophic loss in its power to protect all its less-than vital interests. The opposite risk, also duly noted at the time, was that the new policy was not bluff and that a nuclear war might truly follow in response to merely peripheral aggression, possibly indirect aggression as well—an especially salient danger with the war in Indochina under way.

That the threat was extreme and could therefore be self-inhibiting and that inhibition would allow equal scope for circumvention were dangers too obvious to be missed by academic and journalistic critics. As for the professional military, the code of discipline did not silence all of them either, and they vividly criticized the policy by stressing the near impossibility of purposeful military operations reliant from the start on nuclear detonations.

Eventually, with the advent of the Kennedy administration, these criticisms formed the basis for a drastic change of policy, but an argument can easily be made that massive retaliation was very successful while it lasted. Not coincidentally, in 1955 the Soviet Union carried out its one and only imperial retreat of the postwar era when the occupation of eastern Austria came to an end under the State Treaty. The budgetary savings were substantial, and such evidence as can be mustered does suggest that the principal U.S. allies of Europe, or at least the leaders of their governments, were more secure than ever before or since, in spite of the large superiority of Soviet ground forces. This was not a question of merely subjective feelings because it was during the years of massive retaliation that U.S. desiderata were most readily complied with by allied governments and Soviet desiderata most totally ignored.

In retrospect, we may recognize the 1954–1961 period as marking the culminating point of the importance of nuclear weapons in American strategy, within the overall U.S.-Soviet military balance and, less clearly, in all military balances that they could affect.

No stronger form of warfare has intervened to deprive nuclear weapons of their primacy in destruction. It is, moreover, quite clear that it was not the Soviet Union's success in emulation that has caused the decline now so evident; the Soviet Union was capable of retaliating with its own fusion bombing almost from the inaugural date of massive retaliation. Its bomber forces were, of course, much inferior to those of the

United States in 1954 and every year thereafter but not so utterly incapable as to prevent some fusion bombs from reaching some American cities, more than enough counterpunishment to inhibit massive retaliation for some lesser Soviet aggression.

Certainly there was no important correlation between changes in the relative nuclear capabilities of the Soviet Union and the United States on the one hand and the decline of nuclear weapons on the other. Characteristically the major reduction in the declared U.S. reliance on nuclear weapons—and therefore in their asserted role within the U.S.-Soviet military balance—began with the policy of flexible response enunciated in 1961 (when the U.S. advantage in nuclear capabilities was rapidly increasing) and eventually imposed on the Military Council of the North Atlantic Alliance in 1967 (when the superiority of U.S. intercontinental nuclear forces over their Soviet counterparts was at its peak in both numbers and quality by every criterion of measurement). If the

---

We may recognize the 1954–1961 period as marking the culminating point of the importance of nuclear weapons in American strategy.

---

balance of nuclear capabilities had been the controlling factor, 1967 should have marked the reaffirmation of massive retaliation rather than its final abandonment.

Under the new policy nuclear weapons were formally deprived of their monopoly of serious warfare; they were instead placed in reserve, to provide a higher court of appeal in the event that (nonnuclear) defeat were to become imminent.

Certainly no physical change in the American and Soviet nuclear arsenals can explain what has happened since 1954, to reduce cumulatively the role of nuclear weapons and cause the overall U.S.-Soviet military balance to be determined more and more by nonnuclear capabilities. What has changed is both insubstantial and all important because mentalities have changed. With nuclear weapons scarcely limited in their destructive capacity, their weight in the overall balance must necessarily depend on the readiness to use them, or more precisely on the perceived readiness to use them— credibility, in the reigning jargon.

The risk of a prompt escalation to all-out nuclear war in the event of a Soviet offensive, even nonnuclear and perhaps peripheral, was at least passively accepted by American public opinion in 1954 or 1957 or even in 1959 by all accounts; but it was definitely no longer acceptable a decade later, and it has become steadily less acceptable since then. This was not a one-sided change, the result of some loss of nerve of purely internal origin, but rather reflected a change in the prevailing view of the Soviet threat: from a threat unlimited in scope and in its implications (a lethal threat to a way of life), to a classical, discrete, geopolitical threat, whereby some given Soviet offensive might result in the invasion of a given theater or sector. The appropriate response to such a threat would also be discrete, with a commensurate nonnuclear defense, supplementary theater-level nuclear fires if necessary, and with nuclear retaliation against the Soviet Union itself kept in reserve, to dissuade escalation by the Soviet side, notably to outmatch the defensive use of tactical nuclear weapons. In other words, a discrete threat calls for a graduated response, just as the seemingly all-pervasive threat of Stalin's Communist onslaught on the world called for a massive response.

The Decline of Extended Deterrence

As the acceptability of nuclear use by the United States has continued to become more restricted, the scope of the extended deterrence offered by the United States to other countries, with its implied readiness to respond with nuclear attacks against nonnuclear aggression, has continued to recede. Because perceptions and objective change are one in this matter, it is hard to define with confidence the current boundaries of extended deterrence, though we may recognize with perfect clarity what those boundaries no longer include.

Thirty years ago, the Quemoy and Matsu islands off the Chinese coast, one very small and the other a mere rock, were to be held by nuclear counterattacks against (nonnuclear) Chinese artillery barrages, under joint U.S.–Republic of China defense plans. At this writing, the notion that the United States was ostensibly ready to use nuclear weapons to defend Quemoy and Matsu seems absurd, but it was not so at the time for the officers and officials involved, who would now smile in disbelief at their own thoughts of those days.

Similarly it now seems clear that the drift toward denuclearization has progressed far enough to rule out the use of nuclear weapons for the defense of South Korea against a (nonnuclear) invasion from the North. That was still a highly realistic option during the 1960s, even a prompt necessity in case of an all-out invasion, given the contemporary balance of forces. But nuclear use would hardly be contemplated now, although the United States remains fully committed to the defense of Korea and although it would be difficult both to defeat a surprise invasion and also shield the Seoul area without the use of nuclear weapons.

Japan is still to be defended by nuclear weapons if nonnuclear defenses fail under known plans. Public declarations on the subject mostly address the eventuality of American nuclear retaliation for a prior Soviet nuclear attack, but that is hardly the salient threat, given the extreme vulnerability of Hokkaido at least to nonnuclear invasion from nearby Soviet territory. Even if one considers current American public attitudes toward Japan as merely transitory, it is hard to believe that an American president would authorize nuclear attacks against Soviet bases and military forces in response to a nonnuclear invasion of the thinly populated northernmost island of Japan or perhaps only its northern shore.

With complicated exceptions that commingle third-party protection with the protection of U.S. forces on foreign soil, only the extended deterrence still offered to the NATO allies of Western Europe retains enough plausibility to justify further analysis.

It is hard to say where we might be as the denuclearization drift continues, but the trend is clear enough, and it is best revealed by the size and quality of the nonnuclear forces that the various Alliance members see fit to maintain, especially the most problematic ground forces, whose upkeep imposes the continuation of obligatory military service. In the early 1950s, the various frontages of northern Norway, Italy, and eastern Anatolia, as well as the central front in Germany from the Baltic to the Austrian border, were guarded only by scattered, mostly lightly armed units that formed long, thin, notional lines—a poor defense against concentrated armored offensives but suitable to trigger the nuclear bombardment of the Soviet Union. It is important to recognize that the fragility of the defenses of the 1950s added to the credibility of massive retaliation, for there was no interposed choice, no conventionally secured opportunity for controverted deliberations.

Since those days, NATO ground forces have grown in size, and both formation structures and their greatly strengthened armament belie the constancy of divisional counts. Tactical deployments have become far more realistic, and the logistic capacity of most NATO members for sustained combat has increased most of all, and it increases still.

It now seems clear that the drift toward denuclearization has progressed far enough to rule out the use of nuclear weapons for the defense of South Korea against a (nonnuclear) invasion from the North.

It is obvious that the growth of NATO nonnuclear forces marks more accurately than anything else the continuing advance of denuclearization. Less obviously it is also a cause of denuclearization. Officially it is claimed that stronger nonnuclear defenses add to the credibility of extended deterrence by raising the level of intensity of (nonnuclear) combat and, hence, the visibility of the provocation. But by holding the ring a while, the nonnuclear defenses also defend the political arena in which the imminent possibility of nuclear use will become the only subject of contention. While the nonnuclear defenses defend, newspapers can be published, radio and television can function, parliaments can go into session, all to submit the nuclear use decision to scrutiny much less rarefied than at present. Once the question is thus presented, can there be doubt about the answer, whether in the United States or anywhere in Europe?

The emergence of Europe's postnuclear era, as I have called it, could now be prevented only by an attitudinal reversal that must be judged as improbable (as improbable as the reversion of a decaying Soviet Union to dynamic expansionism). In such an era, still not with us but emerging, peace would have to be secured as it always was before—if only most imperfectly—by (nonnuclear) defense and by diplomatic conciliation, with nuclear weapons finally reduced to the role of reciprocally neutralizing one another. How one views such a future depends on how certain one is that war as a phenomenon will assuredly be confined to less fortunate climes than Europe's. Beyond Europe, on the other hand, U.S. extended deterrence has no future to weigh and contemplate, only a repudiated past.

President Bush's Budget Address
To Congress, February 9, 1989

Chapter 3

The Defense Budget in the 1990s

Gordon Adams
Stephen Alexis Cain

A s it enters the 1990s, the Defense Department (DOD) faces a continuing gap between its planned expenditures and the financial resources it is likely to receive. This dilemma originates in the buildup of the 1980s and the excessive optimism in both DOD and the White House about defense budgets, which were expected to continue to grow into the twenty-first century. Although it has become clear to others that such growth will not occur, the lack of realism continues in the Defense Department and the White House. The task of adjusting plans to resources will be especially difficult because the buildup placed a heavy emphasis on front-loaded investments in military hardware, especially the development of new weapons. For budgets from FY (fiscal year) 1986 through FY 1989 and the budget request for FY 1990, both Congress and the Defense Department failed to address the problem adequately, relying primarily on quick-fix solutions that did not close the long-term gap between plans and resources.

Changes in the international environment present the opportunity to rethink defense policies and plans in ways that could reduce U.S. defense expenditures and significantly change the force structure over the long term. It would make sense to defer production plans for new weapons, favoring instead the efficient production of ongoing programs and the preservation of military readiness and sustainability.

The Gap Between Defense Plans and Resources

The defense budget grew 56 percent after inflation between FY 1980 and FY 1985, reaching constant dollar levels unprecedented during peacetime and higher than even the peak years of the Vietnam War (See figure 3-1). The Pentagon of Defense Secretary Caspar Weinberger, apparently believing that normal peacetime restraints on the defense budget had been eliminated, planned for continued rapid growth. The five-year defense plan (FYDP) for FY 1986 projected growth of 37 percent after inflation through FY 1990, for a total of approximately 110 percent growth after inflation between FY 1980 and FY 1990. But despite the considerable efforts of two skilled and powerful advocates—President Reagan and his secretary of defense—this growth was not forthcoming. Defense funding actually fell 10 percent after inflation between FY 1985 and FY 1989, and although it remained 40 percent higher after inflation than it was in FY 1980, further reductions seemed likely.

The key element in the changed budgetary environment was the explosive growth in the federal budget deficit during the early 1980s, from $74 billion in FY 1980 to $221 billion in FY 1986, and the passage of the Gramm-Rudman-Hollings deficit reduction law in 1985. This law (as amended) mandates a balanced federal budget by FY 1993, to be achieved by meeting a series of progressively lower deficit targets. If the projected deficit from congressional appropriations exceeded the deficit target, automatic spending cuts (sequestration) would take effect, with half of the required amount coming from defense. Thus, Congress had a powerful incentive to restrain growth in defense funding since every additional dollar that went for defense would be taken from other programs or from revenue increases. Congress's inclination to cut defense funding was strengthened when the Democrats recaptured the Senate in 1986.

Figure 3-1. Military Buildup Defense Budget Authority
FY 1946-FY 1993

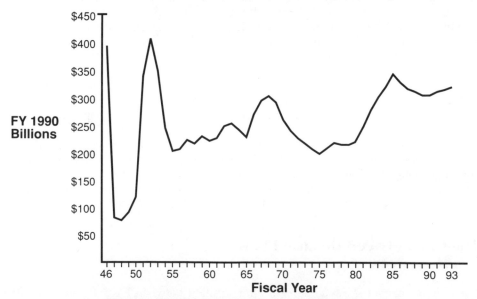

*Figures for 1990-1993 are President Bush's Budget Projections

Popular opinion toward defense spending, as measured in polls, has intensified the downward pressure on the defense budget. In 1980 and 1981, in the wake of the Soviet invasion of Afghanistan and the revolution in Iran, public opinion strongly favored increases in defense spending. This support evaporated by 1983 after the large defense increases in President Reagan's first two budgets. By FY 1983, a majority of the U.S. public favored either a constant level or reductions in defense spending. Moreover, when asked how to reduce the deficit, more people favored cuts in defense than in any other major spending category.[1] The arms control proposals, unilateral force reductions, and the internal reforms of Soviet party general secretary Mikhail Gorbachev added to public resistance to further increase in the defense budget.

Throughout the tenure of Defense Secretary Weinberger, the Pentagon continued to project rapid real growth in its budgets, undeterred by public opinion, Gramm-Rudman-Hollings, and the explicit pleading of congressional leaders to be more realistic. Faint hints that DOD had begun to recognize its new situation appeared in its FY 1988 budget proposal, which projected a 3 percent annual real growth, still unrealistic but down from the higher projections of previous years. Closer investigation revealed, however, that the 3 percent figure was below the rate actually used for internal DOD planning purposes.

In 1987, Weinberger's successor, Frank Carlucci, faced the task of cutting the FY 1989 defense budget request by $33 billion, to a level slightly below the amount needed to keep pace with inflation. This reduction was mandated by a budget summit in which the White House and congressional leaders agreed in advance on the next two years' budget levels for defense, international programs, nondefense discretionary programs, and entitlements. Although Carlucci's FY 1989 budget request made sufficient cuts to comply with the agreement, it projected real growth of 2 percent annually between FY 1990 and FY 1993. Moreover, the military services did not revise their plans and programs to match the 2 percent annual real growth projection since the Defense Department had recently begun to revise its five-year plan in two-year cycles rather than annually. This revision was made only with the FY 1990 budget request, Carlucci and Reagan's last. Even then, the General Accounting Office found that DOD adjusted to the last three years of the FYDP only by counting $15 billion in unitemized subtractions (called "program estimates") each year.[2]

One month after the submission of the final Reagan budget, President Bush announced his intention to reduce FY 1990 defense funds to the level needed to keep pace with inflation. Bush's budget nevertheless projected growth above inflation in future defense funding—1 percent in FY 1991 and FY 1992 and 2 percent in FY 1993 and FY 1994. These reductions were not immediately reflected in actual program changes; the details of the budget plan for fiscal years 1990 and 1991 were to be released in spring 1989. A more long-term adjustment of DOD plans may be delayed until a new five-year plan is developed for the FY 1992–FY 1993 budget cycle.

The danger presented by continued projections of real growth in defense funding is that DOD will begin programs at low initial funding levels, anticipating that future increases will provide the funding needed. When these increases do not occur, adjustments will have to be made.

Like President Reagan's budget, the Bush budget projections made few concessions (beyond the rhetorical) to congressional concerns. The budget proposes severe funding cuts for many domestic programs. While nondefense programs would be cut by over $20 billion, defense would contribute little or nothing to deficit reduction.[3] Congress is likely to restore some of the funds for domestic programs by cutting defense below the rate of inflation and perhaps below the FY 1989 level. Moreover, it may be impossible to implement President Bush's budget plan, under Gramm-Rudman-Hollings, if its highly optimistic assumptions about economic growth, interest rates, and revenues turn out to be incorrect.[4]

If the administration and Congress cannot reconcile their differences over the federal budget, sequestrations under Gramm-Rudman-Hollings are a real possibility. These across-the-board cuts would wreak havoc with defense planning, thwart any attempt to set defense priorities, and disproportionately affect the operations and maintenance accounts, to the detriment of military readiness.

Thus, DOD faces the prospect of adjusting its programs not only to the slower growth budgets projected by President Bush but also to the still lower levels that Congress, or sequestrations, will impose. If defense funding merely keeps pace with inflation from FY 1990 through FY 1994, it will fall $42 billion short of the Bush projections. If defense funding stays level at $299 billion, with no adjustment for inflation (as many expect), it will fall roughly $175 billion short of the Bush projections.

Stern Waves and Bow Waves

Cutting defense funding to cope with this fiscal crisis will be difficult because of the fiscal after-effects of the Reagan buildup, often described as the "stern wave" and the "bow wave" and because most of the quick-fix solutions have been exhausted. The stern wave is defense spending that cannot be controlled because it has already been appropriated for weapons purchases or because it is needed to operate and support the new weapons. The bow wave is the pressure for increased defense budgets that arises as a large number of development programs enter production. These waves of spending clash with pressures for deficit reduction, making it difficult for the Bush administration to implement a sound program without making politically tough decisions and undertaking a fundamental reassessment of U.S. military policy.

The military buildup of the 1980s focused primarily on investment in new military hardware rather than on operations and maintenance or military personnel. The investment accounts—research and development, procurement, military construction, and Department of Energy (DOE) nuclear warhead programs—grew from 37.6 percent of the defense budget in FY 1980 to 48 percent in FY 1986 (figure 3–2).

This rapid growth in defense investment created a large backlog of appropriated but unspent funds as growth in actual spending (outlays) lagged behind growth in budget authority.[5] The backlog results from the practice of providing, in a single appropriation, all the funds needed to procure the weapons authorized that year, though the funds will be spent over the several years it takes to build the weapons. As a result of the growth in investment funding, the backlog of unexpended funds grew 183 percent, from $92 billion in FY 1980 to an estimated $260 billion in FY 1989, approximately 80 percent of it already obligated to contracts.

Once backlogged funds are obligated, it is virtually certain that they will be spent since canceling contracts is expensive and politically difficult. The share of defense outlays considered relatively uncontrollable (due to prior-year contracts) rose from 20 percent in FY 1976 and 27 percent in FY 1980 to an estimated 40 percent by FY 1987,

Figure 3-2. Investment Account as Component of Defense Budget Authority

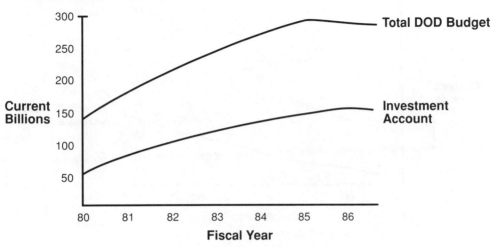

Source: Data derived from OMB estimate

according to Office of Management and Budget (OMB) data (figure 3–3). In addition, roughly 45 percent of defense spending is spent on payroll and pensions. In sum, roughly 85 percent of any year's defense spending cannot be controlled without canceling contracts or reducing personnel. In FY 1986, for example, defense outlays grew 6 percent above inflation despite a 4 percent cut in budget authority that year. Furthermore, outlays kept pace with inflation in FY 1987 and FY 1988 although defense budget authority was cut below the rate of inflation during those years.

Thus, efforts to reduce defense spending have to be planned in advance since each year's spending is determined largely by commitments made previously. The uncontrollability of defense spending is significant because actual spending, not budget authority, contributes to the deficit and determines whether Gramm-Rudman-Hollings deficit targets have been reached.

The other aspect of the stern wave is the increase in the requirement for operations and support (O&S) funding, which follows some years after a buildup in procurement funding.[6] The source of this problem is not growth in force structure; in fact, force structure has stayed basically stable except in the area of combat ships. The problem is, rather, the procurement of increasingly complex and expensive weapons. As a general rule, the more technologically complex a weapon is and the more expensive it is to procure, the more expensive it will be to operate and support.[7]

Since many of the weapons funded during the 1980s will not be deployed until the early 1990s, O&S funding needs will continue to grow. Assuming a continuation of the historical relationship between the cost of acquiring weapons and the cost of operating and supporting them, O&S funding requirements will increase 2.3 percent to 5.5

Figure 3-3. Uncontrollables in Defense Outlays

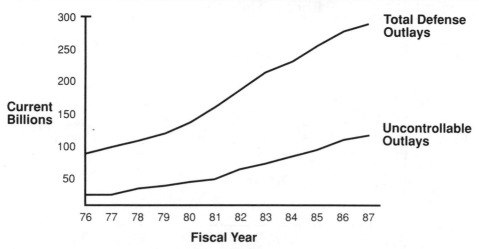

Source: Data derived from OMB estimate

percent per year in the early 1990s, according to the Congressional Budget Office (CBO).[8]

The defense budget could probably manage the stern wave were it not for the imminent arrival of a bow wave of spending on weapons procurement. Rapid growth in funding weapons development has brought a large number of programs to the production stage, where they will require substantial funding increases.

DOD research and development (R&D) funding grew 92 percent after inflation from FY 1980 to FY 1989, faster than any other element of the defense budget. Since DOD funding for basic research held fairly steady during this period, nearly all of the growth was devoted to the development of new military hardware.

Funding growth was especially strong. Strategic R&D funding, including for the Strategic Defense Initiative (SDI), more than tripled after inflation between FY 1980 and FY 1988. Even excluding SDI, funding for strategic R&D grew 140 percent after inflation. A large number of strategic systems began production in the late 1980s or were scheduled to do so in the early 1990s: the B-2 (Stealth) bomber; advanced cruise missile; Trident II missile; short-range attack missile (SRAM II), rail-garrison basing for the MX missile; and the Midgetman missile. In addition, the Reagan administration left office planning to deploy the first phase of a land-and-space-based strategic defense in the mid to late 1990s.

The priority given to strategic programs within the R&D budget mirrors the overall priority of the Reagan buildup. Funding for strategic forces grew roughly 66 percent after inflation between FY 1980 and FY 1989, whereas the defense budget as a whole grew 40 percent after inflation. Under current plans, funding for strategic forces would continue to grow at a more rapid rate than overall defense funding.[9]

Several large conventional weapons programs were approaching production during the same time period, including the Army's tactical missile system (ATACMS) and forward area air defense system (FAADS), the Navy's advanced tactical aircraft (A-12), V-22 Osprey tilt-rotor aircraft, and SSN-21 attack submarine, and the Air Force's C-17 transport and Tacit Rainbow antiradiation missile. Additional programs were moving from advanced development to the engineering development stage, the final stage before production, in the late 1980s and early 1990s. These include the Army's LHX helicopter and advanced antitank weapon system, the Navy's advanced air-to-air missile, and the Air Force's advanced tactical fighter (ATF).

It seemed unlikely that sufficient funding would be available for all of these new weapons, and the gap between funds and plans will be especially large if costs have been underestimated. It would be prudent to anticipate that the bow wave will require even more funds than projected, given DOD's long history of underestimating the costs of its new weapons.[10]

Despite budget reductions since FY 1985, DOD has not proposed canceling any major new weapon system, except the Midgetman missile and an antisatellite (ASAT) weapon, both of which DOD proposed to cancel in the FY 1989 budget request. The Midgetman, however, has persisted as an R&D program, and it may be revived by supporters in Congress and the Bush administration, and the ASAT has been replaced by several new ASAT R&D programs.

Although new weapons programs are the source of the pressure for budget growth, DOD and Congress have so far dealt with the budget crunch largely by cutting funds for military readiness and sustainability and stretching out production of ongoing weapons programs (buying fewer weapons per year than previously planned). In the FY 1989 budget request, budgetary pressures led DOD to seek additional savings by making modest cuts in the force structure, for instance, cutting two Air Force air wings and sixteen Navy frigates.

The FY 1990–1991 Defense Budget:
Avoiding the Tough Choices

The Bush administration initially laid out only its proposal for overall defense budget levels without submitting a detailed defense budget; however, President Bush stated that his detailed plan would follow the overall priority set out in President Reagan's FY 1990–1991 budget proposal, though $6 billion would need to be cut in FY 1990 and $10 billion in FY 1991.

The final Reagan budget placed a high priority on bringing new weapons, especially strategic systems, into production and on preserving the current force structure while stretching out procurement of current production programs and cutting funds needed to maintain military readiness and sustainability. By protecting the entire new generation of weapon systems, it avoided making the difficult choices needed to bring defense programs in line with budgetary resources in the 1990s.[11] President Reagan's final budget canceled no major weapons programs. Cancellations of minor programs would save $1.1 billion from previous budget projections in FY 1990 and $4.3 billion over the course of five years. The largest program canceled, an upgrade of the Navy's A-6 attack jet, would save half of this amount, with the rest of the savings attributed to ten small programs such as a sonobuoy and an improved 155 mm conventional munition.

The Reagan budget proposal would also gain short-term savings—at a long-term cost—by stretching out a large number of current weapons production programs. For example, the budget request called for production of thirty-six F-15 fighter aircraft, down from the forty-two projected in the last five-year plan, and 150 F-16 aircraft, down from a projected 180. Other major program stretch-outs included the Army's Bradley fighting vehicle, the Air Force's KC-135 reengining program, and a number of missile programs including the advanced medium range air-to-air missile (AMRAAM), laser Hellfire, MK 48 advanced capability (ADCAP) torpedo, high-speed antiradiation missile (HARM), Chapparal, multiple launcher rocket system, Standard, Trident II, and the imaging infra-red (IIR) Maverick.

These stretch-outs would allow DOD to avoid cancellations while gaining savings that could be used to provide funding to move new weapons toward production. They would, however, decrease production efficiency, adding to long-term costs, especially since production rates for most major weapons systems have already been reduced to the minimum economic rate, below which cuts would lead to major increases in the cost of each unit. Some weapons are already being procured below the minimum economic rate, including the M1 tank, Bradley fighting vehicle, Blackhawk helicopter, tube-launched optically-sighted wire-guided (TOW) missile, and the F/A-18 and F-15 aircraft.

The other major source of savings in President Reagan's budget request would be reductions in training, maintenance, and production of ammunition. Operations and maintenance funding, which supports programs related to readiness, would grow only 1 percent in FY 1990 and 0.9 percent in FY 1991, after adjusting for inflation and for funding transfers to cover foreign currency costs, reserves readiness, drug interdiction, and the cost of closing military bases.[12] This slow funding growth, together with the increased costs of operating and maintaining new weapons, will cause a decrease in training. Army ground training operations would drop from 850 miles per combat vehicle in FY 1989 to 800 in FY 1990 and FY 1991 under the Reagan request, and large-scale Marine Corps exercises would be cut more than 50 percent from the FY 1989 level. In addition, the amount of equipment that goes unrepaired due to lack of funding will grow. The financial backlog in depot-level weapons maintenance would increase 18 percent in FY 1990 and 15 percent in FY 1991, and the backlog of unfunded property maintenance would increase 24 percent in FY 1990 and 16 percent in FY 1991.

Funding for major new weapons systems will also continue to grow at the expense of ammunition funding. According to the Defense Department total FY 1990 ammunition funding will be 12 percent below the FY 1989 level in nominal terms, and FY 1991 funding will be 7 percent below the FY 1989 level. In addition, funding for four categories of equipment that are less glamorous than aircraft, ships, or strategic missiles but are important to military sustainability fall below the FY 1989 levels adjusted for inflation, according to the CBO: support equipment, tactical missiles, vehicles, and "other weapons."[13]

Funding the Bow Wave

Stretch-outs of current weapons programs and cuts in military readiness and sustainability would provide funds for the entire procurement bow wave of new weapons programs emerging from the R&D budget. The Reagan administration requested substantially more real growth for procurement funding—3.1 percent in FY 1990 and 6.6 percent in FY 1991—than for the defense budget overall (which was to grow 2 percent after inflation per year). Continued procurement funding growth was projected through FY 1994, for a total of 27 percent real growth from FY 1989 to FY 1994. If the Bush administration seeks to control defense spending over the long term, it will need to cut this growth.

Strategic Systems

The Reagan budget request gave priority to the new generation of strategic nuclear systems entering production in the following two years; the B-2 bomber, advanced cruise missile, rail-garrison MX missile, and SRAM II. The MX rail-garrison program would move forward especially rapidly under the budget request as a result of the decision to proceed with the deployment of one hundred MX missiles in rail garrison—fifty new missiles plus the fifty already deployed in silos. Total funding for the MX, including missiles, rail-garrison basing, and construction, would be $2.4 billion in FY 1990 and $3.1 billion in FY 1991.

Funding for the B-2A Stealth bomber is classified, but DOD data indicate that production funding for it is growing rapidly. Procurement funding requests for FY 1990 and FY 1991 were above the FY 1989 level by $747 million and $3.7 billion, respectively. Requested FY 1990 and FY 1991 production funding levels for the advanced cruise missile, which is also classified, were $289 million and $339 million, respectively, above the FY 1989 level.[14] The SRAM II missile would receive advance procurement funds in FY 1990, and the first twenty-five missiles would be purchased in FY 1991.

Funding for the SDI would grow especially rapidly under President Reagan's final request: 47 percent in nominal terms in FY 1990 and another 18 percent in FY 1991. SDI funding would increase from $4 billion (including $337 million in the DOE) in FY 1989 to $5.9 billion in FY 1990 ($311 million in DOE) and $7 billion in FY 1991 ($276 million in DOE). By FY 1994, SDI funding (DOD portion only) would reach $10.7 billion, according to DOD projections (figure 3–4). The SDI request includes the addition of funds for full-scale engineering development. These funds, $262 million in FY 1990 and $427 million in FY 1991, would be used to develop hardware for the first phase of a series of SDI deployments.

DOD, moreover, is requesting funding increases for the air defense initiative (ADI) program to develop defenses against Soviet bombers and cruise missiles. Funds for ADI would increase from $156 million in FY 1989 to $257 million in FY 1990 and $296 million in FY 1991. The Defense Department is also attempting to revive ASAT programs after the cancellation of the F-15-launched miniature homing vehicle in FY 1989. Funds were requested for a new Navy mobile sea-based antisatellite weapon, as well as Army and Air Force ASATs and the ASAT capabilities being developed under the SDI program. The Reagan request also projected increases in funding for the DOE's nuclear warhead programs (which are part of the national defense budget) but not the level required to clean up the environmental problems that DOE created and to modernize DOE facilities so that they can operate safely. The Reagan request projects growth in DOE-military funding from $8.1 billion in FY 1989 to $10.4 billion in FY 1994. CBO projections of needed DOE-military funding show a much more rapid increase—

to $16.4 billion by FY 1994. Thus, the Bush administration may face the need for rapidly increasing DOE budgets during a time of no growth in defense budgets as a whole.

Conventional Weapons

New conventional hardware programs also moved rapidly toward production in the final Reagan budget. The most significant new conventional programs are the Air Force C-17 airlift aircraft (six to be procured in FY 1990 and ten in FY 1991), the Navy–Marine Corps V-22 Osprey (the first twelve in FY 1990, another twenty-four in FY 1991), and the Navy's classified A-12 attack aircraft, scheduled to enter production in 1991. The second and third SSN-21 submarines are to be procured in FY 1991, as well as a new long-range antisubmarine warfare aircraft. Other new conventional procurement programs in FY 1990 and FY 1991 include Army families of medium and heavy tactical vehicles and a new forward area air defense system, and the E-8A (JSTARS) aircraft and Tacit Rainbow missile for the Air Force.

In addition, major funding increases are requested for research and development on the Air Force's ATF and the Army's LHX helicopter, which will enter production in the 1990s. The Army has requested $241 million for the LHX in FY 1990 and $447 million in FY 1991; the Air Force has requested $1.1 billion for the ATF in FY 1990 and $1.6 billion in FY 1991. In addition, several new programs would be started in R&D including development of a chemical warhead for the multiple launcher rocket system and a medium surface-to-air missile.

The last Reagan budget suggested that DOD desires to ignore budget constraints and proceed with its new hardware at full speed. Thus, the Bush administration will have to reverse course if it wishes to avoid a budget crunch that will damage readiness or require unplanned cuts in force structure.

Figure 3-4. DOD SDI Funding (Requested)

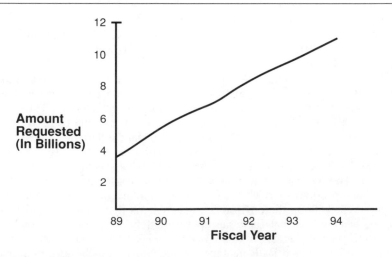

Changes in the Global Arena

Defense planners in Congress and the Defense Department are working within narrow budget constraints in the near term. Changes in the international arena, however, are likely to prove even more important than these short-term constraints. The Reagan defense program and budgets reflected a worldview in which a major defense buildup was needed to counter a decade of defense neglect and significant growth in the Soviet military threat. Whether one agrees or disagrees with that perception, there is no doubt that the 1990s pose significantly different challenges to U.S. national security planners.

The sea change likely to take place in the international environment in the 1990s should ultimately lead to a rethinking of U.S. national security policy of the kind that

The Bush administration will have to reverse course if it wishes to avoid a budget crunch that will damage readiness or require unplanned cuts in force structure.

resulted in the NSC-68 document in 1948. This reassessment could lead, in turn, to a restructuring of and reduction in U.S. military forces, changes in their missions and locations, and a redefinition of the requirements for military equipment.

The changes taking place begin with U.S.-Soviet relations, which could improve to a point that would make the 1970s era of détente pale by comparison. Mikhail Gorbachev appears to be making a major effort to reach an accommodation with the United States that would lower the risk of war and buy time and resources for important domestic changes in the Soviet Union.[15]

U.S. strategic nuclear forces and the large U.S. military presence in Europe may well shrink significantly by the turn of the century as a result of the combined impact of the current U.S.-Soviet thaw, unilateral Soviet conventional arms reductions, new conventional arms talks, a growing Western European resistance to a conventional buildup, and calls in the United States for greater alliance burden sharing. Changes taking place in the rest of the world, from the Middle East to the Pacific to Latin America, will have an important effect on U.S. defense planning, both as a result of a number of current conflicts being resolved and because new ones are likely to emerge in the 1990s. Finally, national security planners will find more of their attention drawn to matters economic and away from matters military, giving U.S. national security policy a vastly different character.

Not all of these changes will be understood in Washington, D.C., and their implications for the size and composition of U.S. military forces may be resisted because of the natural conservatism and inertia of the military services.[16] For the Defense Department, such a reassessment means changing a forty-year-old entrenched way of operating. For the Congress, broad policy scrutiny and careful choice making demand a degree of unity and a willingness to suspend individual district and state interests that is institutionally difficult. There is evidence, however, that some policy planners in the Office of the Secretary of Defense, the services, and the armed services committees of Congress have begun to think through the implications of these changes, foreshadowing conflict in DOD over defense planning in the 1990s.[17] The trends in world politics do not point to a world empty of military conflict or problems for which military forces may be needed. There will clearly be an important role for a significant, ready, and capable military dimension of U.S. national strategy. U.S. strategy, military missions, force structures, and defense budgets could all be significantly different by the year 2000, however, as they are reshaped to fit the needs of the new global realities.

The danger is that policymakers will pursue expensive force structure and modernization plans that do not fit new requirements, locking in programs that make it difficult to reshape forces and security policy. Current budget plans are clearly unrealistic given the constraints on resources. Moreover, the new administration has inherited a mission agenda that is both increasingly inappropriate and sets no limits on defense outlays.[18]

A comprehensive policy review is essential if the Bush administration is to master the budgetary pressures created by the defense legacy of the Reagan years and make sound decisions about the size of the force structure. The military aspects of such a review will not be easy to conduct or to implement. The input of the military services will be necessary, but strong, centralized leadership within DOD and the National Security Council will be required since the services have a large investment in current missions and programs. Furthermore, ground, naval, and air strategies need to be integrated to reduce duplication and improve military effectiveness, and military policy as a whole must be integrated with diplomatic policy and fiscal considerations, a task that the individual services are not structured to perform.

Changes in U.S.-Soviet Relations

Gorbachev is clearly bringing something new to Soviet international policy. His initiatives range from concessions on the treaty on intermediate-range nuclear forces, to a call for rapid conclusion of an agreement on the reduction of U.S. and Soviet strategic nuclear forces (START), to the withdrawal of Soviet occupation forces from Afghanistan, to the December 1988 announcement of unilateral Soviet conventional force reductions in Eastern Europe, the western Soviet Union, and Mongolia.[19]

It may not be prudent for the United States to take rapid unilateral actions in response to Soviet policy changes. Soviet military power remains significant and the important changes announced were only slowly introduced.[20] Moreover, there is bound to be considerable uncertainty about Gorbachev's chances of political survival, given the dramatic nature of the changes he has introduced into Soviet politics and society and, especially, the uncertainties about the nationality question in the Soviet Union. The announced policy changes seem real, however, and while their success would clearly suit Soviet interests, the reduction in international tensions that could follow is clearly in U.S. interests as well. Over time, these changes could lead to agreements that could stabilize the military relationship between the United States and the Soviet Union and make it possible to reduce the size, first-strike potential, and costs of their strategic nuclear arsenals.

During the Reagan years, considerable progress was made toward defining the outlines of the U.S.-Soviet START agreement that could reduce both sides' strategic forces to 1,600 delivery vehicles and roughly 9,000 warheads (4,900 of which could be deployed on ballistic missiles), more than 30 percent below warhead levels of the late 1980s.[21] A START treaty is likely in the near future, with implications for U.S. strategic modernization and strategic defense planning.

Current budget plans are clearly unrealistic, given the constraints on resources. Moreover, the new administration has inherited a mission agenda which is both increasingly inappropriate and sets no limits on defense outlays.

There is clearly some thinking in Washington about the relationship between arms control prospects and modernization plans. Brent Scowcroft, President Bush's national security adviser, argued in 1988 that such a link was important.[22] Les Aspin (D–Wisconsin), chairman of the House Armed Services Committee, proposed that all modernization plans be thrown into a common budgetary basket, with a funding level set for the next ten years. Production programs should then be sequenced so as to stay within the budgetary ceiling.

Despite these initial efforts to examine its relationship to arms control, however, strategic force modernization is likely to continue, with the possible exception of one intercontinental ballistic missile (ICBM) program (MX rail garrison or Midgetman could be dropped). If modernization plans are not changed, the United States would then comply with START treaty limits simply by dismantling older weapons.[23] There should be some room for rethinking this plan that would not entail risks to U.S. national security. The new administration should consider canceling or deferring new strategic hardware production decisions pending a review that considers which programs are truly necessary in the framework of a START treaty regime. It may be possible to negotiate a START agreement that limits modernization on both sides, leaving each with strategic forces consisting primarily of weapons now deployed or already in the pipeline.[24]

It will also be important to scrutinize the SDI and ASAT funding in the context of arms control possibilities. The Phase I system that DOD wants to deploy in the 1990s may not be useful militarily. Along with the larger SDI research program, it would consume significant budgetary resources while detracting from the stability of the strategic relationship with the Soviet Union.[25] It would be wise to continue a long-term research program on strategic defenses, but an early deployment, independent of progress on negotiations over strategic defenses, would be counterproductive. It would be preferable to hold the level of SDI spending down and eliminate Phase I acquisition plans while exploring the opportunities for U.S.-Soviet agreements in this area.

Changes in European Security

While strategic arms are doubtless costly to the Soviets, Soviet conventional forces are far more expensive and must be reduced if significant amounts of Soviet military spending are to be shifted to meet the needs of the civilian economy. This internal economic requirement probably plays a role in the Soviets' apparent willingness to consider major changes in military policy in Europe. Secretary Gorbachev moved quickly to conclude an agreement with the United States eliminating intermediate-range nuclear forces on both sides in Europe, an agreement that went into effect in 1988. The INF treaty reductions, while relatively insignificant militarily, were an important political signal. The treaty may be a precedent for an agreement that significantly reduces conventional forces, decreases the asymmetries in the forces of the two alliances, and permits intrusive verification.

Soviet actions since the INF treaty provide further evidence of this new approach. In December 1988, Secretary Gorbachev announced major unilateral reductions in Soviet conventional forces, including reductions of 240,000 troops in eastern Europe (East German, Hungary and Czechoslovakia) and the western Soviet Union. These reductions include the withdrawal and partial destruction of 10,000 tanks, 8,500 artillery pieces, and 800 combat aircraft, as well as the removal of assault brigades and bridging equipment in Eastern Europe. In addition, the Polish, East German, Hungarian, Czech, and Bulgarian governments have announced unilateral reductions of their own military forces.

The Warsaw Pact released its own data on force comparisons with the North Atlantic Treaty Organization (NATO) in January 1989, the first time that the bloc has been willing to disclose its own figures. The report urged progress toward an accord that would eliminate "existing asymmetries" in military forces, carry out "substantial cuts" in each side's forces, and expand confidence-building measures between the alliances.[26]

The changes in Soviet policy on conventional forces in Europe resonated in Western Europe, where, even before the announcement of Soviet unilateral reductions, governments and public opinion were increasingly unwilling to support renewed growth in defense expenditures or the deployment of advanced tactical nuclear systems in place of those eliminated by the INF agreement.[27] Western European views were expected to have an important role in the new round of conventional arms talks, opening in 1989 in Vienna and slated to included virtually all of the nations of the European subcontinent.[28]

The opportunities posed by the changes in Soviet and Western European policy have not yet been seriously assessed and acted upon by the U.S. government. U.S. policy remains cautious, defining Soviet intentions in Europe as threatening and Warsaw Pact conventional forces as significantly superior to those of NATO.[29] In 1989 there was still some sense in the executive branch and the Congress that NATO needed to expand and modernize its conventional forces to ensure deterrence in Europe. There was also an increasing irritation at what is seen as European (and Japanese) reluctance to carry their "fair share" of the common defense burden.[30]

A detailed review of European security policy, conducted in concert with our allies, could lead to defense options which are less expensive than the current posture, providing equivalent or even greater security to both alliances.

Whatever the conventional military balance in Europe and the non-U.S. contribution to NATO's forces, there is little doubt of two factors in the international atmosphere: the opportunity for significant reduction in conventional forces on both sides now exists, and the countries allied with the United States are unlikely to spend significantly greater resources on the common defense than they did in the 1980s.[31]

A detailed review of European security policy, conducted in concert with U.S. allies, could lead to defense options that are less expensive than the current posture, providing equivalent or even greater security to both alliances. The alliance should not undertake comprehensive and expensive upgrades of NATO's conventional forces without clarifying which upgrades are truly necessary and how they might fit in the framework of conventional arms reductions talks.

Negotiated with care, conventional arms reductions in Europe could limit and stabilize the military confrontation in that theater and constitute a concession to changing international realities. Hasty unilateral U.S. cuts in its European military forces, whether carried out as a reflection of annoyance with the allies or as a unilateral step to parallel Soviet unilateral moves, could well destabilize the U.S. relationship with its allies, especially France, West Germany, and the United Kingdom. Leadership is the crucial ingredient; the United States should be prepared to lead the alliance through these changes over the next five years.

Defense planning in 1989 includes new and costly upgrades of the remaining tactical nuclear forces in Europe and rapidly developing programs for conventional deep-strike technologies and military hardware.[32] These conventional force plans may not provide the most cost-effective means for strengthening deterrence in Europe compared to other improvements such as increased sustainability, better close air support, or barrier defenses such as mines and tank traps.[33] Offensively oriented technologies and tactics may not be desirable given NATO's defense mission and their possible impact on crisis stability in Europe.[34]

Changes in the Third World

The Soviet withdrawal from Afghanistan, completed in early 1989, was only one indication of the significant changes taking place outside Europe. The Middle East remained unpredictable, yet there were growing signs of a possible resolution of the Palestinian question and a settlement of the Iran-Iraq war, a quiescence in Libyan terrorism, and the withdrawal of U.S. naval forces in the Persian Gulf. While the elimination of conflict in the Middle East was not imminent at the end of the 1980s, the justification for a large U.S. military presence may have begun to fade.

Security issues in Africa were also changing as the Polisario-Morocco conflict faded and the agreement on the civil war in Angola and the independence of Namibia began to be implemented, leading to the withdrawal of South African and Cuban troops. While the South African security issue remained unresolved, development and health appeared to be the most pressing issues in Africa for the 1990s. Change could also be seen in Latin America, with a resolution of the Nicaraguan civil war and the withdrawal of U.S. troops in Honduras in sight. Some violent change will continue to occur, however, given the guerrilla struggle in Peru, the Chilean presidential elections, the instability of the governments of Brazil and Argentina, and the continuing conflict in El Salvador. In Latin America, however, development, environmental issues (the fate of the Brazilian rain forest), and the international drug trade seemed likely to pose the greatest security problems.

Change was taking place with equal rapidity in the Pacific. Increasingly Japan was seen as at least a regional power, and the Japanese have expanded their diplomatic, economic, and military resources in the region as part of this change.[35] In addition, the Vietnamese occupation of Cambodia began to wind down, and negotiations leading to a new government were under way. The South Korean and North Korean governments were engaged in bumpy but serious bilateral negotiations, which could open up new opportunities to reduce the military confrontation at the thirty-eighth parallel. Finally, the government of the People's Republic of China was engaged in an important restructuring of the domestic economy while it sought to stabilize its relations with the United States and, after many years, the Soviet Union. In Asia, too, the nature of the security issue was changing, with military problems increasingly taking a back seat to trade and development questions.

These changes in the Third World indicate the need for a reexamination of U.S. military policy and forces. The United States has roughly 760 overseas military installations. Although 75 percent of these are in Western Europe, Korea, and Japan, a number are located in areas where basing rights have become increasingly problematic and may well disappear. By 1994, the United States will need to renegotiate basing agreements with a number of countries, including Morocco, Kenya, Oman, and the

Philippines.[36] The outcome of these negotiations is uncertain. In addition, changes in Central America and Korea will raise basing-rights issues.

The potential loss of basing rights raises questions about the size, location, and mission of the U.S. Navy. It is increasingly clear that the Navy's goal of 600 deployed combat ships will be unattainable for fiscal reasons, making it even more urgent to review the justification for such a large fleet, to consider reducing the number of carrier battle groups, and to rethink the mission of the Navy outside the European and Northern Pacific theaters.[37] In addition, as the nature of U.S. missions changes with respect to the Third World, the Defense Department is beginning a process of restructuring U.S. military forces, which could lead to less emphasis on heavily armored divisions and more emphasis on lighter, more mobile forces intended for low-intensity conflict or special operations, including counterterrorism.[38] A number of military issues need to be addressed in a review of U.S. military policy with respect to the Third World.[39] There is likely to be reason for such forces in the future given the endemic nature of military conflict in the Third World. However, a major change in Soviet policy and similar changes in U.S. policies might extract both superpowers from involvement in such conflicts or from interpreting them as a reflection of superpower competition.

Such a policy change might also provide the basis for greater superpower cooperation, along with other nations, in attempting to limit the expansion of such conflicts. In the Persian Gulf, for example, an area figuring prominently in many scenarios for escalation to global conflict, the United States and the Soviet Union have been making small steps toward cooperating in an effort to limit the consequences of the Iran-Iraq war. President Bush may encounter further opportunities to limit the scope of Third World conflict, decreasing the risk of escalation to a superpower face-off.

Policy Alternatives

Defense planning in the 1990s will take place in a dramatically changed context from that of the early 1980s. The effort to reduce the persistent federal budget deficit puts new constraints on defense resources, and changes in international conditions are opening up significant new opportunities for conflict resolution and arms control.

Both the Congress and the Defense Department may prefer to avoid fundamental changes in programs and policies, however, continuing instead to count on quick fixes. For the Defense Department, such quick fixes include "buy now, pay later" budgeting and cost projections, based on the assumption, contrary to historical experience, that technology will make future weapons cheaper to operate; stretching programs out in order to buy fewer units each year, while buying the full program over a longer period of time and at higher total cost; cannibalizing the force structure or the readiness and sustainability budget without a strategic plan; or repackaging familiar budget plans under a new name such as "competitive strategies."

Congress too could revert to favorite quick fixes: trimming the accounts that fund readiness and sustainability; agreeing to stretch-outs; calling for an elimination of waste, fraud, and abuse; and attempting to legislate a greater sharing of the defense burden by U.S. allies overseas. These too have limits. Readiness cuts and stretch-outs have been discussed. Although eliminating waste is important, it is not a line item in the defense budget, making it difficult to find. Moreover, without program and policy changes, defense spending could still rise, even if the Defense Department achieved new levels of acquisition efficiency, Burden sharing is also more complex than it sometimes appears. There is no general agreement that the U.S. allies are getting a free ride in terms of defense spending or the actual contribution of military capability.[40] Moreover, even if they were, there is little likelihood that congressional legislation will actually lead to greater spending by other sovereign nations on their own defense. Ultimately cuts in U.S. budgets and capabilities will be defined in the framework of the national security needs defined by the U.S. government.

The relaxations in international tensions may actually facilitate both short-term budget control and better long-term policy planning. One possible budgetary approach to the short term would be to delay new defense program starts for a year, pending the

---

The relaxations in international tensions may actually facilitate both short-term budget control and better long-term policy planning.

---

outcome of a broader strategic review and a clearer understanding of the prospects for strategic and conventional arms control.

The U.S. military has made important gains over the past eight years, including a significantly more modern, better trained, readier, and more sustainable U.S. military. A moratorium on hardware new starts would help consolidate these gains by freeing up funds to preserve training, maintenance, and sustainability and to produce current hardware programs more efficiently. Such deferrals would permit the United States to rethink modernization plans in the light of changing international realities, leading to a decision to proceed with some programs while canceling others. They would send a significant signal to the Soviets and U.S. allies about intentions to explore those changes in a sweeping and positive way. Most significant, such a moratorium would save needed budgetary resources, providing control over defense outlays.[41]

Under a new starts deferral, readiness and sustainability would receive the marginal defense dollar. There is no doubt that many measures of readiness and sustainability (quality of personnel, mission-capable rates, training time, equipment maintenance schedules, ammunition, and spare parts stockpile goals) have improved since 1980. However, such progress stopped in 1985–1986, with subsequent decline in some important measures (depot maintenance backlogs, some training indicators). Thus, it is important to ensure adequate levels of readiness and sustainability for current forces.

This deferral concept also means that forces could be restructured in accordance with the opportunities provided by global changes, not cannibalized as a way to obtain adequate funding for new starts. There may well be policy justifications for reductions in Army divisions, Navy and Air Force air wings, or Navy carrier battle groups. They should emerge, however, from a careful consideration of U.S. commitments, goals, and military missions in a changing international environment.

A careful approach to modernization plans should employ the following rules of thumb: efficient production of current hardware programs is preferable to the acquisition of the next generation; if new technology promises great return, it should be obtained, when possible, by integrating it into an upgraded version of a current weapon rather than by starting a new program; careful choices among new programs need to be made, distinguishing between what is necessary and what would be useful but could be done without; no new weapon should enter production without adequate testing of prototypes to verify performance and cost; and all programs should be thoroughly scrutinized and decisions made to cancel, defer, or proceed before the program enters production since, once a weapon reaches production, it is far more difficult to stop. Following such rules, in the framework of a moratorium on new starts, the Defense Department and the Congress could consider the following choices in several areas.

Strategic Programs

The United States faces a critical production threshold for its strategic programs. If all new programs continue as planned, they will cost over $140 billion to acquire. Some of these programs, such as strategic bombers, may be redundant. Some make a questionable contribution to the stability of the deterrent relationship between the United States and the Soviet Union. Without giving up the option to pursue some of them later, now may be an ideal moment to suspend some of them pending negotiations on the START treaty.

The three most important strategic decisions concern ICBMs, bombers, and SDI. Production of MX rail garrison could be canceled, given its inadequate survivability and potentially destabilizing impact, and the Midgetman decision could be deferred for a year pending review and progress in the START talks. Bomber programs illuminate the importance of the rules of thumb. A production delay or even cancellation of the B-2 could be carried out with little damage to U.S. security. The United States has a large bomber capability; it is not clear that another 132 penetrating bombers are needed. Moreover, the B-2 program has encountered production and testing problems, which suggest its schedule could wisely be slowed or terminated, especially with only one test aircraft in existence. There is no reason to repeat the mistake made with the B-1B— rushing into production before conducting adequate testing. Deferring production decisions on ICBMs and the B-2 bomber do not foreclose options that might be desirable over the next two to four years. Making these decisions now, before full production begins, could save considerable money in the 1990s.

With respect to strategic defense, there are sound budgetary reasons for proceeding slowly with a program this unfocused and unpredictable. A moratorium on hardware and deployment decisions while continuing critical research would be sensible as START nears conclusion.

Conventional Modernization Options

The improvements in U.S. conventional forces in the 1980s will be threatened in the era of limited defense budgets unless careful attention is paid to setting priorities among modernization programs. Given international change and the prospects for conventional arms reductions, there may be room for a production moratorium on some conventional programs with minimal impact on current U.S. capabilities.

The Army faces budgetary pressures on its plans for next-generation helicopters and armored vehicles; there will not be adequate resources for both plans and perhaps for neither. Instead of proceeding with full-scale engineering development and, ultimately, production of the new LHX light attack–observation helicopter, it would make sense to purchase AH-64 and UH-60 helicopters at efficient rates and modernize current observation and attack helicopters through the helicopter improvement program. Given possible progress on European conventional arms reductions, it might also make sense to defer production plans for Army air defense systems and such deep-strike weapons (aimed at attacking Warsaw Pact second-echelon forces) as the Army tactical missile system and the JSTARS target location and communications aircraft.

With respect to the Navy's surface fleet, two new aircraft carriers were funded in FY 1988. Given budget constraints and changing carrier missions (particularly the declining attention being given to a Soviet home port attack mission), it may make sense to retire the oldest carriers— the *Midway, Coral Sea,* and *Enterprise*—earlier than planned. In addition, the Navy plans to begin production of a new carrier-based attack aircraft, the A-12, in FY 1991, while it has abandoned plans for a modified A-6G version. It might be wise to reverse course and produce upgraded A-6s through the "G" program and defer the A-12. The Marine Corps' V-22 Osprey transport aircraft could also be deferred. Finally, construction of the first SSN-21 nuclear attack submarine is already under way, but further boats could be deferred.

Air Force procurement plans include continued production of the F-15, F-16, and F-117A (stealth fighter), as well as new production starts for the C-17 cargo plane, the B-2 bomber, and a new close air support aircraft and significant R&D funding for the ATF. The rules of thumb apply: defer funding increases for ATF and C-17 (as well as B-2) while producing F-16, F-117A, and close air support aircraft efficiently, and review the need for additional F-15s with an option to terminate the program.

Some will argue that it is vital to acquire the next generation of hardware as soon as possible.[42] Such thinking, however, ignores changes in the international arena, the evolution of arms control possibilities as a way of buying security at less expenditure, and budgetary constraints. Current production programs provide the services with known capabilities and costs, while new starts involve technological hazards and the risk that rising costs will squeeze future budgets, forcing difficult choices with respect to readiness, sustainability, and the size of the force structure. A more careful approach to defense priorities, with a deferral of some modernization decisions, will help DOD avoid these uncharted waters.

Conclusion

As the Bush administration took office, it faced a major fiscal dilemma in defense. Although defense budgets were cut in each of the preceding four years, the services resisted the pressure to set priorities. Instead a new bow wave of defense procurement was on the horizon, with dangerous consequences for defense resources and military capabilities in the 1990s. Unless early plans were cut back, the result could be fiscal chaos, the cannibalization of force structure, and declining military readiness and sustainability, while defense spending levels, committed to the next generation of military hardware, remain high. Changes on the international scene, which cry out for American leadership, offered an opportunity for major changes in policy, force structure, and procurement plans. The first major test of the new administration was likely to be its ability to hold off the next generation of hardware commitments while policy is reviewed and to implement a new course in which commitments and resources were more carefully matched.

Mobile, rail-based
MX missile.

Chapter 4

Strategic Forces

Jan M. Lodal

A rms control once again was a major determinant of the U.S. strategic force posture in 1988. The year began in the aftermath of a major arms control achievement: the signing of the INF treaty eliminating intermediate-range nuclear-armed missiles from U.S. and Soviet arsenals. The INF treaty, signed at the December 1987 Washington summit between President Ronald Reagan and Soviet leader Mikhail Gorbachev, accomplished much less in quantitative terms than popularly understood. But symbolically it was a major step toward a new accommodation between the United States and the Soviet Union.

The year also saw substantial progress made toward completing the strategic arms reductions agreement (START) between the United States and the Soviet Union, putting the anticipation of START high on the list of considerations for strategic force planners. The likely future role of antiballistic missile defenses (ABMs) became much more realistic in 1988 as managers of the Strategic Defense Initiative (SDI) program moved further away from President Reagan's original SDI goal of "rendering nuclear weapons impotent and obsolete." By year's end, it appeared that the incoming Bush administration would face the prospect of restructuring U.S. strategic forces to fit with START limits and to live within the regime of essentially zero ballistic missile defenses established by the 1972 ABM Treaty.

Budget constraints also remained a major consideration in 1988 and promised to be an even greater determinant of force structure in coming years. For the third consecutive budget year, defense budget authority declined in real dollars; for the first time in a decade, actual defense outlays also declined. There seemed to be a consensus among Democrats and Republicans in both houses of Congress that defense spending would at best stay level in real dollar terms for the next four years as the United States wrestles its budget deficit under control. George Bush also asserted this position during his presidential campaign, although he espoused more programs than can be fit within this budget ceiling.

In quantitative terms, the strategic forces of the United States and the Soviet Union did not undergo major changes in 1988. The steady increase in the total number of on-line strategic weapons continued, with each side deploying 500 to 700 more strategic weapons by year's end than at the beginning, bringing the total number to about 11,000 for the Soviet Union and 14,000 for the United States.

Intercontinental Ballistic Missiles

The United States retired twenty-three additional Minuteman III three-warhead inter-continental ballistic missiles (ICBMs) in order to make way for the final deployment of ten-warhead MX ICBMs in these silos. This modernization will add 350 warheads to the U.S. land-based ICBM force, an increase of about 3 percent in the total strategic force. The 500 deployed MX warheads also have somewhat greater accuracy and yield than the Minuteman IIIs they replaced. But the major development affecting the U.S. ICBM force during 1988 was not a quantitative deployment but rather a change in research and development focus. The Reagan administration dropped the mobile Midg-etman single-warhead missile (officially called the small ICBM, or SICBM) from its initial budget request and proposed a rail-mobile, garrison-based MX as the solution for the decade-old problem of how to modernize land-based ICBMs. Congress restored enough funding to the Midgetman to keep the option open into the Bush administration, but the momentum at the end of the year was away from the mobile Midgetman and toward the rail-garrison MX.

The Soviet Union continued apace with its own deployment of ten-warhead and single-warhead mobile land-based missiles, moving away from a long-standing emphasis on silo-based ICBMs. The Soviets continued the deployment of their SS-24 rail-mobile ten-warhead missile—a weapon with characteristics similar to those of the MX—in-creasing the number of missiles deployed from about ten to about twenty. The Soviets also deployed approximately fifty additional single-warhead road-mobile SS-25s—a mis-sile with some characteristics similar to those of the proposed U.S. Midgetman—bring-ing the total number of SS-25s deployed to about 150. These new deployments of mobile ICBMs were partially offset by the continued phasing out of the older single-warhead SS-11 silo-based ICBMs.

The Air Force's unexpected switch away from the mobile Midgetman to the rail-garrison MX meant that 1988 saw yet another year pass without a consensus on how to modernize the U.S. land-based ICBM force. The mobile Midgetman is strongly sup-ported by many in Congress (most particularly by Les Aspin, D–Wisconsin, chairman of the House Armed Services Committee), as well as by Brent Scowcroft, President Bush's national security adviser. Thus the Bush administration may well reverse course once again and emphasize the mobile Midgetman as a long-term solution to the problem of land-based missile modernization. Budget constraints make it highly unlikely that both projects—the mobile Midgetman and the rail-garrison MX—will proceed. But the same budget constraints also argue against the mobile Midgetman, with its price tag of $40 billion to $50 billion for a 500-warhead force. The rail-garrison MX is estimated to cost only about $15 billion for a force with the same number of warheads.

One possible solution is to continue with the Midgetman missile but set aside for the moment the mobile deployment mode. A single-warhead missile is not an attractive target, even if deployed in a theoretically vulnerable silo, since the Soviet Union would have to use two weapons to destroy only one U.S. weapon. The irrationality of such a first-strike strategy would be ensured if START is completed and each side is limited to equal numbers of total warheads. Thus, single-warhead Midgetmen in silos would be a stable deterrent force despite their theoretical vulnerability.

1988 saw yet another year pass without a consensus on how to modernize the U.S. land-based ICBM force.

A force of 500 Midgetmen deployed in existing Minuteman II silos would cost about the same as the 500-warhead rail-garrison MX force. But completing development of the single-warhead missile would also leave the option of rapidly expanding the force, to several thousand missiles if necessary, in the event of a Soviet arms control break-out or an increased threat to U.S. submarines. Furthermore, research and development could continue on mobility options, providing a further hedge against future threats.

Submarine-Launched Ballistic Missiles

The United States took out of service two additional Poseidon submarines during the year, keeping the total number of MIRVed missiles plus cruise missile–carrying bombers at about 1,345, close to the SALT II limit of 1,320. The Navy had originally proposed to retire only one Poseidon, but Congress required the second retirement to keep from going further above the SALT II limit. The ninth twenty-four-missile Trident boat completed sea trials in December 1988, adding to the total number of launchers counted under SALT, but it will not become operational until late 1989. Thus, in operational terms, the U.S. submarine-based strategic force declined somewhat during 1988. This ninth Trident boat will be the first deployed with the substantially larger Trident D-5 missile. The missile continued its successful test program in 1988.

The Soviet Union continued the construction of both Typhoon and Delta IV SSBNs in 1988, deploying a new boat of each type at roughly twelve-month intervals. In addition, work continued on developing upgraded Delta IV SS-N-23 and the Typhoon SS-N-20 missiles, each capable of carrying ten MIRVs.

Operationally the major development of 1988 was the return of Soviet Yankee-class submarines to their deployment stations near the U.S. coastline. When these submarines were withdrawn earlier in the year, it appeared that the Soviet Union might finally be ending one of the most provocative aspects of its strategic nuclear program. The deployment of these submarines near American shores has threatened a short-warning attack against American bomber bases. But this practice was not terminated.

Strategic Bombers

The United States completed the production of its force of 100 B-1Bs by taking delivery of the last thirty-six aircraft in 1988. Three aircraft were lost on training missions, leading to a net increase of thirty-three and a final force of ninety-seven, organized into four operational wings totaling seventy-four aircraft. Since the B-1Bs were not fully operational by the end of 1988, they represented very little increase in the U.S. striking force capability. The B-1B continues to have problems of such severity that many observers no longer consider it to be much of a technological advance over the B-52 equipped with air-launched cruise missiles (ALCMs).

Approximately twenty-one additional B-52H aircraft were converted to ALCM carriers during 1988. The conversion of the B-52Hs will add approximately 126 weapons; ALCM-equipped aircraft carry, on the average, about six more weapons each than do B-52s intended to penetrate Soviet airspace.

A major development in 1988 was the rollout of the B-2 Stealth bomber and the disclosure of its projected cost—$450 million to $500 million per bomber. The Stealth bomber, shown to the public late in the year, promises to be the major strategic program issue of 1989.

The Soviets put their first Blackjack bomber, an aircraft similar to the B-1, into operation in 1988. By year's end, they had about fifteen aircraft operational, carrying perhaps six weapons each.

Sea-Launched Cruise Missiles

The United States and the Soviet Union continued to deploy sea-launched cruise missiles (SLCMs) during 1988. The United States continued deployment of the nuclear version of the Tomahawk SLCM, and the Soviets continued deployment of the SS-N-21 3,000-kilometer-range SLCM. The United States plans eventually to deploy approximately 750 long-range nuclear-armed SLCMs on approximately 200 surface ships and submarines; the Soviets have proposed in START negotiations a limit of 400 on nuclear-armed SLCMs, but what they might deploy in the absence of a START agreement is not known.

Management of Strategic Programs

Despite the partial implementation of the Packard commission's proposed defense procurement reforms, scandals and procurement failures continued to plague the Reagan administration's Pentagon management. The B-1 bomber and the MX missile fell well short of meeting technological specifications in their initial deployments. In the case of the B-1B bomber, it appears that several of the weaknesses are so intrinsic to the system that they can never be rectified. At a minimum, the cost to attempt to rectify the problems will probably not be affordable, given projected budget constraints.

In the middle of the year, Congressman Aspin delivered a series of speeches, entitled "Acquiring Strategic Weapons: Are Working Nukes Just Flukes?" evaluating major strategic weapons. The speeches were based on an extensive House Armed Services Committee review of the major strategic programs: MX, Midgetman, the B-1B bomber, the B-2 Stealth bomber, the Trident D-5 SLBM, and the Advanced Cruise Missile (ACM). Classification prohibited publication of the results on the B-2 Stealth and the ACM, but the other reports were consolidated and published by the committee in June 1988.

Congressman Aspin gave failing grades to the Air Force for both the management and performance of the B-1B bomber and for ACM management. The Midgetman received generally high grades, but only the Trident D-5 missile received a uniformly positive report.

The B-1B seemed to illustrate all of the problems that have plagued defense acquisition. The entire program had been canceled by President Carter in favor of the B-2 Stealth advance technology bomber, but it was reactivated by the Reagan administration more for political than for strategic and military reasons. Because the projected high cost of procuring and operating two new bombers in the 1990s was ignored, the Bush administration will face extremely difficult choices with regard to these programs.

The B-1B is already procured, but it may not be possible to correct its many problems before Soviet advances in air defenses eliminate the benefits the bomber potentially has over the B-52 equipped with cruise missiles. A major choice will have to be made concerning whether to adjust the bomber's mission and reduce substantially its operational cost, relying on the B-2 and the B-52s equipped with cruise missiles for our strategic retaliatory forces, or to divert scarce resources from high-priority conventional programs to pay for fixing the B-1B.

In contrast, the Navy's management of the Trident D-5 missile program has been a model of success. Its Strategic Systems Program Office (SSPO) has had full responsibility for the service's SLBMs for the last thirty years. It retains responsibility for the missiles not only during development and procurement but through the rest of their life cycle as well, including providing logistics support (repairs and maintenance) during operations. The management of the SSPO has been extremely stable and experienced. In contrast, the programs that have had trouble have been characterized by rapid turnover in management and a strong tendency to pass problems on to the operational forces. Problems are left in systems to be dealt with after they are operational, despite the fact that it is always more expensive to fix them later.

Another major concern with American development and procurement practices has been the tendency to reinvent the wheel. All studies indicate a strong need to use existing components where possible, developing new components only when essential to achieve the mission of the new system. Such an evolutionary approach to developing new systems has long been practiced by the Soviet Union but shunned by many American program managers. Perhaps the complicated and difficult interface between the

U.S. private sector defense contractors and the ever-changing military and civilian managers in the Pentagon makes such a process impossible. But there seems to be no question that failure to adopt it has substantially reduced the effectiveness of U.S. forces.

Dealing with these management problems will have to be a priority of the Bush administration. Budget constraints will no longer permit adding funds to programs in trouble or avoiding choices between competing systems. Congress increasingly will tend to fund only well-managed programs. The developing détente with the Soviet Union, arms reductions agreements, and a high level of confidence in the stability of the nuclear balance will make it difficult to argue that risks should be taken on programs with serious management and performance problems.

B-2 Stealth Bomber

The B-2 Stealth bomber is likely to receive more debate in 1989 than any other U.S. strategic program. Although the excitement and even amazement associated with the bomber's revolutionary and exotic technology will capture the public's imagination, tough cost benefit analysis will seriously undermine support for the program.

Since the United States first developed an effective ballistic missile deterrent in the early 1960s, the role of strategic bombers has been vigorously debated. In the 1960s,

Defense Secretary Robert McNamara canceled the B-70 high-level supersonic bomber and planned to phase out all strategic bombers, relying on a variant of the F-111 fighter to provide a residual force to stress Soviet air defenses. Throughout the 1970s, critics argued that if an air-breathing leg of the triad was needed at all, stand-off cruise missile carriers could do the job much less expensively. This debate notwithstanding, the air-breathing leg of the strategic triad continues to be the most expensive component of the force, consuming close to half the strategic offensive force budget.

Even if most of our ballistic missile force were to fail, a small number of viable ballistic missiles could destroy enough of Soviet air defenses to open a substantial corridor for relatively low-technology bombers to penetrate.

The debate about bombers stems from several factors. Most fundamentally, the question is why the United States needs strategic bombers when ballistic missiles can do the same job so much less expensively. Three answers are usually given. First, bombers act as a hedge against the possible failure of the ballistic missile retaliatory force. Of course, the importance of this point depends on the risk attached to a failure of the ballistic missile force. Second, because strategic bombers can be recalled after launch, it is argued that they are much more flexible than missiles. Those making this argument, however, seem to overlook the fact that ballistic missiles can be retained in their launchers until only a few minutes before they are needed to destroy the target. Bombers, on the other hand, pass their fail-safe point many hours before they strike a target, requiring much earlier decisions about launch. Thus, they are in reality less flexible with regard to the timing of an attack.

The third argument for bombers is that they are needed for conventional war, so keeping them available for strategic missions is not costly. There are two problems with this argument. First, a conventional-only bomber force would cost much less than a force equipped to penetrate and survive in a nuclear environment. Second, if the United States relies on bombers for strategic retaliation, the bombers would have to be withheld in a large-scale conventional war to avoid undercutting this strategic deterrent.

In addition to making the case for retaining the air-breathing leg of the triad, one must as well make the case for penetrating bombers. Even if most of our ballistic missile force were to fail, a small number of viable ballistic missiles could destroy enough of Soviet air defenses to open a substantial corridor for relatively low-technology bombers to penetrate. If all ballistic missiles failed (a highly unlikely prospect), stand-off cruise missiles could probably open such a corridor or perhaps even destroy all necessary targets without penetrating Soviet airspace. The high cost of the B-2 is a result of giving it the ability to penetrate an undegraded Soviet defense; stand-off cruise missile carriers, of which a sizable force already exists, are a small fraction of the cost of the B-2.

During 1988 the Air Force argued that only a penetrating stealth bomber such as the B-2 could seek out and destroy the Soviets' emerging force of mobile ICBMs. But by the end of the year, the Air Force had downplayed this mission, for several reasons. First, to find mobile ICBMs, the B-2 would have to turn on its own radars, giving away its location and undercutting the reason for its existence. Second, Soviet land-based mobile missiles are likely to remain a fairly small portion of the total Soviet strategic force; the remaining invulnerable force would still be quite enough to devastate the United States and its allies. (This has been the reason why all efforts at counterforce have failed for twenty-five years.) Third, such mobile missiles might well have been launched by the time the B-2 finds them. Certainly those mobile missiles remaining after the B-2 had begun to destroy others in the force would be launched before the B-2s found them.

The launch-on-warning problem associated with the B-2 goes further than just the possibility of failing to destroy mobile missiles. The rationale that strategic bombers are not destabilizing to the deterrent balance because they cannot be used as part of a surprise attack disappears if the B-2 operates as advertised. Since the B-2's approach would not be detected by Soviet radars until minutes before it reached its target, some have argued that stealth technology itself, whether applied to B-2s or only to stand-off cruise missiles, renders air-breathing systems potentially destabilizing. Of course, one must take into account the other Soviet strategic forces in evaluating the importance of this effect. But if the counterforce mission is held out as a major part of the rationale for the B-2, one must logically acknowledge the associated destabilizing effect as well.

The B-2 could end up absorbing half of the entire procurement budget for strategic weapons during much of the 1990s. In the end the B-2 may well be worth its immense price. But we should understand the opportunity costs. For example, for the same amount of money 25,000 M1 Abrams tanks could be purchased—enough to offset the Soviets' tank advantage worldwide. Since Soviet offensive armor largely drives the need for flexible response and therefore for a large nuclear deterrent force, meeting the threat directly should at least be considered.

The B-2 will also face questions with regard to its performance and the management of the program. Its prime contractor, the Northrop Corporation, is in legal difficulties and under investigation for failures with the MX guidance system and for other procurement abuses. The intense secrecy associated with the program has led to great suspicion that the bomber's performance is substantially less than advertised. If problems arise in flight testing, the B-2 could face an early death.

The Maturing of SDI

The year 1988 was a time of restructuring and acceptance of reality for the Strategic Defense Initiative Organization (SDIO). Congress again cut the budget request from

$5.1 billion to $4.1 billion. Furthermore, it legislated that no SDI tests violate the traditional (narrow) interpretation of the 1972 ABM Treaty. (The legislation does not refer directly to the ABM Treaty but instead limits SDI tests to those already planned, none of which violates the traditional interpretation of the treaty.) Finally, Congress passed legislation expressing the sense of that body that SDI should concentrate on the first phase of a system to defend against accidental launches of enemy ICBMs. This would move the program dramatically away from President Reagan's stated intention of protecting population centers against large-scale attacks.

Research and development continues to focus on "kinetic kill vehicles" (rockets) for space-based elements of a strategic defensive system. Space-based lasers, the technology that so excited proponents of SDI in its early years, continue to be deemphasized, reflecting the extraordinary technological challenges associated with such lasers. (These challenges were widely pointed out by early critics of SDI.) Testing and full-scale development of any space-based interceptor would violate the ABM Treaty and thus require withdrawal. In any case, according to 1988 testimony by then-SDIO director Lieutenant General James Abrahamson, the space-based interceptor, a key component of a Phase I system, will not be ready for deployment for another ten years.

The SDIO released a new Phase I architecture study in October that reduced the estimated cost of early deployment from $115 billion to $69 billion. The cost reduction was based on the alleged increase in projected performance of space-based interceptors and a shift in priority from space-based to ground-based systems. The number of ground-based exoatmospheric reentry vehicle interception system (ERIS) platforms was increased by 70 percent, while costly space-based rocket-interceptor platforms were decreased by 50 percent, compared to the previous architecture. The proposed architecture raised many questions, however. In particular, the entire system is dependent on a very small number of Space Surveillance and Tracking System satellites, which could be vulnerable to Soviet space mines or other advanced antisatellite weapons. (Presumably the space-based interceptors could destroy simple antisatellite weapons launched at the surveillance and tracking system satellites.) The revised architecture nevertheless would still violate the ABM Treaty, so a decision to deploy it likely would necessitate abandoning efforts to reach new arms control agreements with the Soviet Union. The Soviets have firmly linked such agreements to maintenance of the ABM Treaty.

Both President Bush and national security adviser Scowcroft have expressed some skepticism about a fast pace for SDI. Even the reduced $69 billion for Phase I is an immense procurement cost for a system whose mission is uncertain, survivability questionable, and best possible performance well short of the "astrodome" concept for which President Reagan received such strong public support. Further restructuring and consolidation of the SDI program seems inevitable in 1989.

Production of Nuclear Materials

The previously simmering problem of modernizing the nation's production facilities for nuclear weapons finally reached a full boil in 1988. The Department of Energy (DOE) informed Congress that it will need up to $45 billion to build replacements for some of its aging atomic weapons factories. Even more fiscally threatening is the immense cost projected to clean up improperly disposed toxic nuclear waste resulting from previous production of nuclear weapons. Washington State's Hanford nuclear reservation (closed in January 1988), the facility that produced the plutonium used in the Nagasaki bomb, has more than 1,000 sites where toxic materials were improperly dumped. The DOE has indicated it will need $13 billion in the next five years simply to address problems that pose an immediate threat to safety or the environment. Much waste is being stored temporarily in steel tanks, and many leaks have gone uncontrolled over the years. Both of the department's Savannah River reactors that produced tritium, a gaseous component of fusion weapons that decays rapidly and must be replenished, were shut down during 1988. Both plants are so deteriorated that many experts question whether they can be operated safely at all.

If the potential bill of $200 billion to $250 billion for cleaning up from past nuclear weapons production and building plants capable of supporting future nuclear weapons production is attributed to American strategic programs, as it logically should be, budget constraints will become nothing less than a budget crisis. Calls for the cessation of most nuclear modernization programs, relying on weapons already produced, will undoubtedly increase.

Michael Dukakis proposed slowing down modernization in his presidential campaign. He said on many occasions that he saw no need for additional U.S. nuclear weapons. But his attitude toward nuclear weapons seems to have been strongly rejected by the voting public. Polls indicated that by a three-to-one margin, voters felt that George Bush would be more likely to maintain a strong defense. Governor Dukakis's attitudes on nuclear weapons were cited by many voters as the cause of their preference for Vice-President Bush.

Ironically it is George Bush who will have to face the reality of the immense bill attached to continuing all strategic programs: $50 billion for the Midgetman, $60 billion for the Stealth, $10 billion to fix the B-1, $70 billion for Phase I SDI, $200 billion to clean up nuclear production facilities and build new ones, $40 billion for continuing the Trident program. All of this adds up to procurement programs vastly above the high levels reached at the peak of the Reagan administration's military buildup. But the budget is likely to be inadequate even to continue the Reagan-era programs.

Deterrence as the Basis of Nuclear Strategy

By mid-1987 it appeared that President Reagan was determined to drop nuclear deterrence as the basis for American security policy, although this had been the agreed military strategy of the entire NATO alliance since the end of World War II. His SDI program was designed to substitute an impenetrable shield that would make nuclear weapons "impotent and obsolete." At the Reykjavik summit, he discussed seriously the elimination of all strategic nuclear missiles. The zero option in INF strongly reaffirmed President Reagan's continuing rhetoric favoring the total elimination of nuclear weapons.

Since the 1950s technological and strategic realities have forced the Western allies into a strategy based on nuclear deterrence. By the end of 1988, these realities had once again brought most American programs and arms control proposals back into line with this strategy. Over time, deterrence could be strengthened by developing the capability to use U.S. strategic nuclear forces to attack and destroy the Soviets' ability to wage large-scale conventional war. Such a move would provide justification for substantial strategic forces budgets since this is an extremely difficult (perhaps even infeasible) task.

To justify such an undertaking, one has to believe first that the present nuclear balance is not safe enough. But if, as appears likely, START succeeds and nuclear weapons are reduced, Gorbachev continues to show restraint in regional conflicts, and European allies continue to press for a renewed détente with the Soviet Union, the Bush administration will have great difficulty justifying large expenditures on strategic forces simply to move further away from targeting cities and closer toward deterrence based entirely on the targeting of Soviet military forces.

More than any other single factor, the progress of relations with the Soviet Union will determine the U.S. strategic force posture.

The Primacy of Arms Control

More than any other single factor, the progress of relations with the Soviet Union will determine the U.S. strategic force posture. Achieving a complete settlement of cold war issues with the Soviet Union could permit a move toward minimum deterrence. But well before any such radical change begins, the START agreement will have to be completed.

The preelection statements of President Bush and his advisers indicated a lack of enthusiasm for completing the START agreement in the form it had at the beginning of 1989. In particular, President Bush raised the important issue of needing to agree on a major reduction in the Soviet Union's conventional offensive forces (especially tanks and self-propelled artillery) before taking additional arms control steps that might undercut NATO's strategy of flexible response. Flexible response relies heavily on nuclear deterrence, and the INF treaty was criticized for its potential to undercut nuclear deterrence before eliminating the Soviet conventional arms threat.

On December 7, 1988 at the United Nations, Mikhail Gorbachev announced a 10 percent cut in conventional force manpower (5.5 million to 5.0 million) and a withdrawal from Europe of six tank divisions, 10,000 tanks, 8,500 artillery pieces, and 800 combat aircraft. As dramatic as these announcements were, they leave the Red Army largely intact and still considerably larger and more capable than NATO. Thus, the Gorbachev iniative seems unlikely to bring about any major change in the agreed NATO position that the Red Army must come down to parity with NATO. In these circumstances, START is likely to remain hostage to progress in conventional arms control.

Aside from questions of linkage to conventional arms control, at the outset of the Bush administration there were major issues left in the START negotiations, including how to limit SLCMs, how to handle nonnuclear cruise missiles, limits on mobile missiles, linkage to continuing the traditional interpretation of the ABM Treaty, and the highly complex details of verification.

Despite these challenges, there is a good likelihood that the Bush administration will push for completion of a START agreement, without enforcing strict linkage to conventional arms reductions. The desire for continuity with the Reagan administration, the strong likelihood of a less doctrinaire position on SDI by the Bush administration, the anticipated complexities of conventional arms control, and the need in both the United States and the Soviet Union to control military budgets point toward the early completion of START.

If the START agreement is completed by the Bush administration along the lines already agreed, major changes in U.S. forces would be required. For example, if the existing fifty MX missiles and ninety-seven B-1 bombers are kept, along with 300 of the 500 Minuteman III ICBMs and a Trident force of eighteen boats (versus either the twelve boats deployed or under construction or the twenty-one planned), about half of the cruise missile–equipped B-52s, all single-warhead Minuteman II missiles, 200 three-warhead Minuteman III missiles, and the entire Poseidon submarine force would have to be destroyed. The B-2 bomber would have to be canceled. And almost certainly SDI would be restricted to testing and development within the traditional narrow interpretation of the treaty, eliminating the possibility of any early Phase I SDI deployment. Many other combinations of forces are possible within START restraints, but all combinations have the effect of reducing substantially the overall size of U.S. strategic forces and programs. The same is true for Soviet forces.

Without the constraints of START, the Bush administration will face almost as severe budgetary constraints. The problem of decreasing marginal returns makes it difficult to justify much of a buildup in nuclear forces. Without a major shift in targeting strategy that emphasizes Soviet conventional forces, there are not many more valid targets to cover. Substantial numbers of weapons are already targeted against missile silos that are likely to be empty when destroyed and other facilities whose timely destruction is questionable.

Ronald Reagan did not actually increase the U.S. strategic forces much over what had already been planned by the Carter administration. He did, however, restore confidence in U.S. military capabilities. At the same time, Mikhail Gorbachev came to power in the Soviet Union. Gorbachev's withdrawal of Soviet troops from Afghanistan, his policy of "new thinking" on foreign policy, and his rhetoric of accommodation have left the West less concerned about the risk of war.

Gorbachev's willingness to eliminate a major Soviet advantage in INF weapons admittedly benefited the Soviet Union politically in Europe. But the success of INF has nonetheless set expectations that future arms reduction agreements can be reached. Other symbolic events, such as the U.S. defense secretary in the cockpit of a Soviet Blackjack bomber, Americans visiting the heavily disputed and previously top secret Krasnoyarsk radar site, bilateral INF inspection teams at both U.S. and Soviet factories, and American and Soviet nuclear tests being conducted at the other side's test sites—all events unthinkable prior to Gorbachev—will add to the overall relaxation of tensions. In an age of tight budgets, this relaxation of tension, tentative as it is, will make it impossible to obtain congressional approval for a further buildup of American strategic forces without having first undertaken every effort to negotiate nuclear reductions with the Soviet Union.

M1 Abrams Tanks on REFORGER Exercise, 1988

Chapter 5

Theater Forces

Eliot A. Cohen

Today, as for the past forty years, the defense of Western Europe remains the first charge on the American defense establishment. Depending on how one calculates it, between 50 and 60 percent of the American defense budget goes to NATO-related expenses. Over 300,000 Americans in uniform are stationed in Europe, and most of the rest of the U.S. force structure—even the Army's light infantry divisions—has Europe-related missions. In an age when the American foreign policy consensus shows more cracks than in the past, a commitment to Europe remains more certain than most other elements of American national security policy. During the 1988 presidential campaign, neither candidate suggested that American conventional forces in Europe should be drawn down. Just the reverse, in fact, was true: the more dovish of the candidates, Governor Michael Dukakis, criticized the Reagan administration for doing too little to improve the conventional defense of Europe.

To be sure, neoisolationist sentiments simmered among various groups, represented by left-leaning politicians unhappy with the U.S. role as a global power—Reverend Jesse Jackson and Representative Patricia Schroeder (D–Colorado) come to mind—but also among conservative advocates of minimal government such as economist Melvyn Krauss. Both groups argued that excessive expenditures on NATO defense diverted governmental funds from more worthwhile activities (social spending on the one hand or fiscal soundness on the other). In addition, some neoconservatives, considering themselves global unilateralists, advocated the severing, or at least the dramatic loosening, of a tie with Europe that seemed to them outmoded and confining.

Thus far none of these groups has mounted a successful challenge to the reigning view of U.S. national security interests or to the long-standing strategic decision to deploy large American forces forward, with pledges to reinforce them speedily in the event of a war. This has led many observers of the debate about the U.S. role in Europe to the conclusion that the issues have remained unchanged since the 1950s, when similar views were also advanced, albeit in a more muted fashion. This complacency, however, is illfounded. NATO is undergoing fundamental changes—some driven by particular political decisions or events, others by political, economic, and military trends at home and in the Warsaw Pact.

New Developments: *Perestroika*, Arms Control, and the New European Community

Let us begin with the first category of developments, those brought about by the decisions of statesmen and governments. Most notable here is the rise of Mikhail Gorbachev to power and the advent—or at least the prospect—of major changes in Soviet society and ways of doing business. The Gorbachev era has many aspects, all of which have a bearing on NATO defense. First and foremost, the Soviet Union has made strenuous, and on the whole successful, efforts to appear far less threatening to the countries of Western Europe. These moves culminated in Gorbachev's dramatic declaration before the United Nations in December 1988 that the Soviet Union would unilaterally disband six divisions in Eastern Europe and reduce other forces. As a result of adroit personal diplomacy on the part of Gorbachev and his entourage, as well as a general moderation in the tone of Soviet foreign policy, we reached the curious situation in 1988 in which opinion polls show that some West European publics had more confidence in Mikhail Gorbachev than they did in Ronald Reagan. As a practical matter, the revival of a European détente has renewed the willingness of European bankers and business to loan the Soviet Union money and to conclude large economic deals with it.

Those loans and deals are particularly important to the Soviet Union because under Gorbachev it has become apparent just how badly off the Soviets are. In 1988 Gorbachev told the Central Committee of the Communist party that the Soviet economy had eked out a mere 2 percent annual growth during the early 1980s—and much of the increase came from growth in alcohol sales and the rise in world oil prices. During 1988 experts continued to consider more seriously some of the long-held views of Soviet émigré economists who argued that the Soviet economy was considerably smaller than hitherto thought.[1] Hitherto CIA estimates, which relied heavily on Soviet data, had the Soviet economy at something like 50 percent the size of the American, with an annual expenditure of perhaps 15 to 17 percent of GNP on defense. The new estimates suggested that the Soviet economy might be only slightly more than a third the size of the American, with military spending 25 percent of GNP. The latter figures suggest a country considerably poorer per capita, but no less powerful militarily, than American experts had believed. Although this subject will continue to spark endless disputes among economists, two important facts have become clear: that the Soviet economy has stagnated for at least the last twenty years, growing very slowly and in some cases not at all, and that the system seems poorly equipped to adapt to the new age of information-driven advanced economies.

In 1988, as in the year or two preceding, Western readers learned more and more of appalling public health conditions and ecological catastrophe in the Soviet Union, where life expectancy has steadily decreased and infant mortality has steadily risen. According to one source, infant mortality per live births in the Soviet Union may be as high as thirty-five or forty per thousand, three or four times the U.S. rate, and male life expectancy is at least seven years behind that of the Americans.[2] At the same time, Western and Soviet audiences have seen the unprecedented spectacle of open debates within the leading organizations of the Communist party. Moreover, riots in Armenia and Azerbaijan, coupled with separatist movements in the Baltic republics (including a declaration of quasi-autonomy by Estonia in late 1988), reminded American observers that the Soviet Union is a multinational empire, which has by no means resolved the ethnic and racial hatreds that characterize it.

The sudden appearance of reactive armor on Soviet tanks in Eastern Europe—a development that at a stroke enfeebled most of the West's antitank weapons—confirmed that the Soviets had by no means ceased to develop advanced weapon systems.

There has been talk of new thinking along defensive lines in the Soviet military.[3] Yet here, even more than in economic matters, speech has far outrun deeds. Observers of the Soviet system know that according to Marxist-Leninist doctrine, all Soviet wars are, by definition, defensive. More to the point, there has been not the slightest indication that the Soviets have reduced military spending or changed the patterns of deployment, organization, training, and equipment in Eastern Europe and the western districts of the Soviet Union that would enable them to launch a rapid offensive to the West. The sudden appearance of reactive armor on Soviet tanks in Eastern Europe— a development that at a stroke enfeebled most of the West's antitank weapons—confirmed that the Soviets had by no means ceased to develop advanced weapon systems. Indeed, in many respects the Soviet Union has reduced or even eliminated the old technological disparities that existed between it and the NATO countries.[4]

In the late 1980s, then, NATO's chief opponent is a curious and volatile mix of stagnation and instability, fair promise and unreformed threat, military power and socioeconomic decay. The Soviet Union has good reason to be confident about its abilities today yet gloomy about its prospects a decade hence. Ironically, just as it saw clear-cut military superiority over the West appear within its grasp, it now finds that edge likely to dwindle by the turn of the century. Internally the system has been shaken by its most severe—albeit nearly bloodless—internal crisis since the Great Terror, and despite the urgency of Gorbachev's reformist impulse, it is by no means clear that he will succeed or even remain in power for as long a period as his predecessors. But he and his chosen lieutenants surely represent the shrewdest collection of Soviet leaders since the passing of Stalin. Not surprisingly, they have played one of their strongest cards— nuclear and conventional arms control—very well.

In December 1987 the United States and the Soviet Union concluded a treaty limiting intermediate range nuclear forces (INF), and in 1988 the U.S. Senate ratified it. The treaty banned ballistic and ground-launched cruise missiles (GLCMs) of a certain range (500 to 5,500 kilometers), thereby eliminating an entire class of nuclear as well as conventional weapons. The ratification of the INF treaty and the prospect of revived conventional arms control talks pose some of the most interesting problems to American conventional forces in Europe or destined for that theater. Following bitter internal debates, European leaders had managed to induce their populations to accept the deployment of American GLCMs and ballistic missiles (Pershing IIs) in their countries. They greeted with mixed emotions a treaty between the United States and the Soviet Union that banned all such weapons not only in Europe but globally.

What are likely to be the consequences of INF? First and foremost, in the United States and Western Europe, INF reinforced a sense that a new era had opened in U.S.-Soviet, and indeed Western-Soviet, relations. The complete banning of whole classes of weapons seemed almost as pathbreaking an achievement as the first limitations negotiated on central nuclear systems in the 1970s. Many Europeans were glad to see the departure of any nuclear weapons and looked forward to further agreements to limit or even eliminate shorter-range systems. The acceptance by both sides of the elimination of whole classes of weapons, and the acceptance by the United States and the Soviet Union of intrusive methods of verification of the treaty, seemed to presage a new and altogether welcome period of harmony in Europe and possibly beyond.

The second development, in contrast to the euphoria of the first, was the alarm of some Europeans and Americans (mainly defense or foreign policy experts) at the prospect of decoupling—the severing of the link between the defense of Europe and the main nuclear forces of the United States. The momentum of nuclear arms control seemed to these quiet critics of INF a dangerous thing. One could foresee, they thought, a situation in which the United States would soon pull almost all of its nuclear weapons out of Europe, leaving the continent deprived of a nuclear component vital to deterrence. These critics noted that between its own unilateral decisions and the 1983 Montebello agreement with its allies, the United States had withdrawn some 2,400 nuclear warheads from Europe, reducing the total to 4,600; INF would reduce the total to 4,000, many of these old and extremely short range.[5] In their view, only rapid modernization of these nuclear forces—to include the introduction of surface-to-surface missiles close to the 500-kilometer range limits of the treaty, as well as modernized air-launched systems—could maintain the nuclear guarantee to Europe. The political obstacles in Europe, and in particular in the Federal Republic of Germany, to such modernization appear to be substantial.

The INF agreement had a third consequence: it called attention to NATO's conventional inferiority in relation to the Warsaw Pact. Because the treaty represented a large step toward the denuclearization of NATO, it seemed to many observers that the alliance would have to look again to its conventional forces. Most military leaders and analysts thought that despite certain improvements in the NATO force structure, the Soviets had increased their edge during the 1980s, chiefly by virtue of a steady increase in their defense expenditures by something on the order of 2 percent or more a year. Perhaps such growth had ruined the Soviet economy, but it indubitably created a large and powerful conventional force targeted against Western Europe. Even the substantial increase in NATO-related U.S. defense spending in the 1980s could not compensate for this, given the relative stagnation in European defense budgets. Today, for example, the Belgian defense budget is less in real terms than it was in 1980, the German and Danish budgets are perhaps 3 percent larger than they were then, and even the French and British budgets are barely 10 percent larger than they were in 1980.[6]

The Senate Committee on Armed Services expressed the common view when it declared that "there is considerable risk that NATO forces could be defeated quickly by conventional means."[7] During 1988 General Bernard Rogers, former Supreme Allied Commander Europe (SACEUR), repeated his contention that in the event of a NATO–Warsaw Pact war NATO would have to resort to the use of nuclear weapons within days of the outbreak of hostilities. His successor, General John Galvin, was only slightly more optimistic, suggesting two weeks as the appropriate figure. Careful studies of the quantitative balance between East and West demonstrated that the Soviets had succeeded in increasing their firepower edge steadily over the years, beginning with a ratio of 1.5:1 in 1967, increasing to 1.8:1 in 1977, and rising to 2.2:1 in 1987.[8]

A fourth, though muted, reaction to INF came from those who believed that it revealed two important Soviet advantages over the West. First, during the course of the negotiations, it became clear that the Soviets had rather larger forces than they had been credited with in open sources in the West. Where prenegotiation Western estimates had given the Soviet Union twenty SS-23s, the Soviets informed their Western counterparts that they had 100. Western estimates of missile reloads were similarly off, the Soviets confirming that they had two missiles per SS-23 launcher and five per SS-12 launcher.[9] In some circles, this disclosure shook confidence in the ability of Western agencies to monitor Soviet force structure and deployments. Nuclear-armed surface-to-surface missiles are relatively few in number and, one may assume, high-priority items for American intelligence, and yet the United States may have been unable to track them accurately. All the more, by this logic, should analysts worry about their ability to monitor the quantity and quality of Soviet conventional equipment and organizations. Such concerns gained strength when, for example, in the 1988–1989 edition of its widely used reference work, *The Military Balance,* the International Institute for Strategic Studies (IISS) suddenly decided to credit each of the five Soviet armies in the Group of Soviet Forces Germany with an independent tank regiment.[10] At a stroke of the pen, this added 750 tanks to the institute's assessment of Soviet strength in Eastern Europe. Similarly the institute accepted, for the first time, that Soviet motorized rifle divisions were completely equipped with modern infantry fighting vehicles rather than only half-equipped with such weapons. Such large swings in estimates may reflect only the uncertainties of particular open sources of information; they may also reflect fundamental uncertainties about the very data themselves.

Some critics of the INF treaty concentrated on a second disturbing aspect: the treaty's ban of certain promising conventional weapons. They pointed out that the treaty did not, in fact, require the destruction of a single nuclear warhead; rather, it prohibited ground-launched cruise and ballistic missiles of the 500- to 5,500-kilometer range. They pointed out that this ban, which applied to conventional systems as well as nuclear ones, would constrict NATO force developments, which had looked to the development of new technologies for striking deep into the Soviet rear. To be sure, air- and sea-launched missiles of this intermediate range remained permitted—for the moment. But, these critics argued, it would have been preferable for NATO to have mobile, ground-based systems capable of delivering conventional munitions with extreme accuracy against bridges, airfields, supply dumps, and the like in Eastern Europe and beyond.

A general thinning out of NATO forces is probably not desirable, since it will make it easier, in the event of war, for the Soviets to achieve breakthroughs against a less thickly occupied NATO front line.

It is precisely these kinds of conventional systems that the Soviet General Staff finds acutely threatening to its ability to launch a decisive campaign against Western Europe. If they regretted, as they undoubtedly did, the loss of disproportionate numbers of their own intermediate-range missiles, they gained certain benefits:

The treaty removed a class of nuclear weapons that could strike the Soviet homeland with very little warning.

The treaty sharply limited a class of conventional weapons the Soviets believe could threaten their forces in Eastern Europe, while letting them retain (through shorter-range systems) the ability to strike at Western airfields and choke points in the Federal Republic of Germany, the main battleground and rear area in a future European war.

The treaty pushed the denuclearization of Europe one step further, a welcome development, because since at least the 1970s Soviet military doctrine has found purely conventional operations considerably more attractive than operations that would involve even limited use of tactical nuclear weapons.

From the political point of view, the INF treaty had only desirable consequences in terms of the relationship between the Soviet Union and Western Europe.

The United States had little choice but to accept the INF treaty in its current form once it became clear that the Soviets would accept a complete ban on all these systems; the costs in Europe of rejecting such an agreement, originally proposed by the United States, would have been too great. On the other hand, many observers found the large costs imposed by the treaty almost too much to accept.

This is particularly true given the rising popularity of some kind of conventional arms control negotiation in Europe.[11] To be sure, for some fifteen years the Mutual and Balanced Force Reductions talks have gone on in Vienna without much progress toward an agreement. But political developments in West and East will make it much more difficult for governments to avoid coming to grips with this issue and, at the very least, engaging in a far more public and politically sensitive negotiation than hitherto. In this connection Gorbachev's surprise announcement in April 1986 that he would accept arms control negotiations covering forces from the Atlantic to the Urals was a major departure from previous Soviet policy.[12]

From the outset the odds against achieving a serious conventional arms control agreement appear substantial. The large number of participants in the talks—no fewer than twenty-three nations—the vast geographical purview of the negotiation (from the Atlantic to the Urals—see figure 5-1), and the large number of weapon systems make the matter one of Olympian complexity. Furthermore, the problems of intelligence and verification are immense and grow in magnitude with the increase in the areas and weapon systems covered by the negotiation.

The overwhelming size of the task does not mean, however, that Western powers will be able to avoid it, largely because of domestic political pressures. Here, the asymmetries between NATO and the Warsaw Pact are particularly troubling. Soviet divisions withdrawn from Eastern Europe will simply retire, by land, to the Soviet Union; American divisions withdrawn from Western Europe will not only have an ocean between them and Europe, they may be disbanded upon their return. A general thinning out of NATO forces is probably not desirable, since it will make it easier, in the event of war, for the Soviets to achieve breakthroughs against a less thickly occupied NATO front line. Cuts of selected numbers of tanks or artillery pieces, even if they asymmetrically favor NATO, will codify the vast existing disparity between NATO and Warsaw Pact conventional forces. One RAND study recently concluded that only very large cuts at a NATO: Warsaw Pact ratio of 1:5 could maintain or improve NATO's current material position, leaving aside the political and organizational consequences of such a move.[13]

The third political development of 1988 was the remarkable resurgence in European economic self-confidence based on the assumption that the appearance of a truly open market in 1992 will produce considerable economic benefits. Whether the payoff from 1992 will indeed be as great as promised, the key point is that more European unity is evident today than in the past, British Prime Minister Thatcher's mistrust of pan-Europeanism notwithstanding. Such symbolic events as the reinvigoration of the West European Union, the agreement by France and Germany to create a joint military force, and France's decision to allow British forces to exercise movement through France to reinforce Germany augur a closer European defense relationship. In January 1988 France and Germany created a joint Defense Council to discuss mutual security concerns; in 1987 70,000 French and German troops participated in a joint exercise in Bavaria. Moreover, cooperative weapons development in Europe continues, albeit with hesitation and false starts. There has been talk of Anglo-French cooperation in the development of nuclear delivery systems and continuing cooperative ventures with respect to many other weapon systems, from antitank missiles to fighter aircraft.

At the same time some European countries—Spain and Greece most notably—have shown increasing impatience with American military bases on their territory. The departure of seventy-two American F-16s from the Torrejon air base in Spain was another symbolically important event in this context. These airplanes will be redeployed in Italy, at considerable cost, but the overall message was clear: in a number of NATO countries, interest in an American presence is declining.

Figure 5–1.

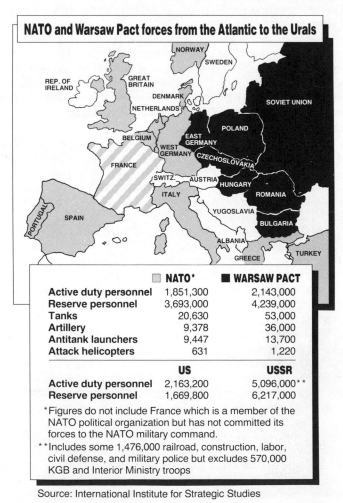

NATO and Warsaw Pact forces from the Atlantic to the Urals

	NATO*	WARSAW PACT
Active duty personnel	1,851,300	2,143,000
Reserve personnel	3,693,000	4,239,000
Tanks	20,630	53,000
Artillery	9,378	36,000
Antitank launchers	9,447	13,700
Attack helicopters	631	1,220
	US	**USSR**
Active duty personnel	2,163,200	5,096,000**
Reserve personnel	1,669,800	6,217,000

*Figures do not include France which is a member of the NATO political organization but has not committed its forces to the NATO military command.

**Includes some 1,476,000 railroad, construction, labor, civil defense, and military police but excludes 570,000 KGB and Interior Ministry troops

Source: International Institute for Strategic Studies

How do these three developments affect American theater strategy and forces? Since the late 1960s American strategy in Europe has rested on several assumptions: that the United States would lead the alliance in the conventional field, maintaining between four and five heavily equipped divisions in the front line, and promising to provide ten divisions shortly after a mobilization decision. Those forces would be deployed for a forward and essentially linear defense, along the inter-German border, as part of a larger NATO "layer cake" of national corps sectors extending from the Baltic to the Austrian border. Supporting those forces would be an array of nuclear weapons stationed in Europe to provide a link with the main American nuclear force. An American SACEUR would control the alliance's military forces in war.

Behind all this lay NATO's fundamental strategy of flexible response, codified in MC 14/3 in 1967. Under flexible response NATO would have conventional forces strong enough to block a Warsaw Pact conventional attack for a period of time, during which NATO could prepare, and if necessary use, tactical and theater nuclear weapons to convince the Soviets to stop the conflict and withdraw to prewar borders. MC 14/3 did not envision a purely conventional defense, but it called for a conventional force capable of serving as more than a mere tripwire.

Perestroika, arms control, and growing European unity may undermine some of the public support for NATO's current strategic arrangements in various ways. Flexible response came into being, after all, at a time when the United States had clear supe-

riority in intermediate-range and tactical nuclear weapons and an edge in strategic nuclear weapons and when NATO had a far better conventional defense than it does today. In the late 1960s the United States dominated the global economic order far more clearly than it does today, and its economy still accounted for over a third of global GNP (as opposed to something like a quarter today). No strategic doctrine is immortal, and if the mere passage of time can erode the premises of a concept such as flexible response, so too can the developments discussed above, and the forces currently loose in Europe and the world.

Long-Term Trends: Turmoil in the East, Tight Budgets in the West, and the Revolution in Military Affairs

On the Soviet side of the Iron Curtain, turmoil will continue, whether *perestroika* succeeds or not. In the Baltic and Central Asian republics, in Czechoslovakia, Hungary, and Poland, various forms of political unrest look likely to remain for the rest of this century and beyond. Zbigniew Brzezinski, national security adviser to President Jimmy Carter in the late 1970s, told the Senate Committee on Armed Services in 1988:

> We are now entering, in my judgment, a phase in which in the East the Soviet type system is going to be faced with a protracted crisis, and particularly so in Eastern Europe, to some extent in the Soviet Union itself; and I would not even dismiss the possibility of some truly explosive events transpiring in Eastern Europe in the not too distant future. Several of the East European countries are today in what might be called a classical prerevolutionary situation.[14]

Despite nearly a decade of military rule, Polish authorities have been unable to quash social upheaval or even avoid negotiating with Lech Walesa, the former leader of Solidarity. The scourge of double-digit inflation—between 25 and 50 percent—continues to reduce living standards, and there is virtually no hope for a restoration of the legitimacy of the Communist party. Hungary, whose partial freeing of its economic system was once a model to the Eastern bloc—and specifically to the Soviet Union— finds itself burdened by a debt nearly two-thirds the size of its GDP. Its economy barely grew at all in 1986 and at only 2 percent in 1987. Within the Soviet Union, the mass demonstrations and rioting in Armenia and Azerbaijan—disturbances that the central government seemed unable or unwilling to crush—testified to the instability of the imperial power itself. And on the periphery of the Soviet empire, Yugoslavia looks to be a fertile area for ethnic tensions every bit as great.

In the short term, this turmoil poses a paradoxical problem for American theater strategy. On the one hand, the weakness of the East European economies, and the apparent willingness of some East European leaders to move further than Moscow (as evidenced, for example, by Hungarian arms control proposals that would involve the withdrawal of Soviet forces from Hungary), may convince some in the United States and in Western Europe that the Soviet empire is a feeble opponent. The more Westerners see Soviet and East European leaders and their societies caught up in domestic turmoil, the less of a threat those leaders and societies will appear to pose, no matter how large or well equipped the armed forces under their control. As a result, it will probably prove impossible to secure support for additional spending on conventional defense in Europe. Indeed, for this and other reasons, the relevant question is whether defense budgets will shrink and, if so, by how much and in what areas.

Western leaders, intelligence services, and universities have no idea what is likely to happen when Communist states undergo the kind of domestic turbulence and reform efforts that we see unfolding in the East.

At the same time, political turbulence in the East has the potential to increase the dangers for NATO. Riots in the streets of East European cities, civil war in the Balkans, the collapse of Communist parties: these could make the security of Western Europe more rather than less precarious. Should such events make the Soviet leadership desperate, the danger of confrontation between East and West may increase. One can imagine many possible sparks of confrontation, particularly mass flights of refugees to the West. It is possible that, as in the Polish crisis of 1980, West European states may find themselves more inclined to come to terms with Communist governments in the interests of stability, while the United States may take a less sympathetic view of the predicament of those leaders.

The fact of the matter is that Western leaders, intelligence services, and universities have no idea what is likely happen when Communist states undergo the kind of domestic turbulence and reform efforts that we see unfolding in the East. The problem is new and quite unfamiliar. To be fair, it does not appear that the leaders of the Communist parties in Eastern Europe and the Soviet Union have a much better understanding of these processes. For the moment, all that we can safely say is that they are unprecedented and have the potential either to tame the East or to make it much more dangerous, by reason either of instability or desperation-driven aggressiveness.

Equally important are trends within the West. Here the most notable are the demographic and budgetary pressures that will make it exceedingly unlikely—barring some catastrophic developments—that either Americans or West Europeans will increase their defense spending. These developments are most vividly seen in the Federal Republic of Germany, where a sharp shortfall in the population of draft-age men will force a shrinkage of the Bundeswehr by over 30,000 to some 455,000 despite longer terms of military service. Yet even this number may well prove unreachable (it would require that the Bundeswehr have almost as many conscripts under arms in the 1990s as it does today). In the new German army even the most ready maneuver brigades will have just 70 percent of their wartime strength, and many will have only half.[15]

In the next twenty years the Soviets see the maturing of technologies currently in place, which will enable quantum increases in the range, precision, and lethality of conventional weapons.

In all European states the proportion of GDP devoted to social welfare spending has grown spectacularly, leaving little room for increased defense spending. Here too demography will be a powerful influence. Today, for example, West Germany has three workers for every retiree: early in the next century it will have two. At the same time, taxes (chiefly for social welfare expenditure) have risen to between one-third and one-half of GDP in most European countries. These facts, together with the steady rise in the expense of certain weapon systems, have led more than one expert to speak of structural disarmament in NATO. A good example is Belgium's decision to refuse to replace the aging Nike air defense missile system, which is being succeeded elsewhere by the Patriot system. The result will be a gap in NATO high-level air defenses at a time when Soviet aviation has increased in range and payload.[16] The marked shrinkage in the size of some European air forces is also testimony to the problem of maintaining balanced forces in an age of rapidly rising costs.

The United States is not immune from such pressures—it too faces a shrinkage in its manpower pool and a slowly rising social welfare budget—although in these two respects, it is better off than its European allies. But defense budgets look likely to face other, no less severe, constraints. First and most important of these is the federal budget deficit, but also important is the rise in new areas of defense spending, such as SDI and other space-related expenses, as well as Pacific and Central American contingencies. Thus it is hard to see whence additional funds for European defense will come.

The final trend stems from what has been termed in the Soviet Union "the revolution in military affairs."[17] In the view of Soviet experts—and the Soviets have a far more developed analytical infrastructure to study these matters than does the United States—the world is on the verge of a revolution in military technology as profound as that caused by the advent of the tank and the airplane or indeed of the atomic bomb. Approaching the problem of warfare holistically, the Soviets see this transformation as the result of the convergence of many different kinds of technology.

In the next twenty years the Soviets see the maturing of technologies currently in place, which will enable quantum increases in the range, precision, and lethality of conventional weapons. Each of these attributes requires some explanation. Since World War II, nations have had the capability to strike deep into an enemy's rear areas but only if they had high-performance aircraft and, in general, if they were able to gain air superiority against an opposing air force. Modern cruise and ballistic missiles do not require general air superiority to be effective, although they do require other kinds of support for accurate targeting. Highly efficient turbofan engines mean that weapons that fit on a rather small truck can strike very close to their targets hundreds or even thousands of kilometers in an enemy's rear. The Iran-Iraq War, which saw the use of some 500 surface-to-surface missiles at these kinds of ranges, pointed the way to more warfare of this kind.

At the same time, guidance systems have improved tremendously. Indeed it was the accuracy of the Pershing II, as well as its high speed, that so alarmed the Soviets. Terrain-contour-matching radars, improved inertial guidance systems, and the use of navigation satellites to provide accurate positioning data to ballistic and cruise missiles mean that the superpowers—and, in the future, the medium powers—can hurl missiles at each other with accuracies of tens of meters rather than, as previously, hundreds of meters.

Finally, the Soviets pay particularly close attention to the spectacular increase in the lethality of new munitions. For example, they estimate fuel-air explosives to have five times the explosive power of conventional explosives, and they have a high regard for smart submunitions that can seek out and destroy tanks and other targets or lay mine fields. The increased accuracy of such systems increases their lethality; the result is that advanced conventional munitions can, in the Soviet view, have the same destructive effect on military forces as do tactical nuclear weapons.

The result of these trends will be warfare that is conducted throughout the depths (extending to hundreds of kilometers) of one's own position and that of the enemy. It is war that will be extremely costly to both sides and one in which the management of information—including not only target acquisition but deception and concealment of one's own forces—will play a central role. It cannot be determined a priori whether this change will favor the tactical, operational, or strategic offense over the defense, although the Soviets appear to believe that it will enable them to move from one to the other with greater speed. It will, in the Soviet view, change the very pattern of war.

Beyond this first stage of the revolution in military affairs, the Soviets look to a second stage, some twenty to thirty years from now, when weapons based on new physical principles will be introduced: beam weapons of various kinds, electromagnetic rail guns, exotic biological agents, and the like. But it is the first stage that is the most arresting and important for Western military theorists to consider. Unlike the Soviets, Americans and Europeans tend to approach the issues raised by the term "revolution in military affairs" in a narrow and fragmentary fashion, considering particular technologies in isolation from larger issues. Not the least urgent item on NATO's agenda is an intellectual one: coming to grips with the revolution in military affairs and what it might mean.

To sum up the argument thus far, NATO's conventional posture and the role of the United States within it look remarkably stable. American forces have retained the same shape and missions over the decades, although the advent of AirLand Battle doctrine in 1982 changed its operational concepts considerably. But we have seen a variety of political, economic, social, and military forces—some the product of particular political decisions, some the result of deep-seated trends—eating away at the assumptions on which that force structure and strategy have been based. In ways that would have been unthinkable a decade ago, prominent American foreign policy experts have called for fundamental changes in U.S. policy toward NATO.[18] How the United States might change its theater forces, in cooperation with its NATO allies, is an important issue for analysis and reflection, yet there has been little creative thinking on this score.

The Culture of Analysis

There are two reasons for the stagnation of American thinking on the future of NATO. First, and more important, large and powerful institutions, and the men and women who inhabit them, find it understandably difficult to grapple with the implications of a changing world. The U.S. Army is, and since Vietnam has been, almost exclusively oriented toward the problem of strategy in Europe along the lines laid down in the 1960s or even earlier.[19] Even its light infantry divisions have now received European missions, and it concentrates most of its intellectual efforts on preparing for a conventional battle in Europe. The foreign policy elites of the United States have traditionally been oriented toward Europe and have found in the exploration of the nuances of NATO strategy a satisfactory substitute for an examination of its foundations. At the same time, the shrillness of most critics of NATO, their eagerness for a brusque disengagement from the Continent, and their seeming fecklessness about the consequences discredits for many the enterprise of rethinking American strategy in Europe.

But there is a second reason for American failure to come to grips with strategy in Europe, and that has to do with the kinds of analysis of NATO military affairs fostered in government and out. A vast industry, which includes universities, think tanks, and governmental research organizations, churns out vast quantities of studies of many aspects of the European balance. Yet for all the resources devoted to this effort, and despite the undoubted talent of many engaged in it, the effort is very largely sterile.

The analytical effort is a compartmentalized one. For example, one of the most interesting developments over the last two decades has been the emergence of a talented group of analysts studying Soviet military doctrine, largely on the basis of the extraordinarily rich open Soviet sources. Researchers at Sandhurst in England and at the U.S. Army's Soviet Army Studies Office at Fort Leavenworth have added immeasurably to an understanding of how the Soviet military understands its problems, how it intends to fight, and what many of its strengths are. Yet rarely is this work integrated into overall studies of the military situation in Europe. For example, it is still commonplace for Western analysts to look at the readiness of Soviet units in terms of three categories ("A"—more than 75 percent of manpower and equipment; "B"—50 percent to 75 percent; and "C"—strength of 10 percent to 33 percent of manpower and 33 percent to 50 percent of equipment).[20] In fact, the Soviet system is quite different and distinguishes chiefly between combat-ready and noncombat-ready units. Combat-ready forces can be "unready" by Western standards—because of the numbers of men and equipment they have—but "ready" by Soviet standards, the latter looking at readiness defined by mission rather than unit strength.[21] Rather than study carefully Soviet operational practices and concepts and look closely at how these might interact with Western organization and doctrine, analysts argue over such abstract, and not overly useful, questions as whether battle is a "dynamic process" (how could it be anything but?) or they construct computer-driven models that provide the Soviets with stereotyped and sometimes implausible options. There are some notable exceptions—RAND's Strategic Assessment System is certainly a major step in the right direction—but those closest to such efforts fully understand their difficulties.[22]

Political concerns are intrinsically difficult to model, intangible, and ambiguous, and many of the analysts feel more comfortable with seemingly "hard" data on weapons inventories, tables of organization and equipment, or quantitative models of combat.

The analytical effort is further compromised by the reluctance of analysts to incorporate political considerations into their studies. A great deal of ink has been spilled in the examination of scenarios in which NATO and Warsaw Pact forces mobilize simultaneously or with NATO lags ranging from four days to a week. Virtually no one, in the open literature at any rate, takes a hard look at scenarios in which mobilizations are partial or inhibited by domestic politics. Yet history would surely tell us that alliances do not mobilize for war simultaneously or anything like it. Almost never do scenarios explain why a war might break out, a question of critical importance in understanding how it might unfold. Almost all who engage in the debate about the conventional balance in Europe pay lip-service to Clausewitz's view that war is all about politics; almost none of them act accordingly.

One may speculate why this is the case. Part of the reason is that "military" analysts frequently lack some of the language skills or knowledge of history and politics to address these issues. Political concerns are intrinsically difficult to model, intangible, and ambiguous, and many of the analysts feel more comfortable with seemingly "hard" data on weapons inventories, tables of organization and equipment, or quantitative models of combat. At the same time, political analysts, who exist in plenty, tend to lack detailed knowledge of weapon systems, command structures, and the like—the details that make real strategic analysis possible.

Some analysts believe that one can parcel out these analytical missions among the different groups and that the cumulative result will be sound analysis.[23] This is as misguided as thinking one can put together piles of peel, pulp, and pips and call the result an orange. Strategic analysis is an organic whole, not a collection of discrete parts. This is particularly true when the compartmentalization has occurred between "political" and "military" matters—issues that are, in practice, indissolubly united.

In its quest for certainty, the American analytic community has turned increasingly to the use of computer simulations and simplified analytical models. These tools, which undoubtedly have real merit in this work, are poor at capturing many of the most important aspects of war. It is difficult to get a computer to take into account the differences in operational style and method between Warsaw Pact and NATO forces, to model the dynamic interactions between many different kinds of weapon systems, or indeed to measure accurately the combat worthiness of forces untested in battle. Formal models and computer simulations can help analysts raise and explore issues, but they should be the starting point for analysis, not the culmination of it.

The extreme advocates of these models often tout them as an alternative to the use of mere bean counts—static comparisons of numbers of weapons on either side.[24] Yet in fact most of those models merely rearrange those beans and in some cases render them less informative than before. The use of elaborate scoring systems such as weapons effectiveness indexes/weighted unit value to create armored division equivalents (ADEs) or analogous measures merely reproduces the defects of bean counting in less obvious ways. This is so because ADEs and their equivalents cannot capture critical aspects of military effectiveness such as morale, skillful generalship, coalition cohesion, and the like. Once again, this is not to deny the usefulness of such aggregated measures. A look at armored division equivalent scores over time, for example, can improve a sense of trends in the balance of forces. The difficulty comes from the overselling of such models.

The practical consequences of an analytical mind-set calcified by obsession with quantitative modeling are two. First, it appears that our understanding of the balance has deteriorated over time. Where students of the conventional balance used to worry chiefly about the Soviet threat to Western Europe, too many now waste their time inveighing against or rendering homage to the three-to-one rule or Lanchester's Theorem.[25] All too often, analysis has degenerated into pitched battles over the merits or defects of a pet model rather than a quest for the truth about an exceedingly complicated problem. It appears, then, that in the field of strategic analysis, unlike practical science, it is possible to decrease one's understanding over time by becoming fixated on more and more rarefied studies. Moreover, the putative object of all this study—the correlation of forces in Europe—is not sitting still waiting to see which model best describes it. If the Soviets are indeed right in their assessment of an impending revolution in military affairs, the old analytical perspectives may become increasingly misleading. Old-fashioned firepower scores, which failed to describe morale and training accurately, will have even less relevance if they fail to consider information management. And firepower scoring itself has become more difficult in an age when a thirty- or sixty-kilometer range rocket can carry such different payloads as scatterable mines, fuel-air explosives, or smart antitank munitions that home in on their prey. Ironically enough, it may appear in retrospect that the analytic tools for modeling a confrontation in Europe may have reached the peak of their refinement just as they finally became irrelevant to it.[26] To convince skeptics otherwise, it would be a worthwhile investment of time and money for government or private institutions to commission unbiased tests of current analytical models against real-world campaigns. It should be noted that when this has been done, the results have made contemporary analytic tools seem all the more inadequate.[27]

The current debate about American strategy in Europe is too narrow for other reasons as well. Few analysts bring to the subject a comprehensive interest in the politics and economics of Europe—thus the failure to think through the importance of developments in the European Economic Community (EEC) for NATO. And similarly, few participants in the debate consider at any length the other dimensions of American national security policy. Specializing in European defense issues, they forget to ask about—or dismiss with scant analysis—competing demands on American military forces.

Today many discussions of the shape of a possible war in Central Europe resemble disputes between physicists about thermodynamics rather than arguments among citizens, statesmen, and soldiers about war. Unfortunately, no clear-cut alternative method is available, although certain guiding principles for analysis seem applicable.[28] Faulty modes of thought can have painful practical consequences. In particular, if the dominant modes of analysis in American strategic studies are used to evaluate various proposals for conventional arms control talks with the Soviets, American and West European publics and statesmen may misjudge the attractiveness or undesirability of various arms control proposals. A mechanical attention to firepower ratios may obscure strengthened Soviet capabilities to overwhelm Western Europe; similarly, the West should not overlook proposals that, if accepted, would weaken the Soviets' confidence in their ability to conduct a successful attack on Western Europe. For example, by banning particular classes of equipment—even those without high firepower scores—NATO may hope to augment its security in such talks.

Alternatives for American Theater Forces

The United States has two broad options for dealing with the set of problems and challenges discussed in this chapter and largely ignored by contemporary analysis. The first and more likely is that of incremental adjustment. Under such an approach, American forces, commitments, and organizational structures would remain roughly unchanged, although budgetary pressures would force some retrenchment. The United States would continue to cajole or bully (albeit in a mild fashion) its European partners into greater defense efforts. American statesmen would try to maintain a credible nuclear force in Europe by modernizing short-range missile systems and American attack aircraft; other gaps (the air defense belt hole in the Northern Army Group region, for example) would also be plugged if possible. The objective over the next decade or two would be for the United States to retain roughly its current position in Europe, both materially and politically.

Such an approach should not be rejected merely because it is conservative and unimaginative; not all bold and innovative courses of action are desirable or possible.

Advocates of a standpat strategy could argue that internal NATO tensions and differences of opinion have always blown up in the past, only to subside in the face of reasoned compromises. NATO has, after all, held together for forty years, a remarkable feat in view of the wide variety of nations involved in it; and, just as important, Europe has remained free from Soviet conventional or nuclear blackmail. The successful—though extremely painful—deployment of cruise and Pershing missiles to Europe in 1987 testifies to the strength of will that NATO still retains. And in any case, one can argue, no drastic overhaul of NATO is feasible. The doctrines of forward defense and flexible response, codified in MC 14/3 some twenty years ago, remain the basis for a consensus among European members of NATO. There is no clearly visible alternative. Particularly at a time when the Soviet threat may diminish, why tamper with success?

There are, however, considerations suggesting that some reassessment is overdue.[29] First, social and demographic pressures are likely to strain American and European defense budgets. Not only will these constraints make it difficult to sustain the minimum of forces required to meet the demands of NATO's current strategy, they will increase the likelihood of intra-alliance acrimony as Americans call for more burden sharing and Europeans deny the justice of or necessity for the implied demands on their resources. From the purely American point of view, the pressure on the defense budget will stem not merely from the budget crisis but from the rise of competing claims on the American defense budget—antiballistic missile defenses of some kind, for example, which may be introduced on a modest scale. Space, already critical for communications and reconnaissance, will become ever more important as an arena of strategic competition between the United States and the Soviet Union. In the next two decades, the United States will have to compensate for the steady shrinkage of its basing structure, particularly if, as appears quite possible, it will lose the use of air and naval bases in the Philippines and Greece. The result may be not only the creation of new bases but increased expenditure on strategic mobility and sustainability, that is, on forces that will depend less than ever before on forward bases in order to operate. Turmoil south of the border may draw American attention increasingly to Central and South America, a region in which, since 1940 at any rate, the United States has had a free ride. The advent of expensive new technologies of war may force the United States to put more money into research and development in the immediate future. The United States will, in particular, wish to invest in these technologies not only because they will shape the means of warfare in the next century but because they offer a natural competitive edge over the Soviet Union. Finally, as the center of gravity of the global economy shifts to the Pacific, so too, in some measure, will American security interests. Whereas in the immediate postwar period, Europe was, unmistakably, the chief prize of the cold war, the only center of economic cum military power beyond the two superpowers, that is no longer the case. A fourth region has emerged, and increasingly it will attract American interest and concern.[30]

Thus, it is inevitable that the current level of U.S. commitment to NATO will prove unsustainable over the next decade or maintainable only at the cost of starving other equally important portions of the defense budget. In practice, one might get the worst of both worlds, eroding NATO's strategic position, patching rather than repairing cracks in the alliance, while leaving other, important challenges unmet. From the point of view of American interests alone, an attempt to cling to the status quo is unacceptable.

Furthermore, even if change in NATO has been slow, it has occurred. The INF treaty did remove an entire class of nuclear weapons from the continent; domestic pressures in Europe, and new arms control initiatives from the Soviets, look likely to weaken even more the nuclear link to the American arsenal—a link whose credibility many have doubted for some time. France's role in the alliance has certainly changed since de Gaulle's brusque withdrawal of that country from NATO's military organization; its open and tacit cooperation with its European allies has increased steadily over the last decade and looks likely to continue. At the broadest level, the EEC seems to have increased its solidity, albeit in very small increments. How it handles the economic integration due in 1992 will indicate whether even further consolidation of the EEC is possible. And finally, the revolution in military affairs may make NATO's current de-fense strategy less and less tenable. That strategy is based, after all, on an essentially linear conception of defense, which may prove hard to support as the lethality of new munitions forces greater dispersal in both offense and defense and as rear-area combat operations grow in importance.

It should be stressed that all these trends are just that—pressures that will require decades, not years, to come to fruition. Nothing could be more foolish than to move hastily to reshape NATO, particularly by unilateral moves such as a reduction of forces

By David Seavey, USA TODAY

Copyright 1988, USA TODAY. Reprinted with permission.

in Germany. At the same time, however, there is little to suggest that these trends will be derailed or reversed; the problem therefore is one of managing long-term change.

An alternative strategic approach to NATO might begin by acknowledging that Europe is, and will remain for the foreseeable future, an overwhelmingly important focus of American national security policy but not the only one. The maintenance of a free Europe, not intimidated by the Soviet Union and its allies, and able to endure with equanimity whatever storms may blow up in the East will remain a central American objective. Furthermore, American forces will remain committed to the defense of Europe.

That said, the broad objectives of American strategy should be two: the strengthening of the European pillar of NATO, including its nuclear forces, and the adaptation of NATO forces to new modes of warfare. These seemingly simple and reasonable objectives are, however, remote from the reality of American theater strategy today. For example, the United States reacted with distinct coolness to the recent rehabilitation of the West European Union and to the creation of a Franco-German brigade in West Germany. Instead the United States should openly and energetically encourage such consolidation of European defenses, even, when necessary, refraining from attempting to sell American defense products in order to allow greater European standardization of European products. The United States would, under this approach, do whatever it can to increase French integration into NATO as well. If this process required that the United States forego some of its current prerogatives in the NATO command structure—even its control of the position of SACEUR—it should be willing to do so. Indeed, such a policy should go even further, to encourage the development of multilateral European nuclear forces. The nuclear weapons stockpiles of Great Britain and France are now quite large; within a few years France, for example, will have approximately a thousand nuclear weapons in its arsenal. The United States should endorse, and if necessary support with technology transfers, the development of Franco-German or Anglo-German nuclear forces to compensate for the diminished American nuclear forces—and their reduced credibility—in Europe.

Most advocates, responsible and otherwise, of a restructuring of the U.S.-European security relationship have concentrated on the issue of the U.S. role, usually assuming that European NATO would automatically move to fill gaps created by a reduced American presence. It is unwise to assume the existence of a compensating mechanism of this kind. By concentrating on building up the European pillar of the alliance—even, occasionally, at the expense of its own short-term interests—the United States can pave the way for a readjustment of alliance responsibilities without causing panic among its partners.

In addition to lending its encouragement to a more cohesive and active West European security alliance, the United States should foster a fundamental rethinking of NATO's operational concepts and organization. This has a precedent in the U.S. Army's development of AirLand Battle doctrine, which, if different from the Follow-on Forces Attack (FOFA) concepts of NATO's military headquarters, clearly had some influence on it. As the means of warfare change with the advent of new technologies and as some new systems become too costly for European nations to bear alone, it might make sense to urge NATO to rethink MC 14/3 and its current dispositions in Europe. Should NATO, for example, invest more heavily in research and development of the new technologies, so that in ten years more of its firepower will come from long-range weapon systems? Does the advent of the armored, all-weather combat helicopter suggest that a more fluid style of operations will be required than in the past? The new Bundeswehr force structure, which will incorporate two airmobile divisions, suggests that some European armies are thinking along these lines; the same might be said of the French Force d'action rapide.

The Defense Department's current competitive strategies initiative can provide some useful guidelines for thinking about new modes of warfare for NATO. Rather than binding NATO to old force structures, which are, in any event, being washed away in spots by structural disarmament, American and European soldiers and statesmen should take a fresh look at the nature of future war. Under the competitive strategies approach, efforts would be (and are) made to find key vulnerabilities in the Soviet military system and to target them, to capitalize on innate Western strengths and minimize equally innate weaknesses. Such forward thinking requires a level of intellectual effort that thus far NATO has not undertaken. Until NATO can combine the technological advantages of its constituent economies with the thoroughness and seriousness of Soviet-style analysis, it will fail to redress the conventional imbalance in Europe. If ever it does combine the two, however, it will quickly produce a defense far more robust than that existing today.

The United States must make clear, insofar as it can, that a rethinking of NATO's doctrine and organization is not an attempt to punish the Europeans for inadequately supporting NATO. Rather, it should be presented for what it is: an attempt to come to grips with changed realities as NATO enters its fifth decade. Such a policy is no counsel of pessimism about NATO or hostility toward allies. To the contrary, it is, and should be presented as, an effort to maintain the vitality of the alliance into the twenty-first century. In the end, the United States and its allies must realize, strategy is about choice, and the time has come once again to face that fact.

Terrier Missile Fired By USS Constellation

Chapter 6

Seapower

James L. George

O n the eve of a new decade, there are two questions most naval analysts are pondering: what is the future of the 600-ship navy, and what is the future of the maritime strategy? Although both were still official Navy policy in 1989, many felt the future for them looked bleak. Indeed the new phrases might well be the "584-ship navy . . . and (hopefully) holding" and "whither the maritime strategy?" Before turning to these questions, it may be useful to look back at 1988, where many actions foreshadowed the bleak outlook for the future.

Events of 1988

Two events dominated naval affairs in 1988: a series of tough fiscal year (FY) 1989 budgetary cuts and events in the Persian Gulf, including the unfortunate *Vincennes* incident and the termination of the Persian Gulf patrols.

After several years of relatively minor across-the-board budget cuts, stretch-outs, deferrals, and other bookkeeping gimmicks, reality finally hit the Department of Defense (DOD) budget. For the first time, all services were required to make real cuts. Those affecting the Navy are shown in table 6–1.

Although most of the delays, postponements, or terminations were individually relatively insignificant, when seen in totality, there seems no question that FY 1989 will be remembered as the year that budget realities finally hit all the services. Of all the cuts, the most damaging to the Navy, at least symbolically, was the decision to retire sixteen older, but still useful, frigates at a date considerably earlier than expected. Ironically their retirement came precisely in the year the Navy had predicted reaching its long-sought goal of a 600-ship navy. Secretary of the Navy James Webb resigned in

Table 6-1. U.S. Navy FY 89 Budget Cuts

CHANGES IN STRUCTURE

Retire 16 frigates
Cancel stand-up of 14th air wing
Deactivate one strategic submarine
Decrease Navy & Marine Corps reserve strength
Savings: $749m; 28,333 personnel

PROGRAM TERMINATIONS

A-6F medium attack aircraft
Naval airship
Anti-radiation seeker
High frequency anti-jam radio
5-inch general purpose ammunition
Savings: $1,077m; beyond: $6,194m

DEFERRALS

Advanced air-to-air missile
Mk 48 advanced-capability torpedo
Mk 50 torpedo
Vertical launch anti-submarine rocket
Savings: $295m

NEW STARTS DELAYED

Low cost sonobuoy
Passive signal monitoring system
ASW variant of V-22 "tilt-rotor" plane
■ New warhead for Mk 50 torpedo
Savings: $441m

SOURCE: Department of Defense.

protest, but as a result of the continued concern over the budget deficit, his resignation soon became yesterday's news. Although the 600-ship fleet is still the goal, budget realities indicate that the Navy might be lucky to lose "just" the sixteen frigates over the next few years, maintaining a 584-ship navy.

The other major seapower event took place in the Persian Gulf.[1] In 1987, the main story centered around the *Stark* incident. In 1988, the main story was the *Vincennes* incident. In the *Stark* incident, the captain and crew were generally criticized for not taking appropriate action to shoot down the incoming plane or take proper evasive measures. In the *Vincennes* incident, the captain and crew were generally criticized for taking action too quickly. In short, in the tough Persian Gulf patrol, the Navy found itself in a classic "damned if you do, damned if you don't" situation.

The downing of the Iranian airliner with the loss of 290 lives was a tragic mistake, but there are several mitigating factors to consider. First was the earlier *Stark* incident in which hesitation cost the lives of thirty-seven Americans. Surely the memory of this earlier incident was fresh in the *Vincennes* captain's mind. More important and often overlooked in the reporting, the *Vincennes* was at the time engaged in a minor scuffle with some Iranian gunboats. While this might not go down in naval history as another Battle of Jutland, the fact remains when someone is shooting at you, whether with 16-inch guns or .50-caliber machine guns, it tends to focus your attention.

With hindsight, it is a wonder that after eight years of fighting, both *Stark*- and *Vincennes*-type incidents had not happened earlier and with more frequency. After such a lengthy period, to have only two incidents is, in some respects, remarkable. That does not mean the Navy can rest on its laurels. In fact, one problem may be that the Navy has focused too much attention on the maritime strategy and its World War III scenarios and not nearly enough on its traditional naval missions of naval presence, sea control, and force projection ashore.

Finally, despite the tragedy of the *Vincennes* incident, many observers felt that the event contributed to the end of the Iran–Iraq War. Although all regretted the loss of life, Iran found itself increasingly isolated in world opinion and finally decided to sue for peace. Thus, despite the many criticisms of American reflagging of Kuwaiti ships and the subsequent escort duty, in the long run, it appears to have worked. Once again the superiority and flexibility of Western seapower was displayed. And it should not be forgotten that it was Western seapower—the United States with help from many North Atlantic Treaty Organization (NATO) allies normally reluctant to participate in out-of-area operations.

Naval Force Structure

In 1989, the U.S. Navy has approximately 580 ships (table 6–2). The 600-ship navy has always been built around fifteen carrier battle groups (CVBGs) with four battleship battle groups (BBBGs), approximately 100 antiair warfare (AAW) guided missile cruisers and destroyers, 100 frigates, 100 nuclear attack submarines with additional underway replenishment (UNREP) and other support ships, and mine and amphibious warfare ships. The Navy is close to its goals. The question is whether it will be able to sustain the force. Normal ship life is approximately thirty years, although through certain service life extension programs (SLEP), these are often extended. For example, the two-year SLEP for aircraft carriers is adding fifteen years to their life. Nevertheless, thirty years is the accepted norm.

Thus, just to maintain, not grow to, 600 ships requires an annual shipbuilding rate of approximately twenty ships. During the 1970s when the size of the fleet decreased from approximately 900 to fewer than 500, the average shipbuilding rate was approximately fifteen per year. During the first several years of the Reagan administration, the shipbuilding rate was well over the twenty per year needed to reach and maintain the 600-ship navy. From 1986 to 1988 the rate slipped below that norm. In 1988 only seventeen ships were requested, with sixteen approved. Thus not only will the Navy fail to grow to 600 ships; given normal retirements, it will probably continue to shrink.

Table 6-2. Force Structure Progress and Goals

Ship Type	FY 80	FY 87	FY 89	Goal
SSBN	40	37	37	20-40
Aircraft Carrier	13	14	14	15
Battleship	0	3	4	4
AAW Cruiser/Destroyer	63	73	77	100
ASW Destroyer	44	32	32	37
Frigates	71	115	100	101
Attack Submarines	79	102	103	100
Mine craft	3	4	9	14
Amphibious Ships	66	63	67	75
Patrol Combatants	3	6	6	6
Combat Logistics Ship	48	56	60	65
Support & Auxiliaries	49	63	71	60-65
TOTAL	479	568	580	600

Under one optimistic projection using a thirty-five-year ship life, the Navy will have to retire some sixty-six ships during the first years of the next decade, with over ninety more retiring by the turn of the century.[2] In shipbuilding terms, when it takes up to ten years to get a ship from drawing board to deployment, the year 2000 is almost tomorrow.

Aircraft Carriers

At the end of the 1970s, after a tremendous fight over building one "last" carrier over President Carter's initial veto (which in the heat of the 1980 presidential race he finally retracted), many, if not most, naval analysts thought they would never see another carrier, at least not more Nimitz-class large-deck carriers. The major reason was cost. When President Reagan requested two Nimitz-class carriers in his 1982 budget, most observers of the congressional scene thought this was simply the old ploy of requesting two in the hope of getting one. It was a bold request, and it succeeded. Even more surprising was the approval of two more carriers in FY 1988. There had been requests for so-called long-lead funding of a few hundred million dollars to start the process, but in the confusion over the budget in late 1987 and a quirk in the law, full funding could be granted for both without breaking the budget ceiling. Since the Gramm-Rudman-Hollings law requires ceilings on current-year dollars, out-year dollars are not affected.

Thus, at the end of the 1980s, it appeared the Navy might reach its fifteen carrier group force, if only for a short time. At that time the Navy had fourteen deployable carriers. Another had been in the two-year SLEP program and was out of commission, and four more were under construction. The fifteenth deployable carrier, the *Abraham Lincoln,* was scheduled for commissioning in 1990, with the *George Washington* to follow in 1991. The fifteen carriers, however, include the World War II-era *Midway* and

Coral Sea. Original plans were for the *Abraham Lincoln* and *George Washington* to replace the latter two, but to maintain fifteen carriers, that plan was changed to keep one until the late 1990s when one of the new ships could replace it. Now, with budget cuts, there is considerable pressure not only to return to the original replacement plan but to retire the *Midway* and *Coral Sea* as well. There is even some pressure to rescind funds for either one or both of the two recently approved Nimitz-class carriers. Nothing would be more devastating to the future of the 600-ship navy than the early retirement of the *Midway* and *Coral Sea*, except perhaps rescission of funds for one or both of the Reagan-approved carriers.

Thus, not only will the Navy fail to grow to 600 ships; given normal retirements, it will probably continue to shrink.

Battleships

Perhaps the biggest surprise of the Reagan naval buildup was the commissioning of all four mothballed battleships. The idea of commissioning one or more of the four Iowa-class battleships built during World War II had been discussed for years. In terms of use, they were relatively young ships, with fewer than fifteen years of commissioned service. The Marine Corps has long desired the fire support of the battleship's 16-inch guns, and they also make good firing platforms for long-range Tomahawk cruise missiles. The major problem with commissioning these ships has been the cost in manpower. As designed, they originally had a complement of almost 3,000 men, which the Navy could ill afford, but with slight modifications in mission, the ships are able to operate with a crew of 1,500.

Whether reactivating the battleships will prove wise in the long run remains to be seen, but so far their deployment in the Caribbean and off the coast of Lebanon seems to have proved their worth. They are still formidable ships with flexible capabilities.

Cruisers

All twenty-seven proposed CG-47 Ticonderoga-class cruisers have been approved, with many, including the new vertical launch system (VLS) modes, now in the fleet. These ultrasophisticated Aegis-class ships with their phased array-radars and semiautomatic air defense systems are reportedly working well—perhaps too well. One criticism of the *Vincennes* incident was that the system was too sophisticated for that Persian Gulf role. The system was not necessarily designed for closed waters or for peacetime use with restricted rules of engagement. The nine-ship CG-16 Leahy-class built from 1962 to 1964 and the nine-ship CG-26 Belknap-class built from 1964 to 1967 will be nearing the end of their useful life in the late 1990s, but the incoming Ticonderogas should more than adequately compensate.

Destroyers

The thirty-one-ship Spruance-class antisubmarine warfare (ASW) destroyers (DDs) built from 1975 through 1983 are relatively new and are being constantly modernized with new VLS systems. However, thirty-one modern, fast ASW destroyers must be considered a minimum number for the size of the fleet. That allows only two per CVBG and none for battleship and amphibious groups that need their 5-inch guns as well as ASW protection.

More disturbing to many analysts is the upcoming block obsolescence of almost the entire AAW guided missile destroyer (DDG) force. Both the ten-ship DDG-37 Farragut-class built from 1960 to 1961 and the large twenty-three-ship DDG-2 Charles F. Adams–class built from 1960 to 1964 are near the end of their useful life. That will leave only the four-ship Kidd-class, often sarcastically referred to as the "Ayatollah-class." These four ships were originally ordered by the shah of Iran, but after the revolution, the U.S. Navy took them over.

The Navy has started a new program, the DDG-51 Arleigh Burke–class, but they may not be built in sufficient numbers or quickly enough to fill the upcoming DDG gap. These Aegis-equipped ships have also been criticized as being too expensive and underarmed. The lead ship will cost approximately $1 billion dollars, and ships of the class will have only limited ASW facilities (no embarked helicopter, for example, although they will have a landing pad). Many critics, including some on Capitol Hill, pointed out that about the same amount of money could buy a CG-47 cruiser with a much larger magazine capacity, crucial for any AAW ship.

Frigates

The only ships built in quantity during the 1970s were the FFG-7 Oliver Hazard Perry–class frigate. Over fifty were built. These much maligned "lo" ships were the only result of Chief of Naval Operations Admiral Elmo Zumwalt's "hi-lo" mix concept of the early 1970s. During that period Admiral Zumwalt proposed that in order to keep numbers up, the Navy had to balance "hi" technology ships, which could be built in only small numbers, with less expensive "lo" technology ships that could be built in some quantity. Unfortunately, very few of the "hi" ships were ever built.

Although severely criticized by many as being slow and underarmed, the Perry-class ships have proved to be useful. Interesting to many observers was that these supposedly underarmed ships were chosen for Persian Gulf escort duty. Although the retirement of the sixteen frigates was a blow to the Navy, between the over fifty Perry-class and thirty-eight FF-1052 Knox-class frigates built in the early 1970s, the numbers should stay up during the 1990s.

Submarines

The U.S. Navy has started building its new SSN-21 Seawolf-class attack submarine (SSN), having completed requests for their SSN-688 Los Angeles–class with a total of some sixty ships. The SSN-21 has been described as "the most controversial ship in the Navy," a view shared by many in Congress.[3] What should have been a relatively happy occasion, starting a new class, was marred late in 1987 when a powerful House Armed Services Committee staff member blasted the Navy by calling the new Soviet

Akula-class submarine the best in the world and charging that the Navy should go back to the drawing board on the SSN-21. The SSN-21 (for "twenty-first century") lead ships will cost over $1 billion each. The Navy's response is that the 1960s-era design Los Angeles–class, although it has been updated, has reached its growth potential and must be replaced. After working on the SSN-21 design for over a decade, the Navy wants to proceed with it.

Since many now consider the submarine, not the aircraft carrier, to be today's capital ship, this is more than just a minor academic dispute between Capitol Hill and the Navy. The SSN-21 should be built, but research should also begin immediately on a follow-on. Also, the notion of building extremely large classes and then looking for quantum leaps in technology for the next class must be reconsidered.

Finally, the Navy should take a new look at nonnuclear submarines. Among recent developments are better nonnuclear submarines and combined nuclear-nonnuclear power proposals. Even poorer countries like Turkey are looking at low-cost combined systems that need only small, low-powered nuclear reactors to charge the ship's batteries. The Navy has always feared that once starting down this road, Congress would force it to buy only cheaper, and admittedly less capable, submarines. As one who worked on Capitol Hill for nine years, I sympathize with these fears. This practice did occur to a certain extent in the 1970s with the building of many "lo" frigates. However, there is probably no more responsible, or respected, leader on Capitol Hill than the chairman of the Senate Armed Services Committee, Sam Nunn (D–Georgia), and a gentleman's agreement could probably be struck for some kind of SSN "hi-lo" mix. In the early 1990s, the thirteen-ship Permit-class will start to fade out, followed by the large thirty-seven-ship Sturgeon-class—a loss of half the current SSN force. Something will have to be done to keep the numbers up.

Amphibious Ships

The Navy is in the midst of a well-planned amphibious force modernization program. Six new amphibious assault ships (LHDs) with both helicopter and Harrier vertical and/ or short take-off and landing (V/STOL) capabilities (also capable of carrying traditional landing craft) are currently under construction or planned for the 1990s. This program will give the Navy eighteen amphibious mini-carriers. In addition the Navy is completing procurement of a new class of dock-landing ship (LSD), the LSD-41 class, and a so-called LSD-41 cargo variant. While well balanced, the seventy-odd ship fleet might be too small for the 1990s.

Auxiliary Ships

With the possible exception of the mine warfare force, the stepchild of most of the world's navies has always been the auxiliary force. Yet the force that really makes a blue-water navy "blue" is not only battleships, cruisers, and aircraft carriers but also auxiliaries, especially UNREP ships, now called combat logistics ships. During any type of combat or even sustained crises, repair ships and tenders are also needed. One reason most analysts still do not consider the Soviet Navy a true blue-water navy is their extremely limited auxiliary force. The United States is building new fleet store and oiler combat logistics ships but perhaps not in sufficient quantity.

Minecraft

After a self-imposed thirty-year naval holiday, the Reagan administration started build-
ing new minecraft. It proposed both a larger oceangoing craft, the mine countermeasure
(MCM) Avenger-class, and a smaller coastal ship. That might be called the good news.
The bad news is that American shipbuilders apparently do not know how to build small
ships. The minesweeper mess is surely worthy of former Wisconsin senator William
Proxmire's Golden Fleece award. After numerous delays and cost overruns, the
Avenger, the first ship of this class, was launched in 1987. The seventeen smaller minecraft have yet to be built. The shipyards and Navy went through several proposals,
none of which worked. They finally decided to turn to a proven Italian class, the Lerici,
which ran into congressional opposition. A modified Lerici is now under construction in
the United States. The importance of minecraft was vividly brought home during the
recent Persian Gulf escort operations where relatively simple, World War I–era design
mines caused havoc. A better example might be the 1984 mine incident in the Red Sea,
where a few mines disrupted normal merchant shipping for weeks.

In sum, as a result of the shipbuilding programs of the early Reagan years, the Navy
should be in relatively good shape, at least through the early 1990s. The only major
ship gap that might appear is in the flexible AAW destroyer category. The Navy should
reach, or at least come close to, its goal of fifteen carrier groups. All twenty-seven
sophisticated CG-47 Aegis cruisers will soon be joining the fleet; the SSN numbers will

remain up with the Los Angeles-class coming in quickly; and most other forces are being modernized. Thus the Bush administration has a year or two to rest on the Ronald Reagan–John Lehman shipbuilding decisions. But fairly soon, some tough decisions must be made with the major block obsolescence facing most forces in the late 1990s. This raises the other major issue, the future of the maritime strategy, and, more important, if it will be appropriate for the 1990s.

A Maritime Strategy for the 1990s

In 1988 Ronald O'Rourke stated that although the "vocal vanguard" of Navy Secretary John Lehman and Chief of Naval Operations (CNO) Admiral James Watkins had "faded from view," the Navy should "not abandon the maritime strategy as a forceful document."[4] Although still part of the Navy's lexicon, there is no question that the maritime strategy has taken a back seat since the departure of Admiral Watkins and Secretary Lehman.

A more appropriate question might be not "Whither the maritime strategy?" but whether focusing on just the maritime strategy is appropriate for the 1990s. When the roots of the maritime strategy were first enunciated by Admiral Thomas Hayward, chief of naval operations, in the late 1970s, the main threat was the emerging Soviet Navy. While the U.S. Navy was going through one of its worse times in the 1970s, the Soviet Navy was going through both a quantitative, and perhaps more disturbing, qualitative growth in forces. Then after staying in home waters for years, the Soviet Navy started to deploy out of area. It also began conducting worldwide exercises (the various Okean exercises), and many analysts were predicting the final emergence of a true blue-water navy.[5] The main U.S. commitments were still to NATO and the Pacific. These three factors—the declining U.S. Navy, the emerging Soviet Navy, and the U.S. commitments in both NATO and the Northwest Pacific—led Admiral Hayward and others to believe that a forward strategy was needed. The U.S. Navy could not, as was generally assumed, simply block the narrow passages such as the Greenland—Iceland—United Kingdom (GIUK) gap and expect to win a war. It had to go after the Soviet Navy in its own bastions. There would be no sanctuaries for the bear. In the environment of the late 1970s and 1980s, the forward strategy, since renamed the maritime strategy, was most appropriate.

Although making predictions can often be a fool's game, there do seem to be some discernible trends for the 1990s. During the next decade, the United States could well see major erosions in the alliance system it has had for almost forty years. Cracks are beginning to show in NATO, and a major European arms control forum will start in 1989, the new Conventional Forces in Europe talks (CFE). While anyone familiar with the sixteen-year-old Mutual and Balanced Force Reductions (MBFR) talks might question whether progress can be made in the CFE, there does seem to be a more genuine desire for progress. The main impetus behind the MBFR talks was to forestall the Mansfield amendment that would have unilaterally cut U.S. strength in Europe. By contrast, CFE follows the Conference on Disarmament in Europe (CDE) talks, which in only two and a half years, a remarkably short time for these sorts of negotiations, produced a series of confidence-building measures. In the Pacific, many are predicting changes in Korea. In both Europe and the Pacific, many are wondering about the future of American bases. Although two-year extensions were recently granted for the large

American bases at Subic Bay and Clark Air Force Base in the Philippines, many feel their days are numbered.

If there are major changes in NATO and Korea, the major U.S. commitments, the direct effect would fall on the Army and Air Force, and the indirect and long-range effects would seem to fall on the Navy. Forward bases might be useful for the Navy, but they are crucial for the Army and Air Force. Certain measures such as prepositioned overseas material configured unit sets (POMCUS) can help the Army, but they still require secure bases. Airlift is also important but, for example, the one battle tank a C-5 can carry means literally nothing in the European theater and, of course, secure air bases are required. On the other hand, although it might have longer steaming times, the Navy can still operate.

There could also be some major changes in Third World areas, where all post–World War II conflicts and most crises have occurred. On the one hand, times have changed. The United States remains in its "no more Vietnams" syndrome. Who would have predicted in 1980 that the Soviet Union would pull out of Afghanistan? The recent Iran-Iraq War has not only left those two countries exhausted; it has also caused much rethinking in Washington. While the United States did what used to be called tilt toward Iraq, few raised the implied Carter Doctrine requirement for actually intervening. If there were ever any thoughts about major intervention in the Middle East, after the Iran-Iraq War, which some have compared to World War I, complete with trench warfare and poison gas, those thoughts have long been forgotten. On the other hand, there will probably always be some type of crisis or low-intensity conflict.

In short, there seem to be some discernible trends for a possible erosion of such long-standing alliances as those the United States has had with NATO, Korea, and the Philippines, all with major American bases, and there are other changes in the Third World. Thus, for the 1990s the proper maritime strategy might be a return to traditional naval missions: naval presence, sea control, and force projection ashore.

Naval presence has been appropriately called "the misunderstood mission."[6] If there was ever a clear example, it was the Persian Gulf experience. Considering all the restrictions and sensitivities, the Navy performed well. Often derogatorily called gunboat diplomacy, naval presence today rarely means intimidating the local natives but rather protecting one's own nationals and freedom of the seas. And problems have become more complex. The required naval presence in the Persian Gulf in 1988 was considerably different from the old show-the-flag mission of the Middle East Force, which has been there since 1948. Today's terrorist attacks and complex Third World political-military situations require the same amount of thought and study that went into the maritime strategy. The lessons, including problems, of the recent Persian Gulf crisis should be thoroughly explored.

Projection ashore, another traditional Navy–Marine Corps mission, also deserves new thought and study. Situations requiring the emplacement of U.S. troops on hostile soil will probably continue to arise, and such actions should be taken with an eye toward preventing a repetition of incidents like the tragedy in Beirut in 1983 in which 241 Marines died. The Army today is not configured for any prolonged intervention since most of its logistical tail is now in the reserves. Thus, a major Army intervention would require at least limited mobilization with a probable triggering of the War Powers Act, unlikely in today's political environment. Only the Navy–Marine Corps team with its own logistical tail from auxiliaries to amphibious ships and the maritime prepositioning ships with carrier air cover and surface ship gunfire support can adequately protect

American interests. With the possible loss of overseas bases, these requirements will probably increase. The Navy might have to increase both its auxiliary and amphibious forces for the environment of the 1990s.

Finally, the Navy must look at its traditional sea control mission. With possible pullbacks or at least reductions in forces from Europe and Korea, missions like protection of sea lines of communications (SLOCs) will become even more important. And, as we have learned from the recent Persian Gulf experience, sea control includes such traditional missions as convoy duty and mine sweeping.

There were two problems with the maritime strategy. First, some of the early pronouncements made it sound like a "charge of the light brigade" to the Kola peninsula. That was never the intent. It was to be a phased rollback. More important, as Secretary Lehman explained in congressional testimony, the United States could not simply give the Soviet Navy a secure sanctuary above the GIUK gap, as many suggested. And, as

---

Thus, for the 1990s the proper maritime strategy might be a return to traditional naval missions: naval presence, sea control, and force projection ashore.

---

he also pointed out, "if the NATO treaty means anything, it means that we are to protect and hold Norway."[7] Fully and adequately explained, the maritime strategy made good sense. It certainly complicated Soviet planning, which is the basis for any good strategy. The second problem was that the maritime strategy seemed to neglect similar thought and analysis of some of the more traditional and day-to-day missions such as naval presence, projection ashore, and sea control.[8] Yet in the 1990s, these tasks seem to be the ones most likely to occupy the Navy.

The Navy and Arms Control

Arms control measures could have a major effect on the Navy. There are three different measures for consideration: the 1987 Intermediate Nuclear Force (INF) agreement, the Strategic Arms Reduction Talks (START), and an agenda item that has simmered below the surface for several years, naval arms control.

Intermediate Nuclear Force Agreement

The INF agreement signed at the Washington summit in December 1987 was hailed by most as an agreement of major importance. The United States would eliminate some 500 Pershing IIs (P-II) and ground-launched cruise missiles (GLCMs), while the Soviet Union would destroy some 1,600 systems, including the modern, mobile, three-warhead SS-20. Looking at the numbers, INF was surely a victory for the United States.

Why then did so many national security experts such as Henry Kissinger, James Schlesinger, Supreme Allied Commander Europe (SACEUR) General Bernard Rogers, and Senator Nunn, among others, express reservations? They did so for reasons of strategy. From the Montebello agreement of 1983 by the United States and its NATO allies, there are some plans to modernize certain nuclear systems, including building a new follow-on to Lance, but the elimination of the P-II and GLCM left SACEUR with only extremely short-range battlefield weapons and some dual-capable aircraft (DCA).

The major concern is how to restore NATO's nuclear credibility in the wake of INF. All of the current modernization programs, even if completed, are too short range. In theory, DCA such as the F-111s have the necessary range to hit most territory in Eastern Europe and perhaps even some in the Soviet Union. As the name suggests, however, this dual capability means they also have conventional roles and missions. And during a prolonged conventional war, attrition could be heavy.

There are two systems that could take up the slack: the Navy's Tomahawk land attack missile/nuclear (TLAM-N), a sea-launched cruise missile (SLCM), and the proposed new Navy medium-attack stealth advanced tactical aircraft (ATA), now designated the A-12. Of the two, the TLAM-N SLCM is more appropriate. It has the range and capability to hit all the targets previously designated to the P-IIs and GLCMs, which were eliminated by the INF agreement. Better, because they are based on ships and so cannot be overrun by enemy forces, SLCMs are not faced with the "use 'em or lose 'em" dilemma of European-based systems. Most suitable for this role would be the new VLS Los Angeles–class SSNs now joining the fleet. According to congressional testimony, the Navy plans to equip all one hundred SSNs and ninety surface warships with

Reprinted by permission: Tribune Media Services

equipment necessary to launch the TLAM SLCM (although all may not carry the nuclear TLAM-N variant).[9]

The Navy's new stealth ATA, scheduled to join the fleet in the 1990s, should also be useful. The ATA will be a follow-on medium-range bomber to the Navy's A-6. Considering that European-based DCA will be both busy and vulnerable during any war, especially a protracted war, the ATA could prove important in later phases. In short, after INF, to restore NATO's nuclear credibility, the only answer might be INNF—intermediate Navy nuclear forces.[10]

Strategic Arms Reductions Talks

It seems likely that the United States will sign a new START treaty, which will have a major impact on today's triad-based force mix of long-range bombers, intercontinental ballistic missiles (ICBMs), and submarine-launched ballistic missiles (SLBMs) on strategic nuclear submarines (SSBNs). Although the details await finalization, it appears that the SSBN force will shrink from the forty-one operated for years to fewer than twenty, and the number of ICBM launchers could be cut by up to 80 percent, especially if more ten-warhead MX are procured, as the Air Force requested. Such reductions have led Henry Kissinger to charge that the START treaty is now being negotiated in a "strategic vacuum."[11]

Less noticed are two new Navy systems that can help fill the strategic gaps. First is the TLAM-N. The TLAM-N SLCM could well turn out to be the only single-warhead nuclear weapon in the U.S. inventory after START. It now appears that the single-warhead Midgetman is about dead due to rising costs. This leaves only the quarter-century-old, inaccurate Minuteman II. Thus, for some of the more limited nuclear options, the TLAM-N might be crucial.

Also important will be the new, accurate D-5 SLBM, scheduled to join the SSBN fleet in 1989. For the first time, an SLBM will have the accuracy of an ICBM, negating one of the primary reasons for not moving all ballistic missiles to sea. Historically there have been two reasons for maintaining an ICBM force even though it has become vulnerable: accuracy and better communications, command, and control (C^3). The D-5 will negate the first reason by providing a survivable weapon with accuracies and throw-weights comparable to ICBMs, and, according to some discussions, SSBN C^3 is not that bad. In fact, after a first strike, naval communication systems such as the airborne TACAMO might be more viable than so-called secure land-lines.[12]

Naval Arms Control

Another item that could surface in the next few years is naval arms control. This is not traditional naval arms control such as the 1920–1930 Washington-London type agreements that set actual limits on ships and tonnage. Nor is it like the nuclear issues, although both INF and START will have great impact on the Navy. Rather, the new naval arms control measures fall under the generic term of confidence-building measures. It includes such items as nuclear-weapon-free zones (NWFZ), ASW-free zones, limits on operations (such as amphibious operations), and advance notice of (usually major) naval movements and exercises. Many of these measures and proposals have been around for years, with some in existence. For example, a Latin American NWFZ treaty was signed in 1967, and the United States has signed the protocols.

What is new and alarming to the naval leadership is the frequency and high source of some of the latest proposals. At a major speech at the Naval War College in 1988, CNO Admiral Carlisle Trost commented on "the well-orchestrated campaign of Soviet naval arms control proposals." He continued, "The proposals are not new. . . . What is new is the frequency of their appearance and the apparent willingness of many well-meaning but naive audiences to accept Soviet declarations at face value."[13] A few months later, as if on cue, Marshal Sergei F. Akhromeyev suggested a series of new measures, including restrictions on missile-carrying surface ships and submarines and prohibitions on deploying amphibious forces within reach of each other's coasts.[14] There have been many more Soviet proposals such as "swapping" Subic Bay for Cam Ranh Bay and limiting both sides to fifteen warships in the Mediterranean.

Not all proposals are initiated by the Soviets. Sweden, for example, has been trying to get the United Nations interested in naval arms control for years. At the 1988 United Nations Disarmament Committee meeting, Sweden introduced a naval arms control study resolution, which the United States vetoed. Many of the NWFZ proposals have come from the littoral states. While all of these proposals are not necessarily bad and some deserve further study, most would restrict traditional naval freedom of the seas and passage. Since the Soviet Navy rarely strays far from home, restrictions would fall most heavily on the U.S. Navy.

The Reagan-Lehman Navy

There has been a fair amount of "Lehman bashing" in the popular press and even some naval professional journals. Many seem to have short memories. To appreciate fully the state of the Navy in the 1990s, it might be well to remember the Navy's condition at the beginning of the 1980s. The following assessment of the U.S. Navy in 1980 by Norman Polmar appeared in the authoritative *Ships and Aircraft of the U.S. Fleet*:

> During the 1980s the United States Fleet will decline in size, from the current 460-odd active, Navy-manned ships to possibly as few as 350 ships. At the same time, the Navy will have difficulty in manning even these ships with the quality of personnel needed to operate them effectively and continuously.[15]

In 1980 few would have argued with that assessment. Shipbuilding rates were down. Enlistments were declining. Captains were refusing to go to sea for lack of crew. There were sea stories about ships stopping mid-ocean to transfer weapons since stocks were down.

That assessment should be compared to the situation only five years later. Testifying before Congress in 1985, Secretary Lehman said, "From the 479 battle force ships in the fleet when President Reagan took office, the fleet has grown to 530 ships today and 545 by the end of the fiscal year [FY 1986], reaching 600 by the end of 1989." Commenting on the personnel situation, he said: "From the worst retention and recruiting in postwar history in 1979 and 1980, we have risen to the highest figures achieved since we began keeping records. We are meeting 100 percent of our recruiting goals." Finally, he commented on readiness: "The fleet is more ready to go in harm's way than at any time in recent peacetime history. In the past four years, combat readiness for surface ships has improved by 29 percent, for nuclear submarines by 34 percent, and aviation squadrons by 42 percent."[16] Since then recruitment has generally stayed up, the readiness bins are close to full, and the 600-ship Navy goal was almost met (it might have had not the sixteen frigates been retired early).

After being criticized for many years for not having a strategy, the U.S. Navy developed and refined its maritime strategy. There are many specific areas for criticism for the Reagan-Lehman years, but overall it will undoubtedly be recorded as one of the best eras in post-World War II naval history.

Conclusions

Because of the shipbuilding decision of the early Reagan-Lehman years, the Navy can rest on its laurels for a few years. Some eighty ships are being built or approved, most readiness bins are once more full, and current manpower problems are still tolerable. Fairly soon, however, some decisions must be made. The Navy should first evaluate the political-military environment of the 1990s rather than just letting sophisticated and expensive weapon programs drive the budget. Once that is done, it might find that a return to basic naval missions—naval presence, projection ashore, and sea control—is more appropriate. It might also be able to return to the old "hi-lo" concept of balancing—for example, expensive Aegis-class destroyers with less expensive ships, as Admiral Harry Train suggested a few years ago, or perhaps even looking at new, less expensive submarine alternatives. It seems certain that at least for a few years, and probably for the rest of the century, defense budgets will never again see the significant rise of the early 1980s. New thinking is required for the 1990s.

Chapter 7

Forces for Projecting U.S. Power

Paul F. Gorman

Power Projection Concepts

Neither *force projection* nor *projection forces* appears in the *Department of Defense Dictionary of Military and Associated Terms*.[1] This lexical anomaly probably reflects a surfeit of claimants for the terms among the armed services and the unified and specified commands, who constitute the dictionary's editorial board. After all, if one discounts military contributions to internal defense of the United States and its possessions, all U.S. forces, both active and reserve components, have been raised and trained for operations abroad, and the phrases are probably too indiscriminate for inclusion in the joint dictionary. Nonetheless, preparing U.S. military forces to influence events abroad, especially to project power in regions where their presence is non-existent or transient, has been a recurrent strategic concern.

Strategic Zones

In contemporary strategy, the United States guards, besides its homeland, four strategic zones: NATO's territory and sea lines of communications (SLOCs); Northeast Asia and the Northwest Pacific; Southwest Asia's strife-torn lands and surrounding seas; and the Caribbean and its problematic insular and littoral nations. The first two requirements stem from common political, cultural, and economic interests so extensive as to have warranted forward deployment, for the past forty years, of a significant proportion of U.S. standing forces; in the current context of relaxed tensions between the United States and the Soviet Union, and between North and South Korea, these deployments can no longer be taken for granted. The Caribbean is of importance not only because of its proximity to the United States, and Cuban and Soviet activities there, but also because of the oil, coal, other raw materials, and trade goods that flow through the region, all as important to U.S. allies as to the United States itself. "Force projection" is of less moment there in that most of the region lies within striking range of forces stationed within the United States. In contrast, Southwest Asia is beyond the range at which any permanently based U.S. forces can protect oil shipments to Japan, Korea, and European allies, and the region's persistent instability has therefore engaged U.S. interests at maximum geostrategic disadvantage.

Implementing Strategy

For decades, the United States has sought to protect its strategic zones by containing the Soviet Union to the extent of its World War II conquests by deploying forward forces to buttress coalitions, holding ready strong forces within the territorial limits of the United States capable of rapid movement overseas in an emergency, maintaining a qualitative edge over potential adversaries through superior military technologies, and providing security assistance to allies and friends. Its efforts have been more successful in Europe and the Northwest Pacific than elsewhere. The series of Middle Eastern crises of the 1970s, culminating in the collapse of the shah of Iran in 1979, refocused American strategists on the importance of maintaining freedom of the seas and the classic oceanic defiles, or choke points, and of the advantaged central position of the arch-adversary, the Soviet Union.

Power Projection

If those words then came more trippingly to the lips of Navy admirals or Marine generals than to those of Army or Air Force counterparts, it was not that the latter were not trying as ardently to narrow the gap between presidential rhetoric and force capabilities. During the Reagan years, military planners of all services often reminded legislators and the public that they had to provide against "firstest with the mostest" competition in which prospective opponents could drive overland to any strategic destination, while the United States, using every means of transport at its disposal, could barely array sufficient force to contest their arrival. U.S. means included (1) deploying forces forward, an expedient as politically onerous as it was economically burdensome; (2) posturing forces for rapid airlift to a threatened theater from the United States; (3) prepositioning matériel in an overseas theater so that relatively fast and plentiful passenger aircraft, possibly from the Civil Reserve Air Fleet (CRAF) could quickly fly in personnel in the event of an emergency; and (4) opening a SLOC to convey personnel, equipment, and supplies to reinforce forward forces and sustain operations. U.S. military planners thought of their problem in something like the scheme shown in figure 7–1.

Forward-deployed forces—whether maritime or land based—are clearly advantageous but costly. Forces delivered by air from strategic reserves in the continental United States or other theaters are strategically crucial in that they are usually the first arrivals after recognition of an emergency and as such may be the first indicator of U.S. resolve to act against a developing threat. But air-delivered forces are severely constrained by the kinds and amount of available airlifters and by the requisite access for overflight or bases for en-route refueling, reception at destination, and refueling upon egress. Prepositioned forces are usually a special case of air-delivered forces, those generated by marriage of units flown in without major impediments with such items stored in theater, provisioned by heavy or bulky supplies also stocked there. But the strategic make-weight is sealift: personnel, equipment, and supplies delivered by ships.

Implementing Strategy

Obviously emergencies against which to develop equipment, structure forces, and conduct training differ depending upon the threat, preparations made in anticipation, distances that must be traversed, and competing demands for scarce resources. The budgeting guidance issued to the armed services by the secretary of defense over the eight years of the Reagan administration called upon them to structure forces to meet a war that begins in Southwest Asia and then spreads to Europe and the Northwest Pacific. Among the upward pressures on Department of Defense (DOD) expenditures during the Reagan administration were consequent efforts to improve airlift and sealift and to enhance strategic prepositioning. But much more has been involved than budgeting. As in other eras, strategy was given form and substance by the president and the Congress through four avenues:

1. *Reorganization: Setting up a new command apparatus to signify to prospective foes, and to Congress and the American people, watchfulness and intent to use force if*

Figure 7-1. U.S. Force Projection Capability

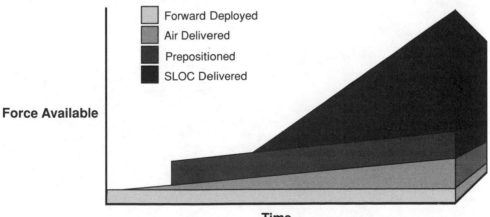

necessary. President Carter established the Joint Caribbean Task Force at Key West to meet anxieties generated by "discovery" of Soviet troops in Cuba in 1979 and set up the Rapid Deployment Joint Task Force to act on his Persian Gulf pronouncement. President Reagan embodied his endorsement of that Carter Doctrine on the Persian Gulf by establishing the U.S. Central Command, and he brought the U.S. Transportation Command into being to unify the planning and concert the operations of the Air Force's Military Airlift Command, the Army's Military Traffic Management Command, the Navy's Military Sealift Command, and the Joint Deployment Agency. More recently, Congress established the U.S. Special Operations Command (USSOCOM) and a new assistant secretary of defense for special operations and low-intensity conflict, and it called for a cabinet-level committee within the National Security Council to overwatch interagency preparations for low-intensity conflict (LIC).

2. *Diplomacy: Initiating action to alter strategic relationships by forming new alliances, revising old ones, or negotiating arms control agreements.* U.S. diplomats have faced daunting tasks in providing bases for U.S. forces overseas, access to ports and airfields to support movement of U.S. strategic reserves, and agreements constraining proliferation of nuclear and chemical weapons, as well as for eliciting other forms of cooperation from allies and friends in the interests of mutual security.

3. *Restructuring: Directing alterations of force structure.* Examples of these changes include the case of the Army's forming light infantry divisions more amenable to intercontinental air delivery or the augmentation of the special operations forces (SOF) of the Army, Navy, and Air Force.

4. *Reassignment: Changing the disposition of U.S. forces.* This is accomplished through efforts such as moving the 7th Fleet to the Indian Ocean or otherwise changing the composition of forward-deployed forces in Southwest Asia. An alternative approach is assigning new missions. The Strategic Air Command has begun serious efforts to equip and train for conventional operations, including reconnaissance, antiship missile operations, sea and land mining, and land interdiction and strike missions.[2]

The most exotic and dangerous weapons in use by either antagonist originated with neither of the two superpowers. China and Brazil became prominent as purveyors of armor, guided missiles, and other advanced military matériel.

Strategic Lessons from the Persian Gulf

Events in Southwest Asia have taught American strategists four salient lessons: the importance of increasing interdependence, the necessity of concerted action by U.S. military forces, the unique requirements of SOF, and the need for alternatives to overseas bases.

International Interdependence

The Persian Gulf is a paradigm of the multipolar world. The United States could tolerate interruption of gulf oil shipments, but its allies could not. In their interests more than its own, the United States provided not only forces but essential common ground for cooperation among nations of the region with each other, European nations, and other states. Absent U.S. action, the Iran-Iraq War would almost surely have spread, and shipments of oil almost certainly would have been impaired. It is also significant that since there were ample suppliers of arms and munitions other than the Soviet Union and the United States, neither was able to influence decisively the course of the conflict. The most exotic and dangerous weapons in use by either antagonist originated with neither of the two superpowers. China and Brazil became prominent as purveyors of armor, guided missiles and other advanced military matériel.

Importance of Unified Action by U.S. Armed Forces

Over thirty years ago (April 13, 1958) President Eisenhower, in his message to Congress on the 1958 reorganization of the DOD, stated that "strategic and tactical planning must be completely unified, combat forces organized into unified commands, each equipped with the most efficient weapon systems that science can develop, singly led and prepared to fight as one, regardless of Service." One of the incidents often cited by proponents of the Goldwater-Nichols Defense Reorganization Act of 1986 was the failure of joint interoperability at Desert One, the aborted Iran hostage rescue mission. The Goldwater-Nichols legislation inserted the JCS chairman into the chain of command over the unified and specified commanders in chief, subordinated the Joint Staff in Washington to him, enjoined simple, clear lines of command responsibility, and provided theater commanders new authority over their service components. Nonetheless, when the United States began employing forces to ensure freedom of navigation in the Persian Gulf, Admiral William Crowe, JCS chairman, encountered objections from the Navy to subordinating elements of the Pacific Fleet operating there to the commander in chief of the U.S. Central Command (USCINCCENT), although that region had long been assigned to him for eliciting cooperation from allies, and planning and conducting U.S. operations, and USCINCCENT already had under his command Air Force, Army, and Marine Corps elements, as well as U.S. Navy ships. In retrospect, the chairman was eminently correct: the projected forces needed more unification, not less.

Unique Requirements of SOF

The failures that led to Desert One were many, but salient among them was an attempt to conduct an intricate raid with forces poorly prepared for the job: fleet helicopters committed to a long overland night flight to a rough landing strip crowded with Air Force fixed-wing aircraft, Army troops, and equipment that were assembled for such purposes for the first time. The new U.S. Special Operations Command, also set up by Goldwater-Nichols, is a congressional remedy for perceived service shortsightedness, an effort to raise the equipping and training of SOF to the same status and priority for resources the services accord forces for more conventional missions. USCINCSOC, as the new commander is labeled, is unique: he is the only commander of a unified or specified command with his own budgetary authority and a dedicated assistant secretary of defense to act as his advocate in Washington. Should a president ever decide to undertake an application of military force like that directed by President Carter, USCINCSOC is responsible for turning out forces capable of doing the job.

Need for Alternatives to Overseas Bases

Neither President Carter nor President Reagan was able to obtain bases for U.S. forces in Southwest Asia, and the U.S. Central Command (CENTCOM) continues to be headquartered in Tampa, Florida. Probably the aura of success surrounding recent CENT-

COM operations in the Persian Gulf militates against resolving its grave difficu[...] remoteness from the region. Some forces assigned to CENTCOM had to operate in the gulf from adapted oil company platforms, with equipment awkward for their tasks. For example, lacking robotic aircraft, they remained dependent for nighttime surveillance of a suspected Iranian minelayer upon relatively short-range manned rotary-wing aircraft flying from barges. Yet a captured U.S. pilot being paraded in Tehran could have severely degraded prospects for CENTCOM's success, and the region's chances for peace. CENTCOM forces did not appear to have been "equipped with the most efficient weapon systems that science can develop," as called for by President Eisenhower. USCINCCENT and USCINCSOC, who provided the forces in question, have a clear congressional mandate to ameliorate such shortcomings.

"Low-intensity conflict" then is high-probability conflict, and includes both terrorism and guerrila warfare . . .

Looking Ahead: 2000 and Beyond

Strategic Requirements

The Commission on Integrated Long-Term Strategy, in its report of January 1988, *Discriminate Deterrence*, foresaw no diminution in the need for projection forces:

> The decades ahead are likely to bring drastic changes: China, perhaps Japan and other countries, will become major military powers. Lesser powers will acquire advanced weaponry, diminishing the relative advantages of both U.S. and Soviet forces. Arms agreements may have sizable impact on nuclear and conventional forces. Major U.S. interests will continue to be threatened at fronts much closer to our adversaries than to the United States. Our ability to deter aggression at these distant places will be impaired by uncertainty about allies and friends granting us access to bases and overflight rights, or joining us in defense preparations to respond to ambiguous warning signals. Our difficulties of access may worsen as a result of Third World conflicts that jeopardize U.S. bases or lead to Soviet expansion in areas previously free of Soviet forces. Military technology will change substantially in the next 20 years. . . .If Soviet military research continues to exceed our own, it will crode the qualitative edge on which we have long relied.[3]

The commission's Regional Conflict Working Group characterized the future as follows:

> By the first decade of the next century, we must anticipate a world in which groups hostile to the United States—governments and non-governmental political or criminal

organizations—will have access to both weapons of devastating power and reliable means to deliver them. The United States and its traditional allies of the Northern Hemisphere could possibly be attacked, and must certainly expect to be threatened, by diverse nations and groups who, compared with the current set of such foes, will be both more numerous and more dangerous. . .a world in which trained terrorists and subversives abound, some operating in league with drug cartels, and irresponsible governments and radical political groups possess deadly weaponry. These trends in the Third World portend for future presidents of the United States problems of national security more diverse, urgent, and potentially destructive than those faced by their predecessors. . . . Moreover, presidents in the first decade of the next century will have to deal with these involvements without many of the overseas bases that have underwritten the strategy of the United States in the Third World for most of the 20th Century.[4]

Useful for considering future conflict is the depiction of a continuum of possible wars in figure 7–2, or warlike uses of violence, in which U.S. interests might be involved. In this paradigm, "low-intensity conflict" occupies the left sector, where probability of occurrence is high, but intensity, referring to weapons employed, casualties, and damage, is relatively low. "Low-intensity conflict" then is high-probability conflict and includes both terrorism and guerrilla warfare (figure 7–3).

Using such a construct, a military planner could visualize the sort of forces his or her service might need to achieve national objectives. There are two contextual imperatives: (1) strategic or national intelligence, which provides a means of assessing threats, of anticipating their actualization, essential for deciding if, when, where, and

Figure 7–2. Possible Conflicts

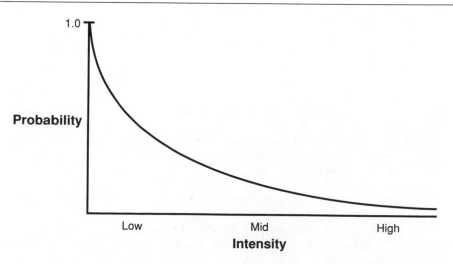

Figure 7–3. Low-Intensity Conflict

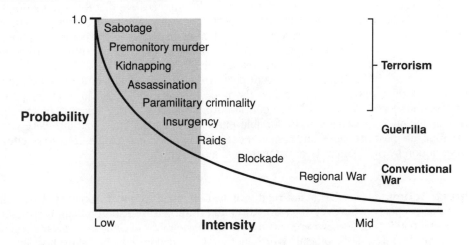

how to commit U.S. forces, and (2) mobile forces, especially naval forces, which can collect intelligence and convey to potential adversaries the potential of the United States to use force should its interests so require. Admiral James Watkins, the former chief of naval operations, used the diagram in figure 7–4 to describe naval contributions to low-intensity conflict.

Figure 7–4. The Spectrum of Conflict

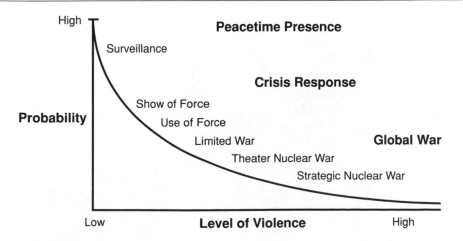

But if the fundamental goal of the United States in low-intensity conflict is to help others to defend themselves, then U.S. forces would avoid direct action except in those rare circumstances where speed, surprise, or lack of alternative dictates the use of its own SOF. Rather than engagement (fire support or maneuver), the force functions most likely to be needed otherwise are security assistance, intelligence, and communications. Figure 7–5 portrays U.S. force functions in the order in which they are likely to come into play inside a country afflicted with low-intensity conflict.

Adroit use of U.S. forces capable of performing the cited noncombatant functions in Third World countries might obviate the need to proceed beyond logistical support of indigenous forces to use of U.S. general-purpose forces for fire support or maneuver—including force projection by forcible entry—and concomitant mid-intensity warfare. But the most probable, and hence, most critical, functions are the first three cited: direct action by SOF, security assistance, and intelligence.

Direct Action. U.S. SOF stand ready for instant employment to protect American lives and property wherever they are threatened abroad by saboteurs or terrorists. The likelihood is that somewhere, even now, some member of SOF is at hazard somewhere, protecting a U.S. official. Were another U.S. diplomat to be taken hostage or another civil airliner hijacked, projection of U.S. SOF would be one option the president would have.

Security Assistance. The security assistance programs of the United States—referring to funds, goods, or services sent overseas to bolster the security of a friend or

Figure 7–5. U.S. Force Functions in Low-Intensity Conflict

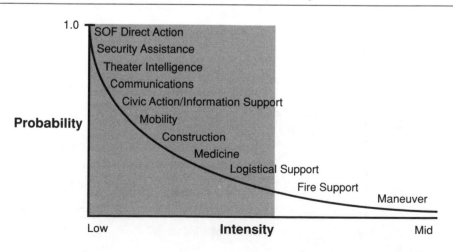

ally—have underwritten American foreign policy for forty years and are regarded worldwide as tangible evidence of American commitment to national independence and peaceful development. The needs of the recipients of this aid have changed less over time than we who have given it. In the years since the wars in Southeast Asia, the government of the United States has adopted legislation, policy, and procedures that have severely limited the flexibility and utility of its security assistance. While U.S. military aid served Presidents Truman, Eisenhower, Kennedy, and Johnson as a mainstay of policy, Presidents Nixon, Ford, Carter, and Reagan were increasingly constrained in its use. The U.S. government is likely to suffer grievous setbacks unless future administrations are provided with improved means for protecting U.S. interests. Current security assistance programs, variously legislated as economic support, military assistance, foreign military sales credits, or international military education and training, are seriously underfunded for pursuing an integrated, long-term strategy and too micromanaged by Congress to enable any administration to deal with crises. Absent President Bush's proposing reform—the Commission on Integrated Long-Term Strategy has recommended to him twelve basic revisions to current law and regulation—and favorable congressional action, security assistance is not likely to be an important strategic instrument.

Mobilizing U.S. ingenuity and technology to assist others in dealing with conflict will require setting aside the notion that security assistance is some sort of U.S. domestic job support program, a way of disposing of surplus or obsolescent U.S. equipment, or a way of reducing the unit price of new equipment for a U.S. service because of larger purchases to accommodate a foreign user. U.S. military matériel and doctrine are not readily adaptable to the needs of the armed forces of most friends and allies. To the contrary, they often require different equipment from that used by U.S. forces and different tactics. If the United States is to help more effectively in the future, American industry may be only marginally involved. Indeed, one U.S. purpose ought to be to use its assistance as an incentive to encourage other friends and allies to manufacture and provide relevant equipment. Moreover, any future U.S. security assistance program should have a strong thrust toward endowing the aid recipient with self-sufficiency and self-reliance.

Intelligence. One senior U.S. diplomat remarked that in low-intensity conflict as in real estate, there are only three things that matter. In real estate these are location, location, and location; in low-intensify conflict they are intelligence, intelligence, and intelligence. The cornerstone for U.S. dealings with regional conflict in the Third World is the ability to collect, analyze, and disseminate information that enables U.S. planners to anticipate not only threatened violence but also political and economic trends with long-term portents of violence, to devise effective counters, and to ensure discriminate responses by allied or U.S. forces. As a direct function of U.S. technological leads in sensors, platforms, and advanced means of interpretation and dissemination, intelligence is the greatest comparative advantage of the United States and probably will remain so for the foreseeable future.

Intelligence is the most efficacious military source of power and influence worldwide. Such successes as the United States has enjoyed in forestalling terrorist acts abroad or in dealing with insurgency, either through a friend or ally or on its own, must be attributed, in large measure, to U.S. intelligence—information collected by or corroborated through the various methods employed by the intelligence community and correlated with existing data and analyses; the whole assessed by experts; and facts and judgments disseminated to those who need to know for diplomatic, operational, or planning purposes. The key presidential decisions concerning any U.S. response to conflict—whether it is in the U.S. interest to act, and if so when and how—depend crucially upon the cogency of intelligence. Moreover, should the president decide to act, the adequacy of U.S. intelligence will influence, often crucially, how much support he will be able to muster among leaders of American opinion, members of Congress, the public, or allies and friends abroad for his initial commitments and for continuing understanding and support in a protracted struggle.

Prospects for Forward Deployments

Forward-deployed land and air forces in NATO-Europe and in Korea will probably encounter intense political pressures for withdrawal. Objections to their presence will include environmental concern over maneuver damage and noise pollution, cultural and racial chauvinism, conviction that international tensions or political divisions would disappear upon their eviction, and hope that their departure would increase chances of avoiding the casualties and damage of war of any intensity. Withdrawals accommodating such pressures could become necessary to preserve a capacity to reinforce in the event of renewed international tensions. If so, force projection from the United States may become newly prominent in U.S. strategy for protecting NATO-Europe and the Northwest Pacific.

The so-called Third World will present other problems, and other possibilities, chiefly in the realm of "low intensity conflict." Over the past forty years, U.S. bases abroad have been reduced in number fourfold, largely reflecting closure or abandonment of bases in the Third World. As recognizably American military installations abroad have diminished in number, constraints have multiplied on U.S. access to foreign airspace for overflight or airfields or ports for transiting forces. These trends will probably continue. The current U.S. basing agreement with the Philippines expires in 1991, and thereafter U.S. forces at Clark Air Force Base and Subic Bay will be subject to removal upon one year's notice. The Panama Canal Treaty, which entered into force in 1979, mandates closing of all U.S. military bases in Panama by the end of 1999. While there is a possibility in either of these cases that negotiations ad interim could extend U.S. tenancy or lead to opening comparable U.S. installations elsewhere, the United States cannot count on such favorable outcomes and must be prepared in the future to support national strategy with fewer, or perhaps no, such footholds.

The United States will undoubtedly have to place increasing reliance on the range and striking power of units of the U.S. Navy and the U.S. Marine Corps. The sea services are well practiced in configuring, training, deploying, and sustaining task-oriented forces for overseas missions. Navy and Marine projection forces, however, will be strained to meet their worldwide responsibilities, including continuing to pose the principal counter to Soviet naval power and providing best prospects for forcible entry in most regions. For military missions in low-intensity conflict, especially those of long duration, it will remain important for the United States to be able to draw upon Army and Air Force capabilities as well. Use of land and air forces will require overseas basing in some form, or changing these forces to adapt to the new strategic circumstance.

. . . any U.S. military unit, whether on a U.S. overseas base, or simply operating temporarily on the territory of another nation, becomes a magnet for saboteurs, terrorists, and political demonstrators of all stripes.

Alternatives to the Present Structure

The difficulties encountered by Presidents Carter and Reagan foreshadow the problems their successors will almost certainly face. The United States must begin seriously to develop, by exploiting all the ingenuity of its military planners, and its scientists and engineers, alternative ways of performing the functions for which U.S. forces have heretofore depended upon terrestrial facilities in the Third World: support of forward-deployed forces, staging and sustainment of reinforcements, command control, communications, and intelligence. The United States should look now for alternatives in how and from where its forces operate.

Through the unified command plan, U.S. strategists carve up the world beyond U.S. borders into theaters, fiefdoms for regional CINCs who are expected to provide ports, airfields, maintenance, supply, and personnel depots and intratheater transportation for forces projected from U.S. strategic reserves. Much more subtle support arrangements will be needed. Few foreign nations will be willing to accept the apparent surrender of sovereignty associated with turning over to U.S. forces ports, airfields, or other territory. U.S. overseas bases will provide a focus for xenophobes, nationalists, and religious fundamentalists. The inflationary impact of American dollars on weak economies, the cultural impact of American service personnel on traditional societies, the fear of AIDS, and the inevitable charges by the domestic opposition that a cooperating government has become a Yankee puppet, will combine to make granting base rights or even temporary access a politically risky undertaking for any government. Moreover, any U.S. military unit, whether on a U.S. overseas base, or simply operating temporarily on the territory of another nation, becomes a magnet for saboteurs, terrorists, and political demonstrators of all stripes. Therefore, U.S. forces must be structured, trained, and equipped to cope with circumstances which, in the aggregate, call for capabilities different from those needed to meet conventional threats amid wartime missions. Measures indicated include the following:

Rearward-Echeloned Units

Current assumptions for organizing and equipping U.S. Army and Air Force units for operations overseas are that the entire outfit will be transported overseas as an entity. Severance with the base of origin is expected to be virtually complete. Overseas, the theater commander is expected to provide the unit support, especially in furnishing expendable supplies, food, and spare parts. But otherwise the unit is expected to bring the wherewithal for self-sufficiency.

All of these notions are invalid in any nation afflicted by low-intensity conflict. There the fewer U.S. personnel who are deployed forward, the better. Theater infrastructure is likely to be minimal to nonexistent. The logistic and security burdens imposed on the host nation and the gaining commander by each deployed U.S. serviceman or service-woman argue for restricting numbers to those essential to performing the mission. The unit itself should be configured so that it can operate in echelons, with that portion of the unit sent forward into the country of interest severely constrained in manning and equipment to the minimum necessary and the remainder positioned on board a ship operating in nearby international waters or retained in the continental United States (CONUS). Echeloning dictates dedicated communications capabilities for the transmittal of voice, imagery, and data among the several echelons and may entail exceptional transportation support, such as helicopter service between ship and shore echelons or regular intercontinental airlift between overseas and CONUS echelons.

The relatively new technologies that make possible audio and visual conferencing centered on high-resolution digital images of maps, documents, or other imagery are particularly relevant to the concept of echelonment rearward. Fully integrated multi-point image communications systems, which operate over narrow bandwidth commu-nications channels (such as voice-grade telephone lines), make feasible staff reductions in headquarters and relocation to CONUS or other secure locations the majority of personnel and equipment that might be deployed for higher intensity warfare.

New Forms of Temporary Shelter

If recent experience is any guide to the future, the administration will have to run the military construction hurdles in Congress if it expects to do much for the projected force beyond using local buildings or erecting tents. U.S. temporary construction tech-niques leave much to be desired. The sandbag, that bane of the World War I doughboy, is still used in profusion to protect personnel and facilities, despite its propensity to sag and deteriorate and its vulnerability to modern ordnance. Concertina barbwire, more of an irritant than a barrier, still delineates secured areas. Canvas tents have major draw-backs in most of the world: hot, dank, vulnerable to insects and reptiles, susceptible to wind and solar damage, mildew, and rot, expensive to repair or replace.

Four related concepts should bear upon future decisions concerning facilities for the forward echelon. First, physical security should be a primary consideration. Application of sensors and processors can help here, and we ought to provide for rapidly erectable, strong fortifications, barriers, and bunkers. Projectile-proof mats and rigid composites, plus hollow, stackable forms to be loaded with soil on site, using portable machinery, are indicated. Second, shipping containers ought to double as shelters. Containers of commercial-standard size could ease deployment and obviate much on-site construction. Third, for large shelters like hangars, rapidly erectable, transportable buildings should be used. Fourth, designs for indigenous materials should also be available.

New Doctrine and Matériel for Unit Security

In many situations, the forward echelon will find itself secured by host nation guards and operating amid the comings and goings of indigenous employees, curious visitors, children, and domestic animals of all descriptions. In such circumstances, the U.S. commander will find pistols, rifles, and machine guns of little use against security problems presented by thieves, prostitutes, and drug peddlers. In most cases, he will not be able to rely on the use of deadly force. Low-intensity conflict requires new security concepts and new matériel. One proposal of merit—an adaptation of a demonstrated technology—would require all personnel authorized in or near the unit's vital areas to carry coded identity tags, which could be remotely and continuously interrogated, so that the commander would have twenty-four-hour-per-day accountability for all U.S. personnel and for foreigners with authorized access. Outer security would rest less on perimeter fences than on sensors capable of detecting any unauthorized intruder within his security zone and of providing close-up visual inspection, coupled with means for deterring or stopping any intruder intent on harm.

Sea-Based Platforms

Most areas of the Third World where U.S. forces are likely to be deployed are accessible by sea and can be supported from sea-based platforms. Sea-based options can also ameliorate many of the political, economic, and security problems associated with stationing U.S. forces in a Third World country or even exercising transient rights there. Operating in international waters or in a nation's territorial sea but outside the view of the population, U.S. sea-based units would be politically, economically, and culturally less intrusive. Sea-based platforms would also be inherently more secure than land bases from attacks by saboteurs, terrorists, paramilitary criminals, or guerrillas. (But, as Iranian guerrilla-launched attacks and minings made evident, naval combatants may have to be deployed to secure unarmed or lightly armed platforms.) Sea-based options can also significantly reduce the time and money required to establish a secure operating area overseas in that the United States can prepare for such operations in advance and deploy platforms only when the situation requires. Finally, sea-based assets are fully recoverable.

The United States could augment the Navy and the Marine Corps with additional amphibious and fleet-mobile logistics ships and strengthen their ability to sustain forces at sea with minimal dependence on forward bases for long periods of time. Or it could look for cost-effective sea-basing alternatives developed expressly to support U.S. air and land operations, for which there are five promising concepts. The first entails configuring a specific type of land or air unit (for example, a helicopter maintenance unit) to fit into shelters identical in shape to standard shipping containers. These could be readily deployed on chartered, container-carrying merchant ships. The unit would be self-sufficient within its containers in that it could perform its mission wholly from them, on ship or shore, without external power or plumbing. The second is new construction of very fast container ships (fifty knots or more), a commercially attractive prospect for the faltering U.S. merchant marine. A third, deployable waterfront facilities, is under investigation by the Navy for a variety of peacetime and contingency port functions: berthing, cargo throughput, and other support for sea-borne forces. The fourth, studied in depth by the Navy a decade or so ago, is a module-assembled island-size base on a floating oceangoing platform. The fifth, also studied years ago, is a "super ship," a huge, mobile airfield at sea capable of supporting operations of the largest U.S. aircraft.

New Mix of Aircraft

One important function of overseas bases is to support U.S. air operations. For low-intensity conflict, intelligence collection and airlift are the most important such operations. While space-based platforms have redoubtable intelligence capabilities, they are unlikely to be able to substitute for air-breathing collectors in all respects and cannot be used for hauling freight or passengers. Sometimes military airlift operations can be conducted through commercial facilities or through the air bases of allies and friends, as routine undertakings. Some airlift operations, however, especially those in support of SOF or other special activities, will have to be conducted directly from U.S. bases, and virtually all intelligence collectors prefer to operate from U.S. bases. This suggests aircraft for SOF and intelligence quite different from those now available or contemplated. It also suggests that the services should reconsider the interservice agreements that led to dividing intelligence collection among the aircraft flown by the various U.S. armed services.

Intelligence

Some of the intelligence systems most valuable in contemporary crises situations are available only on short-range, limited endurance Army aircraft. Yet the United States will often require very long-legged intelligence collectors. Several technologies promising long-endurance, atmospheric platforms should be pursued.

Capabilities for continuous wide-area surveillance will almost certainly be needed. When continuous coverage does not exist, targeted activities can be altered and phased to take place during uncovered periods. Today's surveillance platforms (fixed-wing aircraft, satellites) provide only sporadic coverage, and their presence on station is either predictable or detectable. Additionally manned fixed-wing aircraft, both current and future, require substantial land- or carrier-based support.

One developmental program of promise aims at lighter-than-air ships designed to provide long-endurance, atmospheric platforms. An airship incorporating modern technology could provide a critically needed long-endurance surveillance platform to support

U.S. interests in many regions of the world. Airships could operate independently of foreign bases, in either international or national airspace with the consent and protection of the supported country. Recent Navy, Air Force, and DOD science boards have independently concluded that airships (lighter-than-air technology) have the potential to be the most, and possibly only, cost-effective platform to provide sustainable, continuous airborne surveillance. Mission needs range from surveillance of allied airspace and terrain to defense of the continental United States against cruise missiles.

An airship could be designed to serve as mother-ship for unmanned air vehicles (UAVs), known also as remotely piloted vehicles (RPVs). These robot aircraft could cooperate with the airship for discriminating sensor work at very low altitudes and for extending the range of the airship's sensors. They could even provide it with standoff offensive and defensive weapons.

Unmanned air vehicles could also ease requirements for overseas bases and aid projection forces. The theoretical cost-effectiveness of robotic aircraft for missions in which manned aircraft would be exposed to unacceptable risk has been clear for several decades. Unfortunately the practical difficulties of developing robotic aircraft that are functional, reliable, and affordable have thus far proved to be greater than their proponents had expected. However, between now and the first decade of the next century, successful, cost-effective UAVs will almost certainly become available. It now appears possible to build robots that can be launched from and recovered onto a ship at sea and that can be controlled during flights of long duration from a command center located continents away.

Airlift

In many countries the sinews of nationhood include a fleet of rickety but still-serviceable C-47 (DC-3) aircraft built in the United States three or four decades ago. Crisis creates urgencies for use of air transportation—those old two-engined, unpressurized C-47s constitute strategic airlift. But there is no American-manufactured aircraft that is a modern equivalent of the C-47 in versatility of operations, simplicity of maintenance, ease of manning, or cost of operation. The current U.S. Air Force counterpart, the C-130, is much too complicated and demanding for most countries. In Central America, the C-130 could land on only thirty or so airfields of the entire region, the C-47 on more than ten times that number. The C-17's ability to land on fields comparable to those on which the C-130 can land will not help. At issue is real mobility: the United States may be able to project forces over intercontinental distances, but if it cannot concentrate them at the point of decision or support its own or allied forces operating within the overseas theater, transoceanic airlift capability is more a snare and a delusion than a strategic asset.

No U.S. manufacturer builds a rough field, short-takeoff-and-landing aircraft because no service has announced a requirement for one and offered to buy. Competing demands for funds and the lack of a constituency for so modest an airlifter within the Air Force all but ensure that there will be no domestic Third World airlifter to offer conflict-beleaguered friends anywhere. But foreign manufacturers do make transports that come close to filling the need. The administration ought to direct DOD to purchase at least two squadrons of an appropriate foreign aircraft equipped with the latest U.S.-

made avionics, ordnance and fire control devices, sensor suites, refueling gear, and other ancillary equipment for issue to units of the U.S. Air National Guard or Air Force Reserve. This will ensure that the United States has a training base and a logistic infrastructure for the aircraft. At the same time, the administration should initiate action to make the same aircraft, minus some or all of the high-technology used in the U.S. version, available for the U.S. security assistance program. Both moves will require soliciting the understanding and support of Congress. But they ought to be salable in that they will help the United States project force abroad and help others help themselves.

Space Platforms

U.S. space programs have heretofore aimed at versatile, durable, long-lived satellites. These perforce have also been expensive, large, and heavy, requiring special, powerful booster rockets to attain orbit. It now appears possible to consider a new class of light satellites, which would be much cheaper, smaller, and orbited with an ordinary missile booster but somewhat less mission capable and long-lived. One characteristic of these especially attractive for low-intensity conflict is low-cost, transportable ground stations. The Commission on Integrated Long-term Strategy has endorsed light satellites as a way to improve the redundancy and robustness of U.S. space systems against the prospect of conflict in space and to improve U.S. capabilities to provide what most nations require most: better intelligence and secure communications for disseminating it.

Special Operations Forces and Low-Intensity Conflict

SOF have missions across the entire spectrum of war. Both U.S. SOF and their Soviet counterparts were conceived for the apocalyptic contingencies of a world war. Many of the capabilities with which the United States endows SOF have little or nothing to do with combating terrorists or training Third World forces to cope with guerrillas. Most of the money spent to procure matériel for SOF has purchased elaborate transportation means for projecting them into a defended objective area or extracting them once their mission is completed. The main strategic contribution of SOF has been to lend an unconventional dimension to deterrence, and in particular to pose a threat of exploiting Soviet vulnerabilities to nationalist dissidence. To be sure, they are manned by the sort of individuals one would want for any dangerous, chancy, unstructured operation. And SOF have shown that they can be effective individually and collectively in low-intensity conflict. But they are much more than forces for combating terrorists or guerrillas.

The British have pointed out how useful it is for a nation possessing nuclear weapons to remind itself in its strategic doctrine that there are forms of conflict for which the possession of nuclear weapons is irrelevant—a number of possible cases of recourse to violence for political purposes that are unlikely to be deterred by a nuclear arsenal, or resolved by its use, and for which other kinds of force must be readied. Whether or not those who teach strategy at the Soviet war colleges point out that supporting international lawlessness, terrorism, and insurgency is a low-risk, low-cost way of achieving the stated objectives of Leninism, recent Soviet strategy in the Third World would certainly suggest that such is the case. But the Soviets have not made extensive use of their special operations forces outside their borders (with the significant exception of Afghanistan). Rather they have pursued their ends indirectly through training, aid, and advice for Third World proxies, avoiding direct action by elite combat forces. One telling fact about the Soviet role in Central America has been that two-thirds of the Russians in Nicaragua have served in a military field hospital; they appeared as benefactors to a people sensitive to foreign domination.

U.S. force structure, equipment, and doctrine, designed for accustomed combatant missions, are not well suited to pursuing noncombat roles in assisting any Third World nation.

However much Goldwater-Nichols may have advanced the fortunes of U.S. SOF, the law has thus far done little to enhance overall U.S. readiness for low-intensity conflict. The newly-created assistant secretary of defense for special operations and low intensity conflict has a legislated charter to concern himself with low-intensity conflict, but virtually every other DOD official of comparable rank has overlapping responsibilities, and low-intensity conflict should be the concern of a number of cabinet officers other than the secretary of defense. The mandated deputy national security adviser for low-intensity conflict might be in a better position to deal with the interagency issues that such conflict presents, but the Reagan administration never acted on the sense of Congress in that respect or upon the proposed low-intensity conflict board within the National Security Council to formulate relevant policy. The Bush administration faces unresolved tough questions, including what strategy to pursue, how to organize to implement it, how and for what to obtain funding, to what ends diplomatic action, and what forces where. To be sure, better SOF will help the U.S. posture for low-intensity conflict, but special operations are not coextensive with low-intensity conflict, and making SOF a better competitor for defense resources may make other worthy claimants for resources, in the budget shouldering ahead, less likely to receive the support they deserve.

The United States should not commit its forces to combat in any conflict unless it can do so decisively, swiftly, and with discrimination. Where there are treaty obligations to an ally, combined U.S.-allied forces might be positioned to exploit comparative advantages and to deter aggression, as has been the case in South Korea. But U.S. strategy should emphasize using U.S. forces to complement its security assistance, exploiting their potential for helping friendly forces engaged in low-intensity conflict with training, intelligence, communications, transportation, construction, medicine, logistics, and management.

The American view of war, which has served well for more than 200 years, has led the U.S. armed services to design units, equipment, and doctrine for projecting force to engage and defeat a foreign force in combat operations. Future conflict portends operations short of war, indirect undertakings involving military support for objectives fundamentally political, economic, or psychological in nature. Yet none of the U.S. armed services has yet considered such missions sufficiently in developing doctrine, training programs, force structure, or matériel, although hopeful beginnings have been made.[5]

U.S. force structure, equipment, and doctrine, designed for accustomed combatant missions, are not well suited to pursuing noncombat roles in assisting any Third World nation. Usually the presence of any foreign military force stirs nationalist abhorrence, and in some places, U.S. military forces will operate encumbered by historical burdens, so that their mere presence creates political problems for a host nation. U.S. general-purpose forces are usually too heavily or inappropriately equipped and too elaborately manned for probable missions—prepared as they are for the exigencies of high-intensity conflict. Often they are not well trained for other missions. Often military roles will be best performed by specially trained individuals or detachments as small and unobtrusive as feasible.

The foregoing statements frequently strike U.S. military officers, doctrinally conditioned to believe in the primacy of the combat function, as startlingly novel. These concepts assign priority to such military functions as training, intelligence, communications, mobility, construction, medicine, and logistical support ahead of fire support or maneuver—but this inversion is commonplace among practitioners of unconventional warfare worldwide, most notably in Southeast Asia. However, as the instances of Grenada, Tripoli, and the Persian Gulf underscore, there will be times in regional conflict when a president decides to commit U.S. forces to combat. Such a decision will be made normally only in extremis, to deal with circumstances beyond other means. The criteria for decision ought to include whether U.S. forces can succeed rapidly, with minimum cost and minimum damage. To ensure that the answer is affirmative, the United States must continue to develop the forces, doctrine, and tactical equipment capable of rapid, decisive, and efficiently discriminate force projection anywhere.

The development of such military forces and capabilities is the responsibility of the JCS. The newly created assistant secretary of defense for special operations and low-intensity conflict and the Special Operations Command have been assigned particular roles in readying SOF. The regional commanders, who plan for and direct employment of U.S. forces, have been given new strategic authority and influence over service procurement and force structure. In short, Goldwater-Nichols provided organizations and individuals within the U.S. government the ability to bring before the national command authorities the issues that need to be resolved to ensure the president's having forces capable of supporting U.S. strategy.

Proposals for the Bush Administration

For the foreseeable future, the United States will face requirements, stemming from its overarching objectives of peace and security, to project its power and influence with military forces. It can prepare for the future from a position of strength, but much of its national potential for dealing effectively with likely challenges is as yet unrealized. The traditional roles and missions of the services have obtruded, and the government as a whole has not been mobilized. Portended conflict threatens all Americans and can be met effectively only with a response from the whole government, through all of its departments and agencies.

The United States is not now well postured for the more probable forms of conflict; it needs to contemplate a major new bipartisan effort to enlighten public understanding of, and to win support for, new concepts for bringing U.S. military power to bear abroad. Management cannot be relegated to the DOD, nor can it be regarded simply as one aspect of peacetime foreign relations and assigned to the Department of State. Rather, it requires drawing on all elements of national strength, concerted by the president and the National Security Council, developed in conjunction with the Congress, and resting ultimately upon support of an informed people.

The resources required will be much less quantitatively than the 1980–1984 defense rebuilding but qualitatively perhaps more demanding. The key resource will be people: cadres to create intelligence, transfer technical skills, plan development projects, shape technology, and train future leaders of other countries. Even were the United States to start tomorrow, with very strong backing, it would be years before all the people, with the proper training, were available.

There remains the question of funding. Without adequate funds, any strategy will lack substance. The reforms proposed are not expensive compared with other undertakings of the U.S. government, and the payoff appears to be highly significant. The administration could act with confidence of not impairing other facets of national strategy.[6]

Troops On Golden Pheasant,
April 1988

Chapter 8

Manpower

James L. Lacy

O ne of the most important issues in U.S. military manpower policy in the 1990s is not, strictly speaking, a manpower issue at all. It is a question of force structure: specifically, how many and which kinds of forces should be kept active, ready to use on little or no notice, and how many and which kinds should be in reserve, available only upon call-up. How the question is decided will have far-reaching effects on manpower priorities and practices throughout the 1990s.

In the face of little or no real growth in defense budgets in the period ahead, pressures to transfer more military functions and manpower strength from the active forces to the reserves are bound to intensify. As a rule, reserve forces are less expensive to maintain in peacetime than active-duty forces performing the same missions. This is especially true of manpower-intensive missions. Not only are activity rates (such as training days, vehicle miles, flying hours) generally less for a reserve unit than for a similar active unit, but because most reservists are part time, pay and related costs also are appreciably less.

The inclination to find budgetary savings by substituting reserve forces for active forces continues a pattern set in motion in the early 1970s and accelerated by the Reagan administration in the 1980s. Under the banner of a total force policy, the National Guard and reserve components that together make up the Selected Reserve have assumed a vastly expanded role in the force structure and missions of the nation's armed forces. Not only have the reserve components grown dramatically in manpower strength (a 40 percent increase between fiscal years 1980 and 1989), they have also replaced the active forces in a growing share of missions, functions, and accompanying deployment requirements. This shift of responsibilities is without precedent in U.S. history. As more missions and manpower are relocated from the active to the reserve sides of the force structure, it is less possible to think wholly in terms of forces-in-being when fashioning military responses to external challenges. In the case of the U.S. Army in particular, there are few ground campaigns of anything more than limited duration, anywhere in the world, that can be undertaken without an activation of the reserves.

The underlying principle of the total force is not the issue. The total force idea, in the words of the Department of Defense (DOD), is that "in structuring our forces, units are placed in the Selected Reserve whenever feasible to maintain as small an active component peacetime force as national security and our strategy permit."[1] This is not a new concept. "It is the traditional policy of the United States," the War Department's General Staff wrote in nearly identical fashion in 1912, "that the military establishment in time of peace is to be a small, regular Army and that the ultimate war force of the Nation is to be a great Army of citizen soldiers. This fundamental theory of military organization is sound economically and politically."[2]

What is new, and not widely appreciated, is the extent to which the theory has been converted to practice in recent years. The present total force policy was the handmaiden of the All-Volunteer Force (AVF), embraced at the same time and in response to much the same set of circumstances. Without a total force concept, the logic of the AVF was incomplete. However, unlike the AVF, a widely debated change that, once decided, was implemented in open and unmistakable fashion, transformation of the force structure under the total force has taken place mostly off-stage, in a series of incremental steps, year by year, with little fanfare and almost no public debate.

Yet in terms of the composition and capabilities of the armed forces, the aggregate effects of substituting reservists for active-duty personnel under the total force banner may well be as far reaching as the earlier decision to substitute volunteers for conscripts under the AVF. Questions about force structure are closely linked to military manpower procurement policy; a military force with a heavy emphasis on part-time reserves is a different force-manning proposition from a heavily active-duty force, with considerably different demands on recruitment and training. More important, adjustments in force structure are also linked to broader strategic policy questions of how many and what kinds of forces realistically will be available for use in response to external challenges and emergencies.

Given the political and budgetary environment the United States faces entering the 1990s, it is difficult to imagine a reversal of present patterns. In the face of serious prospects for East-West negotiations on conventional arms reductions in Europe and stiff budget deficit pressures at home, an expansion in the peacetime strength of the active components is highly improbable. At a minimum, the reserve components will continue to grow, while the active forces will at best maintain, and more probably reduce, their manpower strengths. That alone has important implications for future military recruitment and training.

The key questions will be how far and in which directions this already unprecedented reliance on reserves can and should be pushed. Pressures for more of the same will be considerable. But is more of the same a prudent national policy? Is it reasonable to expect that increasing numbers of part-time reserve forces can be substituted for active forces while still preserving acceptable levels of military preparedness and responsiveness? Can we continue to shift manpower from one account and one side of the force structure to the other, merely adjusting at the margins (as has been the pattern and practice to date), or have we reached a point in the transformation of the force structure at which the structure itself requires a reappraisal and overhaul?

Is it reasonable to expect that increasing numbers of part-time reserve forces can be substituted for active forces while still preserving acceptable levels of military preparedness and responsiveness?

The questions will be difficult for both the administration and the Congress for several reasons. Military requirements seldom can be defined precisely, and military capabilities in the absence of an actual engagement are always difficult to assess. Requirements are all the more difficult to estimate in cases where forces need to be bolstered and deployed primarily in pursuit of diplomatic objectives. In the case of reserve forces, the problem is compounded by the nation's limited and dated experience in using them. Despite fifteen years of converting the force structure in total force directions, the total force policy itself has never been put to the test in a crisis or emergency. In order to acquire an appreciation of how activations of reserve forces have worked in the past, one must reach back to the draft era, and then the experience was scarcely reassuring. It is possible, nonetheless, to establish what is involved and in this way help to clarify the character of the choices that will be presented.

Beginnings

Although the total force principle is as old as the republic, its current expression owes its impetus, and to a large extent its terms, to the beginnings of the AVF. The end of the draft in the early 1970s forced a significant change in thinking about the place of reserve forces in national security. Until then, the Guard and reserves were viewed rather hazily as a force in reserve—something that would be mobilized and deployed considerably after the regular forces were engaged in a military conflict. Reserve forces were a hedge against a long war in Europe. For any other contingency, they were largely superfluous. When the nation needed manpower to sustain and bolster the active forces in crisis, its first and consistent choice was to induct men directly from civilian life into full-time active duty. Apart from the early months of Korea, reserves were activated infrequently, and with generally unimpressive results. Expanded draft calls did just as well in terms of increasing the active forces and signaling resolve to adversaries with much less domestic political fuss. Expanded draft calls avoided the need to declare a national emergency or to seek special authorization from the Congress on a case-by-case basis. A presidential declaration of national emergency was a prerequisite to a reserve call-up except when Congress provided specific call-up authority for specific circumstances. In the view of succeeding administrations, such a declaration would be dangerously (or at least prematurely) provocative, unnecessarily arousing domestically, and too blunderbuss in terms of the psychology and machinery that would be set in motion. Seeking special legislative authority on a case-by-case basis was only slightly less arousing.

The anticipated conversion to the AVF presented two problems in this context. First, in the absence of a draft, the nation would need some plausible capability to expand its active forces in two situations: in emergencies short of all-out general war and in circumstances of general war until a wartime draft could be reestablished and made to function. Second, although advocates of the AVF were sure that volunteers would be available to fill out an active force as large as those during the draft era, a smaller force was both the preferred course and an immediate priority of the Nixon administration.

The answer to both problems, the early planners of the AVF argued, was a total force concept. This meant that the reserves would now do what the draft had done

previously. When external circumstances required a surge in military capabilities, the reserves would fill the gap. Henceforth, Secretary of Defense Melvin Laird told the services, "Guard and Reserve units and individuals will be prepared to be the initial and primary source for augmentation of the active forces in any future emergency requiring a rapid and substantial expansion of the active forces."[3]

The second element was related but aimed more directly at the size of the armed forces. In the total force, missions and responsibilities previously housed exclusively in the active forces would be shifted, where possible, to the reserve components. In Laird's words, "Emphasis will be given to concurrent consideration of the total forces, active and reserve, to determine the most advantageous mix to support national strategy and meet the threat."[4] Sound budgetary and force planning policy was the prevalent rationale. According to Laird, "Lower sustaining costs of nonactive duty forces, as compared to the cost of maintaining larger active duty forces . . . allows more force units to be provided for the same cost as an all-active force structure, or the same number of force units to be maintained for lesser cost."[5]

Domestic politics and concerns about giving the reserves a genuine military mission were also important factors. Apart from a token call-up of reserves in 1968, the Johnson administration had fought the war in Vietnam with draftees. That reservists were paid regularly to drill in local armories at home while men were drafted from civilian life to fight in Vietnam did not sit well with a public already greatly disillusioned by the war. The absence of any real military mission for the reserves had troubled administrations in the past (Eisenhower spent his last year in office inveighing against excessive reserve strength that was of no military value and cost an additional $80 million a year). Unless serious and visible military functions were transferred to the reserves, the probability was high that they would continue to be largely superfluous. The total force, accordingly, would begin to provide these missions while allowing for a smaller active force. In elevating Laird's total force concept to formal DOD policy in the wake of the last military induction in 1973, Secretary of Defense James Schlesinger told the armed forces that what was intended was a policy that "integrates the Active, Guard and Reserve forces into a homogeneous whole."[6]

Importantly, however, this "homogeneous whole" took the reserves as they were. The conversion from draft to AVF and the companion total force policy did not result in the development of new kinds of reserve forces or any new organization of existing reserve forces. Nor were basic training requirements in the reserves adjusted to meet the new roles that total force planning implied. In an organizational patchwork whose basic structure had not changed appreciably since the early 1950s, the reserve side of the total force would continue to consist of six reserve components—the Army National Guard, Army Reserve, Naval Reserve, Marine Corps Reserve, Air National Guard, and Air Force Reserve—serving the four military services, at more than 5,000 separate installations in the United States, with the fifty Army and Air National Guards still structured on a state-by-state basis (although in principle subsumed in the national military structure) and each still subject to considerable state influence. Despite the new roles these components were to assume, training requirements would be essentially the same as in 1952: normally one weekend a month and two weeks of summer training per year.

Little thought was given to changing the manpower content of the reserves. Endowed since the mid-1950s with the spectacular recruiting device of a draft deferment, the reserve components had little difficulty enlisting men directly from civilian life. Between these non-prior-service (NPS) accessions and more experienced personnel leaving the active forces with time remaining on their statutory military service obligation, filling the reserve ranks was a political problem, not a force-manning concern.[7] The assumption was that somehow this mix of direct enlistments and residual service could be and should be continued in the total force AVF.

The Reagan Transformation

In the five years following its inauguration, the total force was mostly aspiration. Rhetorical genuflections in its direction were ritual but without much effect on force manning or force structure. Enlistments in the early AVF proved troublesome for both the active and the reserve components. The active forces declined in manpower strength (from 2.25 million in 1973 to about 2 million in 1978), and so did Selected Reserve strength (from 919,000 in 1973 to 788,000 in 1978). The recruitment priority was on getting enough manpower into the active forces; the reserves, not previously in need of mechanisms to recruit from civilian life, had none.

The decline in the size of both forces bottomed out in 1978. For a host of reasons (not the least of which was substantial military pay increases) that are not particularly relevant here, enlistment goals in both began to be met with increasing consistency thereafter. In 1980, for the first time in the AVF, the manpower strength of both the active and the reserve components was increased over the year before.

The real change began in 1981. The Reagan administration took office committed to an across-the-board buildup in military capabilities. In manpower, however, the emphasis was squarely on the reserves. Echoing Laird a decade earlier, Secretary of Defense Caspar Weinberger renewed the pledge. "We can no longer consider Reserve forces as merely forces in reserve," Weinberger told a gathering of reservists in 1982; "they have to be an integral part of the total force, both within the United States and within NATO."[8] The Reagan administration was serious about this pronouncement. Flush with resources and facing a remarkably favorable recruiting environment, growth in the manpower strength of the reserves has far outpaced that of the active components since 1980. The transformation is most pronounced in the Army. "For the first time since World War II," the Department of Defense reported to the Congress in 1988, "the citizen-soldiers of the Army Selected Reserve . . . will exceed the strength of the Active Army."[9] While developments are not nearly so far along in the case of the other services, the department noted that fiscal year (FY) 1987 recorded "another all-time high" in the growth of the Selected Reserve in general, an increase of 20,755 reserve members over the previous year.[10]

The arithmetic of force manning in the 1980s is illuminating. Between FY 1980 and 1989, the manpower strength of the active components increased by 98,000 (about 5 percent) to 2.1 million—about where the active forces were in 1974. Most of the additional manpower, however, will have gone to the Navy to man a fleet of substantially increased size. The active Army actually is smaller at the end of the 1980s than at the beginning and the Air Force and the Marine Corps only slightly enlarged (table 8-1).

Table 8-1. Active-Reserve Military End-Strength, Fiscal Years 1980-1989 (In Thousands)

	Actual								Programmed		Percent Change	
	FY80	FY81	FY82	FY83	FY84	FY85	FY86	FY87	FY88	FY89	1980-1989	1987-1989
Army												
Active	777	781	780	780	780	781	781	781	772	772	-0.6	-1.2
Reserve[a]	580	621	665	683	709	732	756	772	781	804	+38.6	+4.1
Navy												
Active	517	529	542	558	565	571	581	587	593	593	+14.7	+1.0
Reserve	97	98	105	109	121	130	142	149	153	162	+67.0	+8.7
Marine Corps												
Active	188	191	192	194	196	198	199	200	197	197	+4.8	-1.5
Reserve	36	37	40	43	41	42	42	43	44	45	+25.0	+4.7
Air Force												
Active	558	570	583	592	597	602	608	607	576	576	+3.2	-5.4
Reserve[b]	156	160	165	169	175	184	192	193	198	204	+30.8	+5.7
Total												
Active	2,040	2,071	2,097	2,123	2,138	2,151	2,169	2,174	2,138	2,138	+4.8	-1.7
Reserve	869	917	975	1,005	1,046	1,088	1,130	1,157	1,176	1,213	+39.6	+4.8
Active/Reserve Mix (%)	70/30	70/30	70/30	68/32	67/33	66/34	66/34	65/35	65/35	64/36		

SOURCE: Adapted from Department of Defense, *Annual Report to the Congress, Fiscal Year 1989* (February 1988), p. 305.
[a] Includes Army Reserve and Army National Guard
[b] Includes Air Force Reserve and Air National Guard

In contrast, Selected Reserve manpower has grown by 344,000, or nearly 40 percent, since 1980, to a total of approximately 1.2 million in 1989. The greater emphasis on boosting reserve strength is evident across the board. While the active Navy has benefited the most among the services in additional manpower, the Naval Reserve has grown by a striking 67 percent over the course of the decade. Similar, although less dramatic, growth patterns have been the case in the reserve elements of the other services as well. The ratio of active force–to–Selected Reserve manpower will have shifted from 70:30 in 1980 to 64:36 by the end of 1989.

The increase in the Selected Reserve manpower share is shown by service in table 8–2. If nontraining members of the Individual Ready Reserve, whom the armed forces count as critical augmentees to both the active forces and the Selected Reserve in a major conflict, are added to the equation, the dependence on reserve manpower at decade's end is all the more pronounced: 60 percent of the manpower in the Army, 31 percent in the Navy, 32 percent in the Marine Corps, and 31 percent in the Air Force will be in reserve status in peacetime.

There is more to these developments, however, than merely shifting manpower accounts. Beginning in the 1970s and accelerating in the 1980s, missions have been shifted as well. In the words of a 1987 DOD summary:

> We have substantially increased our reliance on Reserve Component units for more and more complex missions. The Army relies heavily on Reserve Component units to fill

Table 8-2. Percent of Available Manpower: Active Forces and Selected Reserve, Fiscal Years 1980, 1989

	1980	1989
Army		
Active	76	49
Reserve[a]	33	51
Navy		
Active	84	78
Reserve	16	22
Marine Corps		
Active	84	81
Reserve	16	19
Air Force		
Active	78	74
Reserve[b]	22	26

SOURCE: Adapted from Department of Defense, *Annual Report to the Congress, Fiscal Year 1989* (February 1988), p. 305.
[a] Includes Army Reserve and Army National Guard
[b] Includes Air Force Reserve and Air National Guard

out its active divisions and to provide essential tactical support to both active and re-serve combat forces. Naval Reserve units form an integral part of the Total Force in most mission areas of the Navy including surface combatants, carrier air wings, mari-time patrol, airlift and medical support. The Selected Marine Corps Reserve provides a division-wing team with balanced combat, combat support and combat service support forces of the same type as active force counterparts. Air Force Reserve Component units bear considerable responsibility for many combat and support missions, including tactical fighter, airlift, continental air defense and aerial refueling missions.[11]

In the space of fifteen years, the Selected Reserve was transformed from a military capability that mattered scarcely at all to a force that is increasingly viewed within DOD planning as the near equivalent of the active forces. Units and individuals of the Guard and reserve are now expected to be among the earliest deployed forces in contingencies ranging from limited conflicts to a major war in Europe. "In the Selected Reserve," according to DOD, "units would mobilize and deploy almost immediately alongside active-duty units" in a full-scale mobilization. "The missions of these forces demand that they be as capable and ready as their active-duty counterparts."[12] In the first thirty days of a European war, about 10 percent of all Army combat units, 60 percent of the combat support missions (such as artillery and engineering), and nearly 60 percent of the com-bat service support missions (such as truck companies and medical units) must now come from deployed reserves. To meet this schedule, round-out reserve units with a

NATO mission will have to be available for deployment in the first ten days and the remainder in the next ten to fifteen days.[13] Although the Navy and Marine Corps have less of their wartime force structure in the reserves, three-fourths of the Navy's ocean-going minesweepers and an entire Marine Corps division/air wing would need to be activated on similarly ambitious schedules.

With over a third of the Army's combat support and combat service support now in the reserves, there are few campaigns of more than very limited duration that can be undertaken without involving the reserve elements.

In less demanding contingencies, the situation differs only in degree. With over a third of the Army's combat support and combat service support now in the reserves, there are few campaigns of more than very limited duration that can be undertaken without involving the reserve elements (a circumstance that may partly explain why the Marine Corps, not the Army, was dispatched to peacekeeping duties in Lebanon from 1982 to 1984). But even in the case of the less reserve-dependent Navy, dependence is a factor of increasing note. In deploying minesweepers to the Persian Gulf to support the Kuwaiti oil tanker reflagging operation in 1987, for example, the Navy had to turn to its reserves for six minesweepers (which it deployed, however, without activating their reserve crew members). In the assessment of James Webb, assistant secretary of defense for reserve affairs in 1986:

> The Total Force Concept of the early 1970s is a reality in 1986, so much so that contingency plans to counter aggression in both hemispheres cannot be effectively executed without committing National Guard and Reserve forces in the same time frame as active forces. We have increasingly staked our national security on the ability to mobilize, deploy, and employ combat ready National Guard and Reserve members and units anywhere in the world rapidly.[14]

Webb might have overstated the point but not by much. Resource constraints are bound to push further in these directions. In the face of budgetary pressures, the active forces of the Army, Air Force, and Marine Corps were pared back between fiscal years 1987 and 1988, while the reserve components have continued to increase in strength (table 8–1). Former defense secretary Frank Carlucci argued that additional transfers of missions and manpower to the reserves will be unavoidable in the absence of real growth in defense expenditures, a situation that itself seems unavoidable.[15] Although the Bush administration is not on record on the matter, the early signs are that it will look at active force manpower as a way to constrain defense spending growth. Before assuming office as national security adviser General Brent Scowcroft suggested placing more active Army units in reserve status as a way to trim defense spending.[16] For its part, the Congress, with few exceptions, supports the general trend and can be expected to be an additional driving force. In the view of the House Armed Services Committee in a recent assessment, "The Total Force concept has proven to be an effective method of increasing U.S. national security—and at only 40 to 70 percent of the cost of active duty personnel."[17]

The Shadow of the Past

Behind this remarkable series of events is an equally remarkable absence of experience with actually using (that is, activating and deploying) reserve forces. Since the total force policy was adopted in 1973, there has never been an involuntary activation of a reserve unit. Individual reservists have served on active duty in a voluntary capacity on occasion, but the true test, the involuntary activation and call-up, has yet to be met.

This is not from want of legal flexibility to activate reserves. Sympathetic to concerns voiced from earlier periods that a call-up requiring a presidential declaration of national emergency might set in motion too blunderbuss a political psychology at home and send a too strong (or the wrong) message abroad, the Congress has steadily increased the president's flexibility to call to active duty both units and individuals of the Selected Reserve for operational missions that require augmentation of the active forces. In 1976 Congress granted the president authority to activate up to 50,000 Selected Reserve members for a period of up to ninety days by issuing an executive order and notifying the Congress within twenty-four hours. Four years later the authority was doubled: from 50,000 to 100,000. It was doubled again, to 200,000, for up to ninety days (or 180 days if the president deems necessary) in 1986.

Nor is it from want of incidents and crises involving U.S. forces in which augmentation by reserves would seem appropriate in the total force era. Between 1976 and 1984, U.S. Navy and Marine Corps forces alone responded to forty-one incidents or crises, with an average duration in some geographical areas in excess of 100 days.[18] In each case, active naval forces were stretched, deployments were altered and extended, exercises and training were canceled, and leaves were delayed, but no reservists were activated for augmentation or relief. In peacekeeping operations in Lebanon from 1982 to 1984, a task not normally associated with the Marine Corps but one at least imaginable if undertaken by the Marine Corp Reserves, it was the active force that was dispatched for extended deployment. (As noted, the more heavily dependent Army probably could not have been dispatched at all without a reserve activation.) In the Persian Gulf minesweeping operation in 1987, the Navy reached into the Naval Reserve for the minesweepers (it had no other choice) but, in the absence of a reserve activation, it left the bulk of the reserve crew members behind. The Persian Gulf naval build-up required extended deployment of the active fleet; frigates and destroyers in reserve stayed in reserve, as did their crews.

In order to acquire some sense of any experience with activating and deploying reserves, it is necessary to reach back much further. The occasions are few and give little cause for optimism. Apart from the early months of the Korean War, U.S. reservists have been called into action only five times: the Berlin crisis (1961), the Cuban missile crisis (1962), the *Pueblo* affair (1968), the limited Vietnam call-up (1968), and the New York City–area postal strike (1970). All of these mobilizations and deployments took longer (by as much as a year) than anticipated. In Korea, National Guard divisions mobilized in September 1950 were not ready for overseas deployment until November and December 1951. (This, however, was an improvement over the World War II experience, when it took National Guard divisions an average of 27.9 months between

---

Despite the infusion of additional resources in equipping and training as well as manning the Selected Reserve components in the 1980s, reserve readiness is still troublesome.

---

mobilization and readiness to deploy overseas.) In Berlin, activated Army Reserve components averaged only 68 percent of required personnel, and some units took up to a year to achieve combat readiness. The Naval Reserve call-up in Berlin, while more rapid, still took four months to execute. In the *Pueblo* affair, the six Naval Reserve air squadrons activated on twenty-four-hour notice were still short of equipment and operational duties four months after the call-up, and none was ever actually deployed. Naval reserves called up in Vietnam in 1968 took four months to deploy and then managed to do so only by cannibalizing equipment and jerry-rigging full-time manpower from "general Navy resources." Nearly half of the Army Reserve units activated in Vietnam were deficient in occupational qualifications, and 17 percent of the activated reservists were totally unqualified for their assignments. Only the postal strike call-up, in which more than 3,000 Navy reservists were dispatched to postal duties in New York City for three days in March 1970, was reasonably trouble free.[19]

Each of these situations was a partial, not a full, reserve mobilization, and that seems to be a relevant point. Rather than an easier, lesser-included case, partial mobilizations appeared to present a range of distinctive problems. Not only was it more difficult (and in most of the call-ups, nearly impossible) to define the relationship between the kinds of reserve units called and the external events that triggered their activation (naval destroyers activated in the Berlin crisis, for example, spent much of their time in the Pacific on splashdown duties in the space program), it also proved difficult to lift a discrete slice out of the reserve structure for activation. Both problems

Table 8-3. Percent of Selected Reserve Units at C-4/N-4 in Measured Readiness, Fiscal Years 1985-1987

	1985	1986	1987
Army National Guard (ANG)	40	29	24
Army Reserve (AR)	60	55	44
Naval Reserve (NR)			
Commissioned	22	10	3
Reinforcing/Sustaining	24	22	19
Marine Corps Reserve (MCR)	50	45	33
Air National Guard (AFNG)	17	13	6
Air Force Reserve (AFR)	24	23	10

SOURCE: Adapted from Annual Report of the Reserve Forces Policy Board, *Reserve Component Programs, Fiscal Year 1987 (February 1988), p. 162.*

were especially acute when the call-up was employed as an instrument of diplomacy (Berlin, Cuba, *Pueblo*).

Structural Factors

The historical record is dated, of course. Reserve forces certainly have been improved in the total force period and especially over the course of the 1980s. The question is whether current facts warrant an optimism that historical experience clearly cannot provide. Generally speaking, the case is rather doubtful. Despite the infusion of additional resources in equipping and training as well as manning the Selected Reserve components in the 1980s, reserve readiness is still troublesome. In terms of condition ratings (C-ratings)—a standard measure that incorporates four categories of readiness: personnel, equipment on hand, equipment condition, and training—there is little question about progress in the 1980s, but there is also little question about serious gaps. These gaps are most substantial in the ground force reserve components—precisely those components where the dependence of reserve capabilities has been placed most strongly in the total force. In FY 1987, nearly a quarter of the units in the Army National Guard, over 40 percent of Army Reserve units, and over a third of Marine Corps Reserve units were given the lowest readiness rating of C-4 ("not ready") (table 8–3).

These low readiness ratings can be explained by any number of factors that can be fixed (equipment shortages, for example), but there would appear to be something more fundamental involved as well. Because of the part-time nature of most reserve service, the typical reservist trains a total of thirty-eight days a year, compared to an average of 161 days for his active-duty counterpart.[20] This may be less a problem for that segment of the Selected Reserve that joins directly upon leaving active military service (although most of these prior-service accessions require retraining for qualifi-

Table 8-4. Selected Reserve Enlistments
(Non-Prior/Prior Service, in Thousands)

	FY80 (Actual)	FY86 (Actual)	FY87	FY88	FY89
ANG	50/47	44/39	69/36	69/36	69/36
AR	26/34	34/54	37/40	37/40	37/40
NR*	3/25	7/39	12/28	12/28	12/28
MCR	5/4	9/6	8/6	8/6	7/6
ANG	7/10	6/9	7/11	7/11	7/11
AFR	3/10	3/11	4/11	4/11	4/11
Total	94/130	103/148	136/122	136/122	136/122
% Non-Prior Service	42%	41%	53%	53%	53%

*Includes TARs & Cat. D IMAs
SOURCE: Department of Defense Annual Report, Fiscal Year 1989.

cation in their reserve assignments),[21] but more than half of Selected Reserve enlistments (66 percent in the Army National Guard) are directly from civilian life (table 8–4) and enter reserve status with only (at best) initial entry training.

In the light of this, are assumptions in current plans that reserve units are equivalent to their active-duty counterparts realistic? According to the Department of Defense itself, the answer appears to be no:

It is in the area of training that the major capability differences between active and reserve components become apparent. . . . Greater opportunity to train allows active units to be more effective and to train to the organizational level at which they will be employed, including brigade and division level operations. Reserve component units, because of time-to-train constraints, normally train at a lower organizational level, such as platoon or company.

One might assume that given equal amounts of equipment and personnel, active and reserve component units of the same type would have equal combat capability. However, the major differences in available training time between active and reserve component units generally result in a greater initial capability for the active unit.[22]

Where To from Here?

Because no administration has seen fit to use the reserve components of the total force, it is difficult to reach firm conclusions about the adjustments in force structure that have been made to date. History and logic certainly do not lend great support for such applications. The historical experience has been uniformly unreassuring. Although certain kinds of reserve units (air units, for example) tend to outperform their active-duty counterparts, it does stretch the logic to assume that major part-time ground units, for example, can ever be made the equivalent of similar full-time active forces, and thus suggests pause about plans that would treat and deploy them in the same manner. That there are cost savings to be made in shifting ground forces from active to reserve status is unmistakable; that the shift can then be treated as little more than a bookkeeping transaction, with the same deployment plans and schedules left unaffected, defies common sense. With sufficient strategic warning of Warsaw Pact preparations for war in Europe, the reserves may be able to mobilize and deploy in time (although nothing in history lends support to this), but in short-warning crises, mobilization is not likely to be anywhere near the equivalent level of readiness that current plans assume. In the case of other challenges and provocations, the total force probably means that any sustained response will be weakened (and may not even be possible) absent a reserve call-up—a step seldom taken in the past due to concern that calling up the reserves would be riskily (or at least prematurely) provocative and unnecessarily arousing domestically. That the president can now do so without a declaration of national emergency may mean very little in this regard. A reserve call-up will still be a reserve call-up, which may explain why the total force reserves have yet to be activated. In the case of the Army especially, such a set of circumstances means that, in anything more taxing than another situation like Grenada and less threatening than general war, it probably will not be employed at all. In the case of the other services, it means investing in reserve forces that are unlikely to be used at the expense of active forces that are most likely to be called upon. The economies in such circumstances are not self-evident.

Among the possible alternatives, reversing the leakage from the active to the reserve forces of combat support and combat service support missions that already has taken place is improbable, since it would mean adding requirements for active-duty manpower at a time when providing such manpower would be especially difficult. Yet merely doing more of the same on a piecemeal basis seems highly undesirable. The problems are created by force structure, and any realistic solutions would seem to lie in force structure.

One course is to continue with the total force policy but to take it to its logical end points. At a minimum, this would require the wholesale reexamination of reserve organization, training, and funding that was not done when the nation began to convert to a total force. There is little doubt that both economies and increased military effectiveness could be realized in reserve reform. Burdened with mysterious redundancies (a National Guard and a separate reserve for the Army and the Air Force), heavy with undifferentiated structure, employing across-the-board training requirements better suited to the 1950s than the 1980s, and expected to function as an expeditionary force according to an unprecedented deployment schedule, the reserves as currently configured are a major chokepoint in U.S. military preparedness. To be sure, the political obstacles to any serious reexamination of the institutional dimensions of the Selected Reserve are imposing, a fact that has left the reserve side of the total force nearly impervious to change in the postwar years. But adding more missions and manpower to a structure better suited to the draft era than to the responsibilities of the AVF scarcely seems a more reasonable way to proceed.

Taking the total force at its own logic would suggest fairly sweeping adjustments in the active force structure as well. If, as trends already suggest, the U.S. Army is moving in the direction of becoming a general-war force only, with limited real capabilities for responding to anything less, it may well be sound policy to elevate the trend from the piecemeal to the strategic and consciously begin to design the Army solely for these purposes while bolstering the active Navy and Marine Corps as the nation's decisive power projection force. This, too, would pose not insignificant political problems. It would mean an even smaller active Army in peacetime; it probably would mean a strengthened Marine Corps with a somewhat different mix of support assets for an expanded role.

To continue the present drift is to shift eventually to a strategic posture that defies both history and logic. The homogeneous whole of the original intent will not come about by clumsily stitching together preexisting active and reserve force structures or by merely shifting the manpower accounting between the two. That part has already been done. The hard part is for the generation of political and military leadership that assumed power in 1989.

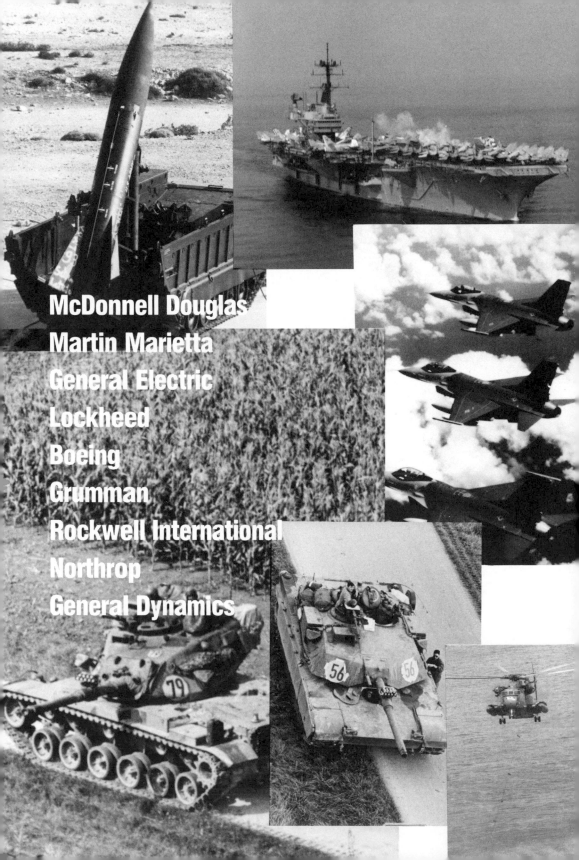

McDonnell Douglas
Martin Marietta
General Electric
Lockheed
Boeing
Grumman
Rockwell International
Northrop
General Dynamics

Chapter 9

Obstacles to Improving the Defense Acquisition Process

J. Ronald Fox

E very few years government commissions are appointed to study problems in defense procurement. They highlight cost overruns, high-priced spare parts, incorrect billings, schedule delays, and technical performance shortfalls. Each time the commissions recommend most of the same cures: more competition, more prototypes, multiyear procurement, economic order quantities, better cost estimates, less gold plating. The recommendations are adopted, but within a year or two key defense managers change, implementation efforts fall short, recommendations fade away, and a new set of problems emerges into public scrutiny. Today the publicized defense acquisition problems may take the form of consultants leaking proprietary government information. Last month the publicized problems might have been contractors making false charges to government contracts; last year, technical failures in defense programs; the year before that, unanticipated cost growth; and the year before that, high-priced spare parts.

Although the focus of publicity changes, many of these problems are long-standing ones. The practice of leaking proprietary government information has occurred for years; it was well established in 1974, when I described it in *Arming America*.[1] Thomas

I wish to acknowledge those who have made helpful comments and suggestions on the topics contained in this chapter. They include John Cataldo, Colonel Robert Drewes, James L. Field, Dr. David Graham, General Frank Hinrichs (ret.), Marshall Hoyler, General Henry A. Miley (ret.), Thomas D. Morris, Robert Murray, George Rabstejnek, Mary Schumacher, Larry K. Smith, Robert J. Stohlman, the members of the Procurement Round Table, the Harvard National Security Program, and Business Executives for National Security.

Muldoon, a key figure in the defense procurement probe that began in 1988, said in a published report that the practices under investigation by the FBI had been going on for twenty years: "This is like that great quote from the Humphrey Bogart movie 'Casablanca' when they close down the joint and the guy says, 'I'm shocked there's gambling going on here.'"[2]

But the year 1989 provides a rare opportunity to make significant improvements in the defense acquisition process: a new Congress and a new administration are searching for ways to deal with a large federal deficit; senior defense officials estimate that $30 billion to $40 billion a year might be saved by management improvements; and the president has made a commitment to major reform in defense acquisition. There has never been a greater need, and the Department of Defense (DOD) has never had a better opportunity to produce substantial acquisition improvements.

To begin to deal with these problems, the secretary of defense must confront four major obstacles to long-term reform:

1. Too few government managers, at all levels of the acquisition process, have the necessary understanding, skills, and experience in business management and industrial cost control to manage the acquisition process effectively.

2. Government managers often enter the acquisition field too late and leave too early in their careers for the DOD to develop an institutional memory. Necessary career-furthering assignments in acquisition are rare.

3. Incentives offered to defense contractors tend to reinforce present methods of operating; they often penalize those who reduce costs and reward those who increase costs.

4. There are too few acquisition manager role models who have achieved effective control of cost. By role models I mean individuals who are singled out, rewarded, promoted, and retained in the acquisition field.

The first part of this chapter discusses the role of acquisition managers, their skills and their experience; the second deals with incentives for government and industry managers.

Background

In his first annual message to Congress, President Andrew Jackson wrote, "The duties of all public officers are, or at least admit of being made, so plain and simple that men of intelligence may readily qualify themselves for their performance."[3] Although the "plain and simple" approach may have been effective in the 1830s, it is far from satisfactory for today's defense acquisition managers. The complexities of managing the development and production of billion-dollar weapon systems require highly developed skills in planning and evaluating the technical and financial progress of a program, understanding complex contract terms, and overseeing and controlling the industrial firms performing the work.

The military services are designed for combat. Consistent with that function, the current military promotion and retirement system is designed to force out most officers in their forties in order to maintain youthful forces for combat. In the past three decades, however, U.S. military operations have shifted increasingly toward the use of high-technology weapons and equipment. As a result of that change, the military services have been given an added mission of great complexity, one requiring training, career development, duration of assignments, and length of career radically different from that required for combat. This added mission—managing the defense acquisition process—requires skills in planning, overseeing, and controlling the largest, most complex industrial programs in the world: the development and production of weapon systems, among them, aircraft, ships, satellites, missiles, and electronic systems, each requiring the expenditure of hundreds of millions of dollars each year.

The Defense Acquisition Management Task

The functions of DOD managers of large acquisition programs are not those classically associated with the term *manager*.[4] This is because the DOD does not develop or produce its weapon systems in-house; rather, the development and production work is contracted for through prime contractors. Hence the principal functions of the program manager and staff are planning, contracting, monitoring, controlling, and evaluating the technical performance of contractors and the government agencies that provide service and support. This range of activities includes design, development, procurement, production, training, testing, and field support. The term *technical performance* is used here in the broadest sense to include not only the engineering aspects of a weapon system but also the contractor's management of resources (costs) and subcontractors.

Managing technical performance, in this sense, poses demanding industrial management challenges. Government managers are required to oversee several industries involving hundreds of the largest firms in the country—firms managed by experienced managers, familiar with the defense acquisition process, and with methods of estimating costs, measuring progress, allocating overhead, calculating profits, and measuring return on investment for high-tech programs. Most of the recurring problems of cost growth, schedule delays, and failure to achieve technical performance in this environment cannot be solved simply by better engineering, better forms of contracting, multiyear procurement, or more prototypes. Solutions to these problems require frequent negotiations with industry (monthly, weekly, and sometimes daily) in situations that require government managers to be knowledgeable about the industry in which they are working, experienced in the acquisition process, and highly skilled in applying the tools of industrial management.

Relationship between Government and Industry

The relationship between a government program office and its major contractor on a large program is necessarily close. In this environment, a contract form does not exist that can substitute for the judgments required for daily decisions involving schedules, costs, and technical performance. On most large development and production programs, a fixed-price contract jeopardizes the quality of the product and restricts the information available to the Department of Defense. Over the past twenty-five years, the Defense Department has found repeatedly that fixed-price contracts cannot substitute for—indeed they inhibit—the week-to-week evaluations of progress, correlations of cost and progress, and negotiations of the thousands of changes proposed by both government and contractor personnel.

Although some commercial business management techniques are appropriate for this environment, many are not. Most commercial industrial firms manage by removing uncertainties in the work to be performed. In the defense acquisition environment, however, it is often impossible to remove most uncertainties; they are inherent in the nature of the work in large development programs.

Managing the defense acquisition process effectively and efficiently requires a critical balance between the adversarial and the pure partnership roles.

Adversarial Relationships

The relationship between government and industry in this uncertain environment is complex. Some government managers deal with contractors as adversaries, failing to achieve the informal cooperation so necessary between buyer and seller in any large development program. In an adversarial relationship, government managers have attempted to use fixed-price contracts (often dictated by senior Pentagon officials) for engineering development work, where cost-reimbursement contracts would be far more appropriate. Or they treat cost-reimbursement contracts as fixed-price contracts, trying to enforce rigid task statements when the work requires flexibility.

Partnership Relationships

Other government managers operate as no more than partners with industry, accepting industry estimates without question, apparently unaware of the mixed motives inherent in the buyer-seller relationship. They share industry's goal of producing technically excellent programs, but they lose sight of the need for arm's-length buyer-seller negotiations on programs where changes often occur weekly or even daily. These government managers often express the erroneous view that "we know how much the program should cost because that's how much the contractor spent." They are proud, as they should be, of their products. But unlike their peers in commercial business, they usually incur no penalty for programs exceeding their original budgets. Managing the defense acquisition process effectively and efficiently requires a critical balance between the adversarial and the pure partnership roles—a balance that produces what I call the "wise buyer." Achieving that balance requires skill in coping with the complexities of the process, frequent negotiations, and marketing tactics within government, within industry, and between the two. What is needed is not an adversarial relationship of animosity, suspicion, and mistrust but (paraphrasing an American Bar Association report) a business relationship characterized by rigorous bargaining and tenacious regard for the best interests of one's own side.[5]

Differing Perceptions of Defense Acquisition

One impression that stands out from my conversations with people involved in defense acquisition is that government and industry managers have very different perceptions of the current condition of the acquisition process. Some describe it as poorly managed and plagued by serious problems; others see it as having few problems. These differing perceptions do not reflect the conventional dichotomies of military versus civilian or government versus industry. Rather, they reflect differing views of the government's role in managing the acquisition process.

The Liaison Manager

Some people in government and industry limit the job of government program management to promoting a program, preparing progress reports and briefings, negotiating with officials at the Pentagon and various military commands, and resolving technical conflicts between these organizations and contractors. They believe the responsibility for cost control belongs solely to the contractor. I call this the liaison manager view; it is based on the belief that the defense business is part of the free enterprise system and is therefore regulated by competition in the marketplace.

The Active Manager

Others describe the program manager's role more correctly as one of planning and making key decisions associated with rigorous oversight of, negotiation with, and control of industrial firms doing the development and production work. They believe the responsibility for cost control belongs to the program manager and the plant representative, as well as the contractor. They also believe that significant cost reductions are often possible, depending on government managers' abilities to establish challenging cost incentives for contractors. I call this the active manager view; it is based on the belief that in this environment, the competitive forces of the marketplace do not alone produce the desired cost, schedule, and technical performance, for these forces are usually frustrated by contract changes occurring throughout the life of a program.

People holding the liaison manager view often talk about cost control in managing programs but fail to understand that the planning and control of large industrial programs are achieved neither by proclamation nor by good intentions. They occur only as the result of careful analyses and trade-offs associated with program and engineering changes and difficult day-to-day negotiations. The skills needed for these tasks require intensive practical training and experience.

Those with the liaison manager view believe government program managers do not need years of training and experience in business management and methods of industrial cost control. If the program manager is limited to promoting the program, preparing progress reports, and performing technical liaison, then experience as a pilot, tank commander, ship captain, or engineer, and possibly fourteen to twenty weeks at the Defense Systems Management College may be sufficient. But for those who hold the active manager view, as I do, military experience and twenty weeks of training are insufficient for the job.

Acquisition Careers

There is no doubt that most government acquisition managers and their staffs are intelligent, hard working, and dedicated. They genuinely want to acquire weapon systems and other products that meet performance standards at reasonable costs. Unfortunately, however, in recent years, those assigned to key acquisition positions—at most levels of the Defense Department, from program managers to presidential appointees in the Pentagon—are often seriously unprepared for their jobs. The skills required to manage the acquisition process effectively are often outside the training and expertise of these otherwise capable and dedicated under secretaries, assistant secretaries, senior military officers, and program managers.

The Defense Department often places military officers and civil servants in impossible situations, asking them to control complex industrial programs yet failing to equip them with a working knowledge of the acquisition process, with skills in analysis and technical negotiations, and with the stable assignments required to deal with contractors on an equal footing. Too few government managers know much about contractor financial incentives, negotiating changes, or controlling costs and technical performance in large industrial firms. Consequently they rarely make the difficult acquisition decisions required to create and reward lean industrial organizations.

During the past twenty-five years, Pentagon officials have assumed that the acquisition process could be managed effectively at any level by generalists, technology specialists, and military officers whose primary training and experience has been in military field operations and who have had little practical training or experience in industrial management and only one or two acquisition assignments. That assumption has proved to be mistaken. It is obvious that a program manager cannot be assigned as a wing commander without years of carefully programmed flight training and experience. By the same token, a pilot cannot manage effectively a complex industrial program without extensive experience and carefully programmed assignments in the acquisition process, business management, and industrial cost control.

In a 1986 study of defense acquisition, the General Accounting Office found that many government program managers were not equipped to tackle the intricate problems of weapons procurement.[6] That finding was supported by extensive congressional testimony about the limited qualifications of program managers. During September 1984 Senate Armed Services Committee hearings, Senator Jeff Bingaman (D–New Mexico) asked Norman Augustine, chairman and chief executive officer of Martin Marietta Corporation and former under secretary of the Army, "In your view, do the people we put in positions of managing these programs have the necessary training and qualifications to do these jobs?" Mr. Augustine responded:

> I would say that in many cases they truthfully don't. We do much better than we did 10 years ago, but it is not uncommon for someone who has been commanding a ship at sea or a division or squadron to suddenly be placed in a position where they have the job of overseeing the work of an industrial giant.
>
> It is pretty tough to be equipped to do that when one comes out of a military operating force. It would be much the same as taking somebody like myself and putting them in charge of an air wing; it would be a terrible mistake.
>
> I think we would need much more training for these people before we put them on the firing line.[7]

The appraisals of the General Accounting Office and Mr. Augustine were supported by views the committee heard from other respected industry spokesmen. Carl Harr, president of the Aerospace Industries Association, observed:

> You cannot underestimate the importance of the quality of the people in the process, obviously. We would agree . . . anything that can be done [to improve the quality] will be helpful. . . .
>
> Sure, one of the ways to improve performance is to upgrade quality, but much more practical I suppose, in the immediate area is to make sure they get trained. Training is a function of time and organization.[8]

Another industry spokesman, Roy Anderson, chief executive officer of Lockheed Corporation, commented:

> In addition, more can be done, in my opinion, to train and attract more qualified military personnel into the procurement process. The services must realize the vast amount of dollars that must be expended and prudently managed to carry out their missions. I believe some sort of business education should be offered in the military academies, and a career in procurement elevated as a factor for promotion, equivalent to strictly military paths including potential for flag positions.[9]

In considering the training and qualifications of acquisition managers, it is noteworthy that most military officers have extensive academic education and general service training. Besides a bachelor's degree, officers often acquire more education by one-year assignments at mid-career to the command and staff college or its equivalent. Many officers obtain master's degrees in one or two years or through evening programs. At the grade of lieutenant colonel or commander, they are sent to the war college for about one year.

But academic degrees rarely provide the industrial knowledge and skills required to cope with the aggressive business tactics of the acquisition process. Academic degrees are no substitute for more practical training and practice in evaluating contractor schedule, cost, and technical performance; in identifying and negotiating solutions to day-to-day problems; or in motivating government and industry personnel involved in the day-to-day management of large, complex programs. Unfortunately, much of the acquisition training available to government acquisition managers is confined to introductory descriptions of types of contracts, regulations, reporting systems, and related topics. Little time is spent practicing implementation, using management tools, or testing the reasonableness and validity of data.

In 1987 I talked with a group of industry managers new to the defense business and unaccustomed to DOD methods. As expected, they were unhappy with detailed government specifications, burdensome audits, monthly reports, and changes in fund-

---

Given little authority and few tools to manage their programs, program managers are often relegated to functioning as briefing specialists and marketing managers, spending much of their time seeking additional funds and continued support for their programs.

---

ing. But they were stunned by the department's attempt to manage complex industrial programs with military officers who have little or no experience in industrial management. Indeed, at two major defense acquisition commands with thousands of personnel, about half the military officers are lieutenants on their first tour of duty. The following comments from the industry managers are typical:

> If we did this in the commercial world, we would be out of business in six months.

> These government managers have little idea how our organizations work and what incentives apply to our managers.

> The government invites contractors to play games by assigning inexperienced government managers to key positions and then changing them every two or three years.

Given little authority and few tools to manage their programs, program managers are often relegated to functioning as briefing specialists and marketing managers, spending much of their time seeking additional funds and continued support for their programs. This is an unreasonable assignment for military officers. It is not a prescription for high-quality management, no matter how dedicated the personnel.

Defense industry managers stress the need for dedicated acquisition careers. The following statements from four industry managers are typical of the views expressed:

> Acquisition should be conducted by professionals who have only one career motivation—to be the best acquisition professional in the system—and who see only that profession as the means of promotion. Setting aside a number of high-level military ranks for procurement assignments does not alone ensure the professional needs of acquisition.

> There is a need for much more care in translating policies down through each organizational level within the Department of Defense. The military services need to do much more in training their procurement personnel and in creating a clear procurement field. There needs to be a separate career ladder for procurement, and the career assignments need to be under the control of the people in charge of procurement.

> There should be career progression ladders for procurement officers and program managers, separate from the career progression ladders for operational personnel. We see no advantage to the country in taking a good boat commander and making him a program manager.

> You will find very few military officers who have had more than one assignment as a program manager. The promotion system usually doesn't give credit for having the same ticket punched twice.

A retired lieutenant general, formerly in charge of a buying command, reflected on his experience:

> There is a widely held belief in the services that the weapons acquisition process is a "secondary specialty" that anyone can learn. In reality, we need to create a program management career and a professional program management organization, not half a career in acquisition and half a career in operational commands. I have really turned around on this point. I used to think that the fifty-fifty arrangement was the best one.

In November 1983, David Packard appeared before the Senate Armed Services Committee and stated:

> I believe that each service should be restructured to have two clearly defined and separate career paths for the development of officers. One should be to train men and women as commanders of military forces. The other would be to train men and women as managers in procurement.
>
> At the present time, officers often rotate back and forth from military assignments to procurement and almost without exception, project managers are not allowed to stay with that program long enough to actually see it to completion. [10]

Acquisition managers' careers should follow a path comparable to those of Army brigade and division commanders, Air Force wing commanders, and Navy wing and ship commanders. These paths are centrally managed to ensure that all supervisors are fully aware of the career requirements. Well-defined career paths include training and practical experience, with successive assignments in the same field, to positions of progressively greater responsibility.

The Air Force has developed a promising acquisition manager career program for nonrated officers. The Navy uses a centralized approach through its Weapon Systems Acquisition Management and Material Professional programs, but for unrestricted line officers, they fall far short of their stated goal. The Army Materiel Acquisition Management program, established in 1983, lacks central control and authority and provides too little training and practical experience too late in Army careers.

If the Army and Navy continue their current practice of managing the acquisition process with combat arms officers who are fifteen years into their careers before they enter the program and are then given a broad array of assignments in supply, maintenance, procurement, contracting, and deployment, it is unlikely the officers will master the specific tasks required to be well-qualified program managers.

Although the twenty-week Defense Systems Management College course is an important first step in training acquisition managers and their staffs, much more must be done to achieve an acceptable level of performance. The current policy of limiting this training to 138 days (because of regulations concerning moving expense reimbursement) must be changed. The moving expenses saved are trivial compared to the potential savings of billions of dollars annually from improved management in the acquisition process.

Future acquisition managers should be required to complete a program of at least one year of practical training in industrial management, designed to develop a familiarity with the acquisition process, typical problems, and practical alternatives for dealing with these problems. The training should include hundreds of examples of the daily dilemmas acquisition managers encounter, exploring the strengths and weaknesses of alternatives to deal with the dilemmas. Instructors should be skilled in conducting interactive sessions and have practical knowledge of the field.

The program should develop the wise buyer skills needed to resolve the complex problems in major research and development and production programs. It should stress analyses and decision making, using simulation exercises, role playing, and case studies. An internship in a program management office should precede and follow the one-year practical training program; carefully chosen program managers could serve as supervisors. Favorable results from such a program need not be years away. The Defense Department could produce major improvements in two years.

Acquisition executives and senior officers at the Army, Navy, and Air Force acquisition commands should have many years of experience on large acquisition programs. Once selected for these positions, they should have sole responsibility for materiel acquisition and personnel recruitment, selection, and assignments. To separate these responsibilities is to perpetuate the problems of the past three decades.

If program managers and their superiors are assigned to acquisition career fields, who will bring the operational knowledge and perspective to the program office? Combat arms officers can perform that function as they have in the past. One or more must be assigned to each major program office but not as program managers responsible for overseeing, negotiating with, and controlling contractors. A program manager for the development and production of a new manned satellite system does not need several years' experience as an astronaut, but he should understand astronauts' needs and have ready access to experienced astronauts familiar with operational requirements.

The Defense Department must be prepared to demonstrate to members of Congress that poor performance will not be tolerated.

Incentives for Industry and Government

The Defense Department customarily manages acquisition programs with rewards and penalties that are the reverse of what they should be. Contractors are often rewarded for higher-than-planned program costs with contributions to overhead, increased sales, and profits. And government managers are often rewarded for placing a higher priority on gaining congressional approval to begin a new weapon program (or to obtain additional funding for an ongoing program) than on controlling costs for existing programs.

The acquisition cost problems of the 1970s and 1980s are not aberrations; they are the result of many government and industry participants reacting in perfect accord with the rewards and penalties inherent in the acquisition process. More fixed-price contracts, better planning and reporting systems, improved cost estimating systems, change-control systems, or multiyear contracts have little likelihood of success unless government managers and contractors are rewarded for quality performance at lower cost.

Reluctance to establish more appropriate contractor incentives has been a serious deficiency in most DOD improvement programs during the past three decades. If the acquisition process is to run efficiently, it should be structured so that contractors have a reasonable opportunity to earn returns comparable to commercial returns, without undermining government program objectives. When contractors perform well, government managers should be able to reward that performance with improved opportunities for future defense business. On the other hand, when contractors fail to meet contract terms, government managers must be sufficiently trained, experienced, motivated, and supported to identify and report inadequate performance and to take corrective actions, including penalties and contract termination where appropriate. DOD officials at all levels must be prepared to support this kind of responsible management. The Defense

Department must be prepared to demonstrate to members of Congress that poor performance will not be tolerated. Defense analyst Richard Stubbing has observed:

> Contractors should be rewarded with higher profits for complying with schedules, satisfying promised performance standards, and delivering goods and services at or below contracted cost. Conversely, penalties, in the form of reduced profits, should be imposed for late delivery, substandard work, and cost overruns. The source selection process should make prospects for obtaining future contracts closely linked to performance on existing contracts. [11]

Equally fundamental changes should be made in incentives for government program managers. They should be rewarded for effective use of analysis and control techniques; for early identification of problems; and for success in controlling program schedules, costs, and technical performance. Managers who handle crises effectively are now given high performance ratings. Often, however, timely preventive action could have corrected problems before the crisis. And because preventive action requires daily attention to management detail, inexperienced supervisors controlling rewards are unlikely to appreciate the work of a good manager. As a result, there is often insufficient incentive to identify potential problems early and to exercise rigorous, systematic control.

There are also few incentives for talented officers to remain in military service beyond twenty to twenty-five years. Indeed, military personnel who begin to develop experience in the acquisition process are effectively forced out of the service when they have heavy financial commitments, including mortgages and children in school. Understandably they seek positions in the private defense industry, where their knowledge and skills are useful and the incentives of rewarding salaries and career status are compelling.

The knowledge that one will eventually need to obtain a job in industry can easily have a subtle effect on a person's performance while in government service. Private industry understandably offers positions to those who have demonstrated an appreciation of its particular problems and commitments. Unfortunately, government and industry goals regarding costs are rarely identical. To address this predicament, government acquisition careers must be made attractive enough to encourage officers to extend their service five to ten years longer than at present, perhaps by offering incentive pay. If an extra $15,000 to $20,000 per year were paid to selected military officers (at the rank of colonel/Navy captain and above) and if career regulations permitted these officers to remain in the acquisition field, incentives to retire from active duty and join the defense industry would be minimized. The extra cost would be negligible compared with the benefits of retaining experienced managers. (If an incentive pay plan were adopted, there would need to be a group of senior acquisition officials to determine the eligibility of those choosing an acquisition career. Otherwise program management could become a haven for officers not qualified to enter the competitive world of private industry.)

Such a proposal is not without precedent. Medical and dental officers and military personnel on flight status and submarine duty now receive incentive pay. Sweden's government acquisition agency attracts and retains senior people (both military and civilian) by a special law that allows an added salary increase for crucial acquisition positions. A Swedish colonel serving as a program manager can receive a significantly higher salary than other colonels and even the director general of the agency receive. This provides prestige and draws highly qualified, experienced people to senior acquisition positions.

One alternative is the establishment of a separate service for acquisition managers, an approach that has produced considerable success in France. The service would need elite managers dedicated to achieving the goals of the acquisition process. Applicants would face a highly selective screening program to remove those not meeting the high standards. Advancement would be based strictly on management ability and performance. Senior acquisition officers, with no interference from combat arms officers, would control assignments and promotions. The service would also need a sufficient number of senior positions consistent with the heavy responsibilities of billion-dollar acquisition programs critical to the national defense.

The service would consist of persons who, by virtue of their education, skill, and assignments, could become experts in managing large development and production programs. They could broaden their expertise in several aspects of defense acquisition, with assignments to buying organizations and laboratories, program management offices, the service headquarters staff, or advanced training courses and tours with industry.

If a more attractive government career in acquisition management were made available, either within the existing services or as a new service, conflicts associated with widespread military retirements to industry could be minimized while preserving the rights of individuals to full-length careers. The basic goal of any change in the career system must be to build competence, integrity, and prestige into the defense acquisition process and to provide appropriate incentives and prestige for government personnel choosing that career. Many competent military officers and civil servants now avoid assignments in acquisition and to the faculty of the Defense Systems Management College because these assignments have not conferred prestige or made promotion more likely.

To create the acceptance, dedication, prestige, and high level of competence needed in defense acquisition, senior civilian managers and military officers need to make convincing statements and promotion decisions consistent with the view that defense acquisition is a desirable career field. Until the secretary of defense and the military chiefs of staff make clear by their words and actions that it is prestigious to be selected to manage the acquisition process, difficulties in attracting and retaining competent people will continue.

This analysis assumes that the defense acquisition process will continue to be managed predominantly by military officers. Most senior defense officials, past and present, military and civilian, recommend that course of action because they have found, as I have, that the uniformed military service brings to the acquisition process a much-needed esprit de corps, a willingness to work long hours and to travel wherever necessary on short notice, and a psychic income to supplement the below-industry pay levels of government service.

Conclusions

Many in government and industry want to improve the acquisition process. But it is unrealistic to expect any lasting improvement unless major changes are made in management skills and unless more appropriate incentives and disincentives are established and enforced. For example:

Unless changes are made in the current practice of waiving training requirements and offering short training courses that cover only introductory subjects rather than important subjects in depth, it is unrealistic to expect improved training for acquisition managers.

Unless changes are made in military careers that now provide few opportunities beyond age forty-five or fifty, it is unrealistic to expect military officers not to seek second careers in the defense industry. (In addressing this problem, DOD needs to hear the views of colonels and lieutenant colonels and Navy captains and commanders on the advantages and disadvantages of the acquisition career field.)

Unless changes are made in the current military personnel system that makes short-term assignments necessary for military officers to acquire the number and variety of assignments needed for promotion, improved continuity in defense program offices is unlikely.

Without genuine promotion opportunities for individuals who make the difficult decisions associated with successful negotiating and wise buying, it is unrealistic to expect to retain in government service experienced program managers able to do much more than the routine tasks of promoting their programs, preparing progress reports, and conducting briefings.

Unless changes are made in the current profit system that demands higher costs as a prerequisite for higher profits, it is futile to expect lower program costs.

Unless changes are made in the current process of contractor source selection, which makes optimistically low-cost estimates a significant advantage in competing for a contract, it is useless to discuss realistic contractor proposals. Criteria for evaluating source selection must give far more weight to cost realism and the contractor's record of past performance.

There will be no lasting improvements in the defense acquisition process until military commanders, beginning with the chiefs of the various services, are sufficiently unhappy with the high cost of weapons and equipment that they will make the changes necessary to produce the management skills needed to capture potential savings. Until steps are taken to create and retain these skills, it makes little difference what other acquisition reforms are attempted.

The mandate to change must come from the top; only then can improvements take place. Military and civilian leaders in the Defense Department will need to be unambiguous in declaring the steps to be taken to improve management of the acquisition process. They will also need to be persistent to ensure that the changes take place. DOD personnel at all levels must be committed to achieving higher-quality products at lower cost. Minor adjustments or corrections to the present system will not accomplish this vital job.

Gilbert Fitzhugh, chairman of the President's Blue Ribbon Commission on Defense Management, noted that when studies are completed and committee members depart, those who remain to assess and implement recommendations are those whose toes have been stepped on in the findings. Not unexpectedly, there is a noticeable lack of enthusiastic support. If significant improvements are to occur, those responsible for implementation need strong advocates remaining on the scene to lend support to the findings, with understanding and conviction.

Destruction Of Ground-Launched Cruise Missile. Davis-Montham AFB.

Arms Control

Kenneth L. Adelman

To reflect on arms control after nearly five years as director of the U.S. Arms Control and Disarmament Agency is daunting. Having left office, however, I no longer need to heed the wise counsel a British diplomat gave his boss, Lord Harrowby, in 1804: to respond to a pleading foreign official in "neutral, unmeaning civilities."

Arms Control in the Past

Before diving for the capillaries—as is the wont in arms control—I should place the field in a larger perspective. Although the impact of arms control upon Western security has been analyzed and written about over the years, it has usually been vastly over-valued. The average citizen has been led to believe that someday, somehow arms control will deliver us from danger. It has often been equated with "peace" by officials who know better and is now so assumed by publics, who should be told better.

The most prevailing and perverse myth equates an arms control agreement with a peace agreement. This assumes that such an agreement would bring lasting peace to our turbulent world. Nothing could be further from the truth.

Arms control has a ring of finality about it that is unwarranted. "When is it going to end?" people ask of the arms race. "When can we do without the nuclear weaponry, soldiers, and big conventional arsenals accumulated all these years?" The answer is, "Just about when we can dismiss the local police force or the national FBI or other domestic security apparatus we have built up over time."

Parchment cannot bring peace; neither can arms control. Maybe it can help improve the political climate, but even that is questionable. That depends primarily upon whether Soviet behavior allows the climate to improve.

If the political climate improves while the Soviets continue fueling and fostering trouble around the world, this new climate is harmful. It would resemble a physician pumping a sick patient up with cortisone to eliminate skin sensations. It can make the patient feel better for a moment but endangers the body by shutting down the system providing natural warning of major problems.

In a nutshell, arms control can never substitute for Western security, determination, and cohesion. At best, it can contribute something to security. At worst, it can harm security quite a bit. Generally arms control can do modest good if handled well and enormous harm if handled poorly.

In the past, however, neither the modest good nor the enormous harm has come about. Despite all the hopes of the liberals and all the fears of the conservatives, despite thousands of analyses like this one, arms control has had scant bearing on Western security. When all is said and done, much more has been said about arms control than has ever been done by it.

A Beneficial But Unappreciated Accord

The United States and the Soviet Union are in the process of implementing an agreement on intermediate-range nuclear forces (INF). It is a rare, indeed to me the sole, good agreement on nuclear arms control because it solves the problem it set out to solve. That is not bad in any endeavor, certainly not in arms control.

The INF Treaty solves the problem that every European government identified in the mid-1970s as a real and grave difficulty. It solves the problem that we conservatives identified then as a real and grave threat: the advent of the SS-20, a triple warhead, mobile, accurate, top-of-the-line Soviet missile aimed at the primary friends and allies of the United States around the world. Moreover, INF set five excellent precedents for arms control that can and should be followed by the Bush administration. History, as Arnold Toynbee put it, is "one damned thing after another." If any lessons are learned from history—and generally they are not—then lessons from these five factors can be learned.

First, the INF accord will lead to reductions in nuclear weapons, even an elimination of an entire category of nuclear arms. We in the strategic fraternity know that reductions can be destabilizing if done wrong, but these reductions have been done right because they do not leave either side at a disadvantage. They are thus welcome, especially in comparison with previous agreements touted as limiting nuclear arms, though they in fact did nothing of the kind. Since the SALT I (Strategic Arms Limitation Talks I) agreements were signed, for example, the Soviets have added some 7,000 strategic ballistic warheads. Since SALT II, the Soviets have doubled the number of their ballistic missile warheads.

Second, INF will result in unequal reductions to equal limits. The Soviets must reduce four to five times the number of warheads that the United States must reduce. Since the Soviets have achieved superiority in critical areas of strategic weapons, conventional arms, and chemical weapons—all areas of active negotiations in the Bush administration—this principle of unequal reductions to equal limits is critical.

Third, the INF accord breaks new ground on verification. The Soviets have agreed to on-site inspection, exchange of data, continuous monitoring around key missile production facilities and other techniques to determine if they cheat—at least, if they cheat easily and cheaply.

Fourth, INF dealt exclusively with American and Soviet INF systems. No restrictions were placed on the Strategic Defense Initiative (SDI), although the Soviets twice tried to tie an INF agreement to SDI, a proposal the United States twice refused. No restrictions were placed on British or French nuclear systems or on German Pershing I-A missiles, although the Bonn government subsequently agreed to scrap them. All this came about despite years of conventional wisdom that the United States had to "give the Soviets something" on weapons of U.S. allies or it would be left without any arms control and instead face the onset of a new cold war.

Fifth—and in many ways most important—INF should stand as a model to the Bush administration on how to negotiate with the Soviets. The approach employed throughout most of the Reagan administration was relatively simple: develop a good proposal—one that solves the problem the negotiations are supposed to solve—and stick with it. If deployments are the alternative, go ahead and deploy while talking. A military buildup in the near term can lead to a mutual military drawdown in the longer term. Whatever happens, U.S. negotiators should not begin with a proposal that puts top priority on being negotiable with the Soviets, one that thus sits midfield between U.S. and Soviet interests. The U.S. team can always count on the Soviets to propose something starkly in their own interest. If the United States proposes something good for both sides, it is then left negotiating between midfield and Soviet territory.

The United States should never get into the drill of negotiating with itself. As former first lady Nancy Reagan said about drugs, "Just say no" to ill-advised Soviet offers. Had the Reagan administration listened to the chorus of voices from the traditional arms control community who often advised "just saying yes," the United States and the North Atlantic Treaty Organization (NATO) would have ended up with no INF agreement at best and a bad agreement at worst. Such individuals time and again gave advice that turned out to be wrong.

When the Soviets threatened to walk out of the negotiations in 1983, the chorus said that arms control would be dead if NATO's deployments proceeded. When the Soviets did walk out, the chorus said that they would not return to the table unless the United States took its missiles out or at least halted their deployment. When the Soviets demanded inclusion of the British and French systems, the chorus said that the United States had to compensate the Soviets for allies' systems. When the Soviets tied progress in INF to SDI, the chorus advised that the United States had to restrict its defense research to make a deal. When the Soviets said that they could arrange something on systems in Europe but not in Asia, the chorus said that this was good enough, at least for a start. When the Soviets wished to restrict U.S. conventional capabilities by including dual-capable systems, the chorus pushed INF proposals that included dual-capable aircraft. All the while, the chorus held that the Soviets would never agree to give up their enormous number of SS-20s for the modest number of INF weapons of the United States. None of their dire predictions came true.

If this field of arms control had any accountability in it, those who made such claims would be held accountable. But there is no real accountability, and so the same individuals who made such wrong predictions in the past are making similar sounds now.

Reservations Still Exist

Even after the Reagan administration resisted repeated temptations to settle for anything less than a solid INF accord, the alliance was not ecstatic. Instead of being greeted with acclaim, the INF accord was generally greeted with apprehension in Western Europe. Instead of realizing that the alliance had withstood the greatest onslaught of Soviet pressure to crack the cohesion of NATO and accomplished what it set out to accomplish, the alliance once again suffered a bout of anxiety. Instead of saying, "We've won!" many grumbled that perhaps we were better off losing or maybe should not have played at all.

Fears that have long (and understandably) afflicted the alliance—fears of decoupling U.S. security interests from those of Western Europe, of European neutralization, denuclearization, and destabilization—once again reared their ugly heads. A *Le Figaro* editorial in September 1987 put it most starkly: "There can be some doubt as to who, the United States or the Soviet Union, comes out the winner. But the identity of the loser appears evident: Europe."

This is utter nonsense yet somewhat understandable. Arms control has long suffered from the psychological syndrome called approach-avoidance. As long as an agreement stays over the horizon, it is universally heralded. Once it comes within sight, the urge to approach transforms into an urge to avoid the object of past adoration. That happened with INF. But leaders of democracies need to accept responsibility; they need to chart a wise course and stay with it, to say what they mean and mean what they say. All elected leaders had been touting the zero option for six years before Soviet leader Mikhail Gorbachev finally accepted it. Foreign and defense ministers had issued communiqués twice yearly proclaiming the glory of eliminating these missiles. They should never have been in a position of telling their citizens that something was good if they actually harbored deep doubts about it. This tack erodes the trust that binds democracies together.

Nor should leaders, as is their wont, especially in the United States, exaggerate what can be achieved in an agreement such as INF. Arms control has long been burdened with a load it cannot conceivably carry. Continuing to claim that arms control can remedy security afflictions, can lead to a new era of East-West relations, can solve the main problems between democracies and totalitarian governments—all this badly misleads citizens and cheapens the endeavor. Overselling will invariably lead to dejection, if not outright rejection of what can be accomplished. It is always shortsighted and self-defeating.

The INF agreement has been criticized for not solving problems it had no possibility of ever solving. No INF treaty could ensure Western security. No INF accord could remedy the long-standing and worsening conventional imbalance in Central Europe. And no INF accord could reconcile the public's growing nuclear apprehensions in Europe with knowledge that nuclear weapons will long be essential to preserving peace on the

Continent. INF will solve the problem it set out to solve: that of the SS-20s. That is not bad. The former British secretary of state, the marquis of Salisbury, said, "There is nothing dramatic in the success of a diplomat. His victories are made up of a series of microscopic advantages."

Looking Ahead to START

With START, hopes are higher—in part because 1989 brought in a new administration eager to achieve an arms control accord and in part because public knowledge about it is slimmer.

The October 1986 Reykjavik breakthrough on START of 1,600 strategic nuclear delivery vehicles was hailed far and wide. Nonetheless, that total is still more than seven times what the Soviets possessed during the Cuban missile crisis, when Ameri-

---

The limitations START attempts to codify are indubitably of greater strategic importance but lesser verifiability than measures in the past.

---

cans worried plenty about the Soviet nuclear arsenal. The 6,000 strategic nuclear weapons, also part of the "Reykjavik breakthrough," is approximately the total the Soviets had when President Reagan took office. It represents more than twelve times the number the Soviets possessed during the 1962 Cuban missile crisis. Moreover, the verification problems in START, which to me seem nigh unto impossible to solve, extend far beyond those of INF. Five conditions mitigate against a successful START agreement.

First, the limitations START attempts to codify are indubitably of greater strategic importance but lesser verifiability than measures in the past. Warheads and throwweight, the key constraints of START, are the truly critical ones strategically but are much harder to verify than strategic nuclear delivery vehicles (the prime measure of SALT I and II). Moreover, the march of technology makes even these increasingly tougher to control by arms control over time. For instance, testing is no longer needed to have high reliability for a certain number of warheads on a missile.

Second, the upcoming strategic systems are smaller and more mobile than their predecessors. Cruise missiles and mobile land-based missiles must be included in any arms accord because they comprise the new generation of strategic forces. Over the coming decade, half of the Soviet ICBMs will be mobile, carrying some 25 percent of their total land-based missile warheads. Yet they are difficult, if not impossible, to detect accurately.

Third, Soviet concealment and deception are far more extensive and sophisticated than before. The Soviets now encrypt (or scramble) just about all their telemetry (or radio signals) emanating from their ballistic missiles in flight tests. Late in the Reagan administration, they agreed to ban all encryption, which seems to solve this problem. Yet difficulties remain because the Soviets can transmit the same information by means other than missile flight telemetry. They know when and where U.S. satellites pass over or around their landmass and are thus able to hide strategic items or practices during the time they can be detected most easily.

Fourth, START requires deep reductions in strategic forces. That is at least how it is billed and how it will be sold (although the alleged 50 percent cuts are not 50 percent cuts at all). The fact of reductions lends greater importance to verification than ever. If the Soviets cheat by 100 units when measuring strategic nuclear delivery vehicles as in SALT II—when they were limited to 2,500 in this category—that is of slight security relevance. If, however, they cheat by 100 when the treaty limits the number of missiles to zero, as in INF, this violation becomes a grave security concern.

Fifth, the clear record of Soviet cheating, the pattern of Soviet violations, increases the need for better verification. If a store browser is a well-known shoplifter, the security guard should keep closer tabs on him or her than on a customer of impeccable integrity.

Verification requires detection within the gigantic Soviet Union, a landmass that spans eleven time zones and a government that historically hides nearly everything that can be hidden. As Premier Nikita Khrushchev told the Supreme Soviet on January 14, 1960, "We locate our missiles in such a way as to ensure a double and even treble margin of safety. We have a vast territory, and we are able to disperse our missiles and camouflage them well."

A False Roadblock: SDI

Complicating the strategic talks is SDI. Indeed most commentators assume that SDI is the major roadblock to a strategic accord. This may be an exaggeration in degree but is undeniably true in kind. It will remain so until the Soviets remove it as a roadblock. To handle the key topic of SDI fully, we must back up for a moment. SDI is the subject of much misunderstanding that needs to be set straight.

First, we must address the obvious question of whether it will work. One reads almost weekly in the newspaper that "expert scientists" say it will not. But they can be woefully wrong:

Thomas Edison once forecast: "Fooling around with alternative current is just a waste of time. Nobody will use it, ever. It's too dangerous. . . . Direct current is better."

Expert Simon Newcomb noted in 1903: "Aerial flight is one of that class of problems with which man will never be able to cope."

Lee DeForrest argued in 1926: "While theoretically and technically television may be feasible, commercially and financially I consider it an impossibility, a development of which we need spend little time dreaming."

Admiral William Leahy, President Truman's chief of staff, said shortly before the Manhattan Project proved successful in 1945, "The [atomic] bomb will never go off and I speak as an expert in explosives."

One scientist knew in 1932: "There is not the slightest indication that [nuclear] energy will be obtainable. It would mean that the atom would have to be shattered at will." That was Albert Einstein.

Besides being wrong, expert scientists can also be political. Those now saying blithely that SDI will not work repudiate the essence of scientific inquiry: discovering whether something will or will not work on the basis of hard evidence rather than ideology or politics.

Scientists and politicians who oppose SDI, even if it would work, should logically oppose all research on it. Why would they want to waste money to see if something would pan out if that something is undesirable? Yet no group or individual, no matter how virulently anti-SDI, is honest enough to oppose all SDI research.

The second major SDI question is: "Work to do what?" SDI will not work to remove all danger from nuclear weapons, though it can and probably would reduce that danger. Like everything else in life, SDI does not have to be perfect or be perfectly useless.

Part of the confusion arises from SDI's father who, like most other fathers, bragged excessively about his progeny's potential. President Ronald Reagan inadvertently put up an inviting target, a leakproof SDI. A perfect defense should be SDI's goal but not its promise. And like most other presidential goals—no drugs, no inflation, no unemployment, no crime—it should be sought with the understanding it can never be reached. Critics who mock an SDI with "only" a 60 percent or 70 percent effectiveness oddly prefer 0 percent effectiveness against incoming ballistic missiles.

What can SDI do? It can work to help prevent a nuclear attack by the Soviets. It can so complicate Soviet targeting that they would never launch missiles in the first place. Some defenses blunt all precision offenses, making a militarily successful attack impossible. That is, after all, the essence of deterrence.

Second, SDI can work to prevent an accidental or unauthorized attack. Accidents can happen, leaving a president with the Hobson's choice of either sending condolences to Americans or sending retaliatory missiles to Soviets. SDI could provide another alternative by creating another "red button," a button to destroy weapons coming at the United States to put alongside the button of retaliation aimed at the Soviet Union.

And third, SDI can work to prevent a third country from attacking the United States with nuclear weapons on ballistic missiles. At a time when unpredictable rulers hold sway in some Third World countries and ballistic missiles are spreading around the world, the United States should develop some protection against an Idi Amin or Khomeini's obtaining such deadly wares.

The Soviets realize these benefits, which is why their attacks on SDI are so hypocritical. That is also why over the years Moscow has devoted between ten and fifteen times as many resources to its SDI program as the United States has to its. The Soviets do not want a world without SDI, just a West without SDI. They like their own SDI program fine.

Although the Soviets have made SDI an obstacle in the strategic arms talks, it should not be one. Indeed the goals of strategic arms control and SDI are the same: to prevent or lower incentives for the Soviets to develop a first-strike capability. Moreover, SDI brought the Soviets back to the negotiating table, where they walked out in December 1983 and stayed away until March 1985, and provides the engine driving deeper reductions.

The Reagan administration, like the Carter, Ford, and Nixon administrations, sought deep reductions before SDI came along and continued seeking such reductions after SDI was introduced. Yet it was only after SDI came on in force that the Soviets accepted the notion of deep reductions and began to negotiate seriously on the basis of that approach.

The goals of arms control and SDI encompass increasing strategic stability by increasing deterrence and also limiting damage to the country should deterrence fail. SDI would help considerably with nuclear winter, a serious problem (though not as grave as some like Carl Sagan maintain). And the synergistic relationship between arms control and SDI goes deeper. SDI would undoubtedly be helped by serious reductions in offensive forces since it then has fewer nuclear weapons to defend against. In turn, SDI can help spur deep reductions by discounting the importance of new nuclear offensive weapons.

The goals of strategic arms control and SDI are the same: to prevent or lower incentives for the Soviets to develop a first-strike capability.

The United States must also resist the much-touted grand compromise: making concessions on SDI research—and/or pledging not to abrogate the Anti-Ballistic Missile (ABM) Treaty for a specified number of years—in exchange for deep offensive reductions.

Although the notion is initially appealing, some thought reveals that it is hollow. The United States has entered one grand compromise already, the ABM Treaty and SALT I, which did not work out well. It threatened to withdraw from the ABM Treaty within five years unless the Soviets agreed to deep reductions, which they did not do and which the United States did not do. Also the presumption of today's grand compromise is all wrong. Strategic defenses would become more important, not less, in the case of fewer offensive arms. For these reasons, I do not hold much hope for this approach.

Conventional Arms Control

Hope springs eternal for conventional arms control, although the difficulties here are enormous. The disparity between level of negotiating input and amount of agreement output is staggering, even by arms control criteria. East and West, the Warsaw Pact and NATO, have wrangled for thirteen years over what, how much, to what level, and where to reduce conventional arms in Europe. During this time, the parties could not even agree about the title of these talks, the West calling them Mutual and Balanced Force Reductions (MBFR) and the East, not content with a tie but seeking superiority, omitting the word *Balanced*.

The odds of producing a worthwhile agreement have fallen since MBFR's heyday, for four reasons: (1) the French joined the talks; (2) the reductions area has grown from Central Europe to all the territory from the Atlantic to the Urals; (3) neutral and nonaligned states from Monaco to Scandinavia can now affect the talks in one way or another; and (4) the focus changed from reductions of troops to reductions of weapons. There is no valid objection to any of these new elements—each in fact is beneficial—but each also makes any agreement even more unlikely than MBFR was. Getting France into the negotiations, for instance, puts the brakes on most diplomatic efforts since the French are so skeptical of any arms agreement and so difficult, at times, to deal with. Yet it serves the Soviets right to have to negotiate with the French (and vice-versa). As for adding nonaligned states, George Kennan said it best: "The failure of any negotiation correlates with the square of the number of participants." There is no real harm in conducting such diplomacy; there is harm only in counting on it to produce worthwhile results.

Nonetheless, something has to give in Europe, given the rise in American impatience. Europe has insufficient funds to boost its own defense yet sufficient funds to boost Gorbachev's economy. In times of severe budget crunch, the United States still allots most of its military muscle to the region least likely to face military aggression. In fact, it spends more to defend Europe than the Europeans spend to defend themselves. One expert, Canadian Richard Gwyn, estimates that the United States allocates $134 billion for Europe's defense versus $83 billion for their own defense funds. Samuel Huntington estimates that the United States bears 70 percent of total allied defense spending, though its GNP is less than 50 percent that of NATO nations and Japan. It furnishes 40 percent of total allied active military manpower, though it has less than a third of the total allied population.

NATO would be well advised to use its fortieth anniversary, celebrated in 1989, to pave the way for forty more successful years. It could begin by establishing a high-level group to write something like the celebrated Harmel Report of 1967, which has guided NATO's way since. This new group should look at the entire picture: U.S. defense posture in Europe, flexible response, the role of nuclear weapons there, ways to fortify conventional deterrence, Third World or out-of-area contingencies; and the Continent's political transformation, with the tremendous changes afoot in Eastern Europe.

Where would such a path-setting group lead? If cleverly chosen, it should lead to a new NATO division of labor. On the macrolevel, the key would be burden relief. U.S. resources would be freed from NATO so the United States could better balance the Soviets in strategic nuclear power and in various trouble spots around the globe. The United States could fulfill more global responsibilities if the Europeans fulfilled more European responsibilities.

On the microlevel, the watchword would be burden sharing. This division of labor would lead the United States to capitalize on its comparative advantage of providing air, sea, and nuclear forces, the capacity for rapid resupply of men and equipment to Europe, and a strong production and technological base to outsmart, rather than outman or outgun, Warsaw Pact forces. The Europeans should build up their men and equipment on the ground as the United States draws down its forces. The United States can retain just enough for a reassuring trip wire, to show the Soviets that an attack on Europe instantly involves the United States.

This approach would not shock the Europeans. Gradual change prevents sudden change. As one of the Continent's most influential commentators, Ralf Dahrendorf, says, "A U.S. withdrawal is virtually inevitable. What matters is how that withdrawal is managed."

The countries shopping for chemical weapons—or worse yet, for plants to make their own chemical weapons— include the world's worst characters: Libya, North Korea, Syria . . .

Chemical Weapons

Iraq's chemical assaults in 1988, first against Iran and then its fellow countrymen, the Kurds, constitute the opening salvos of a race between civilized behavior and barbarism. After a half-century of fairly consistent success in banning chemical warfare, gas is back. Chemical weapons are the poor man's weapon of mass destruction and the poor state's weapon of mass annihilation. They are a handy weapon for conflicts in the Third World: fairly cheap, quite effective, and increasingly available.

Our era undoubtedly suffers from a tremendous nuclear fear, even though not one soul has perished from nuclear weapons for four decades. And, God willing, none will for forty more decades. But hordes have already been strangulated by chemical weapons over the past decade.

As many as 3,000 may have perished by cyanide and mustard gas in one week in Iraq. The gruesome scene of an Iraqi gas attack to drive Iranians from a town was described by *London Daily Telegraph* reporter Norman Kirkham on the scene: "ruined and deserted—an open grave. Bodies lie in the dirt streets or sprawled in rooms and courtyards of the deserted villas, preserved at the moment of death in a modern Middle East version of the disaster that struck Pompeii." I have spoken to victims of chemical attacks in refugee camps in northern Thailand. I have seen convincing evidence of Vietnam's use of chemical weapons against the Hmong peoples. And I have learned how many died of "yellow rain" by choking on their own blood, their skin burning away with blood pouring out of all bodily openings.

The problem of chemical weapons use is growing, not shrinking, in large part because chemical arsenals are growing. At the end of the 1960s, only five nations possessed chemical weapons. At the end of the 1980s, nearly twenty do. Before long, nearly forty may. And the countries shopping for chemical weapons—or worse yet, for plants to make their own chemical weapons—include the world's worst characters: Libya, North Korea, Syria, and some others.

Since 1984, Western nations have joined together to help stop the spread of chemical weapons. They prohibit exports of chemical precursors to problem countries, gather and share more intelligence about chemical arsenals, and work on a treaty banning chemical weapons altogether. Still, the biggest remedy is the toughest: to restore the international norm against any use of poison gas. This means hitting any user, especially a flagrant one such as Iraq, hard. It means orchestrating a universal chorus of condemnation, calling a special U.N. Security Council session to blast such behavior, and breaking off friendly relations. It means, in short, labeling a user state for what it is: an international criminal.

Unless we put the lid on use of chemical weapons now, they will become a staple on the shelf later. As wars arise in the Third World, countries will grab poison gas off the shelf and send it to the front.

Whither Russia?

Although I am not particularly starry-eyed about the prospects of success in strategic, conventional, or chemical arms control, much depends on the big question: Whither Russia? By all accounts, the direction in which Gorbachev takes his country will determine the fate of arms control and, even more important, Soviet behavior and, consequently, U.S.-Soviet relations for the future.

Clearly Gorbachev's reforms are in big trouble; whether he can rejuvenate the system is doubtful. The Soviet economy has gone from bad to worse, with national economic growth practically at a standstill. Rents have not been raised since 1928, bread prices since 1954, and meat prices since 1962. State subsidies cause Soviet farmers to feed their pigs more cheaply with bread than grain.

Gorbachev has yet to come up with big solutions. His refusal to tackle price reform and the retention of government monopoly dooms more minor moves he has made. But he clearly recognizes the problem, having said some time ago, "The economy is in a mess; we're behind in every area. . . . The closer you look, the worse it is." Gorbachev's own top economist, Leonid Abalkin, told the party conference in June 1988 how "the consumer market situation has deteriorated" since Gorbachev took over. "National income in the last two years . . . has grown at a slower rate than the stagnation years" of Brezhnev and the other infirm leaders.

A danger worse than the placid economy is the bubbling nationality issue. The Balkans are boiling again, as they have throughout history, with eruptions in the Soviet republics of Armenia, Azerbaijan, Estonia, and Latvia and the Communist countries of Poland, Yugoslavia, and Czechoslovakia. In fact, the Central Intelligence Agency (CIA) counted some 600 popular disturbances within the Soviet Union since early 1988, nearly half due to ethnic conflicts. More than half—nine of fifteen—of the Soviet republics experienced major nationalistic demonstrations in 1988. The ethnic troubles could drive Gorbachev out of office if the Communist party is seen as losing control in the Soviet Union or Eastern Europe.

Glasnost, while beneficial in highlighting Soviet problems, is detrimental in unleashing Soviet politics. It has set loose forces that cannot easily be contained. In essence, Marxism is catching up with the Marxist state in that the economy is starting to matter to politics. The primacy of politics is starting to diminish.

Gorbachev, to me the most fascinating and (in many respects) historic figure on the world stage today, has put himself into a delicate situation. He is the first general secretary to hitch his fate to the fate of the Soviet economy and the first to show that he both knows and cares about the daily life of his people. Stalin was said to care but not know, Brezhnev to know but not care. From a grander perspective, it is safe to say that Gorbachev's vivid colors seem unnatural in the gray Soviet soil. The personality of the man does not match the personality of the system. He resembles a masterful Western politician more than a wearisome Soviet functionary. And when a leader does not fit the system, something has to give; it is rarely the system.

A host of setbacks at home and abroad, leading Politburo leaders to sense a loss of control, could bring him down or reduce his power. The more that feeling grows, the less Gorbachev governs. Soviet leaders are notoriously risk averse. They can tolerate change but only when tightly controlled by the party. They do not like to live dangerously. This Nikita Khrushchev learned the hard way. Ousted in 1964 for adventurism, which included a stab at *glasnost,* Khrushchev recalled in his *Memoirs,* "We in the leadership were consciously in favor of the thaw, myself included but . . . we were scared—really scared. We were afraid the thaw might unleash a flood which we wouldn't be able to control and which would drown us."

Gorbachev could easily become stodgified—as stodgy as ordinary Soviet leaders and thus blend into that gray soil—or ostracized. Continued economic stagnation and political disruption at home mixed with setbacks abroad may send him down or out. If he goes down, he would follow a long line of Russian leaders, including Catherine the Great and Alexander I, who entered office as ardent reformers and then resigned themselves to being caretakers. If he goes out, he would follow the likes of Nikita Khrushchev and Alexander II, who launched reforms and lost their office (Alexander also lost his life).

Regardless, I believe that the high-water mark of the Soviet empire has passed. If the United States keeps its vigilance, retains a strong defense, learns the lessons of how to negotiate with the Soviets, and refrains from bailing out the Communist system, it can usher in a new situation in international affairs. The Soviet Union will become more a thorn in its side than a dagger at its throat. It will, over time, become a country that will diminish its repression at home and its aggression abroad regardless of the outcomes of the reforms.

For Gorbachev's reforms to succeed, the Soviet Union will have to become a more open, decentralized, nontotalitarian state—precisely the kind of state that will allocate fewer resources to its own defense and to supporting a farflung empire ranging from Cuba and Nicaragua to Angola, Ethiopia, Afghanistan, and Cambodia.

Should Gorbachev's reforms fail, the Soviet Union will become a Third World nation with a bomb—still dangerous in a military way but increasingly irrelevant to the world of the twenty-first century. Just as South Korea's eventual success over North Korea was predictable because it was superior—economically, politically, and in every way—so the West will triumph over the Soviet bloc. When that grand day comes about, the long-awaited goals of arms control will be met, quite regardless of whether agreements are made along the way.

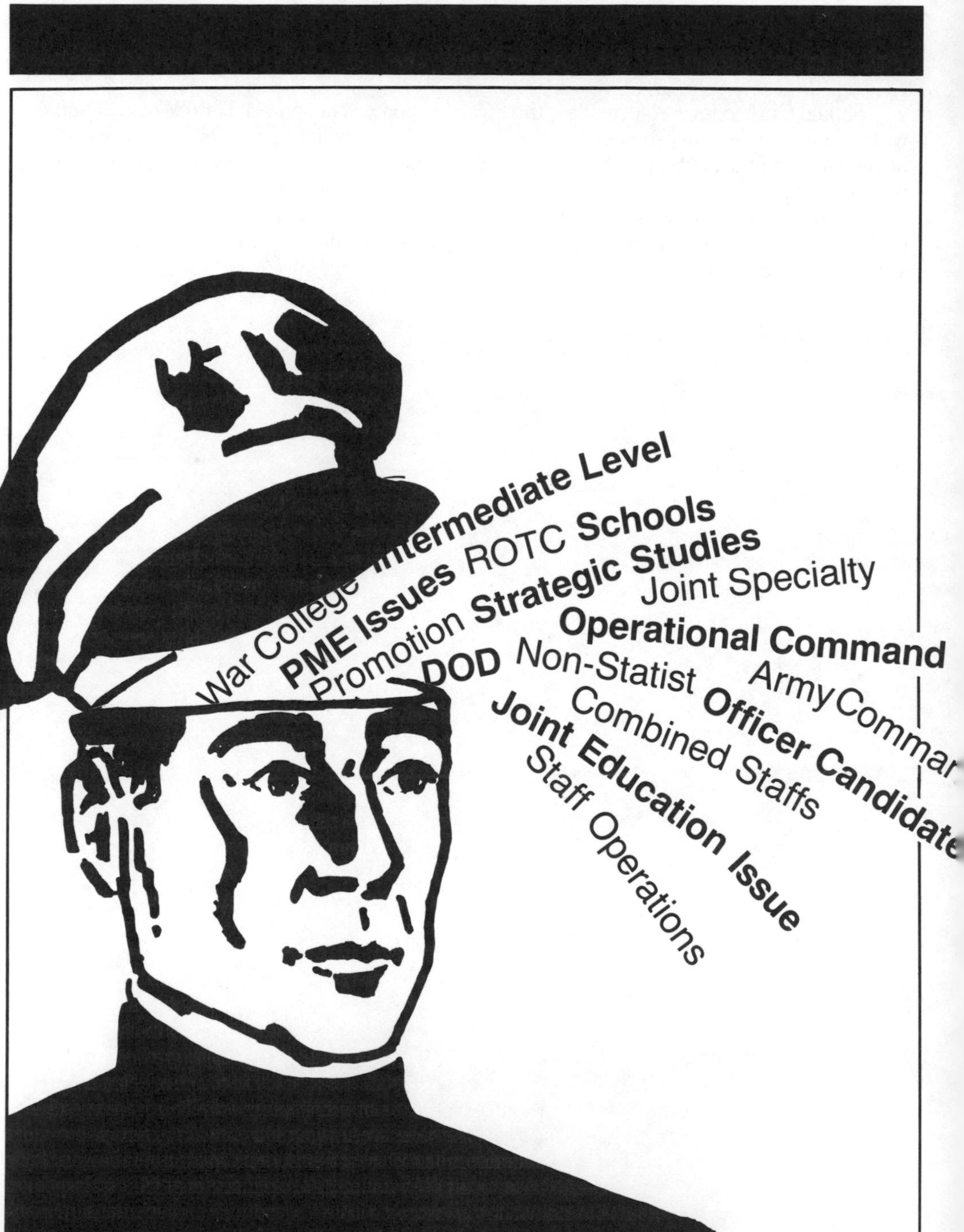

War College
Intermediate Level
PME Issues
ROTC
Schools
Promotion
Strategic Studies
Joint Specialty
Operational Command
DOD
Non-Statist
Army
Officer Candidate
Combined Staffs
Joint Education Issue
Staff Operations

Professional Military Education: Issues for the 1990s

Allan R. Millett
Williamson Murray

I f one could muster all the generals and admirals of the U.S. armed forces in one conference room and require them to swear on a stack of Joint Chief of Staff (JCS) publications to the value of professional military education, the fervor of their pledge would stagger many civilians, who might regard the term *military education* as an oxymoron. Yet professional military education (PME) is always open for debate and disagreement, within both the military establishment and the policy-attentive elite, which includes Congress and the civilians of the Department of Defense (DOD). The issue of PME is a lightning rod for related questions of operational competence, civil-military relations, and national security policy in general. It is hardly surprising that PME issues generate heat and light—and some confusion.

The term *professional* requires some definition since American officers think of themselves as professionals. They believe they have an unusual degree of expertise, that they exercise this expertise for the public good and not primarily for pay, and that they should enjoy a high degree of occupational corporateness and autonomy. They also believe that they merit public trust in defining their own functions, standards of performance, and their system of promotion and rewards. A system of continuing education is an essential ingredient for professional status, and the American officer corps has known this bit of cultural wisdom for more than one hundred years.

American society expects that professionals, at a minimum, start with four-year university degrees, and the military conforms to this expectation. When one eliminates warrant officers and others whose educational achievements are unknown, 96 percent of officers in the armed forces in 1988 held at least a four-year baccalaureate degree.[1] The egalitarian nature of American higher education prevents a precise assessment of the quality of the undergraduate education that American officers receive, but American officers seldom come from the best or worst of the nearly 3,000 American universities and colleges.

Most officers do not consider a baccalaureate degree sufficient for career advancement, a reflection of their professionalization. In 1988 one-third of the entire officer corps had advanced degrees. Whether the degrees have any utility in terms of military skills or professional values is quite another question since a majority of the degrees were in business or educational management.

Why do American military officers place such stock in professional military education? First, they, like other professionals, realize that the educational process affects the future of the profession. All professionals face the same questions: (1) how am I to do "it," whatever the job is; (2) why do I want to do "it"; and (3) why is my willingness to do "it" important to society, whether one defines the society as nonstatist, national, or international? On the surface military officers can easily answer such questions. They are sworn to defend the security of the state as it exists. Furthermore, they understand that this security relates to the well-being of the people inhabiting the state, the values that those people hold, and the processes of change that those people regard as legitimate. Military officers concern themselves primarily with the external threats to these values that come from military capability and secondarily from those threats that come from within the body politic itself when it resorts to violent challenges to the status quo.

The major dilemma for PME is whether it should stress institutional socialization and military skills or the ability of officers to deal with the external political environment. At the officer-candidate and company-grade officer levels, institutional socialization is primary. At the field grades and flag ranks, the emphasis shifts to organizational leadership roles that demand an understanding of the political and social values of American society, sometimes in conflict with professional military mores. The problem for the military establishment lies in the fact that when it shifts from training—the performance-tested achievement of military tasks—to education, it invites civilian comparisons. Career officers at the field and flag ranks must combine technical skills learned through intense formal training and operational experience with leadership abilities that they can develop only through some combination of professional military education and exposure to the political culture in which they must exist.

Professional military education is important to the officer corps because it prepares officers to cope with a diverse set of clients: officers of other American services, military officers of allies, and the civilian political leaders of the United States and its allies. These requirements pose serious choices for American officers. Should a senior officer specialize in learning other services' doctrine and procedures, the functioning of joint and combined staffs, procurement, major (flag rank) operational command within his or her own service, or service within the national security agencies of the American executive branch? The possibilities for ambitious and intelligent officers are multiple and no less bewildering when one weighs them against the opportunities for formal education, whether within the DOD or outside it. Most civilian professionals have a clearer vision of the gates that they must pass to the top rank of their profession, and, to some degree, they can measure their progress by the size of their net wealth. Such a measure does not exist for military professionals, which may make the sense of relative deprivation and sacrifice more acute.

One might accept PME as simply an exercise in progressive institutional socialization, preparing officers only for higher command within their own services. Since the

Goldwater-Nichols Defense Reorganization Act of 1986, however, Congress has expected broader preparation for defense leadership among the military's senior officers. Although the intent of the law is admirable, it remains to be seen whether it will fulfill congressional hopes that the senior officers of the armed forces will reflect visions of defense policy transcending service positions.

Education and the Commissioning Process

America's armed forces lavish considerable attention on the three service academies. All three are commanded by three-star generals or admirals; they are similar in curricula, ambience, and purpose; all produce officers at considerable cost. Ironically, out of the 23,000 young men and women who received commissions in 1988, under 4,000 received their education at the service academies. The great bulk came from the Reserve Officer Training Corps (ROTC) program. In ROTC there are substantial differences in the criteria used by the services. The Army and Air Force are still oriented to mass participation, while the Navy and Marine Corps programs are designed to produce career officers. The Navy and the Marine Corps maintain higher requirements in their demands of how their ROTC cadets shape their academic curricula. Yet even between the Army and Air Force substantial differences exist in ROTC programs, with the latter emphasizing the procurement of engineers and technicians and the former traditionally emphasizing a broad spectrum of interests. In addition to ROTC the services maintain Officer Candidate Schools for a limited number of enlisted personnel and recent college graduates.

As a result of the eclectic sources from which they draw their officers and the diverse educational backgrounds, the services possess a heterogeneous junior officer corps drawn from a spectrum of America's institutions of higher learning. In effect the system of PME attempts to bridge the differences in backgrounds that exist at the beginning. Complicating the process is the fact that the specialties in which the young officers serve exacerbate the differences in background by providing the officers, even within each service, with substantially different perspectives.

Professional Military Education at Midcareer

The military officer has little formal professional military education until he or she emerges from performing duties in a primary military occupational specialty (MOS) between the eighth and twelfth years of commissioned service. Of course, he or she has attended schools, probably several, but the services recognize that schooling at the company-grade ranks (O-1 to O-3) means principally training. The services' first responsibility is to see that officers qualify in their operational specialty and then strengthen these skills with further training to prepare them for additional operational responsibilities.

For all the training, junior officers may also improve their formal educational qualifications. Some return to civilian graduate schools in a duty status to earn degrees required to perform a specific job (a "validated billet") in a specific organization. More generous before the cost-conscious 1980s, fully funded graduate education may be career enhancing, but it is limited to a small number of officers and often has only marginal relevance to service leadership roles—at least in DOD's view. Two services maintain their own civilian-accredited, degree-granting graduate schools—the Air Force Institute of Technology and the Naval Postgraduate School—and part of these institutions' curricula could qualify as PME. American officers have learned that obtaining a civilian graduate degree on their own time (with or without military financial assistance) can help differentiate them from their peers when promotion boards meet. In addition to personal satisfaction and some perceived usefulness in finding postretirement employment, off-duty education probably has some organizational utility as well, but much of the students' work is in management and offered as nonresident courses by universities and colleges that do not rank among America's best graduate institutions.

Since the services have around 53,000 majors and lieutenant commanders who will serve between seven and eight years at that rank, a quick calculation demonstrates how few of these officers will attend a command and staff college.

All four services established command and staff colleges to perform two essential functions: to prepare a field-grade elite for the command and staff duties of major operational units and to prepare the same officers for major organizational leadership roles in their own service. Although the two functions are not inherently incompatible, they are not necessarily the same when one designs a curriculum of a finite number of hours (usually 1,000 to 1,200) or selects a limited number of students. (For example, should technical specialists fill billets that might otherwise go to line officers?)

During World War II the JCS recognized that the service schools did not fill the requirements to provide special education (in fact, mostly training) for officers assigned to joint and combined commands, so it established its own institution, the Armed Forces Staff College (AFSC) at Norfolk, Virginia. The four services continued their own command and staff schools: the Army Command and General Staff College (Fort Leavenworth, Kansas), the Naval Command and Staff College (Newport, Rhode Island), the Air Command and Staff College (Maxwell AFB, Alabama), and the Marine Corps Command and Staff College (Quantico, Virginia).

Although all of these schools have experienced periodic changes in their curricula, method of selecting students, and pedagogy, they have retained an emphasis upon the integration of service arms in the conduct of land warfare, naval warfare, air warfare, and amphibious warfare, respectively. Since American officers reach field-grade rank by mastering only one aspect of their service's operational mission (for example, artillery employment, submarine warfare, air superiority operations, infantry amphibious assaults), education and training in combining service arms in an extended campaign represent a critical requirement. However, the cost of college facilities themselves, the length of the course, and the perceived time "lost" by the students while attending the schools, especially by students with operational specialties in short supply, limits the number of officers who attend resident command and staff colleges. In academic year 1986–1987 only 2,024 officers attended the five command and staff colleges; almost half of these students (1,004) were Army officers (the Army has always placed a higher priority on midcareer education). Since the services have around 53,000 majors and lieutenant commanders who will serve between seven and eight years at that rank, a quick calculation demonstrates how few of these officers will attend a command and staff college.

Continuing a practice that began before World War II, the services send officers to each others' command and staff colleges as well as the AFSC and, in some rare cases, to the staff colleges of allied nations. Table 11–1 shows the 1986–1987 statistics for this practice. All the intermediate-level schools (ILS) offer correspondence courses to non-resident students. The Army regards the completion of ILS as a promotion requirement; the Air Force and the naval services do not. Officers prefer the resident course since selection has a halo effect and reduces the time conflicts between duty and study.

In the post-Vietnam era the command and staff colleges were buffeted by a series of conflicting demands that muted the traditional dominance of operations in their curricula. In the 1970s one pressure was for the colleges to design curricula that could win civilian accreditation to allow successful graduates to earn a master's degree. In practice this meant reducing the attention to operations. The pressure came from several sources: DOD and service concern over defects in officers' undergraduate education, an effort to improve officers' civilian academic certification and thus increase their ability to deal with the civilian political elite, the conviction that a civilian academic degree would improve the retention of talented officers, and the eagerness of civilian institutions to earn DOD dollars. Although combining ILS education and civilian master's study is still possible for a minority of officers (principally at Newport and Fort Leavenworth), this reform waned in the 1980s.

Another stimulus for reform came from the 1975 recommendations of a committee chaired by Deputy Secretary of Defense William P. Clements, Jr., that the staff colleges focus on the study of joint and combined operations as well as provide education in

Table 11-1. Command and Staff College Attendance Distribution*

	Attend Own CSC	Attend Joint/Combined CSC	Attend Other Service CSC
Army	703	214	87
Navy	94	68	16
Air Force	435	148	53
Marine Corps	124	36	82

* 1986-1987 statistics.

Source: Department of Defense

nonoperational matters such as resource planning, defense management, national strategy and security policy, international relations, and civil-military relations in the defense decision-making structure. An additional review spared the staff colleges a major curriculum change by affirming the services' position that the staff colleges must concentrate on the "exacting instruction for selected officers in the essentials of command doctrine and staff operations for ground, sea, and air warfare as well as joint and combined operations."[2] This allowed the staff colleges to devote less than one-quarter of their hours to the Clements core curriculum. The war colleges were not, however, granted a similar reprieve.

Reflecting the views of the services' senior leadership in the 1980s, the command and staff colleges returned to their traditional focus on operations. The operational renaissance represented service conviction and civilian criticism that American officers were not prepared to deter war by combat readiness or to conduct real operations, however small the scale. Some of these concerns were well founded because officer assignment policies tended to place majors and lieutenant commanders in operational billets only once or twice during their service at that rank and then to make these assignments relatively short tours (two years or less). Officers often went to these assignments after several years away from the operating forces. (The Navy argues that it is an exception to this pattern, especially among the aviator and submarine communities.) The staff colleges made operational preparation essential and more a matter of intellectual development (education) than strict training, although operational expertise requires both. While contemporary operations may become more orderly and predictable through staff training, the increasing complexity of combining arms (even of one's own service) requires a degree of creativity and a capacity to deal with uncertainty that the training of officers in routinized procedures cannot meet. The staff colleges try to provide the best of both types of mental preparation.

The manner with which the services provide intermediate-level PME still varies from college to college. The Naval Command and Staff Course devotes twelve weeks to strategy and policy, twelve weeks to national security and decision making (once defined as management), and fourteen weeks to naval operations. Other subjects normally fall in the electives program, only 20 percent of the entire curriculum. The Marine Corps Command and Staff College, which has practically eliminated all electives, requires all students to take nearly 600 hours in landing force operations and another 200 hours in battle studies and strategy, leaving about 350 hours for courses liberally defined as command, a broad field including such topics as effective communications. The common operational curriculum of the Army Command and General Staff College makes up half of the total number of student hours, and the electives program allows students to pursue more specialized strategic and operational topics. In addition, the Army now provides a second year at Fort Leavenworth for sixty officers who have shown special ability as students in the regular first-year curriculum. This program in the operational art and strategy reestablishes an earlier Army practice and is similar to courses in the British Army and the West German Bundeswehr.

The Air Force has a special problem: it has almost 20,000 majors, the largest number in the American armed forces, only 20 percent of whom attend some sort of resident, intermediate-level PME school. Only half of this small group attends the Air Command and Staff College (ACSC). In 1988 the Air Force considered reducing the curriculum at ACSC to twenty-four weeks from forty, making it available to two annual classes, not just one. One purpose of establishing this short course (in addition to doubling the number of Air Force graduates) was to reduce the attractiveness of the AFSC, highly popular with officers who wanted ILS credit without a long absence from operational commands. The new curriculum focuses on the nature, conduct, and management of aerospace warfare, using historical case studies as the heart of the educational effort. The curriculum reduces elective options (less than 5 percent of the long course in any event); since three-quarters of the officer-students already had civilian master's degrees, the college saw no conflict with other academic needs of students. In fact, its commandant believed a shorter course would draw more qualified officers than the college had previously attracted.

The War Colleges

It is at the war college level that PME has received the greatest attention over the past several years. There are five senior or top-level schools (TLS): the National War College (NWC), the Industrial College of the Armed Forces (ICAF), and the Army, Navy, and Air war colleges. (The Marines consider the Naval War College at Newport, Rhode Island, as their war college.) Admiral Stansfield Turner once characterized the mission of the war colleges as

> places to educate the senior officer corps in the larger military and strategic issues that confront America in the late twentieth century. They should educate these officers by a demanding intellectual curriculum to think in wider terms than their busy operational careers have thus far demanded. Above all the war colleges should broaden the intellectual and military horizons of the officers who attend.[3]

Whatever the strengths of Admiral Turner's conception, there has been no unanimity of opinion within the services as to what educational and professional purposes the war colleges should serve. Since a number of the graduates of these institutions will attain flag or general officer rank shortly after graduation, it is not surprising that the war colleges have drawn considerable interest from Congress, outside academics, and military reformers, as well as the services themselves.

The clientele of the war colleges comes from a select group of lieutenant colonels/commanders (O-5) and colonels/captains (O-6). The mission of the war colleges is to provide a higher level of professional education to their student bodies; the war colleges aim to provide highly skilled managers and staff officers to run the bureaucracy and future flag and general officers to *lead* the U.S. military in the next century. Two such divergent aims create considerable tensions in educational policy. Moreover, there is no unanimity, even within the individual services, as to whether the colleges are institutions of rigor in which intellectual and operational excellence is identified and rewarded or whether the war colleges represent institutions for officers to reflect in the midst of their busy operational careers.

All the war colleges purport to provide their students with serious postgraduate-level education, but they differ significantly in educational approaches and policies. Moreover, the educational philosophies that marked American education in the 1960s continue to influence the approach of the war colleges in the 1980s: do students learn best in an environment where there are no examinations? Given the menu of complex issues that confront the services, is it not sensible to allow officers to choose what best will help them on their career paths? Finally, it is worth noting that the war colleges respond to conflicting signals from larger political and societal segments of American life. Congress wants a well-managed, efficient, and inexpensive military; therefore management and organization have received a major emphasis at all the war colleges since the Clements reforms.

Concurrently both from within and outside the military come demands for higher operational competence; therefore strategy and war fighting also receive attention. In fact, there are numerous constituencies that hold strong convictions about what issues the senior service schools need to teach. The war colleges have tended to teach a little bit of everything that these constituencies think senior officers should know. What they should teach and how well they perform their mission are questions that emerged only in the late 1980s as significant points of debate.

At the conclusion of World War II the ICAF was established as a conversion of the Army Industrial College to study the complex issues raised by modern war between industrial nations: how to integrate sources with strategy, how to mobilize a civilian economy for war; and how to manage the complex and interrelated bureaucratic organizations that represent a nation in arms (in peace as well as in war). ICAF would then seem to be ideally placed to train the managers of America's defense establishment. The services, however, have deliberately chosen to mix ICAF's student body with officers from command and operational areas as well as acquisitions and systems analysis. Its graduates are, therefore, fully eligible for command and operational slots as well as assignments as acquisition managers and systems analysts for procurement programs.

The National War College, the Naval War College, the Air War College, and the Army War College claim to provide professional education to the future leaders of America's military forces. The four have substantially different educational philosophies, and there is little evidence to suggest that they are likely to come together in a coherent, consistent approach to educating future service leaders. This may not be a bad thing. The differences between the services in culture as well as in mission suggest that consistency is not only impossible but might be positively harmful.

The National War College (NWC) claims to be the premier senior service school. Certainly it attracts a significant portion of the best officers from the four services. Its location in Washington, D.C., has also been an attraction; officers who attend its course are often able to avoid a move (either coming to Fort McNair from the Pentagon or moving on to the Pentagon after the NWC). The Pentagon, Congress, and executive agencies like the National Security Council (NSC) provide the students at the NWC with numerous opportunities to see the processes of government at work.

Nevertheless, a number of factors work against the NWC's becoming an effective educational institution. One of the unstated purposes of the war colleges is to provide an atmosphere in which cohesion and contacts within the officer corps are established. At the three service war colleges where most officers live nearby, this is not a problem. At NWC, where the cost of living in the area has skyrocketed, students live scattered across Maryland and northern Virginia, often a two-hour commute away. Also the NWC does not possess a service constituency, nor has NWC attracted academic experts in the field of military history or strategy. Student performance is ungraded. The curriculum heavily emphasizes international relations, area studies, and current national strategy. Traditionally there has been little emphasis on military history, although there has been awakening interest in courses in the operational art and military strategy. The NWC's reputation largely rests on the quality of its student body.

The three service war colleges suggest a wide divergence of educational approaches and philosophies. The Naval War College is the most rigorous of the three. In 1972 Naval War College president Admiral Stansfield Turner carried out a drastic reorganization of the curriculum, organization, and faculty. As a result of this revolution, the college has focused on war to a greater degree than the other colleges. The Strategy Department, which teaches a fifteen-week course in strategy and policy, is one of the more impressive departments of strategic studies in the Anglo-American world. Not only does it possess a core of fine academic and military minds in its resident faculty, but it has also been able to attract a number of highly regarded academicians for one-year visiting professorships. It demands serious research papers from its students; its faculty grades those papers rigorously; and the students are graded on midterm and final examinations. Consequently the Naval War College is the only service school with a distinguished graduate program, which demands that the students be ranked on the basis of academic work.

The Army War College has convinced itself that the educational philosophy of the 1960s is the best approach.

Several factors explain the academic excellence and more focused curriculum at Newport. The Turner revolution undoubtedly created an excellent base both in terms of a focused curriculum and in the establishment of a competent, graduate-level faculty. Unfortunately, until the early 1980s, the Navy failed to send its best officers to school in Newport. It was career enhancing to be selected for attendance at the Naval War College and then to avoid the assignment in favor of more critical command or staff duties. This situation changed in 1983–1984 during the tenure of Admiral James D. Watkins as chief of naval operations (CNO). By the mid-1980s virtually all officers coming off command assignments (surface ships, aircraft squadrons, and submarines) attended the Naval War College. CNO Admiral Carlisle Trost made it clear that this policy will not change. The third factor helping the Naval War College has been the high level of support that recent secretaries of the Navy, particularly John Lehman, provided the college. That support has made the Naval War College as attractive a faculty position as many of the best graduate-level civilian academic institutions in the United States in terms of salary, research time, and educational philosophy.

Between 1984 and 1989 the Air War College showed gradual improvement. It does ask students to write papers that are graded but has no examinations or overall grades for performance. In 1985 a blue ribbon panel commission report suggested a number of reforms, including the selection of specially qualified and motivated officers to attend graduate school before assignment to the faculty. Few of the reforms have been implemented, however. In its own defense, the Air War College has replied to its critics that it provides precisely the sort of war college that the Air Force wants. There is considerable interest in the Air Staff in making changes in the Air War College's thrust. A proposed curriculum, circulated at the highest levels of the Air Staff in 1989, would entirely alter the war college's focus from management, area studies, and national security studies to a concentration on the study of war, its grand strategy, military strategy, and the operational sphere. Whether the Air Force and its senior leadership are prepared for such a radical departure is another matter. In early 1989 the betting was on marginal improvements rather than any radical restructuring.

The Army War College has convinced itself that the educational philosophy of the 1960s is the best approach. It presents its students with an ungraded course of study; its emphasis rests on a belief that a relaxed approach is essential to the education of senior officers. A self-study described the war college experience as "a period of broad intellectual and personal growth for an officer: first, in professional knowledge and understanding; second, in his creative, analytical, and verbal capabilities; and third, *in personal and family development.* [authors' emphasis]."[4] The college has doubled the number of electives, and its focus remains scattered over strategy, national security policy, management, and area studies—a little bit of everything. This is not to say that some of the students do not get a good education. In general, the faculty is first rate, with several excellent civilian academics and a number of military officers who are equal in their expertise to the best in the academic world.

Several other issues need to be addressed in terms of the war colleges. Should Congress legislate or the senior leadership dictate what should be taught at the war colleges? Congress and the services should ask (in fact, Congress already has) that some academic rigor be attached to education at the war colleges. The selection process itself weakens the argument that the war colleges teach line service leaders since technical specialists also attend them. Does it make sense to send nurses, doctors, lawyers, chaplains, dentists, and finance officers to the war colleges?[5] Do not such personnel policies detract from the war colleges' sense of mission and purpose? If the war colleges are to prepare the U.S. military services to fight, then one type of curriculum is necessary; if they are to prepare managers and staff officers, a very different set of criteria for curriculum needs to be used.

There will continue to be considerable argument over what the war colleges should teach and how they should teach it. The war colleges can exercise a powerful influence on military institutions and their senior leadership. The interest in war college education may represent the best avenue to reinvigorating U.S. military institutions in the years of budget reductions to come.

Professional Military Education and the Joint Education Issue

Although official concern for the preparation of officers for command and staff service in joint and combined forces or assignments to the Department of Defense (and more specifically the Organization of the Joint Chiefs of Staff) dates from World War II, joint professional military education (JPME) became the military educational issue of the 1980s. Galvanized by the alleged interservice embarrassments in operations in the Middle East and Caribbean, congressional interest placed additional pressure on the senior military leadership to examine the question. In response to this concern—shared by important elements of the military itself (largely in the Army and Air Force)—the chairman of the JCS, Admiral William J. Crowe, created a special investigating board, chaired by retired Air Force general Russell E. Dougherty, to study the staff and war colleges and recommend more reforms. A second group, the Military Education Coordinating Conference (MECC), also considered the issue. Its members, the presidents and commandants of the staff and war colleges, had a direct responsibility for recommending and executing curriculum changes. Both groups received much of their urgency from the congressional debate upon and eventual passage of the Goldwater-Nichols Defense

Figure 11-1. Progression of Military Education

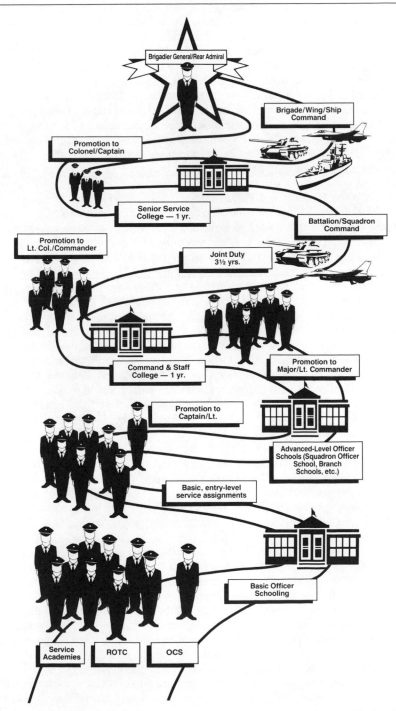

Reorganization Act of 1986. That act required substantial changes in how the services prepared, assigned, and rewarded field-grade officers for service on joint staffs.

The new law, generally supported by the Army and Air Force and resisted by the Navy and Marine Corps, established demanding criteria for joint staff service. First, DOD had to identify what jobs qualified as joint duty assignments; it did so and produced a list of 8,000 officer billets in DOD headquarters, defense agencies, and field joint and combined headquarters that required officers to be knowledgeable in the roles, missions, doctrine, and procedures of two or more of the military services. Another 1,000 billets are still under analysis and evaluation, but the total number of billets was reduced in headquarters cuts announced in December 1988 by Secretary of Defense Frank Carlucci. These billets represented half of all the positions for flag and field-grade officers outside the individual services. The law went on to require that some of these billets be designated critical joint duty assignments and that they be filled by officers who met the most demanding criteria for assignment: graduation from an approved joint service college (initially the National War College, Industrial College of the Armed Forces, and the AFSC) and an earlier full tour (defined as three years) in a joint staff assignment. The law also mandated that half of all joint billets be held by officers who were already joint specialty officers (JSOs) or who had become JSO nominees, a requirement that could be met only by graduation from an approved JPME course before assignment. The services would have to fill these billets as they had filled them in the past, roughly on a proportional basis with one-third from the Army, one-third from the Air Force, and one-third from the Navy and Marine Corps. To establish incentives for officers to seek JSO qualification, Congress directed that all future admirals and generals (with some exceptions) have a joint duty assignment (although not necessarily be a JSO) and that JSOs receive promotion at rates not substantially at variance with the promotion rates of their peers, especially those assigned to the service headquarters. The latter requirement rested upon the perception that talented officers believed they would increase their promotion prospects more on service staffs than on joint duty.

Against the background of the Goldwater-Nichols Act and the general ferment of the question of interservice rivalry and cooperation, the Dougherty board and the MECC proceeded with their separate investigations, both of which were supposed to make recommendations to the JCS chairman. As both study groups continued their reviews into 1987, they found their work of interest not only to the JCS but also to the House Committee on the Armed Services, which approved a proposal by Congressman Ike Skelton (D–Missouri) that he conduct a similar investigation of PME as a follow-up to the Goldwater-Nichols Act. It was inevitable that JPME would dominate all these groups' investigations since the legislation had dramatic implications for officer assignment policies.

The JCS-sponsored inquiries illuminated the critical issues that faced the military in executing the provisions of the Goldwater-Nichols Act. The Dougherty board and the MECC came to similar conclusions about the impact of the Goldwater-Nichols Act on the existing system of PME. Some numbers were intractable. If the services were to provide properly qualified officers for JSO billets, they would have to detail 1,000 to 1,200 officers a year to such assignments. Assuming that the services wanted to continue—indeed, strengthen—their policy of sending staff and war college graduates to service operational assignments, the annual output of the colleges would leave only 1,265 of 2,024 staff college graduates and 502 of 905 war college graduates for assignment outside of joint staff duty. If one regarded the three National Defense University colleges as the only source of JSO candidates, annual output would not meet requirements. Therefore all the service staff colleges and war colleges would have to be part of the process of certifying officers for JSO duty. The Dougherty board recommended that this problem be resolved by accrediting all the staff and war colleges to produce JSO duty officers. The Dougherty board quite properly pointed out that greater attention to joint operations in all the curricula would provide better officers for all the services, regardless of assignment upon graduation.

The MECC incorporated the work of the Dougherty board. It concluded that all of the staff and war colleges were already teaching joint planning and operations but that too many differences existed in course content and the allotment of hours of instruction. It recommended that all the staff and war colleges establish curricula that would qualify selected graduates for JSO duty. At the staff college level this curriculum would provide 240–270 contact hours of special instruction for JSO aspirants; at the war college level the requirement would be 110–120 contact hours since the war colleges already devoted a larger proportion of hours to instruction that could be identified as joint. In addition, the MECC established that the mixed service faculty that taught the joint curriculum should be composed of 75 percent officers who were war college graduates and half of whom had joint staff experience. The student body would have to include a minimum of 15 percent non-host service officers. Nevertheless, the prospect that the staff colleges would have to alter one-fifth of their curricula forced further consideration of how the existing colleges would participate in the process of certifying JSOs, as well as providing an elite group of line officers to the operational commands of the individual services.

Not satisfied that the Dougherty board or the MECC had fully solved the problem of complying with the Goldwater-Nichols Act—and sensitive to the continuing inquiry of the Skelton panel—JCS chairman Crowe in September 1988 ordered the MECC to examine an option that would partially relieve the service staff and war colleges from the problems of major curricula reform. The JCS chairman accepted three premises: that PME and especially JPME made a difference in officers' professional competence; that JSOs must first be experts in their own services' organization, roles, and missions; and that effective JPME required a special curriculum, an elite student body, and a specially qualified faculty that represented all the services. Admiral Crowe envisioned a system (already in effect in West Germany in somewhat different form) that would send officers first to their own service staff or war colleges (or another service's) and then to a course at the AFSC. Instead of offering two courses a year, the AFSC would become a temporary duty assignment (families would not accompany an officer-student at government expense) that would follow ILS or TLS assignments and precede assignment to JSO duty. The JCS approved a modified plan in early 1989. The required annual output of 1,200 officers through the AFSC will be met with a five-week (TLS grads) and nine-week courses (ILS grads). The problem in personnel management was obvious: What would an officer do if he or she did not report to the first class that convened after graduation from a regular ILS or TLS course? While this question is the sort that agitates personnel detailers, it is far less significant than the issue of whether an officer can be educated, not just trained, for joint staff duty in anything less than fifteen weeks. Nevertheless, the focus on the AFSC as a crucial part of the JPME system is a welcome change from the earlier practice of allowing officers to attend it as an alternative to the ten-month courses at the other staff colleges.

Admiral Crowe directed that the National Defense University not only change the curriculum of the AFSC but also examine even more dramatic changes in the NWC. One option the chairman wanted to investigate was the conversion of the NWC to a National Center for Strategic Studies, a military think tank designed as the intellectual home for officers who would devote their energies to research and publication. The

ICAF would sharpen its focus on the resource dimensions of national security policy and strategy but retain its war college character. All the remaining staff and war colleges would provide joint education and training (as approved by the CJCS) as a graduation requirement and as part of the core curriculum. Officers selected for JSO duty would then attend the AFSC for phase II of their JPME. This change, which represented an emerging consensus within the armed forces and Congress, would allow the service staff and war colleges to preserve their focus on service-specific operations and to transfer the responsibility for JSO qualification directly to the AFSC. At the same time graduates of the service staff and war colleges would benefit from increased joint education even though they would not qualify for JSO nomination. The services might actually recover some time for operational matters since the Clements core curriculum and the CJSC-mandated joint service curriculum might be merged in some respects. The issue of rigor and curriculum content for JSO duty will then become the province of the AFSC, which will remain under the supervision of the CJCS.

Conclusion

The three-year inquiry about the current state of PME of field-grade officers has brought a new degree of clarity to the persistent issues of formal schooling. There are four basic questions about PME: (1) What is taught? (2) Who teaches? (3) Who learns? and (4) How do you know whether someone has learned what has been taught?

What Is Taught?

The basic premise is that officers should learn what they need to know to perform the duties of their current rank and, probably, one above it as operational commanders, staff officers, and organizational managers in the defense bureaucracy. Few senior officers have no opinion on curriculum. The problem, however, is that the job description approach to curriculum development is distinct only at the company grade levels where assignments are controlled by primary MOS qualification and entail, principally, training, not education. At the precommissioning level, one constant is that most officers must qualify for civilian-approved baccalaureate degrees; nevertheless, the service academies and the ROTC programs differ on the degree of influence they exercise on officer-aspirants' undergraduate programs in terms of long-term professional development. Nevertheless, both programs stress a broad understanding of communications skills, the values learned in humanistic study, the methodology and knowledge of human behavior produced by the social sciences, the principles of the physical sciences and mathematics, and the methods of information organization and retrieval. The quality of such education is not essentially a matter of curriculum but the quality of the institution at which it is received. The services' challenge is to ensure that new officers have approximately the same quality of undergraduate education, no mean trick given the ideological, regional, racial, and professional diversity of American higher education.

When education becomes an issue at the field-grade level, the inherent tension is between training someone for a specific job assignment and educating him or her for several assignments in the higher echelons of service leadership. Another issue is the debate about whether senior leadership depends upon the mastery of technique or upon the more intangible qualities of mind and character that one usually associates with successful senior-level responsibilities in any organization and whether formal education plays any part in developing these qualities. Like most other important questions, this one defies precise answer, but the weight of fifty years of scholarship and experience suggests that formal education can play a part in leadership development. Concerns about careerism and the ethical dimensions of military leadership are examples of this awareness. The recent emphasis on operations does not necessarily mean that the trainers are in the ascendancy since many officers realize that complex operations require creative thought, not school solution formulas. Even if the staff colleges now send a larger number of their graduates to operational billets, many officers go on to important assignments that require both technical knowledge and professional knowledge not bounded by operational concerns. Although operational education and training should remain the core curriculum at the staff colleges, the war colleges do not require an equal emphasis (certainly not below the joint and combined campaign level), but instead should focus on preparation of officers for service as colonels and flag-rank officers throughout DOD with a heavy emphasis on joint and combined military affairs and civil-military relations.

The problem with curriculum reform is that it is too easy. Unlike civilian academics, military faculty respond to orders. As military presidents, commandants, and directors troop in and out of their martial offices, they can demand almost any curriculum reform they believe their own superiors have ordered or they themselves want. Shuffling multicolored paper labels and filling in master schedules are things military faculty can do, and they can give the appearance of important change. Curriculum reform can also be the moral equivalent of rock painting, bringing distinction to the boss but avoiding the organization's real problems. After the current round of adjustments, the staff and war colleges should try a five-year moratorium on curriculum change and concentrate on other problems.

Who Teaches?

One critical question the services must address is faculty quality, for, as the Skelton panel hearings revealed, an assignment to a military college faculty is not regarded or rewarded with the same enthusiasm that characterized the period between the world wars. One option—most aggressively exploited by the Naval War College—is to civilianize the faculty and to mix some system of permanent and term appointments for civilian faculty. This option has utility but does not fully answer the basic issue: does the faculty have the intellectual and moral authority and legitimacy to teach mature professionals? This issue depends upon the relationship of the subject matter to the teacher's credentials. Only in this context does it matter if a teacher is a civilian or military officer, although the civilian may enjoy an advantage in focused professional interest and job continuity that military careers make difficult. In truth, much military education should come from military officers, especially in operations, and from the elite of the officer corps that has actually performed the duties they teach. The difficulty is that it may penalize officers who seek promotion to colonel/captain and flag rank. In reality, the only subject that really requires exceptional line officers is operations. Other subjects can be taught by civilians, officers in extended assignments, or permanent military professors. These faculty members could maintain their expertise in the same way civilian professionals do: scholarship, the observation of ongoing activities in the their field, exchanges with governmental and nongovernmental agencies, and limited temporary service in the field. In reality, the Air Force (and to a lesser degree the Army) has such a de facto system, which is de jure at the service academies, but all the services need to rethink the value of preparing and assigning qualified officers to long-service academic appointments.

Who Learns?

As civilian universities and colleges learned long ago, the quality of the student body has a strong, positive influence on education since the students teach each other and press the faculty to teach them more. They also compete among themselves for academic standing and other formal recognition. The services, in fact, assume that peer pressure ensures that officer-students will work at learning in order to enhance their professional reputations; they usually beg the question of whether consensual mediocrity may inhibit individual learning. With peacetime assignments and periods between promotion lengthened by a stable (or diminished) force structure and economic constraints in the 1990s, the services should be even more selective than they have been in the 1980s in assigning officers to formal education programs. More interservice mixing of officers (now mandated by the JCS) helps the learning process, even if the officer-students are not their service's best. Service practices still vary widely. The Army is the most insistent that top officers attend ILS and TLS, the Navy the least insistent. The least radical change would be to ensure that students are board selected against the same standards applied to crucial command and staff assignments, a process already institutionalized in the Army. The most radical reform would be to require officers to pass an entrance examination before they qualify for ILS or TLS, a practice common in other nations' armed forces.

How Do You Know If Anyone Learned Anything?

Of all the questions that bedevil professional education of any sort, the issue of evaluation is the most controversial. It can become so serious in civilian universities that some faculty members carry liability insurance to cover "malpractice" if they find themselves the subject of litigation. Students do not relish evaluation, and faculty normally do not regard grading examinations, correcting papers, and conducting oral inquisitions as the most ennobling aspects of their work. Nevertheless, civilian educators generally agree that the educational process does not flourish in the absence of evaluation since most human beings need a variety of carrots and sticks to be assiduous students. Age does not define the question, only the student's antipathy to formal evaluation. In some institutions like the Army Command and General Staff College, tradition dictates painstaking evaluation; in others (like the National, Army, and Air War Colleges), grading seems an insult, a breach of contract that fosters unhealthy competition and a diversion from the tension-reducing expectations of academic duty. As the Skelton panel learned, the question of rigor sets off explosions. The key to the issue is not the form of evaluation, which almost always means whether the students take graded examinations and write graded papers, but whether the students are evaluated at all and whether the evaluations influence their future service careers.

The truth is that all officer-students are evaluated now since they receive fitness reports for their school assignments. Normally these reports are drafted in rough form by the faculty adviser of each student's seminar group and signed by the school director. While this practice may provide insights into a student's character and ability, it can avoid judgment about whether the student learned anything from the curriculum. It also may be too dependent upon the relationship of the student and the faculty adviser, who may have idiosyncratic standards or value qualities not reflective of academic performance. True equity in evaluation requires that students be tested and tested often by the people who teach them and that these evaluations contribute to—indeed, dominate—the evaluation process that already exists. The problem is that the military college must feel confident in its faculty's ability to make such evaluations, that the faculty teach, know what they are teaching, and know whether their students have learned anything. No responsible officer believes that a student-officer's academic performance alone should determine fitness for promotion or high command. To assume, however, that intellectual ability is less important than character, connections, and field performance is to accept the preprofessional standards of nineteenth-century European armies and twentieth-century Third World forces.

In sum, the latest round of curriculum reform should not end the debate on PME. Although they should be cautious about applying all the analogs of civilian education, policymakers should insist that the debate continue within the services and that the nation's needs set the parameters for further change.

Research Notes and Selected Bibliography

Professionalization and Military Education

The relationship between professionalization and education may be examined in Magali Sarfatti Larson, *The Rise of Professionalism (Berkeley: University of California Press, 1977), and Allan R. Millett, Military Professionalism and Officership in America* (Columbus: Mershon Center, The Ohio State University, 1977). For the context of international security studies in general, see Gene M. Lyons and Louis Morton, *Schools for Strategy: Education and Research in National Security Affairs* (New York: Praeger, 1965), and Joseph S. Nye, Jr., "International Security Studies," in Joseph Kruzel, ed., *American Defense Annual, 1988–1989* (Lexington, Mass.: Lexington Books, 1988). For historical perspective on officer education, see especially John W. Masland and Laurence I. Radway, *Soldiers and Scholars: Military Education and National Policy* (Princeton: Princeton University Press, 1957), and Lawrence J. Korb, ed., *The System of Educating Military Officers in the U.S.* Occasional paper N. 9. (Pittsburgh: International Studies Association, 1976).

Precommissioning Education

The best place to start an examination of the service academies is John Lovell, *Neither Athens Nor Sparta? The American Service Academies in Transition* (Bloomington: Indiana University Press, 1979). For current U.S. Military Academy educational policies, we used a draft copy of the Superintendent's Annual Report for 1987, supplemented by "Academic Program, AY 1988–1998," 2 vols., and the annual statistical studies, "Characteristics of the Class of . . . ," for the classes of 1987–1991, furnished by Brigadier General Roy K. Flint, USA, Dean, USMA. For the U.S. Naval Academy, see U.S. Naval Academy *Catalog 1988–1989,* which we supplemented with information from the Registrar's Office for registration statistics. The Air Force Academy data are from two fact sheets, "Academics" (August 1988) and "Statistics" (June 1988). For the evolution of ROTC programs, see Gene M. Lyons and John W. Masland, *Education and Military Leadership: A Study of the R.O.T.C.* (Princeton: Princeton University Press, 1959). The material on the current programs comes from U.S. Army ROTC Cadet Command information pamphlet and statistics, supplemented by information from the command historian; U.S. Air Force, "What's New . . . in Air Force ROTC" (1988), supplemented by two fact sheets, "Air Force Reserve Officer Training Corps" (February 1987), and

"Air Force ROTC Contributions to the Nation" (August 1987); and Commander Naval Education and Training, "The Naval Reserve Officer Training Corps (ROTC) Program" (1987) and "1988 NROTC Situation Report" (October 1988). See also Committee on Government Operations, *Hearings,* "Problems in Administration of the Military Service Academies," 94th Cong. 2d sess., March 1976.

Intermediate and Senior-Level Education

Since 1986 the intermediate command and staff and senior-level (war) military colleges have provided information and analysis to three investigative bodies: Panel on Military Education (Skelton panel), House of Representatives Armed Services Committee; the Military Education Coordination Conference of the National Defense University; and Senior Military Schools Review Board (Dougherty board), Chairman of the Joint Chiefs of Staff. The exchange of documents has been so rapid and comprehensive—and we have drawn basic documents from all three groups as well as the schools themselves—that it is difficult to identify the recipient of the original report. Nevertheless, we have had access to the following college reports: USAC&GSC, "Joint and Combined Instruction Academic Year 1986–1987"; Marine Corps Command and Staff College, "Program of Instruction, 1987–1988" and "Analysis of Joint Instruction" (1987); Air Command and Staff College and Air War College, "A Curriculum Proposal" (1987); Armed Forces Staff College, "How the Armed Forces Staff College Focuses Its Curriculum on 'Jointness'" (1988); Air University, "Assessment of the Air War College Educational Experience" (March 18, 1987); Air University, "Talking Paper on Joint Matters Instruction at Air War College" (1987); Naval War College, "DOD Legislation and Curriculum Review" (November 4, 1986), and "Naval War College Curriculum Review" (1987); Industrial College of the Armed Forces, "Curriculum Analysis" (1987), and "ICAF Report to the MECC and General Dougherty Commission Regarding the Implication of the Goldwater-Nichols Legislation" (December 2, 1986); U.S. Army War College, "Army War College Joint Matters Curriculum Review (1st Revision)" (November 26, 1986); National War College, "Joint Matters in the NWC Curriculum" (December 2, 1986), and "National War College Curriculum" (1987).

We also drew important data and opinions from the testimony of many of the officers who appeared before the Skelton panel: Admiral William J. Crowe, USN, Chairman, JCS (August 11, 1988); General Russell E. Dougherty, USAF (Ret.) (February 2, 1988); Admiral James L. Holloway III, USN (Ret.) (February 2, 1988); General Alfred M. Gray, USMC, Commandant of the Marine Corps (July 12, 1988); Admiral Stansfield Turner, USN (Ret.) (December 9, 1987); Lieutenant General Truman Spangrud, USAF, Commander, Air University (March 18, 1988); Major General Harold W. Todd, USAF, Commander, Air War College (March 18, 1988); Brigadier General Frank E. Willis, USAF, Commandant, Air Command and Staff College (March 18, 1988); Rear Admiral Ronald J. Kurth, USN, President, Naval War College (May 16, 1988); Major General Howard D. Graves, USA, Commandant, Army War College (January 29, 1988); and Major General Gordon R. Sullivan, USA, Deputy Commandant, U.S. Army Command and General Staff College (January 20, 1988).

The Dougherty board findings are found in three key documents: General R. E. Dougherty, USAF (Ret.) to Admiral William J. Crowe, USN (May 7, 1987); Senior Military Schools Review Board, "The Report . . . on Recommendations to the Chairman of the Joint Chiefs of Staff Regarding Professional Military Education in Joint Matters" (May 7, 1987); and "Executive Summary" (May 7, 1987), including responses of military major commanders to questionnaire on the senior service schools.

The work of the Military Education Coordinating Committee (Hosmer committee) may be assessed from the following internal documents: National Defense University, memorandum for the Director, Joint Staff, "Meeting of the Military Education Coordinating Conference (MECC) Review of Senior and Intermediate Service School Curricula" (January 30, 1987); "Accreditation of Service Colleges" (August 6, 1987); "Joint Educational Program" (September 28, 1987); and memorandum for Vice Chairman, JCS, "Educational Program and Specific Standards to Prepare Officers for Joint Duty and Joint Specialty Nomination" (September 28, 1987).

In addition to consulting its hearings, we profited from the following documents on the genesis, activities, and findings of the Skelton panel: House Armed Services Committee, "Armed Services Committee Panel" (February 2, 1987); memorandum for the record, meeting, Congressman Skelton and General Dougherty, (April 13, 1987); five speeches by Congressman Skelton on military strategy and officer education (October 6–November 19, 1987), *Congressional Record,* 100th Cong. 1st sess.; and "Executive Summary," Report of the Panel on Military Education of the Committee on Armed Services, House of Representatives, 100th Cong. 2d sess., Committee Print No. 27, November 18, 1988. Both authors testified before the panel in June 1988 and wish to thank Mark Smith and Arch Barrett, panel staff members, for their assistance. We did not see the Skelton Panel's excellent final "Report" (Committee on Armed Services, House of Representatives, Committee Print no. 4, 101st Congress, 1st sess., April 21, 1989. Washington, D.C.: U.S. Government Printing Office.) until after this chapter went to press.

We also consulted another DOD study: Eugene V. Rostow and John D. Endicott, "Teaching of Strategy and Foreign Policy at the Senior War Colleges: A Personal Assessment," Draft C (May 12, 1987), and final version (June 11, 1987), done for Fred C. Iklé, under secretary of defense for policy.

Joint Staff action on the cascading recommendations from the Dougherty board, the MECC and the Skelton panel have focused principally on the JPME issue. The National Defense University received its latest orders in Director, Joint Staff, memorandum, "JPME Planning Order" (September 21, 1988), which directed substantial changes in the National War College and Armed Forces Staff College. The National Defense University requested service assessment of the change in "Key Questions to Services" (October 1988).

For other assessments of advanced professional education in the armed forces and the issue of joint duty, see Major General Howard D. Graves, USA, "The U.S. Army War College: Gearing Up for the 21st Century," *Parameters* 18 (December 1988): 2–12; Lieutenant General Anthony Lukeman, USMC, "Joint Officer Management: Where We Stand," *Defense 88* (July–August 1988): 24–27; Colonel Norbert Majewski, FRG, and Lieutenant Colonel John H. Peyton, USA, "German Army General Staff Officer Training," *Military Review* 64 (December 1984): 23–34; Williamson Murray, "Grading the War Colleges," *National Interest,* no. 6 (Winter 1986–87): 12–19; and William V. Kennedy, "What Future for the Service War Colleges?" *Armed Forces Journal International* 125 No. 11 (June 1988): 16–17. For the history of two of the war colleges, see Colonel Harry P. Ball, USA (Ret.), *A Responsible Command: A History of the U.S. Army War College* (Carlisle, PA: Alumni Association of the Army War College, 1983), and John B. Hattendorf, B. Mitchell Simpson III, and John R. Wadleigh, *Sailors and Scholars: The Centennial History of the U.S. Naval War College* (Newport, RI: Naval War College Press, 1984).

General Dynamics F-16 Production
Facility, Ft. Worth, Texas

Chapter 12

The Military-Industrial Complex Revisited

James R. Kurth

T here is among American policymakers and policy analysts almost complete agreement about the need to reduce U.S. military spending. A new consensus on increasing détente has replaced that of the early 1980s on increasing defense, just as that consensus itself replaced the consensus of the early 1970s on increasing détente. In fact, there have been three full cycles of ebb and flow between defense and détente, between boom and bust in military spending, since the beginning of the cold war. In each cycle, the military buildup has brought about economic stresses and strains, which eventually dissolved the political consensus behind the buildup and replaced it with a new consensus on the need to reduce military spending and to reform military procurement.

The first military buildup was initiated in 1949 with NSC-68 and culminated during the Korean War. The second was initiated in 1961 with the doctrine of flexible response and culminated during the Indochinese War. And the third was initiated in 1979 with the strategic turnabout of the Carter administration and culminated during what was sometimes called the second cold war.[1]

The first reform movement was initiated by the Eisenhower administration in the late 1950s, particularly with the Defense Reorganization Act of 1958, and culminated in the Kennedy administration, with the efforts of Defense Secretary Robert McNamara to achieve more centralization. The second reform movement was jointly initiated by the Nixon administration and the Democratic Congress in 1969; it culminated in the efforts of Deputy Defense Secretary David Packard to bring more competition to weapons procurement (the so-called Packard Initiatives) and in the efforts of Congress to cancel a number of weapons programs. The third reform movement was initiated by Congress in the mid-1980s and culminated in the Defense Reorganization Act of 1986 (the Goldwater-Nichols Act), which like its predecessors also sought to bring about more centralization of the military services and more competition among defense contractors.[2]

Each of the three waves of defense reform has brought about an examination of the relations between the military services that buy the weapons systems and the defense corporations that produce them, a heightened discussion of the military-industrial complex. The term itself was first used by President Eisenhower in his farewell address in 1961, in the midst of the first reform wave.[3] In the second reform wave, the concept of the military-industrial complex appeared widely and frequently in public discourse, and there was a flood of books on the topic (which, as often happens, reached its height after the reform wave had already begun to recede).[4] It seems likely, then, that the third reform wave will bring about a renewal of public attention to the military-industrial complex. Indeed, excellent works analyzing the contemporary weapons procurement process and the relations between the military services and the defense industry have already begun to appear.[5]

It is useful to look again at these military-industrial relations with an eye to seeing what is new in the third reform era, the late 1980s, and what has remained largely the same since the time of the second reform era, the early 1970s. As we shall see, beneath the ebbs and flows between defense and détente, boom and bust, buildup and reform, there has remained a pattern of continuities, an enduring structure, in military-industrial relations.

Military-Industrial Relations: A Pattern of Continuities

In every reform era, writers on the defense industry have usually begun their analyses with a list of the top defense contractors, the corporations that each year receive the bulk of the Defense Department's (DOD) prime contract awards.

Current Top Defense Contractors

In fiscal year (FY) 1987, fifteen corporations each received more than $2 billion in prime contract awards from the Defense Department (table 12–1). Together they accounted for more than 40 percent of the prime contract awards that year. These corporations form the central core, the commanding heights, of the defense industry.

These fifteen corporations are a varied lot. Some are principally aerospace corporations, which have a particular emphasis on the production of aircraft and strategic missiles (McDonnell Douglas, Lockheed, Martin Marietta, Boeing, Grumman, Rockwell International); they are joined in aerospace production by General Dynamics, a more diversified defense firm, which also produces submarines and tanks. These seven corporations engage in the production of aircraft and strategic missiles. We should also consider Lockheed, normally one of the top three military contractors, as having two main military divisions, Lockheed-Missiles and Space, located in California, and Lockheed-Georgia. There are thus eight major aerospace production lines.

Table 12-1. Top Fifteen Companies Listed According to Net Value of Defense Department Prime Contract Awards, FY 1987

Rank	Companies	Billions
1	McDonnell Douglas Corp.	7.715
2	General Dynamics Corp.	7.040
3	General Electric Co.	5.801
4	Lockheed Corp.	5.573
5	General Motors Corp.	4.081
6	Raytheon Co.	3.819
7	Martin Marietta	3.726
8	United Technologies Corp	3.587
9	Boeing Co.	3.547
10	Grumman Corp.	3.392
11	Unisys Corp.	2.267
12	Rockwell International Corp.	2.237
13	Tenneco, Inc.	2.052
14	Litton Industries, Inc.	2.035
15	Honeywell, Inc.	2.007

Source: Department of Defense

In addition, two corporations produce almost all of the jet engines for aircraft (General Electric and United Technologies). There are two corporations whose principal defense work is in shipbuilding (Tenneco and Litton) and three corporations that are principally electronics firms (Raytheon, Unisys, and Honeywell).

Continuity of Top Contractors

The list of the top fifteen defense contractors has shown remarkable continuity over the years. The particular rank varies, of course, from one year to the next, but many of these corporations have been among the top fifteen defense contractors since World War II.[6]

The pattern of continuity is most pronounced with the corporations producing aircraft or jet engines. Six of the aerospace manufacturers and the two engine manufacturers have been producing U.S. military aircraft since World War II. Indeed seven of these corporations (under their current or former names) have been among the top fifteen defense contractors almost every year for nearly half a century. These are McDonnell Douglas, Lockheed, Boeing, Rockwell International (formerly North American), General Dynamics (formerly Consolidated-Vultee), General Motors, and United Technologies (formerly United Aircraft).

The relative newcomers to the list are the electronics firms that began to enter into the top fifteen defense contractors in the late 1950s. Their contracts have steadily increased relative to other firms as the role of electronics in aircraft, missiles, ships, and land combat has increased. Conversely, with the exception of General Motors, the giants of heavy industry that played so big a role in World War II (Ford, Chrysler, Bethlehem Steel) largely left the ranks of the top contractors by the late 1950s.

There has thus been a series of special relationships between a particular military service and a particular aerospace corporation.

Continuity of Service Affinity

Six of the eight aerospace production lines have had a continuous contracting relationship with one military service, one that has lasted over several decades, in most cases back to World War II. The corporations that have sold almost exclusively to the Air Force have been Boeing, Rockwell, and the aerospace division of General Dynamics. Conversely Grumman has sold almost exclusively to the Navy. Within Lockheed, the Lockheed-Georgia division has sold almost exclusively to the Air Force, and the Lockheed-Missiles and Space Division has sold similarly to the Navy. There has thus been a series of special relationships between a particular military service and a particular aerospace corporation. These might be seen as a series of military-industrial duplexes within the overall military-industrial complex.

There are some exceptions to this pattern of military-industrial monogamy. McDonnell Douglas has been successful in selling aircraft to both the Air Force and the Navy, and Martin Marietta has sold missiles to both the Air Force and the Army.

Continuity of Product Specialties

A third dimension of continuity since World War II relates to aerospace products. Most of the producers have been engaged in the same type of weapons system, the same product specialty, for several decades.

The continuity is especially pronounced with Boeing, which has produced first strategic bombers and then intercontinental ballistic missiles (ICBMs) and air-launched cruise missiles (ALCMs), beginning with the B-17 Flying Fortress of World War II (B-17, B-29, B-47, B-50, B-52, Minuteman, Minuteman III, ALCM, MX subcontract). A similar continuity exists with Lockheed-Missiles and Space, which has produced submarine-launched ballistic missiles (SLBMs) from their origin (Polaris, Poseidon, Trident I, Trident II); Lockheed-Georgia, which has produced military transports (C-130, C-141, C-5A, C-5B); and McDonnell Douglas, which has produced fighters (F-101, F-4, F-15, F/A-18).

Several firms shifted their product specialty during the 1950s from one type of aircraft to another. General Dynamics (originally Consolidated-Vultee) produced the B-24 Liberator of World War II and the giant B-36 of the early cold war but then shifted to smaller bombers and fighters (B-24, B-36, F-106, B-58, F-111, F-16). Rockwell International (originally North American) moved in the opposite direction at about the same time. It first produced the P-51 Mustang of World War II and the F-86 Sabrejet of the Korean War but in the late 1950s shifted to bombers and spacecraft (P-51, F-86, F-100, B-70, Apollo space program, space shuttle, B-1A, B-1B).

These continuities in regard to major contractors, service affinities, and product specialties indicate a certain structure to U.S. weapons procurement and to the relations between military services and aerospace corporations. This structure has endured for several decades, in some cases dating back to World War II, despite the ebbs and flows, the booms and busts, in defense spending.

When these continuities are considered together, they can also suggest answers to some common questions about U.S. weapons procurement: why some weapons systems are bought rather than others, why a particular contractor is chosen rather than another, why a weapons system is bought at a particular time rather than another, and why it is so difficult to control the costs of weapons systems.

Military-Industrial Relations: The Follow-on Imperative

Let us look in more detail at the relations between two variables: aerospace systems that are military or military related (military aircraft, missiles, and space systems) and aerospace corporations or production lines that produce such systems.

We can chart the major military aerospace systems according to the production line to which the DOD, or the National Aeronautics and Space Administration (NASA) in the case of space systems, awarded the contract and according to the years when major development or production phased in or out.[7] Some interesting patterns result (table 12–2).

About the time a production line phases out of one major defense contract, it phases in production of a new one, usually within a year. Since new aerospace systems require a considerable period of development before production, the production line normally is awarded the contract for the new system about three years before production of the old one is scheduled to phase out. In most cases, the new contract is for a system that is structurally similar although technically superior to the system being phased out; the new contract is what is known in the industry as a follow-on contract.

A large and established aerospace production line is a national resource; at least this is how it is seen by most top civilian officials and military officers. The aerospace

Table 12-2. The Follow-on Imperative:
Major Production Lines and Military Aerospace Systems

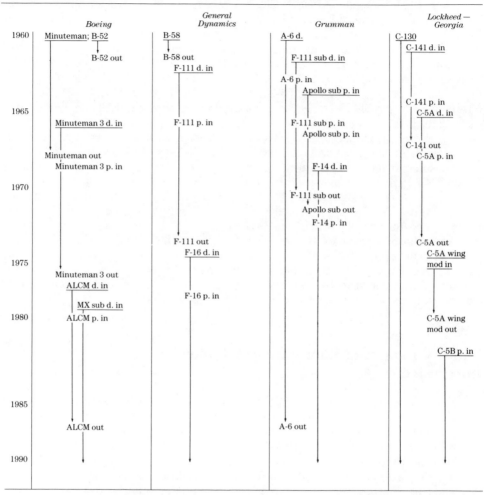

	Boeing	*General Dynamics*	*Grumman*	*Lockheed — Georgia*
1960	Minuteman; B-52	B-58	A-6 d.	C-130 / C-141 d. in
	B-52 out	B-58 out / F-111 d. in	F-111 sub d. in / A-6 p. in / Apollo sub p. in	
1965	Minuteman 3 d. in	F-111 p. in	F-111 sub p. in / Apollo sub p. in	C-141 p. in / C-5A d. in
	Minuteman out / Minuteman 3 p. in		F-14 d. in	C-141 out / C-5A p. in
1970			F-111 sub out / Apollo sub out / F-14 p. in	
1975	Minuteman 3 out / ALCM d. in	F-111 out / F-16 d. in		C-5A out / C-5A wing mod in
	MX sub d. in	F-16 p. in		
1980	ALCM p. in			C-5A wing mod out
				C-5B p. in
1985				
	ALCM out		A-6 out	
1990				

d = development; p = production

Martin Marietta has several diverse production lines, producing a variety of weapons systems. It became a top defense contractor in

corporation's managers, shareholders, bankers, engineers, and workers enthusiastically agree, as do the area's representatives and senators. The Defense Department would find it risky and even reckless to allow a large production line to wither and die for lack of a large production contract.

The reluctance to allow a production line to disappear is especially pronounced because for each type of aircraft (large bombers, fighters and fighter-bombers, military transports), there are actually only a few potential production lines. Large bombers

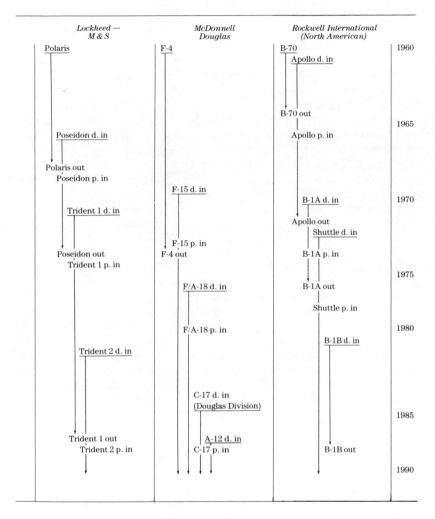

Lockheed — M & S	McDonnell Douglas	Rockwell International (North American)	
Polaris	F-4	B-70	1960
		Apollo d. in	
		B-70 out	1965
Poseidon d. in		Apollo p. in	
Polaris out Poseidon p. in			
	F-15 d. in	B-1A d. in	1970
Trident 1 d. in		Apollo out	
		Shuttle d. in	
	F-15 p. in	B-1A p. in	
Poseidon out Trident 1 p. in	F-4 out		1975
	F/A-18 d. in	B-1A out	
		Shuttle p. in	
	F/A-18 p. in		1980
		B-1B d. in	
Trident 2 d. in			
	C-17 d. in (Douglas Division)		1985
Trident 1 out Trident 2 p. in	A-12 d. in C-17 p. in	B-1B out	
			1990

the 1980s as the primary contractor for MX and Pershing 2.

have been competed for and produced only by Rockwell, Boeing, and in recent years a smaller firm, Northrop. Fighters and fighter-bombers have been competed for and produced only by General Dynamics, the McDonnell division of McDonnell Douglas, Grumman, and Northrop; and military transports only by Lockheed-Georgia, Boeing, and the Douglas division of McDonnell Douglas.[8]

Consequently there has been pressure on the Defense Department from many diverse sources to award a new major contract to a production line when an old major contract is phasing out. Further, the disruption of the production line will be least and the efficiency of the product would seem highest if the new contract is structurally similar to the old; that is, it is a follow-on contract. Such a contract renovates both the large and established aerospace corporation that produces the weapons system and the military organization that deploys it—that is, both halves of the military-industrial duplex.

This constraint, or rather compulsion, imposed on weapons procurement by industrial structure can be called the follow-on imperative and can be contrasted with the official imperative. The official imperative for weapons procurement can be phrased as follows: if strategic considerations determine that a military service needs a new weapons system, it will solicit bids from several competing companies; ordinarily the service will award the contract to the company with the most cost-effective design. The follow-on imperative is rather different: if one of the major production lines is opening up, it will receive a new major contract from a military service (or from NASA); ordinarily the new contract will be structurally similar to the old (a follow-on contract).

The follow-on imperative can perhaps explain the production line and the product structure of sixteen of the twenty major aerospace contracts awarded between 1960 and 1988: (1) Minuteman III follow-on to Minuteman; (2) MX subcontract follow-on to Minuteman 3; (3) Poseidon follow-on to Polaris; (4) Trident I follow-on to Poseidon; (5) Trident II follow-on to Trident I; (6) C-141 follow-on to C-130; (7) C-5A follow-on to C-141; (8) C-5B follow-on to C-5A; (9) F-14 follow-on to F-111 major subcontract; (10) F-15 follow-on to F-4; (11) F/A-18 follow-on to F-15; (12) F-111 after B-58 (superficially a less certain case, but the two planes were structurally similar, with the F-111 being a relatively large fighter-bomber and the B-58 being a relatively small bomber); (13) F-16 follow-on to F-111; (14) space shuttle follow-on to Apollo moon program; (15) B-1A delayed follow-on to B-70; (16) B-1B follow-on to B-1A. And in regard to another contract, Apollo, North American (the former name of Rockwell International) might have been predicted to receive the award since it was already NASA's largest contractor. The three remaining contracts (the B-2 bomber, the A-12 advanced tactical aircraft, and the C-17 military transport) do not fit the follow-on pattern. These were all awarded in the 1980s and will be examined in detail.

The imperatives of the industrial structure are reinforced, not surprisingly, by the imperatives of the political system. Four of the major production lines are located in states that loom large in the Electoral College: California (Rockwell and Lockheed-Missiles and Space), Texas (General Dynamics), and New York (Grumman). Three others are located in states that for many years had a senator who ranked high in the Senate Armed Services Committee or Appropriations Committee: Washington (Boeing; Henry Jackson), Georgia (Lockheed-Georgia; first Richard Russell and then Sam Nunn), and Missouri (McDonnell division of McDonnell Douglas; Stuart Symington). And Texas benefited both from its weight in the Electoral College and from John Tower's tenure on the Senate Armed Services Committee.

It might be said that one should naturally expect most contracts to be follow-on contracts. Production of the original system should give an aerospace corporation a competitive edge in technical expertise that will win for it the next system awarded in the same production sector. But in at least three major cases in the 1960s, the Source Selection Board chose, on technical grounds, a different corporation from the one already producing a similar system; the contract became a follow-on contract only when the board was overruled by higher officials. With the F-111, the original, technical choice was Boeing rather than General Dynamics; with the C-5A, it was Boeing rather than Lockheed; and with Apollo, it was Martin rather than North American.[9]

More important, it is not always obvious that there should be any new version at all of an old type of weapons system. This is especially the case because of the evolution of the different types of systems over the past two decades. Most weapons systems and follow-on contracts are becoming progressively more complex and expensive. Consequently, in some cases there are good arguments that a mission could be performed just as well and at a cheaper cost with a different type of weapons system altogether. In particular, it is not obvious that manned bombers are more cost-effective than cruise missiles. Some types of weapons systems are also becoming progressively more destabilizing and dangerous from a strategic perspective. This is particularly the case with ballistic missiles (the first-strike capabilities of Minuteman III, MX, and Trident II).

B-1 and B-2: A Tale of Two Bombers

Of all the cases of weapons procurement, the ones that have been the most consistently controversial over the past several decades have concerned the manned bomber. It will be useful and illuminating to discuss the procurement of these aircraft in detail.

Bombers versus Spacecraft: Rockwell International and the Two Follow-on Sequences

For most of the period since 1960, procurement of a manned bomber has meant procurement from Rockwell International. But Rockwell has also been the principal contractor for the space program. Rockwell has thus oscillated between two follow-on sequences: one for bombers (B-70, B-1A, B-1B) and one for space (Apollo, space shuttle).

The reason for this oscillation lies in the controversial nature of the manned bomber. On the one hand, there are ample military and industrial forces pushing for the continued procurement of this kind of weapons system. First, within the Air Force, the bomber generals have been dominant since World War II; they have ridden the bomber first to heroic purpose and then to bureaucratic power. Second, within the defense industry, Rockwell has always been one of the most important contractors economically in southern California and politically in Congress.

On the other hand, since the deployment of ICBMs and SLBMs a quarter-century ago, the strategic argument for the manned bomber has always been vulnerable, in part because bombers have appeared less cost-effective than missiles and in part because the bomber itself has been vulnerable to the Soviet air defenses of the time. Thus, when the Soviets shot down the U-2 in 1960, they also shot down the reasons for the high-flying B-70. Consequently Defense Secretary McNamara soon canceled B-70 procurement. Similarly, when the Soviets deployed look-down radars in the mid-1970s they also brought down the reasons for the low-flying B-1A. It became evident that by the time the new B-1 was deployed, it would be about as obsolete as the first B-1 of the 1920s. Consequently President Carter soon canceled B-1A procurement.

B-70 or Apollo

In each case, however, cancellation came at the cost of compensation. In the case of the B-70, as an account by Arthur Schlesinger suggests, the Air Force and its allies in Congress had to be compensated for the cancellation of the bomber with a massive missile buildup, with its attendant costs of a corresponding Soviet buildup and an arms race.[10] Second, as the follow-on imperative suggests, North American (the former name of Rockwell) had to be compensated for the cancellation of the B-70 with another major contract, in this case the Apollo moon program.

The B-2 (Stealth) bomber is probably the most dramatic weapons system of the 1980s; it is certainly the most expensive airplane in history.

B-1 or Space Shuttle

The case of the B-1A replayed this story fifteen years later. First, the Air Force and its allies again had to be compensated for the cancellation of their bomber by the procurement of a new missile, the MX. Second, Rockwell had to be compensated for the cancellation of its B-1A contract with another major contract, in this case for more space shuttles. In any event, cancellation of the B-1 was only temporary. When the Reagan administration took office, it immediately revived the program, this time as the B-1B, a modestly improved version of the B-1A.[11]

Finally, when production of the B-1B was completed in 1988, Rockwell was due by the follow-on imperative for a new bomber contract. However, the contract for the next manned bomber, the B-2 or Stealth, had already been awarded to another production line in southern California, Northrop. Consequently Rockwell has again been compensated for the absence of a bomber contract with expanded contracts for the space shuttle program.

B-2 or Not B-2? Northrop and the California Miracle

The B-2 (Stealth) bomber is probably the most dramatic weapons system of the 1980s; it is certainly the most expensive airplane in history (expected to cost $516 million apiece). The builder, Northrop, normally has received so few DOD contracts that it has rarely been in the top fifteen prime contractors. It spent most of the quarter-century from 1950 to 1975 producing simple and cheap fighters (the F-5 series) for sale abroad, principally to Third World air forces. Why did such an unlikely candidate receive such a spectacular award?

The most obvious explanation is a political one. The Reagan administration was the first truly Californian administration in U.S. history. At one time (1982–1983), the president, the secretary of defense, the secretary of state, the national security adviser, and the White House chief of staff came from California, and from 1982 to 1987 the first three did so. This was a considerably greater representation of Californians than served with Richard Nixon, an earlier Californian president. Consequently it is not surprising that California aerospace firms might have been given favorable attention. By awarding the space shuttles to Rockwell and the B-2 to Northrop, California contracts—and contacts—were maximized.

Still, followers of the follow-on imperative were not surprised when it was finally revealed that the Stealth bomber contract had been awarded to Northrop. It had been Northrop that in the early 1940s had developed and produced the most stealthy U.S. airplane of World War II, the famous night fighter, the P-61 Black Widow. Nor were they surprised a few years later when it was finally revealed that in order to be stealthy, the B-2 bomber shape was to be a flying wing. It had been Northrop that in the late 1940s had developed and produced the only previous U.S. flying-wing airplanes, including the infamous (it was prone to crashing) bomber, the B-49. As it turns out, the wing spans of the two flying wings, the B-49 of 1948 and the B-2 of 1988, are precisely the same length (172 feet).[12]

C-17: Douglas and Another California Miracle

The California preference of the Reagan administration, which may have been a factor in the B-2 contract, probably explains another decision even better. In 1984, DOD awarded the development contract for a new military transport, the C-17, to the Douglas division of McDonnell Douglas. As we have seen, military transports have been produced for many years by Lockheed-Georgia, and the Douglas division had not had any major defense contract since the early 1970s. To deny Lockheed-Georgia a contract for the new military transport while giving it to Douglas, all this while Sam Nunn was the ranking minority member of the Senate Armed Services Committee, was indeed something of a miraculous achievement. In 1984, however, Lockheed-Georgia was busy building the C-5B. In any event, the Douglas division was located in southern California.[13]

The Anomaly of the ATA: A Tale of High Intrigue

The biggest single exception to the follow-on pattern occurred only in the late 1980s. The follow-on imperative would have predicted that the Navy would award the contract for its advanced tactical aircraft (ATA), a fighter-bomber or attack aircraft that will replace the A-6, to Grumman, which produces that aircraft as well as the F-14. Production of both the A-6 and the F-14 was due to phase out in the early 1990s. Further, Grumman has been the primary Navy contractor for half a century, with a distinguished line of carrier aircraft dating back to the F6F Hellcat of World War II. Instead, on Christmas Eve 1987, the Navy announced that the ATA or A-12 contract had been won by a team of McDonnell Douglas and General Dynamics. McDonnell Douglas already had contracts for many more years of production for the Navy's F/A-18 (as well as several years for the Air Force's F-15). Similarly General Dynamics had contracts for many more years of production of the Air Force's F-16.

It is possible, of course, that the technical merits of the McDonnell Douglas–General Dynamics proposal were simply superior to that of Grumman and its teammates of Northrop and LTV. As we have seen, there have been other cases (for example, the F-111, C-5A) when the follow-on firm did not submit the most cost-effective bid.

There is another possible explanation, however. It is an explanation that may be developed not by source selection boards but by courts of law. Six months after the ATA award, it became public that U.S. attorneys and the Federal Bureau of Investigation were investigating possible corruption in connection with billions of dollars of weapons contracts. This became the Pentagon procurement scandal. The inquiry centered on the Navy more than on other military services and on McDonnell Douglas more than on other defense contractors.[14]

Of all the DOD officials who were targets of the investigation, the most prominent was Melvyn Paisley, who had overseen Navy weapons procurement from 1981 to 1987. The leading industry journal, *Aviation Week and Space Technology,* reported that the FBI was looking at "Paisley's efforts to steer" the ATA program to McDonnell Douglas:[15]

> Government documents indicate that while he was assistant Navy secretary for research, engineering and systems, Paisley attempted to ensure that McDonnell Douglas, which later became his client, and General Dynamics won the contract to build 450 A-12 advanced tactical aircraft. They beat the team of Grumman, Northrop and LTV. . . . The initial A-12 contract went for $4.4 billion. Its potential value is in excess of $35 billion.[16]

The Dilemma of the ATF: A Tale of Two Services and Two Teams

At the beginning of 1989, only one planned major weapons program had not yet been awarded to a particular contractor: the advanced tactical fighter (ATF), intended to be the next generation of high-performance fighters and the successor to the Air Force's F-15 and the Navy's F-14. In an effort to increase efficiency and reduce costs, Congress mandated that each of the two services should expect to buy a version of the same basic aircraft; there should be enough commonality in the product so that each service can use it.

Commonality has had a checkered history. Certainly one of the most successful aircraft of the past three decades, the McDonnell F-4 Phantom, began as a Navy fighter and then, under the direction of Defense Secretary Robert McNamara, was also adopted by the Air Force. But one of the most controversial aircraft of the 1960s, the F-111, began as an Air Force fighter and then, again under direction of McNamara, was ordered by the Navy. But the Navy always resisted this intrusion, even when its principal contractor, Grumman, was given the main subcontract for the airplane. In the end, the F-111 never did become a Navy airplane. It seems that commonality was a one-way street, leading from the Navy to the Air Force but not the reverse. A senior Navy official remarked about the possibilities for the ATF, "It is relatively easy for the Air Force to take a Navy airplane and use it, but it is a lot tougher problem for the Navy to employ an Air Force airplane."[17]

Two teams of aerospace corporations are competing for the ATF contract: one composed of McDonnell Douglas and Northrop and the other composed of Lockheed, Boeing, and General Dynamics. The Air Force will select one of the two teams to begin full-scale development in 1991, with procurement of 750 ATF aircraft scheduled to begin in 1993 and the first aircraft entering the combat inventory in 1995 or 1996.[18]

What can one predict about the ATF contract? The technical features of the ATF appear to be indeterminate. On the one hand, it will be the successor to the F-15, suggesting that McDonnell Douglas would have an edge. And it is supposed to be a stealth fighter, which is probably why Northrop (the producer of the stealth bomber) is included in the team. On the other hand, Lockheed has been the producer of the Air Force's small number of experimental stealth fighters (including the YF-19) for many years. More generally, each of the five contractors in the competition has long-established and solid relations with the Air Force.

The decisive consideration will not be technical but political. Which will need the contract? Here the advantage is clearer. Because McDonnell Douglas received the ATA or A-12 contract (never mind how), it does not need the ATF; and because Northrop received the B-2 contract, it does not need the ATF either. One of these firms would need the ATF only if Congress either took away the A-12 because of the scandal or it canceled the B-2 because of the cost. Then the ATF contract might be awarded as compensation. The first possibility appears rather unlikely:

> Senate Armed Services Committee Chairman Sam Nunn (D.–Ga.) voiced the concern that for national security purposes and the amount of money involved, the Defense Department cannot afford to halt major contracts even if they were won illegally. During a hearing, he asked Defense Secretary Frank Carlucci if a banking analogy fit.
>
> "If you're a small bank you can fail," Nunn said. "But if you're a big bank you can't be allowed to fail?"
>
> "It's a possibility," Carlucci answered.[19]

On the other hand, with the completion of C-5A production, Lockheed needs a new major contract;[20] and with the completion of ALCM production, Boeing also may need a new major contract (although it now has a five-year backlog in its commercial aircraft division). Of course, neither the Lockheed-Georgia plant nor Boeing has ever produced a fighter. But General Dynamics has done so (the F-111 and F-16), which is probably why it has been included in the team. The resulting airplane prototype or proposal will likely be a combination of General Dynamics fighter technology, Lockheed stealth technology, and Boeing avionics technology. It will be a rather baroque or even bizarre contraption, but it will probably get the contract award.

What about the Navy? Congress has said that the Navy should buy a version of the Air Force's ATF, whatever that should turn out to be, but the Navy, in this case as earlier, will be reluctant. This describes the Navy's current thinking:

> Congress has increasingly insisted on more commonality between new Air Force and Navy aircraft. But shrinking budget resources have pushed the services toward the less costly alternative of upgrading existing aircraft instead of developing new ones.[21]

The military services continue to pay out vast sums to the defense contractors, but they get fewer and fewer weapons in return.

And what about Grumman? Because it was so confident of receiving the ATA contract (the follow-on practice gave it every reason to be so), it did not compete for the ATF. Consequently it is now shut out of both of the biggest new projects of the 1990s.

For both the Navy and Grumman, there is an obvious solution, one that would kill two birds with one stone:

> The Navy is studying a Grumman proposal to upgrade the F-14D into the Tomcat 21 as a possible solution to conflicting pressures for more commonality in military fighters and growing funding constraints.
>
> Grumman's Tomcat 21 proposal is being considered as an alternative to procuring a Navy version of the Air Force's advanced tactical fighter (ATF).
>
> One high-ranking Navy official said the proposal "looks attractive."
>
> "It was more than just a sales pitch," another senior service official said. "It's definitely something we should chew over."[22]

In summary, it appears that the Air Force may get an advanced tactical fighter whose advances will include an unprecedented conglomeration of diverse contractors. And it appears that the Navy may get an advanced tactical fighter whose advances will consist of upgrading an airplane that first flew a generation ago.

Military-Industrial Relations amid Three Secular Declines

Since the beginning of the cold war there have been three cycles of defense and détente, but beneath this ebb and flow there has been a structure of enduring relations between the military services and the defense industry.

Decline in the Number of Weapons Platforms

There has, however, been one crucial change in the exchange between the services and defense industry, and it is a well-known and much-lamented one: the military services continue to pay out vast sums to the defense contractors, but they get fewer and fewer weapons in return. In the 1950s the normal number of a particular aircraft purchased was several thousand; it is now several hundred. Aircraft manufacture has moved from mass production to customized production. It is not exactly that the services are getting less bang for the buck; each airplane carries many high-yield tactical missiles, and most strategic missiles carry many high-yield warheads. But they are certainly getting fewer weapons platforms for the buck and are therefore putting more eggs in fewer baskets.[23]

The increase in the unit cost of weapons systems and the decline in numbers deployed would not in themselves be enough to destabilize the structure of military-industrial relations. If anything, the small numbers of customized weapons produced by any one contractor make it all the more necessary to maintain a large number of contractors and production lines, at least as long as there is enough money to pay them.

It is this overall amount of money, the federal funds available for military spending, that is now in question, and more so than at any other time since the beginning of the cold war. The military services are only a part of the larger U.S. government, and the defense industry is only a part of the larger U.S. economy. Each of these larger contexts has undergone a massive secular change in the last four decades. And these changes have made the problems of defense spending progressively more severe and the opposition to defense spending progressively more widespread.

Decline of the Defense Budget Relative to the Federal Budget

First, the share of the defense budget within the overall federal budget has undergone a steady decline; there has been a massive increase in federal spending on nondefense programs since the 1950s. On the eve of World War II federal spending on nondefense programs was only 7 percent of the gross national product (GNP), and on the eve of the Korean War it was 11 percent of GNP. Beginning in the mid-1950s, however, spending on these programs (which include support for transportation, agriculture, energy, and education as well as social security, Medicare, and welfare) steadily increased until by 1981 they had reached 17 percent of GNP. During the Reagan administration, federal spending on some social programs declined, but interest payments on the federal debt increased, leaving nondefense spending at a level of 18 percent of GNP.[24]

These increases in nondefense federal spending reflect fundamental shifts in the structure of the American economy and the structure of the American population, and they are supported by powerful political constituencies. This means that military spending must be added to a federal budget, a federal tax burden, and a federal deficit that are already very high compared to the situations in World War II, the Korean War, or even the Indochinese War. Increases in defense spending now affect a wide range of diverse interest groups that are represented more directly and have greater influence in Congress than in any particular presidential administration. Consequently it is Congress that has taken the lead in the third and most recent wave of defense spending cuts and defense procurement reform.

Decline of American Industry Relative to Foreign Industry

Although the defense industry remains one of the largest industries in the U.S. economy and one of the largest sources of U.S. exports abroad, American industry overall now faces intense and effective competition in the world market, resulting in annual U.S. balance of trade deficits on the order of $150 billion.

This, too, is the result of a secular decline over the past four decades. In the 1940s and the 1950s, the United States was extraordinarily competitive in the world market. Virtually anything it produced, it could sell. In part this was the result of World War II, which had destroyed most U.S. industrial competitors. But it was also in part the result of an American monopoly in high-technology industries and American productivity in lower-technology ones. The United States had a handsome surplus in its balance of trade, which could finance large-scale expenditures on U.S. military forces stationed on the territory of allies, such as West Germany, Britain, Italy, and Japan. A productive and competitive economy with high employment also provided a healthy base for federal taxes and federal spending. In such a happy condition, the United States could maintain a vast system of military alliances and spend 10 percent of its GNP on defense. In the slogan of the Eisenhower administration, "peace and prosperity," the former was underwritten by the latter.

These conditions of peace and prosperity among U.S. European and Japanese allies led first to the rebuilding of their old industries (textiles, steel, shipbuilding, chemicals) and then to the building of new ones (automobiles, electronics). These new or renewed industries had "the advantages of backwardness" in their production processes—that is, lower wages and higher technology than their American counterparts. This led in the 1960s and 1970s to the erosion of American competitiveness in the world market, successively in textiles, steel, shipbuilding, automobiles, and finally even electronics.[25] It had been U.S. superiority in these industries, along with the aviation industry, that had been the basis for the American victory in World War II.

At about the same time, in the 1950s and 1960s, the Soviet Union also developed its own formidable industries devoted to military production. It especially emphasized the production of tanks and tactical aircraft, those winning weapons in the land battles of World War II.

Military Allies and Industrial Adversaries

Had the allies of the United States built up their own militaries, at the rate that they were building up their industries, some of the U.S. strategic and economic problems of the 1980s would have been solved or indeed might never have arisen. But the allies did not do this. Indeed there developed by the 1970s a rough inverse correlation between military spending as a percentage of GNP and industrial competitiveness in the world market. A continuum went from high military spending and low market competitiveness to low military spending and high market competitiveness, in a sequence composed of the United States, Britain, France, West Germany, and Japan. This ranking remains largely the same today. But the high military spending of the United States compared to its allies was not the only reason for declining American competitiveness. A large number of other factors were at work too, including the advantages of backwardness.

By the 1970s, U.S. military allies in world politics had become U.S. industrial adversaries in the world market. The allies were undercutting the economic base of the U.S. military defense of them. And with the consequent rise of protectionist pressures in the United States, they were undercutting the political base of the alliance with them. The economic and political bases of U.S. military commitments were being hollowed out by the relentless workings of the world market.[26]

Some economists believe that this process of military spending debilitating commercial competitiveness was aggravated in the 1980s by the Reagan administration's military buildup. The buildup drew engineers and other technical personnel, already in short supply, away from American civilian industries, at the very time that they were needed to maintain these industries or to develop new ones if the United States is to continue to compete in the world market.[27]

THE SPIRIT OF '88   Conrad
Los Angeles Times

Copyright 1988, Los Angeles Times. Reprinted with permission.

The Reform Proposals of the 1980s

The three secular declines have provided the basis in the 1980s for several different programs for the reform of U.S. weapons procurement.

Simpler, Cheaper, and More: The Quality of Quantity

The first problem addressed was the rise in the unit cost of weapons and the decline in the numbers procured. In the early 1980s, there was considerable discussion among some younger Democrats in Congress and some former members of the Carter administration about a different conception of the quality of weapons systems than that which had been prevalent for many years. They believed that most U.S. weapons systems had become so expensive and so complicated that they could no longer be deployed with the numbers, flexibility, and reliability necessary to make them effective in combat. The alternative, it was argued, was to procure greater numbers of less expensive and less complicated systems, such as five F-5s instead of one F-15, four simple tanks instead of one M-1, and two medium aircraft carriers instead of one nuclear-powered supercarrier. As Lenin once observed, "Quantity has a quality all its own." The congressional advocates of this view formed the Military Reform Caucus; their program was "simpler, cheaper, and more." They argued that this procurement reform would result in U.S. conventional forces that would be more effective and more credible.[28]

The program of the quantitative reformers was never adopted by the Reagan administration or even by Congress, and there seemed little likelihood that it would be pursued by the Bush administration. But even if this procurement reform were adopted and were successful in restoring the effectiveness and credibility of U.S. conventional forces, it would not significantly ease the economic stresses and strains. First, it is quite likely that greater numbers of cheaper weapons would still add up to total defense expenditures that would be equivalent to expenditures for the current program of fewer numbers of costly weapons. The economic burden of the defense budget would not really be reduced but would merely be reproduced. Second, this procurement reform would not ease the problems of American industry in the world market. There would still remain the deficit in the U.S. balance of trade and the pressures within the United States for protective trade barriers against West European and Japanese products, and these factors would continue to erode the economic and political bases of U.S. military alliances.

Waste, Fraud, and Abuse: Reform as Reorganization

The next problem addressed was the fiscal burden of military spending. By the mid-1980s, there had developed a broad consensus in Congress on the need to cap or even cut military and other federal spending; this issued in the Gramm-Rudman-Hollings Act of 1985. In addition, some conservative members of Congress sought to reorganize weapons procurement; they wanted to increase centralization within the Defense Department and to increase competition within the defense industry; this issued in the Goldwater-Nichols Act. And as in every other reform era, there was heightened congressional focus on "waste, fraud, and abuse"; this issued in an extensive series of congressional investigations and hearings.

The potential for this reform program is the reverse of the first. Even if the reorganization reformers were successful in easing the economic burden of the defense budget, their program would not significantly increase the effectiveness and credibility of U.S. military forces.

SDI, MITI, and EDI: Defense Policy as Industrial Policy

The third problem, the decline in the competitiveness of American industry, has not generated a defense reform movement with a program directly addressed to the issue. There are, however, two indirect approaches. Some advocates of cutting military spending see hope that this will also reduce the tax burden on American industry and free up a supply of engineers and other technical personnel for commercial production and exports. And some advocates of the Strategic Defense Initiative (SDI) hope that it can also serve as an American version of the industrial policies of foreign competitors, such as Japan. With the research and development contracts for SDI, the Defense Department can bring into being innovations that will have commercial applications and therefore new industries that will restore the U.S. lead in the world market. This would be similar to what the Defense Department did for aviation in the 1940s and 1950s, for computers in the 1950s, and for semiconductors in the 1960s. In this view, SDI is the American equivalent of MITI (Japan's Ministry of International Trade and Industry), and SDI is also EDI, an economic defense initiative.

Even if SDI should help solve the third problem, however, it does not do much for the first or the second. As a strategic defense initiative, it is addressed to nuclear deterrence, not to conventional defense. And it promises to add greatly to the economic burden of military spending, not subtract from it.

Precision-Guided Munitions and a Battlefield Copernican Revolution

There is, however, one reform proposal with the potential to address simultaneously all three problems. Some defense analysts advocate a much greater focus upon conventional weapons systems based on emerging technologies (ET) and competitive strategies. Most of these would be some type of precision-guided munitions (PGMs).

The advocates of PGMs argue that a military strategy based on them would provide both a more effective and a much cheaper conventional defense of such regions as Western Europe and the Persian Gulf than one based upon tanks and tactical aircraft. And they argue that it would provide a far less risky and reckless defense than one based upon tactical nuclear weapons and "limited nuclear war."[29]

These are controversial propositions. Historically, new weapons systems have been used first as merely extensions of old, established systems. The airplane was first used as a reconnaissance vehicle to improve the accuracy of artillery, and the tank was first used as a pathbreaker to ease the advance of infantry. It is not surprising that many current PGMs are deployed on, and are extensions of, tactical aircraft and tanks. And it is not surprising too that such combination systems are even more expensive than the aircraft and tanks they replace.

It is possible, however, that new generations of PGMs will become the center of whole new configurations of weapons systems rather than merely the extension, the periphery, of old configurations centered on the airplane or the tank. In an earlier, analogous case, the aircraft carrier displaced the battleship from the center to the periphery of naval operations in 1941. But unlike the carrier task force, the new configuration of PGMs probably would be able to take advantage of the economies of mass production, increasing returns to scale, and learning curves so characteristic of the semiconductor, computer, and telecommunications industries, which provide the industrial base for PGMs.

If such a Copernican revolution in weapons systems should occur that would place PGMs in the center of the automated battlefield, it could bring about fundamental changes in American military strategy and industrial competitiveness. The United States could be in a better position than any other military or industrial power to excel in the production, deployment, and operation of the new weapons systems. A military strategy centered upon PGMs might at last provide a feasible conventional defense for Western Europe and the Persian Gulf against the Soviet advantage in tactical aircraft and in tanks. And successive generations of automated battlefields might provide technological spinoffs to civilian industry, such as helping to make the telecommunication of information rather than the transportation of persons a central focus of the future economy. Together these new military and civilian products could become major new American exports in the world market.

The Follow-on Imperative and an Aerospace Copernican Revolution

Whatever might be the merits of PGMs, however, they are unlikely to displace military aircraft and strategic missiles from the center of U.S. military strategy soon. The most formidable obstacle in their path is not the Soviet army but the American aerospace industry. The American corporations that focus on the production of PGMs are substantial firms, but most rank in the second fifteen of DOD contractors. As we have seen, the producers of military aircraft and strategic missiles rank in the first fifteen, and they have the economic importance and political influence to stay there. As long as the aerospace firms are in the business of producing military aircraft and strategic missiles, these weapons systems will be at the center of U.S. military strategy. A Copernican revolution on the battlefield will have to wait upon a Copernican revolution in the aerospace industry.

From Aircraft to SDI

There is, however, a possible path along which these contractors might travel from ATAs, ATFs, and ICBMs to PGMs. It is a path that passes through SDI.

In the first five years (1983–1988) of the SDI program, its top eight contractors (those that received total awards for the five-year period ranging from $1.6 billion down to $500 million) were, in descending order, Lockheed, General Motors, TRW, Boeing, Rockwell International, McDonnell Douglas, General Electric, and Martin Marietta.[30] Not surprisingly, California has been the top state on the list. Because they are aerospace corporations, these firms have been able to benefit from SDI, even though it offers no place for aircraft and ICBMs. Their SDI contracts are still small compared with their contracts for military aircraft and strategic missiles; however, the possibility is there for the SDI contracts to grow gradually to the point that they displace the aircraft and missile contracts as the profit centers of the firms. The follow-on contracts would then be for high-tech electronic weaponry rather than for new versions of old aircraft and missiles.

From SDI to CDI

Some defense analysts believe that developments in SDI will bring with them applications for conventional combat on land. SDI would become the seedbed for a conventional defense initiative (CDI), one that would truly organize and automate the battlefield around high-tech command, control, and communication and high-tech electronic weaponry, including massive numbers of PGMs.

If so, the aerospace corporations of today may become the CDI corporations of a generation hence. The corporations would be the same ones that built the weapons that won World War II and defended "the American century" during the long cold war. But the weapons that they would now produce and that would deter another world war would be ones that would be so new that they would be unique to the twenty-first century.

Highlights of the DOD Annual Report to Congress, Fiscal Year 1990

T he defense secretary's *Annual Report to Congress* is usually one of the most eagerly anticipated documents issued by the U.S. government.[1] The federal bureaucracy regularly inundates Washington with reports, books, and memoranda, with most of the paper going unread, but the *Annual Report,* as Edward Luttwak notes, "is in a class by itself: even the censored public version is greatly in demand."[2]

As the official statement of the Department of Defense (DOD) regarding the interplay of budget and strategy in the forthcoming fiscal year, the *Annual Report* represents the incumbent administration's perception of the world, its assessment of the threat, its preferred strategy, and its view of the optimal mix of forces required to advance U.S. interests.

In some circumstances, however, the report may generate less than usual interest, and such was the case with the report issued by Secretary of Defense Frank Carlucci for Fiscal Year (FY) 1990. Prepared by a lame duck defense secretary only weeks before President Bush's budget address to the Congress, the FY 1990 report was dead on delivery. Perhaps anticipating such a reaction, Carlucci's report was less a guide to future action than a retelling of past accomplishments. Wanting to give his successor as much leeway as possible in charting a course for DOD, Secretary Carlucci addressed the future with only the broadest of strokes.

The Nature of the Threat

In 1988 the U.S.-Soviet treaty on intermediate-range nuclear forces (INF) entered into force, Soviet General Secretary Gorbachev pledged unilaterally to reduce Soviet conventional forces in Europe, and East-West relations generally experienced a significant warming. Carlucci acknowledged the new détente—"The changes taking place in the Soviet Union today inspire widespread hopes that the international environment is becoming safer"—but he remained skeptical of a substantial change in the nature of the Soviet system. He warned that many Soviet initiatives were rhetoric that had not yet produced concrete changes in the Soviet defense posture. Indeed, Carlucci attributed any "softening" in the Soviet position to the expansion of U.S. military strength during the first Reagan term. Noting the real decline of U.S. defense spending in the last half of the Reagan presidency and the pressure for continued downward adjustment in the wake of a seemingly favorable international climate, Carlucci warned: "We must be guided by realism, not wishful thinking. The West's security preparations must be based not on Kremlin declarations but on actual Soviet military capabilities."

Carlucci saw a "kinder, gentler" Soviet Union as only one of several possible outcomes. For the near term, he argued that the United States should continue to assume that the Soviet threat is unaltered. "Hope alone is a poor guide to policy. We must cautiously assess the threats to our security, not in light of professions of intent or interpretations of present tendencies, but primarily in terms of the balance of capabilities of the military forces maintained by ourselves, our allies, and our potential enemies."

While the Soviet Union represented the greatest potential military threat in the late 1980s, Carlucci recognized other dangers faced by the United States, including potential aggression by Soviet proxies, independent Third World states, national liberation movements, and terrorist organizations. As the size and lethality of the arsenals at the disposal of various groups increase, the threat they pose will increase as well. Carlucci averred that "a Third World conflict may be the most likely scenario for a chemical or biological attack on U.S. forces."

The FY 1990 report also addressed a popular theme among analysts in the late 1980s: the decline of empire and the waning of hegemonic influence. Paul Kennedy's best-selling book, *The Rise and Fall of the Great Powers*, argued that economic difficulties spelled the end of the American Century and that the economic decline would inevitably lead to military decline. Secretary Carlucci acknowledged a number of adverse global economic trends and conceded that the relative economic advances of a number of countries will result in an "increasingly multipolar" international system. He declared, however, that this did not necessarily constitute the "decline of America" but rather presented an opportunity for expansion of mutually beneficial trade among free market economies.

Arms Control

The FY 1990 report provided little new in the way of positions on arms control. It reported a somewhat more favorable arms control climate in the late 1980s and attributed that development to the military buildup of the first Reagan term. The report summarized the progress in ongoing negotiations and asserted that despite the history of Soviet noncompliance, the Soviet insistence on a suspension of U.S. research and development efforts in strategic defense, and the Soviet radar facility at Krasnoyarsk that the United States charges is a material breach of the ABM Treaty, some progress was made.

Specifically Carlucci reported continued success in monitoring the INF treaty, in efforts to develop a mutually acceptable means to monitor compliance with the unratified Threshold Test Ban Treaty and the Peaceful Nuclear Explosions Treaty, and in preliminary agreements on total numbers of warheads and launchers in the START (Strategic Arms Reduction Talks) negotiations. Even here the message echoed earlier reports, relying on the notion of weapon systems as bargaining chips to facilitate successful agreement. "The INF Treaty shows the wisdom of pressing for a ban on a weapon system while proceeding with its development, both as an incentive for the Soviets to negotiate in good faith, and to deter the increased Soviet threat if an agreement cannot be reached."

Defense Management

The bulk of the defense management section of the FY 1990 *Annual Report* rehashed initiatives that began in the early and mid-1980s. One continuing crisis merited special attention. Noting the ongoing Justice Department investigation of defense contracting, Carlucci argued that a plan for procurement reform was being formulated in the Pentagon. He warned, however, that responsible officials must be wary of "a reform at all cost" mentality. He identified a number of proposals before Congress at the end of 1988—particularly those aimed at creating an independent acquisition agency, removing the inspector general from the Defense Department, and sealing shut the so-called revolving door between the DOD and defense contractors—with the potential for doing "far more harm than good." On the positive side, Carlucci reported that DOD had reduced the cost of acquiring major weapon systems, streamlined the acquisition process, and expanded competitive bidding for defense contracts.

Competitive Strategies

The notion of competitive strategies remained a key feature of U.S. defense planning. Secretary Carlucci reported "significant progress toward further defining and institutionalizing competitive strategy" during 1988. He also announced the formation of a new task force to study nonnuclear strategic capabilities in the competitive strategies framework. In addition, the Senior Intelligence Committee was said to be preparing a study of future Soviet defense policy, outlining "the range and scope of possible changes that Chairman Gorbachev's programs may have on Soviet defense."

NATO

The belief that the burden of European defense falls too heavily on the United States and not heavily enough on Europe continued to gain support in the United States. Secretary Carlucci indicated that European nations may have begun to assume a greater share of the defense burden. Commitments of forces to the Persian Gulf, transfers of funds and equipment to Greece, Portugal, and Turkey, and the agreement to pay the facilities costs of moving the 401st Tactical Fighter Wing from Spain to Italy suggested a willingness to share the burden more equally.

Base Closure and Realignment

As the reality of fiscal limitations became apparent, the search intensified for ways to increase the efficiency and decrease the cost of the defense establishment without compromising national security. That search led, among other things, to the formation of the Commission on Base Closure and Realignment in May 1988. In October the Congress passed legislation giving legal clout to the commission's activities. At the end of 1988 the commission released its report, recommending the realignment of the domestic base infrastructure. In early 1989 the secretary approved the report of the commission.

While motivated by fiscal concerns, the base closing commission was charged with identifying facilities "which no longer effectively support strategic goals and those that are underutilized." The primacy of military utility, however, did not obviate other concerns. The secretary was cognizant of the potential economic effects of base closings on local areas, but the charge that local communities suffer economic dislocations as a result of base closings, he argued, was a misconception. In the past, "100 communities have replaced 93,400 former DOD civilian jobs with 138,000 new jobs on former military bases." And while there were initial costs in the closure process with savings accruing only in the longer term, the annual report argued that the final effect of base closing and realignment will be a leaner, more efficient, and less costly domestic base infrastructure.

FY 1990 Budget Overview

The fiscal message of the annual report was quite clear: provide real increases in defense spending or risk jeopardizing national security. While not returning to the openly confrontational posture of Secretary Caspar Weinberger, Carlucci warned that the 2 percent real increase in the defense budget requested in the report represents hard choices and that "reducing this program implies accepting increased risks to our security, today and in the future. . . . Even though we have rebuilt our defense capabilities, the time for vigilance has not passed."

While the report was more a wish list than a budget request, destined to be overtaken by the budget dealings of the Bush administration and the Congress, it did recognize several limitations in the expansion of DOD even at the level of a 2 percent real increase in the budget. Such restrictions would become more severe under the Bush budget since the rate of spending in that budget would be less than in the Carlucci request, at best keeping pace with inflation. For example, Carlucci admitted that "in light of the Navy's maritime strategy and current global commitments, the requirement for the 600-ship Navy, already delayed in the FY 1989 report, would now have to be postponed until after the year 2000." Readiness, which Carlucci called "our highest defense priority," was similarly held hostage to budgetary concerns as reductions were ordered in training hours and equipment maintenance. Sustainability, a force's ability to fight over time, was threatened by reductions in expenditures for ammunition and spare parts.

Although the secretary called for real increases in spending, he acknowledged that even those increases would leave inadequacies in defense preparedness. The mismatch between commitment and capability would continue. Further reductions by the Bush administration without a corresponding retrenchment of self-determined global U.S. responsibilities would only heighten the mismatch.

Reactions

The *Annual Report* often generates significant reactions. The FY 1989 report, which announced cuts in funding for naval programs, prompted the fiery resignation of Secretary of the Navy James Webb. The FY 1990 report generated no such reaction. It was released by a secretary of defense only days away from leaving office. Secretary Carlucci himself, seeming to sense his declining relevance, delivered "less of a blueprint for the future than a summation of Mr. Reagan's $2 trillion military program and a final echo of his military doctrine."[3]

The report was also overshadowed by other events, most significantly the storm raging over the ill-fated nomination of John Tower. In addition, a massive strategic reassessment, certain to go over much of the same ground contained in Secretary Carlucci's report, was being eagerly awaited. President Bush put a hold on U.S.-Soviet strategic arms negotiations pending completion of a review of the previous administration's efforts in that area and the development of a new approach to strategic weapons negotiations. The Bush administration was attempting to establish its own foreign policy and national security agendas, and the Carlucci report was simply a throwback to an earlier time. Given the additional political requirement that the Bush administration distance itself from, and create an identity independent of, the Reagan administration, the muted official and press responses to the Carlucci report were not unexpected.

Defense Chronology 1988

January

2   Congress approves $84.8 million in construction funding for Whiteman AFB, Missouri, as the first home for the Air Force's B-2 Stealth bomber.

3   Deputy Defense Secretary William Taft IV directs the Army to cut an additional $1 billion from its planned FY 1989 budget request.

5   The Navy awards a $643.9 million contract for a Trident submarine along with options on two others to Electric Boat of Groton, Connecticut. The contract maintains Electric Boat's monopoly on Trident construction.

6   The Pentagon announces plans to cut 20,000 people from the Air Force and 10,000 from the Army to meet the terms of the proposed FY 1989 defense budget.

10   A team of American scientists and technicians arrives at the Soviet nuclear test site at Semipalatinsk in Kazakhstan for a five-day tour and inspection of the site. The visit is the first step in an effort by the superpowers to verify the existing limits on nuclear testing. A Soviet team of equal size is to visit the American nuclear test site in Nevada from January 26 to January 30.

11   Gregory (Pappy) Boyington, a retired Marine Corps colonel and highly decorated World War II ace, dies.

12   A Navy P-3C Orion surveillance plane and a Soviet MiG-23 come within fifteen feet of colliding over the Sea of Japan.

12   A senior House Armed Services Committee staff aid declares that the Navy should cancel its planned Seawolf SSN-21 submarine because Soviet boats have advanced beyond the capabilities of the Seawolf.

13   A consortium led by FMC, a U.S. defense and aerospace group, beats British and West German competition to win a $1 billion contract to manufacture amphibious armored personnel carriers for Turkey.

14   The Department of Defense (DOD) agrees to Spanish demands to remove the seventy-two F-16 fighters of the 401st Tactical Fighter Wing from Torrejon air base near Madrid. The question of a new location for the wing remains unanswered.

14   The Army, citing budget pressures, cancels its LHX helicopter project.

14   A U.S. Army instructor at the Aberdeen Proving Ground's tank turret division is arrested and charged with spying after he attempted to sell sensitive information to an undercover U.S. agent.

14   Round IX of the Defense and Space Talks begins in Geneva.

14   Soviet general secretary Mikhail Gorbachev warns the United States that any deployment of sea-launched cruise missiles (SLCMs) would jeopardize the Strategic Arms Reduction Talks (START).

16   Fred C. Iklé, under secretary of defense for policy, announces his resignation.

19   U.S. cruise missile tests resume in northern Canada despite criticism that since the INF treaty would ban these missiles, there is no need for such tests.

19   Senator Sam Nunn (D–Georgia) calls for a limited SDI (Strategic Defense Initiative) to protect U.S. territory against accidental ballistic missile launches.

20   Rockwell International completes assembly of the last of one hundred B-1 bombers ordered by the Air Force. The completion of the program comes two months ahead of schedule and narrowly within the budget set six years ago.

20   The DOD grants veterans' status to thousands of Americans who served as merchant seamen during World War II.

21   The Navy destroys an unarmed Trident II missile when it veers off course during a test flight.

22   The United States presents the Soviet Union with a draft treaty on antimissile defense systems. The draft calls for the parties to agree not to withdraw from the 1972 Anti-Ballistic Missile (ABM) Treaty through 1994 but sidesteps such issues as the broad interpretation of the treaty and SDI testing.

23   France and West Germany form a high-level military commission to coordinate Franco-German policies on nuclear disarmament and other defense matters.

24   Nicaraguan troops down an airplane carrying supplies to the contras in southern Nicaragua. The plane is part of a CIA contra supply operation.

24   The Reagan administration charges that during the past several years, the Soviet Union has fired ground-based lasers at American reconnaissance satellites.

25   Defense Secretary Frank Carlucci, following a DOD decision to approve the transfer of radar technology between Texas Instruments and Thomson-CSF of France, calls for a major review of Pentagon technology transfer procedures.

25   A Soviet ballistic missile submarine, withdrawn from service to keep within the limits of the unratified SALT II Treaty, is redeployed armed with 100-kiloton cruise missiles in place of its ballistic missiles. SLCMs are not covered by the treaty.

27   The Pentagon confirms that a worker damaged a massive SDI laser facility in southern California earlier in the month, resulting in delays in testing the unit, which is designed to produce a 2 million watt Alpha antimissile beam.

28   Soviet soldiers in East Berlin charge American troops on legal patrol and fire what appear to be blanks at the Americans.

February

2   Defense Secretary Carlucci requests continued funding for the small intercontinental ballistic missile (SICBM) program in the Pentagon's FY 1989 budget.

2   Defense Secretary Carlucci directs the Navy to retire sixteen of its older ships.

3   The Air Force cancels its $4 billion antisatellite (ASAT) program.

4   The DOD quarterly statistics on deaths of active-duty personnel reveal that serving in the U.S. armed forces accounted for 1,527 total deaths between January 1, 1987, and September 30, 1987.

4   The Air Force reduces its proposed budget request for the MX by 50 percent, or about $400 million.

4   The launch of a $200 million SDI research satellite is postponed due to a malfunction in the Delta launch vehicle.

4   Brigadier General Roland Lajoie of the Army is named to head the On-Site Inspection Agency (OSIA), which is responsible for administering on-site inspections under the INF treaty.

6   A Trident I missile carrying a dummy warhead self-destructs shortly after a routine test launch from a submerged submarine. It is the third failure of the Trident series since August 1987.

8   A Delta rocket is successfully launched to test space-sensing technologies. Fourteen test objects are deployed, and a battery of instruments provide data that will be used in designing sensors for strategic defenses. Officials claim the test proves the SDI sensors will be able to distinguish warheads amid a cloud of decoys.

10   DOD procurement chief Robert Costello says that as much as $45 billion of the yearly purchasing budget is lost as waste.

10   U.S. National Guard units find Soviet military equipment on Alaska's St. Lawrence Island.

12   Two U.S. Navy ships on patrol in the Black Sea are bumped by Soviet vessels.

13   The USS *Abraham Lincoln,* the fifth in the line of Nimitz-class carriers, is launched and christened in Newport News, Virginia.

14   Republican presidential candidate Pat Robertson claims that Soviet short-range nuclear-tipped missiles are deployed in Cuba. The White House denies the allegation.

15   Six Pershing II missiles with dummy warheads are test launched in Florida.

15   Round Two of the Nuclear Testing Talks begins in Geneva.

16   The DOD rescinds its order that had barred access to classified information to any naturalized citizen who originally came from one of twenty-nine nations considered hostile to U.S. interests. The new rule promises to consider naturalized citizens on an equal basis with native-born citizens.

17   U.S. minesweeping helicopters end a six-month tour of duty in the Persian Gulf. They leave the gulf aboard the attack carrier *Okinawa,* the first major ship to be withdrawn since the military buildup in the summer of 1987.

17   A U.S. Marine officer attached to the U.N. observer group in Lebanon, Lieutenant Colonel William Higgins, is abducted by unknown gunmen.

17   The DOD reveals plans to remove all nuclear warheads from its fleet of B-52G bombers at four locations: Mather AFB, California, Loring AFB, Maine, Andersen AFB, Guam, and Barksdale AFB, Louisiana.

21   Secretary of State George Shultz and Foreign Minister Shevardnadze meet in Moscow to discuss a range of issues, including a possible summit and the START talks.

22   Navy Secretary James H. Webb, Jr., resigns over budget differences with Defense Secretary Carlucci.

22   Four incendiary bombs explode at the U.S. military facility at Goeppingen in southern Germany. No one is injured, damage is slight, and no one claims responsibility.

23   President Reagan, in a move designed to reassure U.S. North Atlantic Treaty Organization (NATO) partners in the wake of the INF treaty, pledges a continued American commitment to the defense of Europe.

24   The Pentagon approves the development of new long-range cruise missiles to replace some of the systems banned by the INF agreement.

24   Prime Minister Felipe Gonzalez of Spain announces that the United States will withdraw all of its combat troops from Spain as part of an agreement in which it will reduce by 50 percent its military presence in Spain.

25   The Soviet Union withdraws the first of its nuclear missiles from East Germany under the terms of the INF agreement. The SS-12s are being removed prior to the official effective date of the treaty, according to an East German Foreign Ministry statement, to demonstrate the Warsaw Pact's "constructive peace policy."

25   An Army helicopter carrying at least nineteen soldiers crashes and burns in a field in Texas. At least eight people are killed.

25   In a budget-cutting move, the Army announces that it is reducing its active-duty strength by 8,600, including 1,540 officers. The plan includes the appointment of a board to select more than 350 colonels and lieutenant colonels for early retirement.

25   Prime Minister Rajiv Gandhi announces that India has successfully tested a missile capable of carrying large warheads at least 150 miles.

26   The DOD orders military personnel in Panama to remain on their posts or at home and to avoid the political turmoil in that country.

28   Turkey ratifies the extension until 1990 of a pact allowing U.S. air bases and monitoring stations along the Soviet border to remain in exchange for aid.

March

1   President Reagan leaves to meet with European leaders to assure them of the continued strength of U.S. commitment to European defense after the INF agreement.

2   General James Lindsay, US Special Operations Command (SOC), reveals that the Navy SEALs have acquired fifteen minisubmarines to enable them in penetrating naval defenses.

2   Lee Mirecki, a recruit at the Pensacola Naval Air Station, Florida, dies shortly after being pulled from a pool during a program to train naval air crews for search and rescue missions.

3   The State Department notifies Congress that it will seek approval for joint production with Egypt of the M-1 Abrams tank.

3   The House of Representatives narrowly rejects a $16 million package of food, medical supplies, clothing, and shelter for the Nicaraguan contras.

3   At the NATO summit Secretary of State George Shultz tells the allies that their rates of defense spending are too low.

6   American helicopters on a reconnaissance mission draw heavy machine-gun fire from an oil platform and several boats in the central Persian Gulf. No one is injured.

6   Italian Defense Minister Valerio Zanone declares that the F-16s to be transferred from Spain to Italy will not be accompanied by nuclear weapons.

7   Naval officials charge that the latest versions of the Los Angeles–class attack submarines cost $1.2 billion more than projected and are more than eighteen months behind schedule.

7   In an attempt to manage budget cuts the Navy decides to forgo purchases of spare parts and to accept lower aircraft readiness rates and will shift the savings to fund construction of surface combatants and submarines to fill out a 600-ship fleet.

8   Two Army troop transport helicopters collide over Fort Campbell, Kentucky, killing all seventeen soldiers on board.

9   The U.S. delegation to the Nuclear Testing Talks in Geneva tables a draft verification protocol for the 1974 Threshold Test Ban Treaty (TTBT) pending the completion of the joint verification experiment planned for later in the year.

10   The Tooele Army depot in Utah resumes destruction of M-55 nerve gas rockets. Demolition of the obsolete munitions was halted for thirteen months following a nerve gas leak at the facility.

10   A House subcommittee charges that American weapons production and military facilities are responsible for radioactive and hazardous waste pollution, which may cost as much as $100 billion to clean up.

10   The battleship USS *Iowa* returns to its home port of Norfolk, Virginia, after six months in the Persian Gulf.

10   The DOD reports that Soviet arms shipments to Nicaragua continued apace in January and February. The Soviets have delivered $100 million worth of weapons since the beginning of 1988.

11   U.S. naval intelligence reports that the Soviet Union has stopped sending Yankee-class nuclear missile submarines to patrol off the Atlantic coast. They have been patrolling in European waters instead, prompting Naval intelligence to surmise that the ships have been redeployed to cover targets previously held at risk by missiles banned by the INF agreement.

13   Thirty U.S. military advisers are sent to Bolivia on a follow-up to a summer 1987 mission in which U.S. troops and helicopters helped Bolivian troops battle a cocaine ring.

13   Four Soviet colonels tour a major NATO winter exercise, the first such inspection under the terms of an agreement between NATO and the Warsaw Pact intended to help ensure crisis stability.

14   The Army announces the formation of a Space Command at Peterson AFB, Colorado.

14   President Reagan addresses a Washington conference on the first five years of the SDI program, pledging continued development and deployment.

15   Defense Secretary Carlucci and Soviet defense minister Dmitri Yazov hold an unprecedented meeting in Switzerland. Among the issues under discussion, Carlucci asks for an official apology for the 1985 shooting of Army Major Arthur Nicholson.

16   Nicaragua launches a major offensive against U.S.-backed contra rebels. Up to 7,000 Sandinista troops strike contra targets in northeastern Nicaragua and Honduras.

16   President Reagan orders the immediate deployment of four Army infantry battalions to Honduras in response to a Nicaraguan offensive.

16   Soviet leader Mikhail Gorbachev proposes a freeze on Soviet and U.S. naval forces in the Mediterranean.

16   Douglas Aircraft rolls out its first Navy T-45—a two-seat jet trainer.

16   The Air Force charges that the development of the C-17 transport is about eight months behind schedule.

17   The Soviet Foreign Ministry announces that the Soviet Union intends to withdraw its troops from Afghanistan even if the current negotiations fail.

20   In an effort to drive Nicaraguan forces from Honduras, 700 U.S. Army troops are repositioned fifteen miles from the Honduran-Nicaraguan border.

21   An Army helicopter crashes in Honduras, injuring ten soldiers.

21   U.S. and Soviet negotiators agree to a broad framework for the START negotiations. Assistant Secretary of State Rozanne Ridgeway calls it a "monumental accomplishment."

23   Sandinista leaders and contra rebels sign a cease-fire.

23   A House subcommittee deletes funding for the Trident submarine in the FY 1989 budget.

23   President Reagan announces that he and Mikhail Gorbachev will meet in Moscow from May 29 through June 2.

24   The DOD reveals that it is using depleted uranium to upgrade the armor of the M1A1 Abrams tank.

26   The Reagan administration stops sending Stinger missiles to the Afghan rebels.

27   The Pentagon reveals that it is scaling down the SDI program from the initial vision of a leakproof shield over the United States to a more modest system to protect military installations.

28   The first of the 3,500 American combat troops deployed to Honduras on March 16 are recalled to the United States.

29   The House Armed Services Committee cuts $300 million from the requested $800 million for a rail-mobile MX basing mode. The $300 million is then tacked on to the $200 million requested for continued development of the SICBM.

29   Republican and Democratic leaders in the House announce that they have agreed in principle to a package of at least $45 million to aid the contras.

30   William L. Ball III is sworn in as the sixty-seventh secretary of the navy.

30   U.S. officials report that the Persian Gulf nation of Qatar has secretly acquired thirteen American Stinger missiles.

31   In Geneva the U.S. delegation to the Nuclear Testing Talks tables a draft verification protocol for the 1976 Peaceful Nuclear Explosions Treaty (PNET)

April

1   Major General William F. Burns (U.S. Army, retired) is sworn in as the ninth director of the Arms Control and Disarmament Agency (ACDA), replacing Kenneth Adelman.

1   The Air Force trims its SICBM program in spite of the fact that the House Armed Services Committee approved more than the Air Force's original funding request for the project.

1   The DOD sends 1,300 troops to Panama to help protect American personnel and facilities there.

4   The Reagan administration establishes a special task force to begin delivering humanitarian aid to the contras.

4   A federal appeals court upholds the espionage conviction of Samuel Loring Morison, who had given photographs of a Soviet ship to a British military journal. It is the first case in which a federal employee was convicted on criminal charges for disclosing government information to the press.

5   The United States plans to send an additional seventy-five advanced F-16 fighters to Israel for $2 billion.

6   The DOD clears the sale of a highly advanced gyroscope to India. It is to be used in the production of a new jet fighter.

6   A federal judge dismisses fraud charges against Northrop. The charges claimed that the firm regularly sold used and defective parts to the Air

Force, particularly a key component of the MX guidance system. The dismissal was based on a legal technicality.

7   Anti-American riots break out in Tegucigalpa, Honduras. Fifteen hundred demonstrators throw rocks and set the U.S. embassy on fire. At least four of the demonstrators die.

7   The Soviet Union and Afghanistan announce that all remaining obstacles to a peace agreement have been eliminated and that withdrawal of Soviet troops will begin on May 15. The Soviet Union also accepts a U.S. formula that allows both sides to continue to supply arms to their allies in the conflict after the peace accord takes effect.

8   U.S. troops engage in an exercise simulating a takeover of the Panama Canal. The exercise is intended to show U.S. resolve to ensure the security of the canal.

9   The Department of Energy (DOE) shuts down its remaining three weapons production nuclear reactors after seismic experts determine that strategically located brackets might fail and damage the emergency cooling system in an earthquake.

10   An explosion rips through a major arms dump in Rawalpindi, Pakistan. Nearly $80 million in American and Saudi Arabian weapons destined for the anti-Soviet *mujahedeen* in Afghanistan were destroyed.

11   Afghan guerrillas down a Soviet-made An-26 passenger plane over northern Afghanistan, killing twenty-nine people.

11   The Reagan administration rejects a Soviet proposal to conduct tests to determine whether cruise missiles aboard ships are armed with nuclear or conventional warheads.

11   Intelligence sources in Punjab report that Sikh extremists have acquired four to six U.S. Stinger surface-to-air missiles.

12   Army officials disclose that more than 1,000 chemical weapons in storage at various sites around the country are leaking. Officials warn that the problem is likely to worsen.

12   American security forces mistakenly shoot and kill a Marine sentry while investigating a possible intrusion at an American fuel storage depot in Panama.

12   A team of ten Soviets arrive in Washington to discuss and finalize verification procedures for the INF treaty.

13   U.S. intelligence experts report that after a moratorium of more than a year, Iran has resumed terrorist activities.

14   The United States, the Soviet Union, Pakistan, and Afghanistan sign an accord to end the eight-year conflict in Afghanistan and provide for the withdrawal of Soviet troops from that country. In preparation, the Soviets rush 15,000 troops and armored vehicles to Afghanistan.

14   An American frigate, the USS *Samuel B. Roberts,* on escort duty in the Persian Gulf, strikes a mine. The explosion tears a twenty-two foot hole in the ship's hull and injures eleven crew members. Due to the extraordinary efforts of the crew, the ship is saved and moves to dry dock in Dubai.

15   The Sandinista government and the contras begin top-level negotiations to end the conflict in Nicaragua.

18   U.S. Navy ships attack two Iranian oil platforms in retaliation for the mine blast that damaged the U.S. frigate *Samuel B. Roberts*. The platforms are used as command and control radar stations by Iran. Iranian gunboats attempt to return fire. Six Iranian naval vessels are damaged or sunk. One American Cobra helicopter and its two-person crew are missing.

18   By a margin of 17–2, the Senate Foreign Relations Committee favorably reports the INF treaty to the full Senate.

18   An American F-16 stationed at Ramstein AB crashes near the Luxembourg border.

19   The Danish government, fearing its relationship with NATO is damaged by a parliamentary order to enforce its nuclear ban on NATO warships, calls for a referendum on the issue.

20   A test firing of a redesigned shuttle booster rocket is a success. The National Aeronautics and Space Administration (NASA) claims the test results keep plans for an August launch of the shuttle on schedule.

21   The Senate Armed Services Committee cuts the $200 million budget request for the small intercontinental ballistic missile (SICBM) to $50 million.

21   The Pentagon announces that the B-2 Stealth bomber will make its debut in the fall.

22   China informs the United States that it will not abide by an international arms embargo against Iran after the clashes in the gulf between the U.S. and Iranian navies.

24   The USS *Bonefish*, one of the last active Navy diesel submarines, catches fire off the Florida coast. Three crew members are missing, and eighteen are injured.

24   The Government Accounting Office (GAO) reports that more than 500 Phoenix air-to-air missiles designed for Navy F-14s remain unusable because of faulty fuses.

25   Reacting to congressional concern over Saudi Arabia's secret purchase of Chinese medium-range ballistic missiles, President Reagan postpones formal notification to Congress of a proposed $450 million arms deal with the Saudis.

25   The U.S.-Japan Peaceful Nuclear Cooperation Agreement goes into effect, giving Japan a thirty-year blanket authorization to reprocess thousands of tons of spent nuclear fuel into plutonium, initially in Europe and later at facilities in Japan.

27   The House votes to restrict all SDI testing to elements that fall within the traditional, narrow interpretation of the 1972 ABM Treaty.

27   Rupert Scholz, a Berlin senator and virtual unknown, is named to replace West German defense minister Manfred Wörner when Wörner leaves later in the year to become NATO secretary-general.

27   An attempt is made to blow up a U.S. military passenger train in West Germany. The train is damaged, but the thirty-one soldiers on board escaped unharmed.

27   The U.S. airlifts emergency supplies of weapons to the Afghan rebels. The emergency shortage is a result of the explosion at an ammunition dump in Pakistan earlier in the month.

28   The House unexpectedly defeats a measure that would have permanently banned the testing of the F-15-launched antisatellite system.

29   The Reagan administration orders a broadening of the rules of engagement for U.S. warships on escort duty in the Persian Gulf to protect neutral shipping and oil platforms that come under Iranian attack.

30   The one-hundredth B-1B bomber is delivered to the Air Force at Palmdale, California.

May

1   Great Britain makes a commitment of £1.7 billion to develop a European fighter plane. The announcement by British defense minister George Younger is intended to influence decisions on the fighter by the governments of Spain, Italy, and West Germany.

2   In the face of intense congressional opposition, the DOD drops its plan to deploy six Coast Guard cutters in the Persian Gulf.

2   At the semiannual meeting of the NATO nuclear planning group, Secretary of Defense Frank Carlucci reveals that the United States is considering additional deployments of nuclear-capable aircraft in Europe to offset expansion of Soviet theater nuclear delivery systems.

2   The House of Representatives votes nearly unanimously to grant new health benefits to an estimated 250,000 so-called atomic veterans. The bill was approved by the Senate a week earlier.

3   Administration officials reveal intelligence estimates indicating that as many as ten nations are developing biological weapons. The officials refuse to name the nations other than the Soviet Union.

3   In anticipation of legislation to ease the process of base closing, Defense Secretary Carlucci establishes a bipartisan panel to identify redundant domestic military facilities.

3   Secretary of the Air Force Edward C. Aldridge announces that a $500 million contract has been awarded to General Dynamics to build a new medium-sized rocket that will complete the inventory of U.S. launch vehicle requirements for national security and commercial payloads.

4   The House of Representatives votes to spend $3.5 billion on SDI, approximately $1.4 billion less than the administration had requested.

4   A series of explosions destroys the Pacific Engineering & Production Company plant in Henderson, Nevada. The plant produced fuel for the space shuttle program, as well as for ballistic missiles. A spokesperson for Morton Thiokol, the builder of solid propellant motors for both the shuttle and ballistic missile programs, expresses concern over potential fuel shortages.

5   Two years after discovering the problem, the Pentagon warns troops in the field that they have been using potentially defective bolts to repair tanks, TOW missile carriers, and other major weapons systems.

5   The Senate Armed Services Committee agrees to lift partially its directive that the services reduce their number of officers. After cuts of 6,176 officers from 1986, the committee agrees with a similar House panel to suspend similar requirements for 1989 and 1990, provided the services establish a plan to control the number of officers in the future.

5   A meeting of NATO defense ministers in Brussels decides to modernize NATO nuclear weapons positioned in Turkey. Modernization will increase the accuracy of the warheads, but their range will not be affected.

5   Following several years of tough negotiations, India purchases a U.S.-built Cray supercomputer. India says it needs the computer to process climate data, allowing it to predict the beginning of monsoon rains, but Washington has been wary of selling the supercomputer to non-NATO nations because of its potential military applications.

6   A federal judge rules that the Congress and the president can order state National Guard units to go on training missions outside the United States over the objections of a governor, validating a government policy of sending National Guard units on training missions to Central America.

8   Tests of a modified Copperhead laser-guided artillery round provide evidence that it can defeat Soviet reactive armor. The modification involves putting a time-delay fuse on the shell, allowing the steel cone of the shell to crush the reactive armor plates so the warhead can penetrate the tank's armor.

9   A major military supply agency, the Defense Logistics Agency, found that 30 percent of its stock of the Army's most commonly used automotive bolt is counterfeit, and troops in the Army's 7th Infantry Division at Fort Ord said defective bolts have put 75 percent of their new truck fleet in the shop. Spurred by such findings, hearings in the House begin on the subject of defective bolts in military machinery.

9   Charles S. Whitehouse is nominated as a twelfth assistant secretary of defense responsible for the new unified Special Operations Command (SOC). Analysts see this step as a turning point in an eight-year bureaucratic turf war within the DOD.

10   The Soviet Union, responding to last-minute U.S. objections to verification provisions of the INF treaty, claims the problems are "purely technical" and easily resolved. U.S. and Soviet negotiators meet to hammer out the differences.

10   The Air Force announces that 4,000 civilian employees will be required to sign agreements stating that they understand they may be called upon to move permanently to different parts of the country as a condition of employment.

10   DOD discloses plans to sell three Navy P-3C Orion antisubmarine patrol planes to Pakistan for $240 million.

10   The Reagan administration reveals plans to sell up to forty F-18 fighter-bombers to Kuwait.

11   The United States offers to drop the drug trafficking indictments against General Manual Noriega on the condition that he resign and leave Panama.

11   The House of Representatives approves a $299.5 billion DOD appropriations bill that substantially undercuts administration requests for funds for a limited SDI and a rail-basing system for the MX.

11   A Marine Corps CH-46 Sea Knight helicopter with three crew members aboard crashes into the ocean near Oahu. No survivors are reported.

11   Sikorsky Aircraft returns $75 million to the U.S. government, claiming

that it erroneously overcharged the government on a contract for military helicopters. It denies any attempt at fraud.

12   Secretary of State Shultz and Soviet foreign minister Shevardnadze reach full agreement on technical compliance issues, clearing the way for Senate ratification of the INF treaty.

12   Martin Marietta Corp. successfully tests a new missile guidance system that makes use of adjustable control thrusters, allowing for more precise guidance control.

12   A Senate panel overwhelmingly approves the placement of a bronze statue honoring women who served in Vietnam at the site of the Vietnam Veterans War Memorial.

12   The Pentagon announces that beginning in FY 1989 it will raise the rate of its monthly payments to defense firms from 75 to 80 percent of contracting costs.

12   The Justice Department agrees to join an amended complaint against McDonnell Douglas, alleging that the company overcharged the Army by $175 million on the Apache attack helicopter. The suit seeks total damages of $750 million.

13   The United States and the Soviet Union conclude a draft scientific agreement. DOD officials, worried that provisions of the agreement would allow the Soviets direct access to data from American high-tech companies, plan to seek to rescind those provisions.

13   An explosion rips through a Soviet solid fuel propellant plant. The explosion severely limits the fuel available for the new Soviet SS-24s and SS-25s.

13   The DOD agrees to halt or moderate its experiments on electromagnetic pulse (EMP) pending the completion of an environmental impact study.

15   The first Soviet troops leave Afghanistan under the terms of the agreement negotiated between the Soviet Union, Pakistan, Afghanistan, and the United States, signaling the end of eight and one-half years of occupation.

15   The Senate votes overwhelmingly to use U.S. military forces in drug enforcement roles.

15   The Army stops taking delivery of its new 9-mm Beretta handgun after several of the weapons shattered during test firings, injuring the shooters.

15   The Air Force discloses that the estimates of the per unit costs of the Stealth bomber rose about 20 percent to $450 million.

16   The first Soviet troops to leave Afghanistan are returned to the Soviet Union.

16   West Germany, Great Britain, and Italy agree to a joint project to produce an advanced fighter. The United States has attempted to block the venture, claiming that the Europeans could get the same fighter at half the price by buying American.

16   Great Britain announces that it intends to upgrade and modernize its independent nuclear force by equipping its bombers with nuclear-tipped stand-off missiles instead of gravity bombs.

17   The full Senate begins consideration of the INF treaty.

17   The Reagan administration acknowledges that Soviet leader Mikhail Gorbachev has been quietly removing political opponents from important positions, thereby solidifying his base of power.

19   Defense Secretary Frank Carlucci rejects a congressional proposal to use the military in drug enforcement roles.

19   Key Senate leaders propose a sweeping overhaul of the War Powers Resolution, declaring it ineffective as an instrument of congressional control on excessive presidential use of military power.

20   Lieutenant General Frank E. Peterson, commander of the Quantico Marine installation, reduces the thirty-year sentence imposed on former Marine sergeant Clayton Lonetree for espionage. The reduction is related to Lonetree's cooperation during posttrial debriefings.

20   Senate supporters of the INF treaty soundly reject a series of "killer amendments" that would have tied implementation of the treaty to Soviet compliance on other arms agreements and delayed the effective date of the treaty until after NATO stockpiles of fuel and ammunition had been substantially increased.

20   The Pentagon issues a report by the Defense Science Board calling for a more incremental approach to the initial deployment of SDI more in line with the congressionally mandated reductions of the SDI budget.

20   Concerned that the Department of Defense is spending money too quickly, Deputy Defense Secretary Taft orders a ban on all "discretionary spending" in the department until June 30.

23   Pakistan test-fires a missile capable of carrying a nuclear weapon.

25   The Philippine Senate approves a ban on all nuclear weapons in the Philippines. The bill is expected to have an immediate impact on the operations of the U.S. Clark AFB and Subic Bay naval installation in the Philippines.

25   The Italian government agrees to accept the seventy-two F-16s of the 401st Tactical Fighter Wing, which were previously ordered out of Spain. The Italian parliament must still vote on the matter. The government's action is seen as a statement of the importance of a strong southern flank to the NATO alliance.

25   Secretary of State Shultz announces that U.S. efforts to end the crisis in Panama have collapsed and that all proposals have been withdrawn.

26   NATO defense ministers agree in principle to accept the Italian offer to house the 401st Tactical Fighter Wing.

26   Blytheville AFB, Arkansas, is renamed Eaker AFB in honor of the late General Ira C. Eaker, the first commander of the "Mighty 8th" Air Force in World War II.

28   The Soviet parliament ratifies the INF Treaty. The timely action will allow the agreement to be signed by President Reagan and General Secretary Gorbachev at the summit in Moscow.

28   The Soviet Union indicates that it may slow its withdrawal from Afghanistan if Pakistan continues to aid the rebels and U.S. aid continues at "lavish" levels.

28   The Air Force announces plans to develop a B-52-launched three-stage rocket designed to place payloads of up to 600 pounds into low orbit.

29   President Reagan and General Secretary Gorbachev begin their series of meetings in Moscow. The summit is the fourth between Reagan and Gorbachev and is expected to yield results on certain roadblocks related to the START talks. Defense Secretary Carlucci also attended the summit, something former Defense Secretary Weinberger never did, and held meetings with Soviet Defense Minister Yazov and Chief of Staff Akhromeyev.

30   The Army staff agrees to make the 1st Special Operations Command at Fort Bragg, North Carolina, a separate command, the Army's seventeenth, to be run by a three- or four-star general.

June

1   The INF agreement, signed in Moscow, goes into effect.

1   The DOD begins testing recruits for drug and alcohol abuse.

2   The United States announces that China, despite its assurances to the contrary, continues to sell Silkworm missiles to Iran.

2   The summit ends, and although both sides claim better ties because of the meetings and although the INF treaty was signed and activated, there were no substantive breakthroughs on arms control issues.

2   FMC Corp. completes an agreement to sell 200 Bradley fighting vehicles to Saudi Arabia for $400 million.

5   The State Department, bowing to pressures from the Congress, has added restrictions to the pact between the United States and Japan that grants Japan authority to reprocess spent nuclear fuel into plutonium. The restrictions include a ban on flights carrying plutonium over U.S. territory.

5   The Air Force announces that General Electric's F110-GE-100 engines, designed expressly for the F-16 and widely used in other military aircraft, may require a redesign of its compressor blades to prevent engine blades cracking. Fourteen tactical aircraft powered by that engine have been grounded due to engine malfunction.

6   Defense Secretary Carlucci appeals to the Japanese government to bear more of the burden of the cost of maintaining U.S. bases in Japan. Currently the total spent on the U.S. bases in Japan is about $6 billion, of which Japan pays $2.5 billion (40 percent).

6   The U.S. Navy tests the ability of naval ships to operate following the detonation of a nuclear weapon. The test, the first of its kind, involves the release of a burst of electromagnetic energy designed to simulate EMP. A specially equipped barge will test the effect of EMP on various hardware.

6   A group representing the families of American service personnel missing in action in Southeast Asia expresses outrage at President Reagan's pledge to help the Soviet Union recover MIAs in Afghanistan. The group wants to see more action to recover U.S. MIAs.

7   North Korea stations surface-to-air missiles near the demilitarized zone, approximately 70 miles from Seoul.

7   The Soviet Union delivers a squadron of twenty MiG-29s to North Korea, the first such transfer to North Korea.

9   The administration announces that the Pentagon is considering the de-

velopment of a missile defense to protect only the Washington, D.C., area.

12   The Environmental Protection Agency (EPA) charges that the Pentagon is responsible for a significant portion of the hazardous waste problem plaguing the United States. The agency claims that thousands of military facilities are in violation of EPA regulations and that environmental contamination is commonplace.

13   Western diplomats reveal that the Soviet Union has introduced a powerful new weapon in Afghanistan. The Soviets have attempted to slow the advance of anticommunist forces as Soviet troops pull out by using "fuel-air explosive bombs." The weapon creates a fuel-rich, oxygen-rich aerosol cloud in the atmosphere, which explodes with tremendous force. Military planners worry that the weapon would be tremendously effective against concentrations of ground forces, and critics worry that because of its explosive power, it blurs the distinction between conventional and nuclear weapons.

14   The Soviet Union apologizes for the 1985 shooting death of Major Arthur Nicholson in East Berlin.

15   Air Force Systems Command chief General Bernard Randolph announces that Boeing Aerospace Co., Pratt & Whitney of United Technologies Corp., and Autonetics of Rockwell International Corp. will undergo reduced government oversight because they have demonstrated good past performance.

15   The Reagan administration proposes to sell $1.9 billion of sophisticated arms to Kuwait, including Sparrow, Sidewinder, and Maverick missiles, gravity bombs and cluster bombs for use on F/A-18 fighter-bombers the United States had previously sold to Kuwait, the first such sale to a Third World country.

15   Air Force F-15s intercept four Soviet Bear bombers in two separate incidents off the Aleutian Islands, bringing to fifteen the number of intercept missions off Alaska in 1988, involving twenty-seven Soviet aircraft.

16   A federal grand jury issues more than 250 subpoenas for documents and testimony from defense contractors, consultants, and Pentagon officials in a massive investigation into the military procurement process.

16   Alan C. Nelson, the commissioner of the Immigration and Naturalization Service, says that he opposes any efforts to deploy U.S. military troops along the U.S.-Mexican border either to interdict drugs or to monitor immigration.

17   Defective bolts are found in safety-related locations in more than half of the nation's 109 nuclear reactors, the Nuclear Regulatory Commission reveals.

19   House and Senate conferees agree to scrap three older Poseidon SSBNs to keep the United States near the limits of the never-ratified SALT II treaty.

20   The United States and Greece resume talks on the future of U.S. military installations in Greece.

22   The United States sends an additional 250 troops to Panama to improve security at U.S. installations.

22   Two nuclear weapons are detonated simultaneously at the Nuclear Test-

ing Site in Nevada. It is only the third time since testing began at the site in 1951 that two devices were exploded simultaneously.

23 The Nuclear Regulatory Commission levies a fine against the Air Force—its first against a military service—for its handling of a September 1986 spill of radioactive powder at Wright-Patterson AFB, Ohio.

24 An advance team of Soviet inspectors arrives in Utah to begin work on verifying U.S. compliance with the INF Treaty.

25 The DOD releases a report citing a growing potential for the Soviet Union to use Nicaragua for military purposes and warns that the United States may have to send troops and equipment to the region in a crisis.

25 A Marine Sikorsky CH-53D Sea Stallion helicopter slams into a hillside in southwestern Japan, killing all seven Marines on board.

27 Defense Secretary Carlucci and Israeli defense minister Yitzhak Rabin meet to discuss military issues concerning the two countries, including modernization of the Israeli navy and an Israeli proposal to coproduce a new surface-to-air missile with the United States.

27 Qatar refuses to turn over to the United States thirteen Stinger missiles it acquired and refuses to assist the United States in tracking down their source.

27 The U.S. Supreme Court votes five to four to give military and other government contractors broad immunity against liability for deaths and injuries caused by negligently designed equipment as long as they hold to "reasonably precise" government specifications and notify the government of potential dangers. The ruling is expected to result in the dismissal of most of the dozens of personal injury suits pending against military contractors.

28 The United States and the Soviet Union exchange data regarding the size of some previous nuclear tests. It is the first time the Soviets have disclosed the size of any of their test explosions.

28 A federal grand jury indicts three managers at the Aberdeen Proving Ground for felony violations of federal hazardous waste laws.

28 The senior military officer assigned to the U.S. embassy in Athens is killed by a bomb blast in an Athens suburb.

29 The DOD plans to sell eight sophisticated Phalanx radar-aimed antimissile machine guns to Brazil.

30 The Pentagon informs Congress it plans to sell eight F-16s to Malaysia. The deal includes spare parts and support equipment.

30 The DOD announces a month-long joint U.S.-Thailand military exercise to be held near Rayong.

30 In separate incidents, one F-16 crashes into the Black Forest in West Germany, and two others collide near Bodenheim. One pilot dies.

30 Five former Marines go to Vietnam to help clear mines laid by the U.S. forces there twenty years ago.

30 The U.S. Supreme Court removes the last obstacle in the way of settling the Agent Orange class-action suit; $240 million will be distributed to victims of Agent Orange.

30 Manfred Wörner of the Federal Republic of Germany becomes the new secretary-general of NATO, replacing Lord Carrington.

July

1	The United States begins inspections of Soviet weapons facilities to verify compliance with the INF treaty.
1	Italy's parliament votes to approve the transfer of the seventy-two F-16s of the 401st Tactical Fighter Wing from Spain to Italy.
2	General John Chain, command in chief of the Strategic Air Command (CINCSAC), confirms that fifty-one FB-111s will be transferred from the Strategic Air Command to the Tactical Air Command for reassignment in Europe.
3	The USS *Vincennes,* engaged in battle with a number of Iranian gunboats, mistakes an Iranian jetliner for an attacking warplane and shoots it down, killing 290 people. President Reagan announces that there will be no change in policy as a result of the incident, and no charges are to be brought against the captain or crew of the *Vincennes.*
3	Air Force Secretary Edward Aldridge visits space and military facilities in the Soviet Union.
6	Soviet chief of staff Sergei Akhromeyev begins a six-day tour of the United States, including the Pentagon and other military facilities.
7	Chief of staff Akhromeyev visits the USS *Theodore Roosevelt* and is given a demonstration of the military power of an American supercarrier.
8	Brigadier General Gail Reals becomes the commander of the Quantico Marine installation, making her the first woman to command a Marine base. She is the highest-ranking female in the Marine Corps.
12	Two U.S. helicopters answer a distress call from a Panamanian freighter in the Persian Gulf. Upon arriving at the scene, the pilots discover the freighter being attacked by two Iranian gunboats. The Iranian vessels fire upon the helicopters, and the helicopters return fire, damaging both gunboats. The helicopters sustain no damage.
13	Soviet chief of staff Akhromeyev promises that the Soviet Union will begin to match deeds to words and that the United States will begin to see changes in Soviet military spending and force structure.
13	Greece serves notice that U.S. military facilities there must close by June 1990. U.S. officials indicate that the notification is merely a formality and that they expect new negotiations to prolong the American military presence in Greece.
13	The Senate cuts NASA's budget request of $1 billion for a permanently staffed space station to $200 million. NASA officials warn that the cut virtually dooms the project.
13	Space officials warn Congress that space junk—bits and pieces of expended orbital material from paint chips to rocket stages—threatens to curtail the use of space by the year 2000. A collision between a paint chip and a space shuttle damaged the shuttle's cockpit window, and a continued buildup of debris could endanger the survival of any orbiting facility.
14	Forty Soviets arrive in the United States to begin the next round of inspections to ensure compliance with the INF treaty.

14   U.S. and Soviet officials announce that to date there have been no violations of the INF treaty.

14   Secretary of State Shultz petitions Chinese foreign minister Qian Qichen to begin consultations designed to head off the dangerous spread of ballistic missile technology. China is a key supplier of ballistic missiles, especially to the troubled Middle East.

15   The GAO releases a report charging that the Air Force has waived test requirements and is about to purchase 400 advanced medium-range air-to-air missiles (AMRAAM) that have not been rigorously tested. The report asserts that only fifty-nine of the scheduled eighty-nine test firings have been completed and that only three of those involved the advanced version of the missile that the Air Force intends to purchase.

15   Vietnam rescues three Navy fliers missing over the South China Sea since they abandoned their plane three days earlier.

17   A missing former Navy enlistee surfaces in Moscow and is granted political asylum. Glen Michael Souter had special intelligence clearances and had been the subject of an FBI espionage investigation prior to his disappearance.

17   Three members of the U.S. test verification team stationed at the Soviet Union's principal nuclear test site are discovered attempting to ship prohibited, militarily sensitive materials from the Soviet Union. The United States denies charges of espionage but admits the actions of the three violate the test verification agreement between the United States and the Soviet Union. The three are permanently expelled from the Soviet Union.

18   A report shows that U.S. military hospitals have severely curtailed access to abortions over the past decade. The number of abortions performed dropped from over 10,000 in 1977 to thirty-three in 1987.

18   A Navy helicopter on a mine-detecting exercise explodes and crashes into the Pacific. All eight crew members are feared dead.

18   A DOD management study recommends that the Army, Navy, and Air Force Space Commands should be abolished and that greater authority should be given to the U.S. Space Command.

19   Six off-duty U.S. military personnel are injured in a bomb and small-arms attack on a dance club in Honduras. In response to the attack, the United States steps up security at its installations in Honduras.

19   A team of twenty Soviets arrives in Great Britain to conduct inspections to verify compliance with the INF treaty. It is the first inspection under the short-notice provision of the agreement, meaning that the Soviets were required to give only forty-eight hours' notice of the inspection.

21   Cuba, Angola, and South Africa agree on a framework for peaceful settlement of the conflict in southwestern Africa. U.S. officials say the plan does not prevent them from providing aid to UNITA because the United States did not sign the agreement.

21   The United States rejects eight Soviet on-site inspectors proposed by Moscow to verify compliance with the INF treaty. Washington suspects the eight are spies.

22   In a move that could signal the end of the close ties between the Soviet

Union and Peru, Peru approaches the United States for assistance in fighting antigovernment terrorist groups. In exchange for the assistance, Peru offers to reduce its military relations with the Soviet Union.

24   Trying to capitalize on the congressionally motivated delay of the sale of F/A-18s to Kuwait, the Soviet Union offers to sell Kuwait MiG-29s.

24   The Army suspends awarding contracts to seventeen defense firms named in court documents relating to a massive procurement fraud investigation.

25   An Air Force sergeant is shot to death while jogging near Clark AFB in the Philippines. Officials say the killing is not politically motivated.

26   U.N.-sponsored talks begin between Iran and Iraq.

26   The Philippines suspends talks reviewing the final two years of the basing agreement between it and the United States, citing serious disagreement over compensation as the reason for the suspension.

26   President Reagan signs a finding authorizing new covert activities to oust Panamanian dictator Manuel Noriega.

27   The Army announces that it is gearing up to conduct biological war games and is planning a public relations campaign to lessen the stigma associated with such weapons.

27   A $57 million aid package for the contras is introduced in the House. The package includes $30 million in military aid and $27 million in humanitarian aid.

30   The administration and the House of Representatives agree to postpone testing of low-trajectory submarine-launched ballistic missiles (SLBMs).

August

1   The Soviet Union destroys four SS-12s, the first missiles destroyed under terms of the INF treaty.

1   Secretary of Defense Carlucci arrives in Moscow to begin a series of visits to Soviet military installations and to meet with Soviet defense minister Yazov.

1   The United States requests a map showing the location of anywhere from five million to thirty million Soviet mines remaining in Afghanistan, which make it hazardous for refugees to resettle.

3   President Reagan vetoes the defense authorization bill, charging that it calls for unacceptable unilateral defense cuts in many strategic programs.

4   One hundred American National Guard troops are deployed along the U.S-Mexican border to determine if such forces can help reduce the flow of drugs into the United States.

8   The Greek government confirms that the U.S. military installation at Hellenikon will be closed and the troops and equipment there transferred out of the country.

10   *Mujahedeen* rebels fire rockets into a major Soviet base at Kalagay. They set fire to a fuel depot, which spreads to ammunition stores. Chain-reaction explosions destroy tons of ammunition and weapons—including 113 tanks and other armored vehicles—and kill over 700 Soviet troops and civilians.

12   In a nonjudicial disciplinary hearing, Commander Richard Marcinko, a

former head of the SEALs, was convicted of providing false information to officials during an investigation of an alleged kidnapping and beating. He and several other officers are alleged to have beaten a security officer during a training exercise to test his ability to withstand a terrorist attack. Marcinko has requested retirement.

12   A conference committee on the budget provides NASA with $10.7 billion for FY 1989, including $902 million for the space station, which will now be able to continue on schedule.

13   The Army War College begins a five-year plan to reform the professional military educational process. Reforms will include a doubling of electives from four to eight and the hiring of civilians to serve on the faculty.

14   The Soviet Union unveils a new MiG-29 fighter. The public report and picture of the aircraft represent a sharp break with the past practice of military secrecy in the Soviet Union.

14   President Reagan sends a letter to Mikhail Gorbachev detailing American concerns that the Soviet radar installation at Krasnoyarsk is a material violation of the 1972 ABM Treaty.

17   President Mohammad Zia ul-Haq of Pakistan and several American officials, including Arnold Raphel, the U.S. ambassador to Pakistan, and Brigadier General Herbert Wassom, are killed when their aircraft explodes and crashes in Pakistan. Sabotage is suspected.

17   Soviet inspectors monitor a nuclear blast at the Nevada test site as part of a joint verification project between the United State and the Soviet Union, the first joint test ever conducted.

18   The Navy cancels its contract with Boeing to rewing its A-6E aircraft with graphite wings and awards a contract to Grumman to rewing the aircraft with metal wings.

18   A redesigned shuttle booster passes a "flaw test" in which the booster is deliberately riddled with fourteen flaws and then test-fired. The successful test clears the way for the shuttle program to resume.

19   The Pentagon releases the report on the downing of an Iranian airliner by the frigate USS *Vincennes*. The report admits errors were made and attributes them to the stress of battle because the *Vincennes* was engaged in skirmishes with Iranian gunboats at the time of the shoot-down. The report urges that no disciplinary action be taken against the officers or crew.

22   The Congressional Budget Office reports that the total cost of upgrading the B-1 bomber to enable it to penetrate present and future Soviet defenses is approximately $8 billion.

23   The Navy charges Captain Alexander Balian with dereliction of duty for his failure to rescue a boatload of Vietnamese refugees who claim they later turned to cannibalism to survive.

23   Repairs are completed on the USS *Stark*. The ship will be returned to the Navy in about two weeks.

23   The Soviet Union denies that a disastrous explosion occurred at a major ammunition depot in Afghanistan. Contrary to other reports (see August 10 entry), they claim that the facility was a minor one and that no deaths occurred.

24   U.S. and Soviet arms negotiators meet in Geneva to begin a review of

compliance with the 1972 ABM Treaty. The review sessions occur every five years. The United States intends to make the Soviet radar facility at Krasnoyarsk a key issue of the discussion.

24   American and West German security officials uncover a spy ring that has been supplying Hungarian intelligence agents with secret Western military documents for over ten years.

24   The C-17 transport plane designed to ferry huge amounts of gear and troops, which has been months behind schedule, moves to the assembly line at McDonnel Douglas.

28   A military air show at the American Ramstein Air Base in West Germany ends in tragedy when three Italian jets collide and one crashes into the crowd, killing seventy and injuring five hundred.

28   The GAO reveals the results of a study indicating that most of the B-1 bomber fleet is grounded on any given day due to a number of problems, including a shortage of spare parts.

28   The Soviet Union officially begins eliminating its stock of medium-range missiles with the destruction of three SS-20s at a test site near Volgograd.

28   During training exercises in West Germany, two Army Bradley fighting vehicles are struck by armor-piercing rounds from a U.S. tank, killing one soldier and injuring five others. Since practice rounds are less powerful than comparably sized combat munitions, critics claim the damage justifies concerns expressed over the safety of the vehicle.

29   West German defense minister Wörner bans future displays of acrobatic flying over West Germany, the result of the air show crash at Ramstein a day earlier.

29   The aircraft carrier USS *Dwight D. Eisenhower* collides with a Spanish collier at Hampton Roads, Virginia. There are no injuries, but about 100 feet of the starboard side of the ship is damaged. The *Eisenhower* is on its way home from a six-month assignment in the Mediterranean.

29   Republican vice-presidential candidate Dan Quayle says the 1972 ABM Treaty should either be rewritten to allow early limited deployment of an SDI system or the treaty should be scrapped.

30   The hot-line between the United States and the Soviet Union celebrates its twenty-fifth year of service. Congratulatory messages are sent between the two countries.

30   The last of the South African troops who had penetrated 180 miles into Angola are withdrawn. The withdrawal is part of a series of agreements between the warring parties.

30   The Soviet Union steps up military activities in Afghanistan, assisting government troops and attacking rebel positions with ground forces and aircraft. The United States charges that the air assault violates the April 14 accords because the aircraft were brought in from outside the country.

31   The Reagan administration announces that it will complete no new arms control agreements until the Soviets dismantle their controversial radar facility at Kransoyarsk. The administration also threatened officially to label the facility a "material breach" of the 1972 ABM Treaty unless it is destroyed.

31   The administration authorizes military air exercises to take place over West Virginia, Maryland, and Virginia, despite protests that the exercises will be environmentally disruptive.

September

1   Cuban officials meet with U.S.-backed Angolan rebels in the first face-to-face contact between the Cubans and UNITA.

5   A Titan 2 missile carrying a classified payload is successfully launched.

7   The Air Force, responding to a 1987 ground test in which the wing of an F-16 fighter buckled, announces that it is adding reinforcing plates to the wings of existing aircraft and will order strengthened wings on F-16s produced in the future.

7   Defense Secretary Carlucci announces a pledge by the People's Republic of China to halt missile sales that could cause instability in the Middle East and elsewhere, removing a stumbling block to improved U.S.-Chinese relations.

11   The first American missiles are destroyed under the terms of the INF treaty. The sixteen missiles and two spares of the 550th Tactical Missile Wing were the last missiles deployed, and, in keeping with the American last in–first out policy, they are the first to go.

13   125,000 U.S. and NATO forces begin Exercise Certain Challenge in West Germany, one of the largest ground maneuvers since the end of World War II.

13   Nearly 3,000 Marines and Army soldiers arrive in Yellowstone National Park to help battle forest fires that have charred almost one million acres of the park.

14   U.S. officials witness a Soviet nuclear test. It is the first time American officials and sensing instruments have been permitted at a Soviet test, and it follows one month after the Soviet Union had observers at a U.S. test, also a first. The reciprocal test site visits are part of a plan to create a verification regime for the 1974 Threshold Test Ban Treaty and the 1976 Peaceful Nuclear Explosions Treaty.

14   The Soviet Union tests its newest SS-25 mobile ICBM according to launch data gathered at North American Air Defense (NORAD).

14   The United States charges that Libya is on the verge of full-scale production of chemical weapons. The United States calls on the world community to take vigorous action to curb the spread of chemical weapons.

15   The Soviet Union informally invites the United States to inspect its controversial radar installation at Krasnoyarsk. The facility has been unofficially called a "material breach" of the 1972 ABM Treaty, and the issue has been an impediment to continued negotiations between the superpowers. The invitation is intended to convince Washington that the facility is incapable of fulfilling a role in a ballistic missile defense system.

16   Mikhail Gorbachev launches a new diplomatic initiative toward Asia, calling for the dismantling of U.S. and Soviet naval facilities in the Western Pacific and an early Sino-Soviet summit.

16   Congressman Les Aspin (D–Wisconsin) reports that the latest cost es-

timate for the SICBM fell by $4 billion. The cost of 500 of the new single-warhead missiles is $36 billion, down from the original estimate of $40 billion.

20   House Speaker Jim Wright (D–Texas) reveals that the CIA provoked antigovernment demonstrations in Nicaragua. CIA and administration officials charge that Wright breached security by revealing the information, which was provided only to a congressional panel and was classified. Wright denies the charge.

27   Lieutenant General James A. Abrahamson announces his retirement as head of the Strategic Defense Initiative Organization (SDIO).

28   The United States and Spain reach an agreement on the three remaining U.S. military facilities in Spain.

29   The space shuttle *Discovery* is successfully launched, returning the United States to space after a thirty-two month absence following the explosion of the shuttle *Challenger*. James Fletcher, NASA chief, calls the launch "the first step of a new era."

29   The Soviet Union unveils its own version of a space shuttle. Similar in design to the American shuttle, it has been under development since at least 1982.

29   President Reagan reports to the Congress that the United States must continue to expand its nuclear testing program even if arms control talks with the Soviets prove successful. This is an apparent shift from December 1987 when the United States and the Soviet Union agreed to seek further limits on testing.

29   The United Nations Peacekeeping Forces are named the winners of the Nobel Peace Prize.

29   The Air Force abandons efforts to acquire F-15–launched ASAT missiles because Congress has consistently prevented them from testing the system. The Air Force plans to shift to a ground-based laser system for ASAT capabilities.

October

1   President Reagan signs into law a bill providing $27 million in humanitarian aid to the contras. The law calls for aid in the same four areas as previous legislation—food, clothing, shelter, and medical supplies—but the new law does not contain the word *only*. President Reagan plans to take advantage of this "flexibility" by providing training programs intended to make the contras self-sufficient.

1   Apparently reacting to continued operational difficulties with the B-1, the DOD announces more stringent testing requirements for the B-2.

2   The Army drops Colt Industries as the manufacturer of rifles and awards a five-year contract to FN Manufacturing of Columbia, South Carolina. The shift is reported to be the result of Colt's being underbid, not because of a series of strikes that have plagued the operation.

2   The GAO reports that the military unnecessarily bars women from thousands of jobs and has established recruitment goals that further limit the number of positions open to women.

3   The shuttle *Discovery* ends its four-day mission with a tribute to the seven crew members who died in the *Challenger* accident in 1986.

3   The Pentagon suspends initial funding for a new naval surveillance aircraft because the Navy failed to comply with a DOD ruling that the service study alternatives. After the completion of such a study, the funds will be eligible to be released.

3   Saudi Arabia signs the Nuclear Nonproliferation Treaty (NPT).

3   The Air Force assures Congress that the advanced cruise missile (ACM) program is back on track after several of the missiles crashed during test flights. The accurate ACM is said to have a range nearly double that of the current generation of cruise missiles, thereby contributing to the survivability of airborne platforms when the ACMs are used in standoff mode.

4   The Pentagon announces that SDI will not be sufficient to defend the United States. Citing Soviet bomber and cruise missile forces, the Pentagon indicates that U.S. air defenses will have to be dramatically improved as well.

4   *Mujahedeen* leaders claim they have a shortage of Stinger missiles and that the shortage is preventing them from retaking areas abandoned by Soviet troops because Afghan and Soviet aircraft have stepped up their attacks.

4   The Soviet Union recommends steps to strengthen U.N. peacekeeping operations, among them a call for greater authority to set up peacekeeping operations in troubled areas of the world.

5   A conference committee agrees on legislation to close obsolete military bases. The legislation calls for Defense Secretary Carlucci to empower a twelve-member nonpartisan panel to prepare a list of recommended closings to be presented before December 31. Carlucci has until January 16 to accept or reject the list. Congress then has forty-five days, beginning March 1, to pass a resolution barring the closings. If Congress does not take action, the closings will proceed.

5   The State Department reveals that the Soviet Union agreed to include fighter aircraft in the new European Conventional Stability Talks. The Soviet decision removes one of the last roadblocks to the beginning of the talks.

5   Iran agrees to stop searching ships sailing in international waters that it suspects of carrying war supplies to Iraq.

5   The CIA settles the $750,000 claim of nine Canadians who were unknowing victims of brainwashing experiments in the 1950s.

5   The DOE releases a report on the Savannah River nuclear power plant that reveals that the plant has had to shut down nine to twelve times per year for the last two decades, more than twice the rate of shutdowns in the civilian nuclear power industry.

6   The Pentagon cuts the number of weapons it intends to deploy in the first phase of SDI by 50 percent. Estimates of total cost of the initial deployment decrease from $115 billion to $69 billion.

6   The House votes to transfer up to $150 million in unspent DOD funds to the United Nations for new peacekeeping initiatives.

7   President Reagan announces major shake-ups in some of the most senior

posts in the U.S military services. Among others, Lieutenant General Craven Rogers, Jr., currently commander of the 7th Air Force based in South Korea, has been selected as the new deputy chief of U.S. Central Command.

8   President Reagan nominates Lieutenant General George Monahan, Jr., the top Air Force acquisitions official, to replace Lieutenant General James Abrahamson as SDIO director.

12   The Pentagon warns that a prolonged delay in restarting the nation's weapons reactors, all five of which had been closed for safety reasons, could jeopardize national security by precipitating a shortage of tritium.

12   Sundstrand Corp., a major defense contractor, agrees to plead guilty to charges of defrauding the government and to pay $128 million. It is being described as the largest fraud recovery in history.

13   U.S. intelligence officials report that satellite observations detect a significant increase in the number of mobile SS-24s deployed by the Soviet Union.

13   The Reagan administration abandons attempts to secure military aid for the contras, leaving the issue to be resolved by the next president.

14   A congressional panel reveals that the DOE was aware that its nuclear weapons reactor in Ohio was leaking thousands of tons of uranium into the environment over the course of decades and decided not to spend the money required to stop the leakage.

16   The Reagan administration charges that the Soviet Union has refused to permit the operation of equipment needed by U.S. inspectors to verify key elements of the INF Treaty.

17   The United States and the Philippines sign an agreement to more than double the amount of aid to be received by the Philippines in exchange for the continued operation of U.S. military facilities through the remainder of the lease agreement in 1991.

19   The first Pershing II missile launchers in West Germany are destroyed in accordance with the INF treaty.

19   The House rejects a bill that would have authorized disability benefits to Vietnam veterans who were exposed to Agent Orange.

20   A congressional report reveals that the series of spy scandals that broke in the United States in 1987 and 1988 has failed to result in an increase in security.

20   Lawrence Livermore officials report that an earth penetrating warhead was successfully tested in New Mexico.

21   The United States and Argentina conclude their first joint naval maneuvers in seven years. Officials claim the maneuvers are part of a gradual warming in relations between the two nations' military establishments.

22   The battleship Wisconsin is recommissioned and returned to active duty.

23   The Reagan administration announces that tritium needed for the nation's nuclear weapons is in short supply due to the closure of the nation's nuclear weapons reactors. Unless steps are taken to address the problem, officials predict that the supply will be gone by mid-1989.

23   The DOD announces that it has trimmed personnel by almost 38,000 to a total manpower level of just over 2,136,000.

24   Air Force chief of staff Welch says that the problems of the B-2 bomber are far greater than those experienced by the B-1.

24   EDO Corp. has received a $1 million contract from the Air Force for 5,000 visors made of polycarbonate that will protect pilots' eyes from laser beams used to target aircraft in flight.

25   Resolving a dispute between the Department of State and DOD, President Reagan decides on a plan of limited on-site inspection for the START agreement being negotiated with the Soviet Union. Civilian DOD officials favored a more intrusive verification scheme.

25   President Reagan signs legislation raising the Veterans Administration to cabinet level.

26   During training exercises, two Marine Corps helicopters crash, killing all ten service people on board.

27   The United States denies the Soviet Union access to a shipyard next to Subic Bay in the Philippines claiming that there is a risk that the Soviets could spy on the facility.

27   The NATO Nuclear Planning Group is disrupted as Belgium refuses to endorse a report on steps to offset the military reductions of the INF treaty. Belgium later reverses itself.

28   Hughes Aircraft Co. delivers the first production version of the new AM-RAAM missile to the Air Force.

28   State Department officials charge that the Soviet Union has deployed about thirty advanced ground attack planes in Afghanistan. Many officials assert that the planes are designed for offensive operations, while some argue that the planes are merely there to help prevent rebel attacks on retreating columns.

29   The first scheduled launch of the Soviet space shuttle is aborted after an emergency evacuation platform fails to separate from the rocket body.

31   Spain agrees to establish formal intelligence ties with the government of Cuba. U.S. officials worry that the relationship could jeopardize NATO secrets and make it more difficult to protect Cuban defectors.

31   The DOE announces that it intends to cooperate with state and federal agencies to monitor environmental damage caused by radioactive leaks at a number of its weapons production facilities and to clean up the leaks.

31   Two Marine helicopters collide during battle exercises over Okinawa. All four Marines on one of the aircraft die, while the other helicopter is able to return to base.

November

1   The United States and Egypt sign an agreement calling for Egypt to coproduce the M1A1 Abrams tank with the United States. It is the first time any country outside the United States has produced the Abrams tank.

2   The Soviet Union officially recognizes the 1977 Panama Canal Treaty and calls for the neutrality of the canal in both war and peace.

2   The space shuttle *Atlantis* is rolled out to the launch pad. The shuttle is expected to make a secret military flight later in the month.

3   The Reagan administration, citing frustration over the continued refusal of the Soviet Union to dismantle the radar site at Krasnoyarsk, an-

nounces that it will counter with increased offensive capabilities and a speeding up of antiballistic missile development.

3   A virus infects thousands of computers at universities and defense research centers throughout the United States, causing the Internet system to shut down.

3   Avtex Fiber-Fort Royal, a major producer of rayon, closes. Rayon is a critical fiber for the shuttle boosters, as well as missiles. NASA and the DOD express concern over the closing of the facility.

4   DOD officials report that the virus that had infected a defense research network of over 50,000 institutions has been eliminated. A graduate student at Cornell University, the son of a U.S. electronic security expert, is named as the author of the virus program. Officials claim that vital defense and security networks were not affected by the virus and are, in fact, virtually impenetrable.

5   Soviet officials assure the United States that all Vietnamese troops will be out of Cambodia within a year.

7   Genisco Technology Corp. is ordered to pay $725,000 in fines and restitution for falsifying test data on several key military contracts.

8   NASA and DOD officials meet with congressional leaders and officials of Avtex Fibers-Front Royal to find a way to keep the plant in operation.

8   North Korea unveils a proposal for its reunification with South Korea. The proposal includes a phased withdrawal of U.S. military forces from the South.

8   The second operational B-1B crashes near Dyess AFB, Texas. All four crew members eject safely.

9   Air Force Secretary Aldridge announces his resignation. He plans to open a Washington office of McDonnell Douglas Corp. specializing in command-and-control and electronic intelligence systems.

9   The Air Force grounds the entire fleet of B-1 bombers pending a safety inspection to determine the cause of recent crashes.

10   The Air Force unveils its top-secret Lockheed F-117A stealth fighter, releasing a photograph of the aircraft in flight. The Air Force confirms that it has been flying since June 1981 and that some fifty of the fighters are now in operation.

11   A new study sponsored by the American Legion reveals that almost two-thirds of those who saw heavy combat in Vietnam suffer delayed psychological and other health effects.

12   Half of the grounded B-1 bomber fleet is cleared to return to the air.

12   Military sources reveal that chair of the Joint Chiefs William Crowe has no intention of stepping aside to allow president-elect Bush to name a new chair. Crowe wants to serve out his term because he believes the staggered nature of JCS chair appointments, overlapping the arrival of a new president, maintains continuity within the military.

13   Spain and Portugal are admitted into the Western European Union.

14   After a year-long study, the Army opens up over 3,000 active-duty assignments to women.

15   The Soviet space shuttle completes its first flight, a remotely piloted flight through two orbits of the earth.

16   A blue-ribbon panel concludes that unless the U.S. intelligence network

undergoes a major overhaul, it will be unable to compete with the intelligence networks of other countries, with disastrous implications for U.S. national security.

17   The third operational B-1B, the second in less than two weeks, crashes at Ellsworth AFB, South Dakota. All four crew members escape.

18   Attempts to open NATO–Warsaw Pact negotiations on European conventional forces come to a standstill when the United States and France disagree on the inclusion of a European security conference in the negotiations.

18   The Air Force agrees to provide Avtex Fibers Inc. with $20 million in operating capital to keep the rayon manufacturer afloat.

19   U.S. intelligence sources reveal that the Soviet Union has begun deployment of a new, more accurate, more powerful SS-18, the Mod 5. Each Mod 5 warhead is reported to have double the yield of the Mod 4s.

21   The Navy removes the captain of a destroyer twelve days after he fired a volley that landed near a Japanese patrol boat in a crowded waterway.

22   The Air Force and Northrop roll out the prototype of the B-2 advanced technology Stealth bomber.

22   The United States and Australia announce a new agreement extending the U.S. base presence in Australia for ten years.

23   President-elect Bush names Brent Scowcroft to be his national security adviser.

28   The special commission on military bases begins to draft its list of obsolete facilities to be closed.

28   Workers at the Rockwell International plant in Columbus, Ohio, which produced components for the B-1 bomber, claim that flawed parts were used in construction of the bombers.

29   Technicians at Radio Free Europe and Radio Liberty report that Soviet jamming of their broadcasts has stopped.

29   A federal judge upholds a key conspiracy charge against Oliver North, setting the stage for a full criminal trial.

29   President Aquino says that any extension of leases on U.S. military facilities in the Philippines will have to be negotiated by 1991, one year earlier than U.S. officials had anticipated.

December

1   President Reagan rules out a pretrial pardon for Iran-contra defendant Oliver North.

1   The Pentagon announces that White House national security adviser Colin Powell is to be promoted to four-star rank and made commander in chief of the U.S. Army Forces Command.

4   The shuttle *Atlantis* is successfully launched. Part of its mission will be to deploy a new-generation satellite that can "see" through clouds.

4   Soviet officials and Afghan rebels hold their first high-level meeting.

5   Defense Secretary Carlucci announces that the U.S. force in the Persian Gulf will remain at strength until there are clear indications of a peaceful settlement to the Iran-Iraq war.

6   President-elect Bush selects William Webster to remain as head of the CIA.

6   A B-52 bomber on a training mission crashes on the runway. The crew escapes serious injury, and the cause of the crash is unknown. The Air Force grounds all B-52s but lifts the grounding the next day.

6   A federal appeals court, deciding a case brought by the state of Minnesota, rules that the Montgomery amendment is unconstitutional. The Montgomery amendment, enacted in 1986, made it possible for the federal government to order state National Guard units into training missions over the objections of state governors. A district court in a Massachussets case ruled in favor of the amendment several months earlier.

7   General Secretary Mikhail S. Gorbachev, speaking at the United Nations, announces unilateral reductions in Soviet troop and tank deployments in Asia and in the Central European theater.

7   Soviet chief of staff Akhromeyev retires.

7   U.S. officials report that South Africa has signaled its readiness to accede to the Angola-Namibia peace accords.

8   An American A-10 crashes in Remscheid, West Germany, killing the pilot and four people on the ground, injuring fifty, and destroying two dozen homes. That brings to nearly 100 the number of people killed in West Germany this year as a result of crashes of NATO warplanes. A moratorium on low-level training flights is adopted for the remainder of 1988. Resistance to continued overflights is growing.

11   The DOE issues a report calling for expenditures of $50 billion over the next twenty years to improve its bomb production processes and to clean up the environmental damage caused by nuclear weapons facilities.

13   The United States and Greece begin the final round of talks on the future of U.S. military installations in Greece.

13   Palestine Liberation Organization leader Yasir Arafat fails to comply with U.S. demands regarding terrorism and the future of Israel during a speech to the United Nations General Assembly. His failure means that the United States and Israel will not enter into negotiations with the PLO.

13   South Africa, Angola, and Cuba sign a peace agreement calling for the withdrawal of 50,000 Cuban troops from Angola and independence for Namibia. A final treaty signing is planned for December 22 in New York.

14   The Pentagon announces that it intends to expand its review of top military contractors to include an additional eighteen firms. A review of twelve defense firms has already revealed that the United States has been billed for millions of dollars in questionable consulting fees.

15   The Soviet Union appoints Colonel General Mikhail Moiseyev as the new armed forces chief of staff to replace Sergei Akhromeyev. Moiseyev was promoted over a number of more senior officers.

16   President-elect Bush names former senator John Tower to be secretary of defense.

19   Soviet sources indicate that troop withdrawals from Afghanistan may be completed ahead of the negotiated schedule.

21   A Pan Am airliner crashes in Scotland, killing 270 people on board and on the ground. Investigation reveals that a bomb on board the aircraft caused the crash.

21   A U.S. district court judge sets January 31 as the starting date for the trial of Oliver North in the Iran-contra scandal.

21   Two Soviet cosmonauts return to earth after a record-setting 366 days in space.

21   An Army intelligence officer is arrested by FBI agents for selling security information to Eastern bloc agents.

22   The United States refuses to rule out the use of force against a suspected Libyan chemical weapons production facility.

22   Sudan and Ethiopia sign an agreement to "respect each others' sovereignty." Analysts hope this will lead the two governments to reduce their assistance to rebel groups fighting against each government.

22   The Southwest African peace settlement is signed in New York.

28   President-elect Bush names Robert Gates, the second-ranking CIA official, to be the deputy assistant for national security in the new administration. Gates was originally nominated to replace William Casey as the head of the CIA in 1987, but questions about his role in the Iran-contra affair forced President Reagan to withdraw his name.

29   The bipartisan commission on base closings issues a list of eighty-six military facilities it deems militarily suspect and expendable.

29   Border talks between North and South Korea end abruptly when the North issues a surprise call for an end to South Korea's joint military exercises with the United States.

30   Oliver North's attorney issues subpoenas for President Reagan and President-elect Bush to testify at North's trial.

Worldwide U.S. Force Deployments, 1989

U.S./Western Hemisphere
 1 Airborne Division
 1 Air Assault Division
 4 Armored Divisions
 6 Mechanized Infantry Divisions
10 Infantry Divisions
 3 USMC Divisions
25 Combat Brigades
24 USAF Tactical Fighter Wings

Pacific Command
East Pacific (3rd Fleet)
 4 Aircraft Carriers
 5 Helicopter Carriers
 1 Battleship
21 Destroyers
43 Frigates
36 Attack Submarines
20 Amphibious Ships
 7 USN/USMC Tactical Fighter Wings

Atlantic Command
North Atlantic (2nd Fleet)
 5 Aircraft Carriers
 5 Helicopter Carriers
 2 Battleships
 9 Cruisers
35 Destroyers
50 Frigates
49 Attack Submarines
18 Amphibious Ships
10 USN/USMC Tactical Fighter Wings

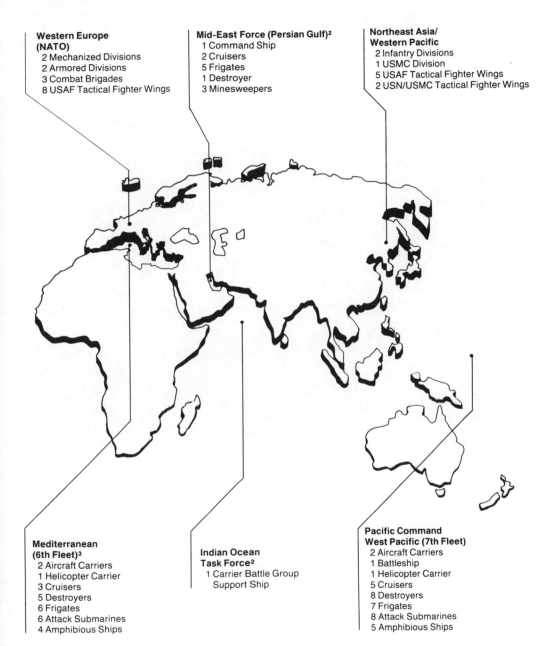

**Western Europe
(NATO)**
  2 Mechanized Divisions
  2 Armored Divisions
  3 Combat Brigades
  8 USAF Tactical Fighter Wings

Mid-East Force (Persian Gulf)[2]
  1 Command Ship
  2 Cruisers
  5 Frigates
  1 Destroyer
  3 Minesweepers

**Northeast Asia/
Western Pacific**
  2 Infantry Divisions
  1 USMC Division
  5 USAF Tactical Fighter Wings
  2 USN/USMC Tactical Fighter Wings

**Mediterranean
(6th Fleet)[3]**
  2 Aircraft Carriers
  1 Helicopter Carrier
  3 Cruisers
  5 Destroyers
  6 Frigates
  6 Attack Submarines
  4 Amphibious Ships

**Indian Ocean
Task Force[2]**
  1 Carrier Battle Group
    Support Ship

**Pacific Command
West Pacific (7th Fleet)**
  2 Aircraft Carriers
  1 Battleship
  1 Helicopter Carrier
  5 Cruisers
  8 Destroyers
  7 Frigates
  8 Attack Submarines
  5 Amphibious Ships

Notes:

[1] Compiled from numerous private and public sources.
[2] Indian Ocean & Persian Gulf surface units rotate out of the Pacific Fleets.
[3] Mediterranean surface units rotate out of the Atlantic Fleet.

Defense Publications 1988

This bibliography cites the major books published during calendar year 1988 on U.S. national security affairs. Books are grouped in the following categories: arms control, conventional forces and strategy, defense budget and political issues, history, NATO, nuclear strategy and weapons, regional issues, personnel, terrorism and other issues, and yearbooks and data bases.

Arms Control

Compliance and the Future of Arms Control. Gloria C. Duffy. Cambridge, Mass.: Ballinger. 320 pp. A complete record of the charges and countercharges of Soviet and U.S. arms control cheating in the 1980s.

Conventional Arms Control and the Security of Europe. Uwe Nerlich and James A. Thomson. Boulder, Colo.: Westview Press. 252 pp. Contains a broad range of European and U.S. perspectives on the historical, political, and military factors shaping the arms control debate.

From the Atlantic to the Urals: Negotiating Arms Control at the Stockholm Conference. John Borawski. Washington, D.C.: Pergamon-Brassey's. 261 pp. A realistic assessment of the successes and failures of the various conventional arms control negotiations in the 1980s.

Iron Destinies, Lost Opportunities: The Arms Race between the U.S.A. and the U.S.S.R., 1945–1987. Charles R. Morris. New York: Harper and Row. 544 pp. Examines the history of the arms race and the people responsible for dealing with it.

The Master of the Game: Paul Nitze and the Nuclear Peace. Strobe Talbott. New York: Knopf. 416 pp. A study of ongoing superpower arms negotiations with an emphasis on the START talks and the person seen as responsible for U.S. negotiating success in the 1980s, Paul Nitze.

Soviet-American Security Relations in the 1990s. Donald M. Snow. Lexington, Mass.: Lexington Books. 256 pp. Focuses on the dynamic nature of the U.S.-Soviet relationship and the role in it played by nuclear weapons and arms control.

Strategic Defenses and Arms Control. Alvin M. Weinberg and Jack N. Barkenbus, eds. New York: Paragon House. 263 pp. Discusses the relationship between SDI and strategic arms limitations. Proposes defense-protected build-down as a mechanism to achieve arms reductions during transition to a defensive force deployment.

Verification and Compliance: A Problem Solving Approach. Michael Krepon and Mary Umberger, eds. Cambridge, Mass.: Ballinger. 328 pp. Suggests solutions for difficult verification problems and ways to minimize disputes over noncompliance.

Conventional Forces and Strategy

Air Defense Systems and Weapons: World AAA and SAM Systems in the 1980s. Christopher Chant. Washington, D.C.: Pergamon-Brassey's. 317 pp. Examines the land and ship air defenses available to military commanders, with a complete listing of specifications.

America Invulnerable: The Quest for Absolute Security from 1812 to Star Wars. James Chase and Caleb Carr. New York: Summit Books. 316 pp. Traces unilateralism as a fundamental U.S. national characteristic from 1812 through today's quest for SDI.

America's Defense. Michael Mandelbaum, ed. New York: Holmes & Meier. 265 pp. An introduction and guide to U.S. military policy over the coming decade and beyond.

American Military Policy in Small Wars: The Case of El Salvador. A.J. Bacevich, James D. Hallums, Richard M. White, and Thomas F. Young. Cambridge, Mass.: Institute for Foreign Policy Analysis. Examines U.S. military involvement in El Salvador as a new approach to an old problem.

Armies in Low Intensity Conflict. David Charters and Maurice Tugwell, eds. Washington D.C.: Pergamon-Brassey's. 270 pp. Case histories of American and other forces and the rise of strategies for small-scale conflict.

Beyond Military Reform: American Defense Dilemmas. Jeffrey Record. Washington D.C.: Pergamon-Brassey's. 184 pp. Takes issue with the military reform movement's approach and examines why U.S. forces often fail at their assigned tasks.

Defending America's Security. Frederick H. Hartmann and Robert L. Wendzel. Washington, D.C.: Pergamon-Brassey's. 365 pp. Provides the analytical tools to understand U.S. defense policies in the wider context of national security and in the overall setting of international affairs.

The Geopolitics of Super Power. Colin S. Gray. Lexington: University of Kentucky Press. 274 pp. Sees U.S.-Soviet competition as a case of the classic competition between a sea power and a land power. Calls on the United States to concentrate on a sea-based defense posture and to end the threat of first use of nuclear weapons to defend Europe.

Guerrilla Warfare and Counterinsurgency: U.S.-Soviet Policy in the Third World. Richard Shultz, Jr., Uri Ra'anan, Robert L. Pfaltzgraff, Jr., Igor Lukes, and William Olson, eds. Lexington, Mass.: Lexington Books. 488 pp. Outlines preferred operational policy choices in future Third World conflicts.

Low-Intensity Warfare. Michael T. Klare and Peter Kornbluh, eds. New York: Pantheon Books. 250 pp. A critique of U.S. plans for use of counterterror and low-intensity conflict techniques.

Modern Amphibious Strategy and Techniques. James D. Ladd. London: Brassey's. 200 pp. A study of modern amphibious warfare from a commander's point of view.

National Security Strategy of the United States. Ronald Reagan. Washington, D.C.: Pergamon-Brassey's. 128 pp. Second annual White House articulation of American strategic objectives.

Naval Command and Control. W.T.T. Pakenham. London: Brassey's. 200 pp. A comprehensive examination of the technical and operational aspects of naval command and control.

Naval Strategy and National Security. Steven E. Miller and Stephen Van Evera, eds. Princeton, N.J.: Princeton University Press. 408 pp. Essays from the journal *International Security* that cover aspects of past and present naval technologies and explore current disparities over U.S. naval doctrine.

Secret Armies: Inside the American, Soviet, and European Special Forces. James Adams. New York: Atlantic Monthly Press. 320 pp. Detailed look at special operations and small-scale conflicts from both the planning and operational perspectives.

Soviet Breakout: Strategies to Meet It. Joseph Churba. Washington, D.C.: Pergamon-Brassey's. 144 pp. Calls on U.S. policymakers to understand the serious nature of the Soviet threat and to develop a long-term strategy to guide policies for countering Soviet expansion.

Warfare in the 20th Century: Theory and Practice. Colin McInnes and G.P. Sheffield, eds. Winchester, Mass.: Unwin Hyman. 256 pp. Highlights key themes of warfare throughout the world, emphasizing the gulf between theory and practice.

1999: Victory without War. Richard Nixon. New York: Simon and Schuster. 336 pp. A warning by the former president that the new face of Gorbachev's Soviet Union belies a continuing desire to dominate the world. Suggests a forceful U.S. response.

Defense Budget and Political Issues

Bureaucratic Politics and National Security: Theory and Practice. David C. Kozak and James M. Keagle, eds. Boulder, Colo.: Lynne Rienner Publishers. 504 pp. A combination of classic scholarly works and original essays that sheds light on the functional activities, policy relationships, and issues of the national security bureaucracy.

Conflict or Codetermination: Congress, the President, and the Power to Make War. Marc E. Smyrl. Cambridge, Mass.: Ballinger. 200 pp. Examines congressional gains and limitations from the 1960s to the present, emphasizing developments in the interpretation of the War Powers Act, as well as new strategies for power sharing.

The Dangerous Doctrine: National Security and U.S. Foreign Policy. Saul Landau. Boulder, Colo.: Westview Press. 201 pp. Argues that U.S. security policy from at least the end of World War II through the present has used anticommunism as a cover for imperialist inclinations. Calls for reprioritization to emphasize domestic social problems.

The Defense Management Challenge: Weapons Acquisition. J. Ronald Fox. Boston: Harvard Business School Press. 368 pp. Detailed examination of the procurement process with recommendations for upgrading Pentagon management.

Diplomacy and the American Democracy. David D. Newsome. Bloomington: Indiana University Press. 226 pp. Explores the peculiarities of American diplomacy.

FEMA and the Politics of Emergency Management. Gregory D. Foster. Boulder, Colo.: Westview Press. 224 pp. Explores the critical domestic side of U.S. national security.

Gorbachev's Russia and American Foreign Policy. Seweryn Bialer and Michael Mandelbaum, eds. Boulder, Colo.: Westview Press. 510 pp. A thoughtful examination of the nature of the changes in Gorbachev's Soviet Union and the potential responsive changes in U.S. foreign and national security policy.

Inside the National Security Council: The True Story of the Making and Unmaking of Reagan's

Foreign Policy. Constantine C. Menges. New York: Simon and Schuster. A behind-the-scenes story of the making of foreign policy during the Reagan years.

Lost in Space: The Domestic Politics of the Strategic Defense Initiative. Gerald M. Steinberg. Lexington, Mass.: Lexington Books. 192 pp. Examines the relationship between SDI and U.S. domestic policy.

National Security and the U.S. Constitution: The Impact of the Political System. George C. Edwards III and Wallace Earl Walker. Baltimore: Johns Hopkins University Press. Explores the consequences of the U.S. constitutional structure for national security.

The New Politics of the Budgetary Process. Aaron Wildavsky. Glenview, Ill.: Scott, Foresman. 468 pp. A close look at the current budgetary process and the political trade-offs between the components.

Nuclear Fear: A History of Images. Spencer R. Weart. Cambridge, Mass.: Harvard University Press. 523 pp. Examines the consistency of nuclear imagery in the United States from the beginning of the nuclear age to today.

Peace, Defense, and Economic Analysis. Christian Schmidt and Frank Blackaby, eds. New York: St. Martin's Press. 481 pp. Explores the models used to analyze arms industries and defense expenditures. Offers a new understanding of arms race dynamics.

Peace Movements and Political Cultures. Charles Chatfield and Peter van den Dungen, eds. Knoxville: University of Tennessee Press. 320 pp. Examines the history of various peace movements, placing them in their cultural and political contexts, to help explain the often agonizingly slow progress society has made toward peace.

The Politics of Resource Allocation in the U.S. Department of Defense. Alex Mintz. Boulder, Colo.: Westview Press. 149 pp. Demonstrates how domestic and international shocks influence deviations from a routinized pattern of resource allocation in the Department of Defense.

The Presidency and the Management of National Security. Carnes Lord. New York: Free Press. 240 pp. Looks at the structures of national security decision making and concludes that centralized executive authority is essential to an effective process.

Reforming Defense: The State of American Civil-Military Relations. David C. Hendrickson. Baltimore: Johns Hopkins University Press. Analyzes the major military reform movements of the 1980s.

Starting with the People. Daniel Yankelovich and Sidney Harman. Boston: Houghton Mifflin. 279 pp. Exposes the discontinuity between public opinion and national security policy. Advocates returning concurrence through huge (90–95 percent) cuts in nuclear weapons.

United States Foreign Policy: Choices and Tradeoffs. Miroslav Nincic. Washington, D.C.: Congressional Quarterly Press. 407 pp. Examines the broad scope of U.S. foreign policy and national security issues.

Wild Blue Yonder: Money, Politics, and the B-1 Bomber. Nick Kotz. New York: Pantheon Books. 313 pp. Uses the B-1 as an instructive case to provide a valuable commentary on the weapon procurement process.

History

Blowback: The First Full Account of America's Recruitment of Nazis, and Its Disastrous Effect on Our Domestic and Foreign Policy. Christopher Simpson. New York: Weidenfeld and Nicolson. 398 pp. Examines the use of ex-Nazis by the United States to carry out foreign policy initiatives in postwar Europe and its effect on U.S. policymaking.

A Bright Shining Lie. Neil Sheehan. New York: Random House. 768 pp. The story of Lieutenant Colonel (retired) John Paul Vann and the American experience in Vietnam.

Brown Water, Black Berets: Coastal and Riverine Warfare in Vietnam. Thomas J. Cutler. Annapolis: Naval Institute Press. 426 pp. A look at the naval war in Vietnam.

The CIA's Secret Operations: Espionage, Counterespionage, and Covert Action. Harry Rositzke.
Boulder, Colo.: Westview Press. 237 pp. The only book by a professional CIA operations
officer to survey the wide range of CIA activities abroad since World War II.

A Death in November: America in Vietnam, 1963. Ellen J. Hammer. New York: Oxford University
Press. 388 pp. Examines the events leading to the assassination of South Vietnamese pres-
ident Ngo Dinh Diem to provide a fuller understanding of the American involvement in
Vietnam.

The Fate of Nations: The Search for National Security in the Nineteenth and Twentieth Centuries.
Michael Mandelbaum. New York: Cambridge University Press. 510 pp. Offers a global perspective on national security policy and identifies and illustrates various approaches to planning and maintaining a strong national defense.

The Forgotten War: America in Korea, 1950–1953. Clay Blair. New York: Times Books. 1,136
pp. A critical, frank history of the U.S. mission in Korea.

*The General and the Bomb: A Biography of General Leslie R. Groves, Director of the Manhattan
Project*. William Lawren. New York: Dodd, Mead. 324 pp. Looks back at General Groves
and the building of the bomb.

George Kennan and the Dilemmas of U.S. Foreign Policy. David Mayers. New York: Oxford
University Press. 416 pp. A comprehensive account of George Kennan's contributions to
and critiques of U.S. foreign policy.

Grenada: The Jewel Despoiled. Gordon K. Lewis. Baltimore: Johns Hopkins University Press.
240 pp. An analysis of Grenadian politics, U.S. intervention, and their implications for other
West Indian nations.

Meeting the Communist Threat: Truman to Reagan. Thomas G. Paterson. New York: Oxford.
317 pp. An examination of what the author sees as the consistent penchant of U.S. policymakers to exaggerate and misperceive the Soviet threat.

Military Effectiveness. Allan R. Millett and Williamson Murray, eds. Boston: Allen and Unwin.
960 pp. A three-volume survey of military effectiveness at the political, strategic, operational, and tactical levels that assesses how various military organizations have performed
in the first half of this century.

The Path to Vietnam: Origins of the American Commitment to Southeast Asia. Andrew J. Rotter.
Ithaca: Cornell University Press. 278 pp. Provides a unique understanding of the U.S. involvement in Vietnam and argues that the commitment to support the French in Indochina
was an essential element of containment and the reconstruction of Europe.

Technology and War. Martin Van Creveld. New York: Free Press. 304 pp. A DOD-commissioned
study of how technology has shaped the conduct of war throughout history.

Vietnam at War: The History, 1946–1975. Phillip B. Davidson. Monterey, Calif.: Presidio Press.
848 pp. A comprehensive account of the three wars that ravaged Vietnam for thirty years.

NATO

ATBMs and Western Security: Missile Defense for Europe. Ronald L. Hafner and John Roper.
Cambridge, Mass.: Ballinger. 352 pp. Examines the technical and political implications of
various proposals for the deployment of antitactical ballistic missiles (ATBMs) in Europe.

Clash in the North: Polar Summitry and NATO's Northern Flank. Walter Goldstein, ed. Washington, D.C.: Pergamon-Brassey's. 208 pp. A collection of articles, originally prepared for

the Standing Conference of Atlantic Organizations, that address the unique problems facing Norway and Sweden as a result of their proximity to the Soviet Union.

The Crucible of Peace: Common Security in Europe. Eric Grove and Stan Windass. Washington, D.C.: Pergamon-Brassey's. 161 pp. A comprehensive account of the problems of European security.

Europe without America? The Crisis in Atlantic Relations. John Palmer. New York: Oxford. 217 pp. Seeing a deterioration of the alliance, this author calls for a unified, independent, and perhaps neutral Europe.

European Security beyond the Year 2000. Robert Rudney and Luc Reychler. New York: Praeger. 317 pp. A collection of twenty-three essays, all by European writers, that establishes the factors that will govern security decisions in the future rather than makes specific predictions in particular policy arenas.

NATO and the U.S.: The Enduring Alliance. Lawrence S. Kaplan. Boston: Twayne Publishers. 256 pp. A comprehensive history of the alliance in celebration of its fortieth anniversary.

NATO Strategy and Nuclear Defense. Carl H. Amme. New York: Greenwood Press. 189 pp. Focuses on upgrading NATO strategic planning regarding tactical nuclear weapons, including the establishment of a definite threshold for the initiation of tactical nuclear use and the creation of additional steps on the escalation ladder between first use and general war.

NATO's Conventional Defenses. Stephen J. Flanagan. Cambridge, Mass.: Ballinger. 176 pp. A balanced approach to the debate over which initiatives to pursue for strengthening NATO's nonnuclear deterrent.

The Politics of European Defense Cooperation: Germany, France, Britain, and America. David Garnham. Cambridge, Mass.: Ballinger. 208 pp. Examines the prospects for strengthened European defense efforts and a consequent reduction of American defense commitments.

Politics and Security in the Southern Region of the Atlantic Alliance. Douglas T. Stuart, ed. Baltimore: Johns Hopkins University Press. 256 pp. Examines the political difficulties facing the nations of the Southern Flank and their implications for NATO security.

The Soviet Biochemical Threat to NATO. John Hemsley. New York: St. Martin's Press. 200 pp. An examination of Soviet perceptions and imperatives that seeks to establish the Soviet view of chemical and biological warfare and the consequent danger to NATO.

Spain's Entry into NATO: Conflicting Political and Strategic Perspectives. Frederico G. Gil and Joseph S. Tulchin, eds. Boulder, Colo.: Lynne Rienner Publishers. 165 pp. A comprehensive discussion of the problems presented by Spain's entry into NATO.

Nuclear Strategy and Weapons

A Base for Debate: The U.S. Satellite Station at Nurrungar. Desmond Ball. Winchester, Mass.: Unwin Hyman. 128 pp. A revelation of the costs and benefits to Australia of the U.S. satellite tracking station.

Claiming the Heavens: The New York Times Complete Guide to the Star Wars Debate. Phillip M. Boffey, William J. Broad, Leslie H. Gelb, Charles Mohr, and Holcomb B. Noble. New York: Times Books. 299 pp. An effort by these Pulitzer Prize–winning authors to present a balanced view of the history and development of SDI.

Crisis Stability and Nuclear War. Kurt Gottfried and Bruce G. Blair. New York: Oxford University Press. 368 pp. Examines the role crises play in conflict in the nuclear age and the abilities of the Soviet and American command structures to maintain control in crisis situations.

Democracy and Deterrence: The History and Future of Nuclear Strategy. Philip Bobbit. New York: St. Martin's Press. 334 pp. A thorough history of U.S. nuclear strategy and differences in strategy associated with specific weapon systems.

Ending a Nuclear War: Are the Superpowers Prepared? Stephen J. Cimbala and Joseph D. Douglass, Jr., eds. Cambridge, Mass.: Institute for Foreign Policy Analysis. 185 pp. Examines a broad range of issues relevant to the termination of nuclear war.

Fateful Visions: Avoiding Nuclear Catastrophe. Joseph S. Nye, Jr., Graham T. Allison, and Albert Carnesale. Cambridge, Mass.: Ballinger. 280 pp. Examines ten of the most influential theoretical alternatives to simple deterrence.

A Fighting Chance: The Moral Use of Nuclear Weapons. Joseph P. Martino. San Francisco: Ignatius Press. 283 pp. Draws on classical literature on morality, international law, and military strategy to make a case for nuclear ethics.

Innovation and the Arms Race: How the United States and the Soviet Union Develop New Military Technologies. Matthew Evangelista. Ithaca: Cornell University Press. 300 pp. A comparative exploration of U.S. and Soviet military innovation.

Making Space Defense Work: Must the Superpowers Cooperate? A. Fenner Milton, M. Scott Davis, and John A Parmentola. Washington, D.C.: Pergamon-Brassey's. 204 pp. An analysis of the technological and political breakthroughs that will be required if SDI is to become an operational reality.

Minds at War: Nuclear Reality and the Inner Conflicts of Defense Policy Makers. Steven Kull. New York: Basic Books. 352 pp. Argues that several U.S. policies, including pursuing strategic defense and seeking equal numbers of nuclear weapons, are inconsistent with the reality of the nuclear age.

New Weapon Technologies and the ABM Treaty. Herbert Lin. Washington, D.C.: Pergamon-Brassey's. 112 pp. Argues that weapon technologies developed since 1972 provide a challenge the authors of the ABM Treaty could not have anticipated. Calls for controls on systems that threaten the treaty as a precondition to reductions in offensive systems.

The Nuclear Age: Atomic Energy, Proliferation, and the Arm Race. 2d ed. William Sweet. Washington, D.C.: Congressional Quarterly Press. 225 pp. A comprehensive treatment of issues arising from the expansion of nuclear technologies.

The Nuclear Dilemma in American Strategic Thought. Robert E. Osgood. Boulder, Colo.: Westview Press. 138 pp. An exploration, published posthumously, of U.S. attitudes toward the use of force and nuclear weapons.

Nuclear Ethics. Joseph S. Nye, Jr. New York: Free Press. 162 pp. A balanced and comprehensive exploration of the ethical dilemmas raised by the existence of nuclear weapons and the various alternative plans for their use and nonuse.

Nuclear Strategy, Arms Control, and the Future. 2d ed. P. Edward Haley and Jack Merritt, eds. Boulder, Colo.: Westview Press. 372 pp. A revised and updated edition of this resource for scholars, researchers, and libraries.

Nuclear Strategy: Deterrence and Reality. Stephen J. Cimbala. New York: Praeger. 306 pp. A criticism of the abstract nature of U.S. nuclear strategy.

On the Defensive: The Future of SDI. Joseph S. Nye, Jr., and James A. Schear. Lanham, Md.: University Press of America. 120 pp. Explores key security and policy issued related to SDI.

Pine Gap: Australia and the U.S. Geostationary Signals Intelligence Satellite Program. Desmond Ball. Winchester, Mass.: Unwin Hyman. 118 pp. Discusses whether stations such as Pine Gap are important to the maintenance of world peace or merely tools used by the United States to augment its strategic nuclear war-fighting capabilities.

Rethinking Nuclear Strategy. Stephen J. Cimbala. Wilmington, Del.: Scholarly Resources. 278 pp. A wide-ranging discussion of nuclear strategy and related issues.

Soviet Ballistic Missile Defense and the Western Alliance. David S. Yost. Cambridge, Mass.: Harvard University Press. 352 pp. A study of the critical strategic challenges to the West posed by Soviet ballistic missile defense programs.

Strategic Defense Initiative: Survivability and Software. Report from the Office of Technology Assessment. Princeton, N.J.: Princeton University Press. 275 pp. Collected reports on the feasibility and survivability of SDI.

Toward a Comprehensive Test Ban. Steve Fetter. Cambridge, Mass.: Ballinger. 224 pp. Examines a number of issues relating to a ban on nuclear tests. Concludes that testing is essential to war fighting but has no impact on deterrence. Fetter favors a compete ban on testing.

While Others Build: A Commonsense Approach to the Strategic Defense Initiative. Angelo Codevilla. New York: Free Press. 256 pp. A sad farewell from an SDI proponent mourning the fact that the proposed system has been progressively reduced in scope.

Without the Bomb: The Politics of Nuclear Proliferation. Mitchell Reiss. New York: Columbia University Press. 336 pp. Examines six nations that did not acquire nuclear weapons and attempts to use them to determine which factors could help prevent proliferation in the future.

Regional Issues

America, the Gulf, and Israel. Dore Gold. Boulder, Colo.: Westview Press. 120 pp. Examines the U.S. military buildup in the Persian Gulf region in connection with the establishment of the U.S. Central Command and the changing strategic role of the Middle East in the 1980s.

American Military Bases in the Philippines, Base Negotiations, and Philippine- American Relations. William E. Berry, Jr. Boulder, Colo.: Westview Press. 272 pp. Assesses the bilateral relationship between the United States and the Philippines.

Arming the Dragon: U.S. Security Ties with the People's Republic of China. James A. Gregor. Washington, D.C.: Ethics and Public Policy Center. 140 pp. Examines the ambiguity of U.S. ties to Taiwan as the United States also courts the PRC. Calls for a defense partner relationship between the United States and Taiwan.

Asian Policy: A New Look for American Defense. Robert Manning. Winchester, Mass.: Unwin Hyman, 112 pp. Examines new challenges to U.S. foreign policy in Asia, the growing Soviet presence, and possible U.S. responses.

Banana Diplomacy: The Making of American Policy in Nicaragua, 1981–1987. Roy Gutman. New York: Simon and Schuster. 352 pp. A detailed account and assessment of the Reagan foreign policy toward Nicaragua.

The Eagle and the Lion: The Tragedy of American-Iranian Relations. James A. Bill. New Haven: Yale University Press. 520 pp. A powerful critique of U.S. policy toward Iran.

Finding Our Way: Toward Maturity in U.S.–Latin American Relations. Howard J. Wiarda, ed. Washington, D.C.: American Enterprise Institute. 304 pp. An examination of the evolution of Reagan policy toward Latin America from January 1981.

The Future of Asian-Pacific Security Collaboration. Sheldon W. Simon. Lexington, Mass.: Lexington Books. 208 pp. An examination of the changing order in the Asia-Pacific region and its effect on the U.S. role in regional security affairs.

Imperial State and Revolution: The United States and Cuba, 1952–1986. Morris H. Morley. New York: Cambridge University Press. 576 pp. A provocative account of U.S.-Cuban relations that accuses the United States of a relentless effort to manipulate and isolate Cuba and destroy the effects of the Cuban Revolution.

Military Basing and U.S.-Soviet Military Balance in Southeast Asia. George Tanham and Alvin H. Bernstein, eds. New York: Taylor and Francis. 200 pp. Contains papers dealing with the political and economic effects of the Soviet and U.S. military presence in Southeast Asia.

A Nuclear Weapons Free Zone in the Middle East: Problems and Prospects. Mahmoud Karem. New York: Greenwood Press. 200 pp. Examines current trends toward the nuclearization of the Middle East and proposes a nuclear-weapons-free zone as the only plausible solution.

Partners in Conflict: The U.S. and Latin America. Abraham F. Lowenthal. Baltimore: Johns Hopkins University Press. 256 pp. Examines the problem of how to restore hemispheric relations between now and the year 2000 by moving from the anticommunist focus of the Reagan administration.

Security in Northeast Asia. Stephen P. Gilbert, ed. Boulder, Colo.: Westview Press. 193 pp. Examines the necessary shift from a Euro- centered U.S. policy to a new focus on Northeast Asia, a region affecting the security and prosperity of the United States to a degree unimagined a decade ago.

Semper Fidel: America and Cuba, 1776–1988. Michael Mazaar. Baltimore: Nautical and Aviation Publishing Company of America. 540 pp. A comprehensive account of U.S.-Cuban relations.

The Soviet-American Competition in the Middle East. Steven L. Spiegel, Mark Heller, and Jacob Goldberg, eds. Lexington, Mass.: Lexington Books. 400 pp. Explores the military, economic, and political-diplomatic context of U.S.-Soviet competition in the Middle East.

Superpower Competition and Security in the Third World. Robert S. Litwak and Samuel F. Wells, Jr., eds. Cambridge, Mass.: Ballinger. 295 pp. A collection of essays on the nature of regional instability and the place of the superpowers in regional conflicts.

The Superpowers, Central America and the Middle East. Peter Shearman and Phil Williams. Washington, D.C.: Pergamon-Brassey's. 240 pp. Examines regional instabilities as factors in the U.S.-Soviet relationship.

U.S. Middle East Policy. Shai Feldman. Boulder, Colo.: Westview Press. 100 pp. Examines the domestic setting that influences U.S. decision making toward Israel and the Middle East.

U.S. Policy and the Two Koreas. Edward A. Olsen. Boulder, Colo.: Westview Press. 115 pp. Focuses on the roots of U.S. commitments to South Korea and its hostility toward the North.

Personnel

A Call to Civil Service: National Service for Country and Community. Charles C. Moskos. New York: Free Press. Argues that the central notion of shared responsibility for society must be reintroduced to young people. Calls for a national, voluntary, decentralized program that links military and civilian service for young people.

He, Too, Spoke for Democracy: Judge Hastie, World War II, and the Black Soldier. Phillip McGuire. Westport, Conn.: Greenwood Press. 154 pp. The story of the fight in the 1940s, led by William Hastie, a civilian aide to Secretary of War Stimson, to integrate the U.S. armed forces.

The Military: More Than Just a Job? Charles C. Moskos and Frank R. Wood, eds. Washington,

D.C.: Pergamon-Brassey's. 305 pp. An assessment by an international team of military sociologists showing the shift in armed forces service from an institutional format to one resembling a civilian occupation.

A Painful Field: The Psychiatric Dimension of Modern War. Richard A. Gabriel. Westport, Conn.: Greenwood Press. 147 pp. Explores the psychological limits of soldiers on the modern battlefield.

To Raise an Army: The Draft Comes to Modern America. John W. Chambers II. New York: Free Press. 386 pp. A history of selective service in the United States in the twentieth century.

The Spit-Shine Syndrome: Organizational Irrationality in the American Field Army. Christopher Bassford. New York: Greenwood Press. 171 pp. Examines the organizational and operational difficulties experienced by units in the field.

War without Men: Robots on the Future Battlefield. Steven M. Shaker and Allan R. Wise. Washington, D.C.: Pergamon-Brassey's. 202 pp. Examines current trends and future options for military use of robotic technology.

Terrorism and Other Issues

Anti-Americanism: Origins and Context. Thomas Perry Thornton, ed. Newbury Park, Calif.: Sage Publications. 497 pp. Analyzes anti-Americanism in eleven nations from Central America to Pakistan.

Best Laid Plans: The Inside Story of America's War against Terrorism. David C. Martin and John C. Walcott. New York: Harper & Row. 391 pp. Covers the period 1980–1987 and the Reagan administration's handling of terrorism.

Beyond the Iran-Contra Crisis: The Shape of U.S. Antiterrorism Policy in the Post Reagan Era. Neil C. Livingstone and Terrell E. Arnold. Lexington, Mass.: Lexington Books. 352 pp. Assesses the events leading up to the November 1986 Iran-contra disclosures and analyzes their impact on the future of U.S. counterterrorism efforts.

Comparing Foreign Intelligence: the U.S., The U.S.S.R., the U.K. and the Third World. R. Godson, ed. Washington, D.C.: Pergamon-Brassey's. 157 pp. Provides expert and up-to-date guidance to the labyrinth of intelligence services.

Current Perspectives on International Terrorism. Robert O. Slater and Michael Stohl, eds. New York: St. Martin's Press. 240 pp. A state-of-the-art examination of international terrorism and the many problems it poses for the global society.

Deadly Paradigms: The Failure of U.S. Counterinsurgency Policy. D. Michael Shafer. Princeton, N.J.: Princeton University Press. 344 pp. Argues that U.S. policymakers have consistently failed to perceive correctly the political context of revolutionary wars, with consequent consistent failure of U.S. responses.

Foreign Intelligence Organizations. Jeffrey T. Richelson. Cambridge, Mass.: Ballinger. 304 pp. Final issue of Richelson's trilogy examining major intelligence organizations worldwide.

Intelligence Requirements for the 1990s. Roy Godson, ed. Lexington, Mass.: Lexington Books. 320 pp. Explores the challenges that the United States will face in the 1990s and evaluates the preparedness of the U.S. intelligence community to meet those challenges.

International Terrorism: An Introduction to the Concepts and Actors. Donna M. Schlagheck. Lexington, Mass.: Lexington Books. 176 pp. An in-depth look at international terrorism.

Merchants of Treason. Thomas B. Allen and Norman Polmar. New York: Delacorte Press. 378

pp. A comprehensive exploration of how disastrous U.S. counterintelligence has been for the last several decades.

Psychological Operations. Joseph S. Gordon, ed. Boulder, Colo.: Westview Press. 216 pp. Examines the nature of Soviet bloc propaganda as an instrument of foreign policy and the extent to which it presents a threat to the West.

Revolutionaries and Functionaries: The Dual Face of Terrorism. Richard Falk. New York: Dutton. 211 pp. A critique of mainstream definitions of terrorism and of measures to combat it, which often put states in the terrorist category. The 1986 U.S. bombing of Libya is one such measure.

Science between the Superpowers. Yakov Rabkin. Winchester, Mass.: Unwin Hyman. 100 pp. Examines scientific exchanges between the United States and the Soviet Union, analyzing the problems that arise in order to suggest changes to ensure the continuation of scientific exchanges and to bring exchanges closer to the ideal of open scientific communication.

Secret Warriors: Inside Covert Military Operations of the Reagan Era. Steven Emerson. New York: G.P. Putnam's Sons. 256 pp. A chronicle of the excesses and absurdities of covert actions during the Reagan administration.

Superpower Détente: A Reappraisal. Mike Bowler and Phil Williams. Newbury Park, Calif.: Sage Publications. 288 pp. Examines the coincidence of interests between the United States and the Soviet Union and the divergent conceptions of détente and the type of behavior it required.

Terrorism: The Cuban Connection. Roger W. Fontaine. New York: Taylor and Francis. 206 pp. Focuses on Havana's particular mode of terrorism, how it is powered, and what implications exist in line with its perceived scope.

Terrorism: Threat and Response. Eric Morris and Alan Hoe. New York: St. Martin's Press. 180 pp. Explores terrorism from its origins to its global growth, analyzing its motives and methods and discussing steps individuals can take to protect themselves from it.

The Terrorism Reader: The Essential Source Book on Political Violence Both Past and Present. Walter Laqueur and Yonah Alexander. New York: New American Library. An examination of recent terrorist groups. Provides historical perspectives as well.

The Terrorist. Maxwell Taylor. Washington, D.C.: Pergamon-Brassey's. 220 pp. A psychological study of modern political terrorism that offers a sophisticated understanding of terrorism.

The Threat of Terrorism. Juliet Lodge, ed. Boulder, Colo.: Westview Press. 280 pp. A wide-ranging survey of contemporary, indigenous, and international terrorism in and against Western Europe.

The U.S. Intelligence Community. Jeffrey T. Richelson. Cambridge, Mass.: Ballinger. 616 pp. One volume of a trilogy. Reflects the most recent information available on the structure of more than twenty U.S. intelligence-gathering organizations.

U.S.-Soviet Security Cooperation: Achievements, Failures, Lessons. Alexander George, Philip J. Farley and Alexander Dallin. New York: Oxford University Press. 768 pp. Builds on a set of case studies to provide an understanding of the potential for and limitations of superpower cooperation.

The Violence Formula: Why People Lend Sympathy and Support to Terrorism. Terrell E. Arnold. Lexington, Mass.: Lexington Books. 224 pp. Explores the visible web of support for terrorist organizations, including fund-raising activities in the United States, media promotion of terrorist activities, and the use of law to protect terrorist organizations.

Whither the American Empire: Expansion or Contraction? Marvin E. Wolfgang, ed. Newbury

Park, Calif.: Sage Publications. 184 pp. Looks at a broad range of international problems—military, economic, and political—and explores their implications for the future security of the United States.

Yearbooks and Data Bases

The ACCESS Resource Guide: An International Directory of Information on War, Peace, and Security. William H. Kincade and Priscilla B. Hayner. Cambridge, Mass.: Ballinger. 280 pp. Comprehensive, worldwide guide to information sources on war, peace, and security issues.

The American Defense Annual, 1988–1989. Joseph Kruzel, ed. Lexington, Mass.: Lexington Books. 352 pp. The 1988 edition of a well-established source book on national security issues.

Combat Fleets of the World, 1988–1989. Jean Labayle Couhat. Annapolis: U.S. Naval Institute Press. 900 pp. A comprehensive naval reference that describes the naval programs of over one hundred nations.

The Concept of Defensive Deterrence: Strategic and Technical Dimensions of Missile Defense. George C. Marshall Institute. Washington, D.C.: George C. Marshall Institute. 137 pp. Presents the technological requirements and capabilities of strategic defense systems.

Dictionary of Military Terms. Joint Chiefs of Staff, comp. New York: Taylor and Francis. 478 pp. A major reference source for researchers and journalists that concisely defines modern military and related terms.

Guide to Modern Defense and Strategy. David Robertson. New York: Gale Research Co. 324 pp. A dictionary of more than 400 words and expressions used prominently in the literature on national security issues over the past forty years.

Guide to Nuclear Weapons, 1988. Paul Rogers. New York: St. Martin's Press. 128 pp. Comprehensive listing of the facts and figures on the nuclear weapons systems of the major powers.

The Law of War. Ingrid Detter DeLupis. New York: Cambridge University Press. 432 pp. The first new survey of the laws of war since 1952.

Nuclear Heartland. Samuel H. Day, Jr., ed. Madison, Wis.: Progressive Foundation. 96 pp. A complete map of U.S. ICBM silos and command centers.

The Nuclear Weapons Databook. Vol. 4: Soviet Nuclear Weapons. Thomas B. Cochran, William M. Arkin, and Jeffrey Sands. Cambridge, Mass.: Ballinger. 360 pp. Provides virtually all information in the open literature about Soviet nuclear weapons.

RUSI/Brassey's Defence Yearbook 1988. Royal United Services Institute for Defence Studies (RUSI). London: Brassey's. 456 pp. An annual review of defense and strategic affairs.

SDI: Technology, Survivability, and Software. Office of Technology Assessment. Washington, D.C.: U.S. Government Printing Office. 281 pp. An analysis of the state of SDI technology and the potential for technological advances in the area of strategic defense.

A Soviet Lexicon: Important Concepts, Terms, and Phrases. Roy D. Laird and Betty A. Laird. Lexington, Mass.: Lexington Books. 192 pp. A dictionary of Soviet and Western terms designed to provide an understanding of the concepts essential to interpreting the Soviet system.

U.S. Arms Exports: Policies and Contractors. Paul L. Ferrari, Raul L. Madrid, and Jeff Knopf. Cambridge, Mass.: Ballinger. 496 pp. Updated and expanded database of the arms trade business.

The World Atlas of Warfare: Military Innovations That Changed the Course of History. Richard
Holmes. New York: Viking Books. 850 pp. A detailed and fully illustrated chronology of the
art and science of warfare.
World Weapon Database. Vol. 2: Soviet Military Aircraft. Randall Forsberg, series ed. Lexington,
Mass.: Lexington Books. 1,088 pp. The second part of a planned twelve-volume set that
will catalog the military hardware of every nation.

Cross Index by Author

Adams, James. *Secret Armies: Inside the American, Soviet, and European Special Forces.*
Allen, Thomas B., and Norman Polmar. *Merchants of Treason.*
Amme, Carl H. *NATO Strategy and Nuclear Defense.*
Arnold, Terrell E. *The Violence Formula: Why People Lend Sympathy and Support to Terrorism.*
Bacevich, A.J., James D. Hallums, Richard M. White, and Thomas F. Young. *American Military
Policy in Small Wars: The Case of El Salvador.*
Ball, Desmond. *A Base for Debate: The U.S. Satellite Station at Nurrungar.*
———. *Pine Gap: Australia and the U.S. Geostationary Signals Intelligence Satellite Program.*
Bassford, Christopher. *The Spit-Shine Syndrome: Organizational Irrationality in the American
Field Army.*
Berry, William E., Jr. *American Military Bases in the Philippines, Base Negotiations, and Phil-
ippine-American Relations.*
Bialer, Seweryn, and Michael Mandelbaum, eds. *Gorbachev's Russia and American Foreign
Policy.*
Bill, James A. *The Eagle and the Lion: The Tragedy of American-Iranian Relations.*
Blair, Clay. *The Forgotten War: America in Korea, 1950–1953.*
Bobbit, Philip. *Democracy and Deterrence: The History and Future of Nuclear Strategy.*
Boffey, Phillip M., William J. Broad, Leslie H. Gelb, Charles Mohr, and Holcomb B. Noble.
Claiming the Heavens: The New York Times Complete Guide to the Star Wars Debate.
Borawski, John. *From the Atlantic to the Urals: Negotiating Arms Control at the Stockholm
Conference.*
Bowler, Mike, and Phil Williams. *Superpower Détente: A Reappraisal.*
Chambers, John W. II. *To Raise an Army: The Draft Comes to Modern America.*
Chant, Christopher. *Air Defense Systems and Weapons: World AAA and SAM Systems in the
1980s.*
Charters, David, and Maurice Tugwell, eds. *Armies in Low Intensity Conflict.*
Chase, James, and Caleb Carr. *America Invulnerable: The Quest for Absolute Security from 1812
to Star Wars.*
Chatfield, Charles, and Peter van den Dungen, eds. *Peace Movements and Political Cultures.*
Churba, Joseph. *Soviet Breakout: Strategies to Meet It.*
Cimbala, Stephen J. *Nuclear Strategy: Deterrence and Reality.*
———. *Rethinking Nuclear Strategy.*
Cimbala, Stephen J., and Joseph D. Douglass, Jr., eds. *Ending a Nuclear War: Are the Super-
powers Prepared?*
Cochran, Thomas B., William M. Arkin, and Jeffrey Sands. *The Nuclear Weapons Databook. Vol.
4: Soviet Nuclear Weapons.*

Codevilla, Angelo. *While Others Build: A Commonsense Approach to the Strategic Defense Initiative.*

Couhat, Jean Labayle. *Combat Fleets of the World, 1988–1989.*

Cutler, Thomas J. *Brown Water, Black Berets: Coastal and Riverine Warfare in Vietnam.*

Davidson, Phillip B. *Vietnam at War: The History, 1946–1975.*

Day, Samuel H. Jr., ed. *Nuclear Heartland.*

DeLupis, Ingrid Detter. *The Law of War.*

Duffy, Gloria C. *Compliance and the Future of Arms Control.*

Edwards, George C. III, and Wallace Earl Walker. *National Security and the U.S. Constitution: The Impact of the Political System.*

Emerson, Steven. *Secret Warriors: Inside Covert Military Operations of the Reagan Era.*

Evangelista, Matthew. *Innovation and the Arms Race: How the United States and the Soviet Union Develop New Military Technologies.*

Falk, Richard. *Revolutionaries and Functionaries: The Dual Face of Terrorism.*

Feldman, Shai. *U.S. Middle East Policy.*

Ferrari, Paul L., Raul L. Madrid, and Jeff Knopf. *U.S. Arms Exports: Policies and Contractors.*

Fetter, Steve. *Toward a Comprehensive Test Ban.*

Flanagan, Stephen J. *NATO's Conventional Defenses.*

Fontaine, Roger W. *Terrorism: The Cuban Connection.*

Forsberg, Randall, series ed. *World Weapon Database. Vol. 2: Soviet Military Aircraft.*

Foster, Gregory D. *FEMA and the Politics of Emergency Management.*

Fox, J. Ronald. *The Defense Management Challenge: Weapons Acquisition.*

Gabriel, Richard A. *A Painful Field: The Psychiatric Dimension of Modern War.*

Garnham, David. *The Politics of European Defense Cooperation: Germany, France, Britain, and America.*

George, Alexander, Philip J. Farley, and Alexander Dallin. *U.S.-Soviet Security Cooperation: Achievements, Failures, Lessons.*

Gil, Frederico G., and Joseph S. Tulchin, eds. *Spain's Entry into NATO: Conflicting Political and Strategic Perspectives.*

Gilbert, Stephen P., ed. *Security in Northeast Asia.*

Godson, Roy, ed. *Comparing Foreign Intelligence: The U.S., the U.S.S.R., the U.K. and the Third World.*

———. *Intelligence Requirements for the 1990s.*

Gold, Dore. *America, the Gulf, and Israel.*

Goldstein, Walter, ed. *Clash in the North: Polar Summitry and NATO's Northern Flank.*

Gordon, Joseph S., ed. *Psychological Operations.*

Gottfried, Kurt, and Bruce G. Blair. *Crisis Stability and Nuclear War.*

Gray, Colin S. *The Geopolitics of Super Power.*

Gregor, James A. *Arming the Dragon: U.S. Security Ties with the People's Republic of China.*

Grove, Eric, and Stan Windass. *The Crucible of Peace: Common Security in Europe.*

Gutman, Roy. *Banana Diplomacy: The Making of American Policy in Nicaragua, 1981–1987.*

Hafner, Ronald L., and John Roper. *ATBMs and Western Security: Missile Defense for Europe.*

Haley, P. Edward, and Jack Merritt, eds. *Nuclear Strategy, Arms Control, and the Future.* 2d ed.

Hammer, Ellen J. *A Death in November: America in Vietnam, 1963.*

Hartmann, Frederick H., and Robert L. Wendzel. *Defending America's Security.*

Hemsley, John. *The Soviet Biochemical Threat to NATO.*

Hendrickson, David C. *Reforming Defense: The State of American Civil-Military Relations.*

Holmes, Richard. *The World Atlas of Warfare: Military Innovations That Changed the Course of History.*

Joint Chiefs of Staff, comp. *Dictionary of Military Terms.*

Kaplan, Lawrence S. *NATO and the U.S.: The Enduring Alliance.*

Karem, Mahmoud. *A Nuclear Weapons Free Zone in the Middle East: Problems and Prospects.*

Kincade, William H., and Priscilla B. Hayner. *The ACCESS Resource Guide: An International Directory of Information on War, Peace, and Security.*

Klare, Michael T., and Peter Kornbluh, eds. *Low-Intensity Warfare.*

Kotz, Nick. *Wild Blue Yonder: Money, Politics, and the B-1 Bomber.*

Kozak, David C., and James M. Keagle, eds. *Bureaucratic Politics and National Security: Theory and Practice.*

Krepon, Michael, and Mary Umberger, eds. *Verification and Compliance: A Problem Solving Approach.*

Kruzel, Joseph, ed. *The American Defense Annual, 1988–1989.*

Kull, Steven. *Minds at War: Nuclear Reality and the Inner Conflicts of Defense Policy Makers.*

Ladd, James D. *Modern Amphibious Strategy and Techniques.*

Laird, Roy D., and Betty A. Laird. *A Soviet Lexicon: Important Concepts, Terms, and Phrases.*

Landau, Saul. *The Dangerous Doctrine: National Security and U.S. Foreign Policy.*

Laqueur, Walter, and Yonah Alexander. *The Terrorism Reader: The Essential Source Book on Political Violence Both Past and Present.*

Lawren, William. *The General and the Bomb: A Biography of General Leslie R. Groves, Director of the Manhattan Project.*

Lewis, Gordon K. *Grenada: The Jewel Despoiled.*

Lin, Herbert. *New Weapon Technologies and the ABM Treaty.*

Litwak, Robert S., and Samuel F. Wells, Jr., eds. *Superpower Competition and Security in the Third World.*

Livingstone, Neil C., and Terrell E. Arnold. *Beyond the Iran-Contra Crisis: The Shape of U.S. Antiterrorism Policy in the Post Reagan Era.*

Lodge, Juliet, ed. *The Threat of Terrorism.*

Lord, Carnes. *The Presidency and the Management of National Security.*

Lowenthal, Abraham F. *Partners in Conflict: The U.S. and Latin America.*

McGuire, Phillip. *He, Too, Spoke for Democracy: Judge Hastie, World War II, and the Black Soldier.*

McInnes, Colin, and G.P. Sheffield, eds. *Warfare in the 20th Century: Theory and Practice.*

Mandelbaum, Michael. *The Fate of Nations: The Search for National Security in the Nineteenth and Twentieth Centuries.*

———. ed. *America's Defense.*

Manning, Robert. *Asian Policy: A New Look for American Defense.*

George C. Marshall Institute. *The Concept of Defensive Deterrence: Strategic and Technical Dimensions of Missile Defense.*

Martin, David C., and John C. Walcott. *Best Laid Plans: The Inside Story of America's War against Terrorism.*

Martino, Joseph P. *A Fighting Chance: The Moral Use of Nuclear Weapons.*

Mayers, David. *George Kennan and the Dilemmas of U.S. Foreign Policy.*

Mazaar, Michael. *Semper Fidel: America and Cuba, 1776–1988.*

Menges, Constantine C. *Inside the National Security Council: The True Story of the Making and Unmaking of Reagan's Foreign Policy.*

Miller, Steven E., and Stephen Van Evera, eds. *Naval Strategy and National Security.*

Millett, Allan R., and Williamson Murray, eds. *Military Effectiveness.*

Milton, A. Fenner, M. Scott Davis, and John A. Parmentola. *Making Space Defense Work: Must the Superpowers Cooperate?*

Mintz, Alex. *The Politics of Resource Allocation in the U.S. Department of Defense.*

Morley, Morris H. *Imperial State and Revolution: The United States and Cuba, 1952–1986.*

Morris, Charles R. *Iron Destinies, Lost Opportunities: The Arms Race between the U.S.A. and the U.S.S.R., 1945–1987.*

Morris, Eric, and Alan Hoe. *Terrorism: Threat and Response.*

Moskos, Charles C. *A Call to Civil Service: National Service for Country and Community.*

Moskos, Charles C., and Frank R. Wood, eds. *The Military: More Than Just a Job?*

Nerlich, Uwe, and James A. Thomson. *Conventional Arms Control and the Security of Europe.*

Newsome, David D. *Diplomacy and the American Democracy.*

Nincic, Miroslav. *United States Foreign Policy: Choices and Tradeoffs.*

Nixon, Richard. *1999: Victory without War.*

Nye, Joseph S., Jr. *Nuclear Ethics.*

Nye, Joseph S., Jr., Graham T. Allison, and Albert Carnesdale. *Fateful Visions: Avoiding Nuclear Catastrophe.*

Nye, Joseph S., Jr., and James A. Schear. *On the Defensive: The Future of SDI.*

Office of Technology Assessment. *SDI: Technology, Survivability, and Software.*

———. *Strategic Defense Initiative: Survivability and Software.*

Olsen, Edward A. *U.S. Policy and the Two Koreas.*

Osgood, Robert E. *The Nuclear Dilemma in American Strategic Thought.*

Pakenham, W.T.T. *Naval Command and Control.*

Palmer, John. *Europe without America? The Crisis in Atlantic Relations.*

Paterson, Thomas G. *Meeting the Communist Threat: Truman to Reagan.*

Rabkin, Yakov. *Science between the Superpowers.*

Reagan, Ronald. *National Security Strategy of the United States.*

Record, Jeffrey. *Beyond Military Reform: American Defense Dilemmas.*

Reiss, Mitchell. *Without the Bomb: The Politics of Nuclear Proliferation.*

Richelson, Jeffrey T. *Foreign Intelligence Organizations.*

———. *The U.S. Intelligence Community.*

Robertson, David. *Guide to Modern Defense and Strategy.*

Rogers, Paul. *Guide to Nuclear Weapons, 1988.*

Rositzke, Harry. *The CIA's Secret Operations: Espionage, Counterespionage, and Covert Action.*

Rotter, Andrew J. *The Path to Vietnam: Origins of the American Commitment to Southeast Asia.*

Royal United Services Institute for Defence Studies. *RUSI/Brassey's Defence Yearbook 1988.*

Rudney, Robert, and Luc Reychler. *European Security beyond the Year 2000.*

Schlagheck, Donna M. *International Terrorism: An Introduction to the Concepts and Actors.*

Schmidt, Christian, and Frank Blackaby, eds. *Peace, Defense, and Economic Analysis.*

Shafer, D. Michael. *Deadly Paradigms: The Failure of U.S. Counterinsurgency Policy.*

Shaker, Steven M., and Allan R. Wise. *War without Men: Robots on the Battlefield.*

Shearman, Peter, and Phil Williams. *The Superpowers, Central America and the Middle East.*

Sheehan, Neil. *A Bright Shining Lie.*

Shultz, Richard, Jr., Uri Ra'anan, Robert L. Pfaltzgraff, Jr., Igor Lukes, and William Olson, eds. *Guerrilla Warfare and Counterinsurgency: U.S.-Soviet Policy in the Third World.*

Simon, Sheldon W. *The Future of Asian-Pacific Security Collaboration.*

Simpson, Christopher. *Blowback: The First Full Account of America's Recruitment of Nazis, and Its Disastrous Effect on Our Domestic and Foreign Policy.*

Slater, Robert O., and Michael Stohl, eds. *Current Perspectives on International Terrorism.*

Smyrl, Marc E. *Conflict or Codetermination: Congress, the President, and the Power to Make War.*

Snow, Donald M. *Soviet-American Security Relations in the 1990s.*

Spiegel, Steven L., Mark Heller, and Jacob Goldberg, eds. *The Soviet-American Competition in the Middle East.*

Steinberg, Gerald M. *Lost in Space: The Domestic Politics of the Strategic Defense Initiative.*

Stuart, Douglas T., ed. *Politics and Security in the Southern Region of the Atlantic Alliance.*

Sweet, William. *The Nuclear Age: Atomic Energy, Proliferation, and the Arm Race.* 2d ed.

Talbott, Strobe. *The Master of the Game: Paul Nitze and the Nuclear Peace.*

Tanham, George, and Alvin H. Bernstein, eds. *Military Basing and U.S.-Soviet Military Balance in Southeast Asia.*

Taylor, Maxwell. *The Terrorist.*

Thornton, Thomas Perry, ed. *Anti-Americanism: Origins and Context.*

Van Creveld, Martin. *Technology and War.*

Weart, Spencer R. *Nuclear Fear: A History of Images.*

Weinberg, Alvin M., and Jack N. Barkenbus, eds. *Strategic Defenses and Arms Control.*

Wiarda, Howard J., ed. *Finding Our Way: Toward Maturity in U.S.-Latin American Relations.*

Wildavsky, Aaron. *The New Politics of the Budgetary Process.*

Wolfgang, Marvin E., ed. *Whither the American Empire: Expansion or Contraction?*

Yankelovich, Daniel, and Sidney Harman. *Starting with the People.*

Yost, David S. *Soviet Ballistic Missile Defense and the Western Alliance.*

Notes

Chapter 1
Perspectives

1. Richard Halloran, "A Cadet Exchange by U.S. and Soviets," *New York Times,* February 3, 1989, p. 7.

2. "Base Alignments and Closures: Report of the Defense Secretary's Commission" (December 1988).

3. Mike Mills, "Base Closings: The Political Pain Is Limited," *Congressional Quarterly,* December 31, 1988, p. 3625.

4. Kevin Sack, "South's Clout Helps Keep Its Military Bases Off Shutdown Roster," *Atlanta Journal and Constitution,* January 1, 1989, p. 1.

5. "Opportunity to Diversify Was Seized in State of Washington," *New York Times,* December 28, 1988, p. B5.

6. "Base Alignments and Closures," p. 88.

7. Bernard Weinraub, "Bush Backs Plan to Enhance Role of Security Staff," *New York Times,* February 2, 1989, p.1.

8. The project is best described by one of its participants. See Daniel Yankelovich and Richard Smoke, "America's New Thinking," *Foreign Affairs* 67 (Fall 1988).

9. Quoted by Francis J. West, Jr., "Secretaries of Defense: Why Most Have Failed," *Naval War College Review,* March/April 1981, p. 92.

10. For a good assessment of various secretaries of defense, see Richard A. Stubbing, *The Defense Game* (New York: Harper & Row, 1986).

Chapter 2
Toward the Postnuclear Era:
The Decline of Extended Deterrence

1. Under the so-called first-use policy, embodied in the official NATO strategy of flexible response that dates from 1967.

2. By a NATO consensus implicit in the frequently reaffirmed need for the first-use policy. The analytical case for the sufficiency of NATO nonnuclear forces now forms a large literature of its own, whose more notable authors include Joshua M. Epstein, William W. Kaufmann, John J. Mearsheimer, and Barry R. Posen; see Elliot A. Cohen "Towards Better Net Assessment: Rethinking the European Conventional Balance" *International Security* 13, no. 1 (Summer 1988): 50ff., for detailed references. Because the purpose of these authors is to translate the exactitude of strategic-nuclear balance calculations to the stubbornly protean nonnuclear balance, as Cohen points out, their analyses must exclude inter alia such nonmeasurables as the varied consequences of surprise and the dislocations of operational maneuver, precisely the effects so strongly emphasized in the Soviet style of war (at the expense of the attrition capabilities on which the analyses of Epstein and others are focused). Further assumptions, not methodologically mandatory and thus more questionable, include the exclusion of preemptive attacks on NATO air bases in Europe and the noninterruption of reinforcements by the full range of available nonnuclear means.

3. Certainly more than strike-back capabilities are required if the latter must remain in reserve throughout.

4. For a broader exposition, see my *Strategy: The Logic of War and Peace* (Cambridge: Harvard University Press, 1987).

5. That is, autonomous invention, unresponsive to material inputs (resource-determined engineering progress).

6. Used throughout to include all theater missions but not strategic bombing.

7. A situation in which only one side can operate its aircraft.

8. Not strategic-level balances, wherein the effect of air power is not definitive.

9. The converse of even seemingly successful countermeasures and circumvention—evasive flight paths, stand off and other prudent tactics, the loading of countermeasure equipment and supplies in lieu of weapons—reduce the positive capabilities of air power even when no aircraft are shot down. For reasons of prestige and also because of the understandable preferences of pilot-dominated air forces, actual attrition, even at low rates, is avoided even at the price of far more consequential virtual attrition.

10. Heinz Guderian's first Panzer division was formed in 1935. Until then all operational applications had been incomplete and/or experimental. At the time, the prevailing doctrine in both the British and French armies still utilized only the tactical potential of the tank as a supporting weapon for foot infantry and as a direct substitute for horse cavalry (accordingly tank designs were sharply differentiated between slow, heavily armored "infantry" tanks and fast, lightly armored "cavalry" tanks; neither was suitable as the weapon of an autonomous new arm).

11. "Hedgehogs" or "boxes," that is, perimeters formed by antitank weapons behind mine fields and barriers.

12. Bernard Brodie, ed., *The Absolute Weapon: Atomic Power and World Order* (New York: Harcort, Brace, 1946).

13. For a critical overview, see David MacIsaac, "Voices from the Central Blue," in Peter Paret, ed., *Makers of Modern Strategy: From Machiavelli to the Nuclear Age* (Princeton, N.J.: Princeton University Press, 1986), pp. 624ff.

14. There is now a serious work on Douhet: Ferruccio Botti and Virgilio Ilari, *Il Pensiero Militare Italiano Dal Primo al Secondo Dopoguerra (1919–1949)* (Rome: Stato Maggiore del Esercito, 1985), pp. 89ff.

15. With aircrews usually having worse survival chances than infantry in World War I trench warfare.

16. The yield of the Hiroshima bomb is usually estimated at 14 kilotons (the blast-only equivalent of 14,000 tons of TNT) and the Nagasaki bomb at 19 kilotons. World War II (four-engine) bomber payloads were normally of 10 tons or less.

17. Five percent losses inflicted per sortie were considered very good in World War II, and anything over 10 percent was a rarity.

18. By the end of the 1950s, every major military vector (rockets, mortars, guns, howitzers as well as air-to-air, air-to-ground, ground-to-air and antisubmarine missiles, depth charges, demolition charges, and attack aircraft of all types) had its nuclear version or nuclear ordnance available for it, in addition to more abundant nonnuclear ordnance.

19. Because it excludes the nuclear content of the general-purpose forces; the latter, however, were more "nuclear" when the relative share of strategic expenditures was larger, and vice-versa, so that the indicator is not misleading.

20. By forcing the frequent upgrading of electronic countermeasures for the B-52s, the provision of standoff weapons for them, and the modernization of the bomber force with the B-1 and currently the B-2.

21. Unlike future money, military power is anticipated rather than discounted. In September 1949 the Soviet Union detonated a nuclear device but still lacked an effective means of delivery, yet it was immediately promoted to the rank of an atomic power.

22. As General Leslie R. Groves had anticipated from the start. When told that below a critical mass the bomb would not explode at all, Groves was displeased: "If you can make it the equivalent of five hundred tons, it will be available for military use without restriction. If you make it much larger, the conditions under which it can be used will become a matter of political decision." William Lawren, *The General and the Bomb: A Biography of General Leslie R. Groves, Director of the Manhattan Project* (New York: Dodd, Mead, 1988), pp. 80-81, citing unpublished Compton text in Groves's personal papers.

23. If followed by overt resistance and bloody suppression.

24. Specifically justified as a deterrent to extra-NATO aggressions.

25. With blast-only effects equivalent to 1 million tons of TNT (1,000 tons for kiloton weapons).

26. Enunciated by John Foster Dulles in January 1954; qualified immediately after, but then restated.

27. Office of the Assistant Secretary of Defense (Comptroller), *National Defense Budget Estimates for FY 1986* (Washington, D.C.: Government Printing Office, March 1985), table 6–1, pp. 60–61.

Chapter 3
The Defense Budget in the 1990s

1. Americans Talk Security Project, *How Much Defense Can the U.S. Afford: A New National Debate,* National Survey No. 3 (NY: Daniel Yankelovich Group, March 1988), pp. 94–95; Gallup Poll, July 10–13, 1987.

2. "Cuts That Don't Hurt," *National Journal,* February 4, 1989, p. 269.

3. Center on Budget and Policy Priorities, *The Bush Budget: Progress toward a Kinder, Gentler America?* (Washington, D.C.: CBPP, February 17, 1989.

4. President Bush's budget, like President Reagan's final budget, is constructed on the assumption that the economy will grow at an annual rate of 3.25 percent compared with CBO's assumption of 2.25 percent. President Bush projects that interest rates on three-month Treasury bills will be 3 percent by FY 1994, compared with CBO's estimate of 5.9 percent. Congressional Budget Office (CBO), *An Analysis of President Reagan's Budgetary Proposals for Fiscal Year 1990* (Washington, D.C.: CBO, February 1989), pp. 9–23. President Bush's budget proposal is even more optimistic than President Reagan's because it projects that a proposed cut in taxes on capital gains will actually increase tax revenue, a projection disputed by CBO and the Joint Congressional Committee of taxation. See Center on Budget and Policy Priorities, *Bush Budget*, p. 14.

5. Defense funding (budget authority) is the authority, appropriated by Congress, to spend money (make outlays). Funding is not necessarily spent in the year it is appropriated. The defense spending of each year results partly from that year's funding and partly from the funds appropriated in prior years.

6. Operations and support funding includes the budgets for operations and maintenance and military personnel. It can also include funds for the procurement of readiness-related items like ammunition and spare parts.

7. Congressional Budget Office (CBO), *Operations and Support Costs for the Department of Defense* (Washington, D.C.: CBO, July 1988).

8. Ibid., pp. 16–20. The impetus behind this cost growth seems to be the increasing technological complexity of new weapons systems. Complex weapons tend to require more expensive maintenance, spare parts, and diagnostic equipment than simpler ones.

9. Stephen Alexis Cain, *Strategic Forces Funding in the 1990s: A Renewed Buildup* (Washington, D.C.: Defense Budget Project, April 1989).

10. "Report of the Working Group on Weapons Acquisition," in Barry Blechman and William J. Lynn, *Toward a More Effective Defense: Report of the Defense Organization Project* (Cambridge, Mass.: Ballinger Publishing, 1985), p. 89; General Accounting Office, *Underestimation of Funding Requirements in Five Year Procurement Plans* (Washington, D.C.: GAO, March 12, 1983), p. 48.

11. See Stephen Alexis Cain, *The FY 1990/1991 Defense Budget: Preliminary Analysis* (Washington, D.C.: Defense Budget Project, January 12, 1989).

12. Without adjusting for these transfers, the real growth in O&M funding would be 2.7 percent in FY 1990 and 1.1 percent in FY 1991.

13. CBO, *Analysis*, p. 36.

14. Data on changes from the FY 1989 baseline were taken from an unpublished DOD document: Department of Defense Comptroller, *Department of Defense Budget Highlights: FY 1990/1991 Biennial Budget* (Washington, D.C.: Department of Defense, January 1989).

15. See John D. Steinbruner, "The Prospect of Cooperative Security," in Barry P. Bosworth et al., *Critical Choices: What the President Should Know about the Economy and Foreign Policy* (Washington, D.C.: Brookings Institution, 1989), pp. 71–95, which argues that Soviet defense policy is shifting to a defensive stance in large part to serve the new goal of avoiding military conflict. Henry Kissinger has argued that the Soviets are "condemned by circumstances to seek a realistic accommodation" with the United States. Kissinger, "Dealing with Moscow: A New Balance," *Washington Post,* February 7, 1989, p. A25. Nixon argued that Gorbachev's changes have been driven by both U.S. strength and internal necessity. Nixon, "American Foreign Policy: The Bush Agenda," *Foreign Affairs* 68, no. 1 (1989): 203–204.

16. See Gordon Adams, *The Politics of Defense Contracting: The Iron Triangle* (New Brunswick, N.J.: Transaction Books, 1982), and Richard A. Stubbing, *The Defense Game* (New York: Harper & Row, 1986), esp. chaps. 6–8.

17. Commission on Integrated Long-Term Strategy, *Discriminate Deterrence* (Washington, D.C.: Department of Defense, January 1988); William A. Owens and James A. Moseman, "The Maritime Strategy: Looking Ahead," U.S. Naval Institute *Proceedings,* 115, no. 2 (February 1989): 24–32. Owens and Moseman argue for a continuation of current U.S. maritime strategy.

18. The U.S. *Defense Guidance* of 1983 laid out a large number of U.S. military missions, including strategic deterrence of the Soviet Union, strategic defense, the defense of Europe with nuclear and conventional forces (including new, deep-strike weapons), the military capability to open a second military front in Asia and to attack Soviet home ports ("maritime strategy"), a military role in the Middle East and Persian Gulf, control over the high seas, and a broad force projection and intervention capability for other theaters. See Richard Halloran, *To Arm a Nation: Rebuilding America's Endangered Defenses* (New York: Macmillan, 1986), pp. 217–222. As Secretary Weinberger stated, "It would be a grave mistake for our strategy to focus only on what seemed the most dangerous threats, or the most plausible ones." Rather, the United States should be prepared to fight "across the entire spectrum of conflict," from terrorism to nuclear war, in virtually any theater. Department of Defense, *Annual Report to the Congress, Fiscal Year 1984* (Washington, D.C.: Government Printing Office, February 1983), p. 37.

19. Richard Nixon notes that Gorbachev outstrips Khrushchev and Brezhnev in "realism, quickness and intelligence," "sees the world without ideological blinders," and recognizes both the defects of internal Soviet economic and political organization and the global reality that the Soviet Union must seek an accommodation. See Nixon, "American Foreign Policy," pp. 199–219.

20. David Holloway, "Gorbachev's New Thinking," *Foreign Affairs* 68, no. 1 (1989): pp. 74–75, notes that the Soviet military is still rethinking its doctrines.

21. This agreement is sometimes described as a 50 percent reduction in strategic warheads from current levels of roughly 12,000 each. However, due to the decision to count non-ALCM bombers as one warhead, regardless of the number of bombs and short-range missiles it carries, the actual reduction would be roughly one-third. See Stephen Alexis Cain, *The START Agreement: Strategic Options and Budgetary Savings* (Washington, D.C.: Defense Budget Project, 1988).

22. Scowcroft urged a rethinking of arms control and modernization plans, proposing that the Midgetman rather than the MX rail-garrison system, be deployed, in addition to the Trident submarine and D-5 missile. He did not discuss the new B-2 Stealth bomber. See Brent Scowcroft and R. James Woolsey, "Defense and Arms Control Policy," in Jimmy Carter and Gerald R. Ford, *American Agenda* (Washington, D.C.: 1989), pp. 1–11.

23. Congressional Budget Office, *Modernizing U.S. Strategic Offensive Forces: Costs, Effects, and Alternatives* (Washington, D.C.: Congressional Budget Office, November 1987), pp. 40–45; Robert S. Norris, William M. Arkin, and Thomas B. Cochran, *Nuclear Weapons Databook Working Paper: START and Strategic Modernization* (Washington, D.C.: Natural Resources Defense Council, December 1, 1987), pp. 14–16.

24. See Cain, *START Agreement,* pp. 8–13. Such an agreement might, for example, make the MX rail garrison unnecessary and limit the deployment of a mobile ICBM such as the Midgetman, in exchange for Soviet limits on mobile forces. It might also restrict Trident II deployment to new submarines, without a retrofit to the first eight, and defer or even cancel plans to proceed with production of the B-2.

25. See Douglas C. Waller and James T. Bruce, "SDI's Covert Reorientation," *Arms Control Today* 17, no. 5 (June 1987): 2–10.

26. "Warsaw Pact Release Figures on Force Strengths," *Pravda,* January 30, 1989, p. 5.

27. See International Institute for Strategic Studies, *Strategic Survey, 1987–1988* (London: IISS, 1988), pp. 81–89.

28. Jonathan Dean, "Will Negotiated Force Reductions Build Down the NATO–Warsaw Pact Confrontation?" *Washington Quarterly* (Spring 1988): 69–84.

29. See North Atlantic Treaty Organization, Defense Planning Committee, *Enhancing Alliance Collective Security: Shared Roles, Risks and Responsibilities in the Alliance* (Brussels: NATO, December 1988).

30. Minus the burden-sharing issue, this cautious perspective on the European conventional security issue is amply reflected in the FY 1989 posture statement of the Joint Chiefs of Staff. See Joint Chiefs of Staff, *United States Military Posture, FY 1989* (Washington, D.C.: JCS, 1988), pp. 1–7, 17–20. A number of Democratic defense spokespersons also endorse this general view of European security. See Democratic Leadership Council, *Defending America: Building a New Foundation for National Strength* (Washington, D.C.: Democratic Leadership Council, September 1986); Democratic Policy Commission, *New Choices in a Changing America* (Washington, D.C.: Democratic National Committee, 1986). On the burden-sharing issue, see House Armed Services Committee, *Report of the Defense Burdensharing Panel* (Washington, D.C.: Government Printing Office, 1988); and Gordon Adams and Eric Munz, *Fair Shares: Bearing the Burden of the NATO Alliance* (Washington, D.C.: Defense Budget Project, 1988).

31. See Adams and Munz, *Fair Shares.* On the complexities of the conventional force balance in Europe, see Joshua M. Epstein, *The 1988 Defense Budget* (Washington, D.C.: Brookings Institution, 1987), pp. 36–45; John J. Mearsheimer, "Numbers, Strategy, and the European Balance," *International Security* no. 4 (Spring 1988): 174–185; Barry Posen, "Is NATO Decisively Outnumbered," *International Security* 12, no. 4 (Spring 1988): 186–202; Carl Levin, *Beyond the Bean Count,* 2d ed. (Washington, D.C.: U.S. Senate, July 1988).

32. The New tactical nuclear programs include more artillery-fired atomic projectiles, a nuclear version of the army tactical missile system (as a follow-up to the Lance), a new air-to-surface nuclear missile, and new dual-capable fighter aircraft. The conventional deep-strike technologies include new intelligence and communications systems to assist in processing combat information and targeting adversary forces and longer-range conventional missiles to target second-echelon adversary forces and supplies. See Office of Technology Assessment, *New Technology for NATO: Implementing Follow-on Forces Attack,* OTA-ISC-309 (Washington, D.C.: Government Printing Office, June 1987).

33. For a discussion of the value and low cost of barrier defenses, see Congressional Budget Office, *U.S. Ground Forces and the Conventional Balance in Europe* (Washington, D.C.: Congressional Budget Office, June 1988), pp. 38–43.

34. Jonathan Dean, *Watershed in Europe: Dismantling the East-West Military Confrontation* (Lexington, Mass.: Lexington Books, 1987), pp. 61–75.

35. See Martin E. Weinstein, "Trade Problems and U.S.-Japanese Security Cooperation," *Washington Quarterly* 11, no. 1 (Winter 1988): 19–33; and Weinstein et al., *The United States and the Asian Pacific Region: Decisions for the Next President,* Significant Issues Series, Vol. 10, No. 6 (Washington, D.C.: Center for Strategic and International Studies, 1988).

36. Basing negotiations will take place during this period with Spain, Turkey, Greece, and Portugal. Although these are NATO allies, U.S. forces in these countries are also used for non-NATO contingencies, and disputes have grown in recent years about the desirability of such forces from the host country point of view. See James R. Blaker, "U.S. Overseas Basing System

Faces a Difficult Transition," *Armed Forces Journal International* (February 1989): 65–67. See also Rochelle L. Stanfield, "Off Base," *National Journal*, February 11, 1989, pp. 339–342.

37. See William W. Kaufmann, *A Thoroughly Efficient Navy* (Washington, D.C.: Brookings Institution, 1987); John Mearsheimer, "A Strategic Misstep: The Maritime Strategy and Deterrence in Europe," *International Security* 11 no. 2 (Fall 1986): 3–57; Congressional Budget Office, *Future Budget Requirements for the 600-Ship Navy* (Washington, D.C.: Congressional Budget Office, September 1985); and Ronald O'Rourke, *The Cost of a U.S. Navy Carrier Battlegroup,* Congressional Research Service Report 87-532F (Washington, D.C.: Congressional Research Service, June 26, 1987), pp. 7–8.

38. While official policy tends toward lighter divisions, the light 9th Division is "heavying up." See *Army Times*, February 20, 1989, p. 4.

39. See, in particular, the discussion of how U.S. forces might need to be restructured in response to future international changes in Commission on Long-Term Integrated Strategy, *Discriminate Deterrence* (Washington, D.C.: Department of Defense, January 1988), and *Supporting U.S. Strategy for Third World Conflict,* Report by the Regional Conflict Working Group (Washington, D.C.: Department of Defense, June 1988).

40. See Adams and Munz, *Fair Shares.*

41. William Kaufmann has proposed a similar concept, which he describes as holding the next generation of hardware at the R&D stage. See Kaufmann, "Restructuring Defense," in Bosworth et al., *Critical Choices,* p. 159.

42. Secretary of Defense Frank Carlucci noted in March 1988: "The weapons [which would be canceled] incorporate technological advantages that help us counter the numerical superiority the Soviet Union enjoys. . . . They are essential components of the next decade's deterrent." See Frank Carlucci, "Why National Defense Can't Wait," *New York Times* March 22, 1988, p. A30.

Chapter 5
Theater Forces

1. Various assessments are briefly discussed in Andrew W. Marshall and Charles Wolf, eds., *Sources of Change in the Future Security Environment: A Paper by the Future Security Working Group,* submitted to the Commission on Integrated Long Term Strategy (Washington, D.C.: Government Printing Office, 1988), pp. 2–4. See also Richard E. Ericson, "Soviet Numbers Game Threatens Perestroika," *Bulletin of the Atomic Scientists* 44 (December 1988): 20–25.

2. "Getting Russia Well Again," *Economist,* November 21, 1987, p. 51.

3. For a description, see Stephen M. Meyer, "The Sources and Prospects of Gorbachev's New Political Thinking on Security," *International Security* 13 (Fall 1988): 124–163.

4. See Ken Brower, *The Warsaw Pact-NATO Military Balance: The Quality of Forces,* Report C66 (Royal Military Academy, Sandhurst: Soviet Studies Research Center, 1988).

5. See U.S. Senate, Committee on Armed Services, *NATO Defense and the INF Treaty: Report, together with Additional, Supplemental, and Minority Views,* 100th Cong., 2d sess., 1988, pp. 83–88.

6. International Institute for Strategic Studies (IISS), *The Military Balance, 1988–1989* (London: International Institute for Strategic Studies, 1988), pp. 250–251.

7. Committee on Armed Services, *INF Treaty,* p. 8.

8. Ibid., p. 61. These numbers were provided by Philip A. Karber and reflect active forces

only (no stored, war reserve, or inoperable equipment) in the NATO Guidelines Area (Belgium, the Netherlands, Luxembourg, the Federal Republic of Germany, Czechoslovakia, the German Democratic Republic, and Poland.)

9. See the discussion in Eliot A. Cohen, "Toward a Better Net Assessment," *International Security* 13 (Summer 1988): 59.

10. IISS, *Military Balance, 1988–1989,* p. 31.

11. On conventional arms control, see Robert D. Blackwill, "Conceptual Problems of Arms Control," *International Security* 12 (Spring 1988): 28–47.

12. See the testimony of Karl Kaiser, Robert D. Blackwill, Philip A. Karber, James A. Thomson, and Charles H. Thomson in U.S. Senate, Committee on Armed Services, *Hearings, NATO Defense and the INF Treaty,* 100th Cong., 2d sess., pt. 4, 1988, pp. 106–338.

13. Testimony of James A. Thomson, in ibid., p. 107.

14. Ibid., pt. 3, pp. 265–266.

15. Brenton C. Fischmann, "West German Defense Planning for the '90s: A New Bundeswehr on NATO's Front Line," *Armed Forces Journal* (September 1988)126: 44–46.

16. See Robert R. Ulin, "Belgium: The Strategic Hub," in Jeffrey Simon, ed., *NATO-Warsaw Pact Force Mobilization* (Washington, D.C.: National Defense University Press, 1988), p. 418.

17. See Notra Trulock, Kerry Hines, and Ann Herr, *Soviet Military Thought in Transition: Implications for the Long-Term Military Competition,* Report 1831 (Arlington, Va.: Pacific-Sierra Research Corporation, 1988), upon which much of what follows is based. See also U.S. Congress, Office of Technology Assessment, *New Technology for NATO: Implementing Follow-On Forces Attack,* OTA-ISC-309 (Washington, D.C.: Government Printing Office, 1987).

18. See, for example, Zbigniew Brzezinski, *Game Plan: A Geostrategic Framework for the Conduct of the U.S.-Soviet Contest* (Boston: Atlantic Monthly Press, 1986).

19. See Andrew F. Krepinevich, *The Army and Vietnam* (Baltimore: Johns Hopkins University Press, 1986), pp. 4–7, and passim.

20. See IISS, *Military Balance, 1988–1989,* p. 34, which applies these categories to the Soviet Union with the curious proviso that they only "parallel to some extent the Soviet system."

21. See "Soviet Plans Stress Force Structure," *Jane's Defence Weekly,* June 18, 1988, pp. 1248ff.

22. See Paul K. Davis, "The Role of Uncertainty in Assessing the NATO-Pact Central Region Balance," Paper P-7427 (Santa Monica, Calif.: RAND, 1988). The RSAS attempts to model the differences between Western and Soviet styles of operational planning and strategic choice: as such it is a great advance over gaming systems that assume that the Soviets behave in ways similar to their NATO counterparts.

23. See the exchange of letters in *International Security* 13 (Spring 1989).

24. See, for example, Joshua M. Epstein, "Dynamic Analysis and the Conventional Balance in Europe," *International Security* 12 (Spring 1988): 154–165.

25. The three-to-one rule is a hoary rule of thumb that holds that an attacker needs odds of that magnitude to overwhelm a defender. The Lanchester Theorem, derived from World War I research on air-to-air combat, holds that combat power is proportionate to the square of the two forces engaged. Thus a force that outnumbers its opponent by three-to-two may actually have a superiority in combat effectiveness of better than two-to-one. There is little empirical support for either proposition.

26. This has happened before in military history. As Martin van Creveld pointed out in a lecture at Harvard University, the battleship reached its most elaborate and even aesthetic form just as it became obsolete (or something like it) in the late 1930s.

27. Philip A. Karber, Grant Whitley, Mark Herman, and Douglas Komer, *Assessing the Correlation of Forces: France 1940,* DNA-001-78-C-0114 (McLean, Va.: BDM Corporation, 1979).

28. See Cohen, "Toward a Better Net Assessment," pp. 84–89.

29. See Eliot A. Cohen, "The Long-Term Crisis of the Alliance," *Foreign Affairs* 61 (Winter 1982–1983): 325–343.

30. These developments are discussed at greater length in Marshall and Wolf, eds., *Sources of Change.*

Chapter 6
Seapower

1. The history and major events are well chronicled by Barry Blechman, "Seapower," in *American Defense Annual,* ed. Joseph Kruzel (Lexington, Mass.: Lexington Books, 1988).

2. Bruce R. Linder, "What Happened to the 600-Ship Navy?" *Navy International,* (July/August 1988): 384.

3. Scott C. Truver, "The Most Controversial Ship in the Navy," *Armed Forces Journal* (April 1988): 56–60.

4. Ronald O'Rourke, "The Maritime Strategy and the Next Decade," *U.S. Naval Institute Proceedings* (April 1988): 34–38.

5. See, for example, Bruce W. Watson, *Red Navy at Sea: Naval Operations on the High Seas, 1956–1980* (Boulder, Colo.: Westview Press, 1982).

6. James F. McNulty, "Naval Presence—The Misunderstood Mission," *Naval War College Review* (September–October 1974) Vol. 27, No. 5: 21–31.

7. U.S. Senate, Committee on Armed Services, *Hearings, Department of Defense Authorization for Appropriations for Fiscal Year 1985,* 99th Cong., 1st sess., 1985, pp. 3870–3871.

8. For an elaboration of this point, see James L. George, "Maritime Missions or Strategy?" *Naval War College Review* (Winter 1989) Vol. 42, No. 1.

9. For a discussion of the Navy's plans on Tomahawk, see Blechman, "Seapower," pp. 131–133.

10. James L. George, "INNF: Intermediate Navy Nuclear Forces," *U.S. Naval Institute Proceedings* (June 1987): 35–39.

11. Henry Kissinger, "START: A Dangerous Rush for Agreement," *Washington Post,* April 24, 1988.

12. For a good pro and con discussion on SSBN-C3, see W.J. Holland, "The Triad's Best," and Richard B. Keeley, "A Bad Connection," both in *U.S. Naval Institute Proceedings* (January 1988): 41–51.

13. C.A.H. Trost, "The Morning of the Empty Trenches: Soviet Politics of Maneuver and the U.S. Responses," *U.S. Naval Institute Proceedings* (August 1988): 13.

14. Michael Parks, "Soviets Propose Reducing Risks of Naval Clash," *Los Angeles Times,* September 6, 1988, p. 1.

15. Norman Polmar, *The Ships and Aircraft of the U.S. Fleet,* 12th ed. (Annapolis, Md.: U.S. Naval Institute Press, 1981), p. 1.

16. John F. Lehman, Jr., "A Report on the Fiscal Year 1986 Military Posture of the United States Navy and Marine Corps," *Hearings,* 99th Cong., 1st sess., February 6, 1985.

Chapter 7
Forces for Projecting U.S. Power

1. Joint Chiefs of Staff, *Department of Defense Dictionary of Military and Associated Terms,* Pub. 1 (Washington, D.C.: Government Printing Office, 100th Cong., 1st sess. 1987).

2. Paul F. Gorman in U.S. Senate, Committee on Armed Services, *Hearings,* 100th Cong., 1st sess., January 28, 1987.

3. Commission on Integrated Long-Term Strategy, *Discriminate Deterrence* (Washington, D.C.: Government Printing Office, January 1988). See also Future Environment Working Group of the Commission on Integrated Long-Term Strategy, *Sources of Change in the Future Security Environment,* (Washington, D.C.: Government Printing Office, 1988); Regional Conflict Working Group of the commission, *Commitment to Freedom—Security Assistance as a U.S. Policy Instrument in the Third World,* (Washington, D.C.: Government Printing Office, 1988); and *Supporting U.S. Strategy for Third World Conflict,* (Washington, D.C.: Government Printing Office, 1988). All three working group reports bear the following notation: "The Report of the Commission on Integrated Long-Term Strategy, Discriminate Deterrence, was published in January 1988 and is available for sale by the Superintendent of Documents, U.S. Government Printing Office, Washington, D.C. 20402. Working Group reports and other separate papers which were prepared in support of the Commission on Integrated Long-Term Strategy are printed in limited numbers by the Department of Defense. There are no restrictions on further reproduction of these working group reports and other papers."

4. Ibid.

5. See, for example, Headquarters, Department of the Army, Department of the Air Force, Military Operations in Low Intensity Conflict, FM 100–20, AFM 2-XY (Final Draft), June 24, 1988.

6. National figures presented to the Commission on Integrated Long-Term Strategy for buying what U.S. departments and agencies have not yet provided for called for outlays of $12 billion per year (an amount equivalent to about 4 percent of the current DOD budget). See Regional Conflict Working Group, *Supporting U.S. Strategy for Third World Conflict,* pp. 86–87.

Chapter 8
Manpower

1. U.S. Department of Defense, *Manpower Requirements Report, FY 1987: Force Readiness Report,* February 1986, p. II-1.

2. U.S. War Department, General Staff, *Report on the Organization of the Land Forces of the United States,* Appendix III (1912), p. 12.

3. Melvin R. Laird, "Memorandum to Secretaries of Military Departments," reprinted in *Congressional Record,* September 9, 1970, p. 30968.

4. Ibid.

5. Melvin R. Laird, *Statement of the Secretary of Defense on the FY 1972–1976 Defense Program and the 1972 Defense Budget,* March 1971, p. 36.

6. James R. Schlesinger, "Readiness of Selected Reserve," Memorandum to the Secretaries of the Military Departments, August 23, 1973.

7. The draft deferment for reserve service was the rub. In 1967 a presidential commission (the Marshall commission) reported widespread favoritism in securing reserve enlistments, observed that professional football teams were preserved intact within reserve units, and protested that blacks were disproportionately underrepresented in reserve ranks. Not only were the re-

serves overwhelmingly white, they were ludicrously well educated for an enlisted force as well. By 1970, 54 percent of reserve enlistments were either college graduates or had some college; 94 percent were high school graduates. See James L. Lacy, "Military Manpower: The American Experience and the Enduring Debate," in Andrew Goodpaster, Lloyd Elliott, and J. Alan Hovey, Jr., eds., *Toward a Consensus on Military Service* (New York: Pergamon Press, 1982), pp. 37–39.

8. Quoted in Edward Philbin and James Gould, "The Guard and Reserve: In Pursuit of Full Integration," in Bennie Wilson, ed., *The Guard and Reserve in the Total Force* (Washington, D.C.: National Defense University Press, 1985), p. 50.

9. U.S. Department of Defense, *Annual Report to Congress, Fiscal Year 1989,* February 1988, p. 161.

10. Ibid.

11. Department of Defense, *Manpower Requirements Report, FY 1987,* p. I-4.

12. Department of Defense, *Annual Report, FY 1989,* p. 217.

13. Actual deployment schedules are classified, but these figures are consistent with Army testimony and have been employed by the Congressional Budget Office. See, for example, U.S. Senate, Committee on Appropriations, *Hearings on Department of Defense Appropriations for Fiscal Year 1985,* 98th Cong., 2d sess., February 9, 1984, p. 162. See also Congressional Budget Office, *Improving the Army Reserves* (Washington, D.C.: Government Printing Office, November 1985), p. 23.

14. Statement of James Webb before the U.S. Senate, Committee on Armed Services, 99th Cong., 1st sess., 1986, p. 2.

15. See, for example, "Carlucci Warns on No-Growth Budgets: U.S. Forces Abroad Would Have to Be Cut, Secretary Says," *Washington Post,* November 29, 1988, p. A8.

16. "Early Deadlines on Arms Issues," *Washington Post,* November 30, 1988, p. A8.

17. U.S. House of Representatives, Committee on Armed Services, *Report: National Defense Authorization Act for Fiscal Year 1988/1989* (Washington, D.C.: Government Printing Office, 1987), p. 186.

18. Unclassified details can be found in James L. Lacy, *Naval Reserve Forces: The Historical Experience with Involuntary Recalls* (Alexandria, VA: Center for Naval Analyses, 1986), p. 19.

19. Details of these call-ups can be found in Martin Binkin, *U.S. Reserve Forces: The Problem of the Weekend Warrior* (Washington, D.C.: Brookings Institution, 1974), pp. 41–44; Lacy, *Naval Reserve Forces,* pp. 6–20.

20. Excluded from consideration here are the increasing numbers of full-time reserve personnel, who in 1989 constitute 12 percent of the Army National Guard and 9 percent of the Army Reserve but who, because they are full time, provide little cost advantage over active-duty members.

21. U.S. Army, Army Training Board, *Enhancing Reserve Component Unit Training* (Washington, D.C.: Government Printing Office, 1987), p. 14.

22. U.S. Department of Defense, *Reserve and National Guard Capabilities,* Report to the Senate Armed Services Committee, March 19, 1984, p. 18.

Chapter 9
Obstacles to Improving the
Defense Acquisition Process

1. J. Ronald Fox, *Arming America* (Cambridge: Harvard University Press, 1974).

2. United Press International, August 28, 1988.

3. "Most Federal Workers Need Only Be Competent," *Wall Street Journal,* May 21, 1986.

4. Personal interview with General Henry A. Miley (ret.), 1987.

5. Richard J. Bednar and John T. Jones, Jr., "The Role of the DOD Contracting Officer," Report of the American Bar Association (ABA) Section of Public Contract Law, Ad Hoc Committee, John E. Cavanagh (Chair), January 11, 1987, p. 120.

6. U.S. General Accounting Office, *DOD Acquisition: Strengthening Capabilities of Key Personnel in Systems Acquisition,* GAO/NSIAD-86-45 (May 1986); *Washington Post,* June 12, 1988.

7. U.S. Senate, Committee on Armed Services, *Hearings, Defense Procurement Process,* 96th Cong., 2d sess., September 20, 1984, pt. 2, pp. 163–164.

8. U.S. Senate, Committee on Armed Services, *Hearings, Implementation of the 1984 Defense Procurement Legislation,* 99th Cong., 1st sess., October 17, 29, November 7, 13, 1985, p. 353.

9. U.S. Senate, *Hearings, Defense Procurement Process,* pt. 3, p. 36.

10. U.S. Senate, Committee on Armed Services, *Hearings, Career Paths and Professional Development for Acquisition Managers in the Department of Defense,* 98th Cong., 2d sess., December 13, 1984, pp. 27–28.

11. Richard A. Stubbing, *The Defense Game* (New York: Harper & Row, 1986), pp. 410–412.

Chapter 11
Professional Military Education

1. The total officer corps is 306,209. Warrant officers and officers whose educational achievements are unknown number 19,352. Of the remaining 286,857, 274,857 hold at least four-year baccalaureate degrees.

2. "Report of the Military Education Coordinating Conference's (MECC) Review of Senior and Intermediate Service College Curricula," January 8, 1987, p. 4.

3. Williamson Murray, "Grading the War Colleges," *National Interest* (Winter 1986–1987): 13.

4. Major General Howard D. Graves, "The U.S. Army War College: Gearing Up for the 21st Century," *Parameters* (December 1988).

5. The services' command and staff colleges similarly devote large numbers of student slots to nurses, doctors, lawyers, chaplains, dentists, and others at the expense of educating combat arms officers.

Chapter 12
The Military-Industrial Complex Revisited

1. NSC-68 was an NSC statement analyzing the Soviet threat and proposing a U.S. military buildup. A comprehensive historical overview of these buildups is given in John Lewis Gaddis, *Strategies of Containment: A Critical Appraisal of Postwar American National Security Policy* (New York: Oxford University Press, 1982). Excellent analyses of the Reagan administration's buildup are given in Richard Stubbing, "The Defense Budget," in Joseph Kruzel, ed., *American Defense Annual, 1987–1988* (Lexington, Mass.: Lexington Books, 1987), pp. 45–68; and Lawrence J. Korb and Stephen Daggett, "The Defense Budget and Strategic Planning," in Joseph Kruzel, ed., *American Defense Annual, 1988–1989* (Lexington, Mass.: Lexington Books, 1988), pp. 43–65.

2. A comprehensive historical overview of these reforms is given in Thomas L. Mc-Naugher, "Weapons Procurement: The Futility of Reform," *International Security* 12, no. 2 (Fall 1987): 63–104; and in his *New Weapons, Old Politics: America's Military Procurement Muddle* (Washington, D.C.: Brookings Institution, 1989).

3. The text of Eisenhower's account of the military-industrial complex is given and discussed in William J. Weida and Frank L. Gertcher, *The Political Economy of National Defense* (Boulder, Colo.: Westview Press, 1987), pp. 28–29.

4. The first book to use the phrase in its title seems to have been Sidney Lens, *The Military-Industrial Complex* (Philadelphia: Pilgrim Press, 1970). Several edited volumes then were published, which contained many diverse articles on the topic: Seymour Melman, ed., *The War Economy of the United States: Readings in Military Industry and Society* (New York: St. Martin's Press, 1971); Carroll W. Pursell, Jr., ed., *The Military-Industrial Complex* (New York: Harper & Row, 1972); Sam C. Sarkesian, ed., *The Military-Industrial Complex: A Reassessment* (Beverly Hills, Calif.: Sage Publications, 1972); and Steven Rosen, ed., *Testing the Theory of the Military-Industrial Complex* (Lexington, Mass.: Lexington Books, 1973). The last book includes a chapter I wrote at the time, "Aerospace Production Lines and American Defense Spending," pp. 135–156, plus a critique of my analysis by Arnold Kantor and Stuart J. Thorson, "The Weapons Procurement Process: Choosing among Competing Theories," pp. 157–196.

5. Richard A. Stubbing with Richard A. Mendel, *The Defense Game* (New York: Harper & Row, 1986); Thomas L. McNaugher, "Weapon Procurement: The Futility of Reform" and *New Weapons, Old Politics;* William B. Burrett and F.M. Scherer, "The Weapons Industry," in Walter Adams, ed., *The Structure of American Industry*, 8th ed. forthcoming. Hedrick Smith, *The Power Game: How Washington Works* (New York: Random House, 1988) also contains a useful discussion of the politics of weapons procurement, especially pp. 160–215. Four books on topics closely related to the military-industrial complex were published in 1980–1982, between the reform waves: Jacques S. Gansler, *The Defense Industry* (Cambridge, Mass.: MIT Press, 1980); Paul A.C. Koistinen, *The Military-Industrial Complex: A Historical Perspective* (New York: Praeger, 1980); Mary Kaldor, *The Baroque Arsenal* (New York: Hill and Wang, 1981); and Gordon Adams, *The Politics of Defense Contracting: The Iron Triangle* (New Brunswick, N.J.: Transaction Books, 1982). A more recent account by Gansler is his "The Weapons Procurement Process," in Joseph Kruzel, ed., *American Defense Annual, 1986–1987* (Lexington, Mass.: Lexington Books, 1986), pp. 155–170.

6. See table 2 in Burnett and Scherer, "The Weapons Industry."

7. The analysis in this section is an expansion of that given in Kurth, "Aerospace Production Lines and American Defense Spending," and in Kurth, "Why We Buy the Weapons We Do," *Foreign Policy*, no. 11 (Summer 1973): 33–56. The original analysis covered the period 1960–1973; the present analysis covers the period 1960–1988. The data are drawn primarily from the leading industry journal, *Aviation Week and Space Technology* (hereafter cited as *AWST*).

8. Gansler, *Defense Industry*, p. 180.

9. The F-111 is discussed in Robert F. Coulam, *Illusions of Choice: The F-111 and the Problem of Weapons Acquisition Reform* (Princeton, N.J.: Princeton University Press, 1977).

10. Arthur M. Schlesinger, Jr., *A Thousand Days* (Boston: Houghton Mifflin, 1965), pp. 499–500.

11. The B-1 is discussed in Nick Kotz, *Wild Blue Yonder: Money, Politics and the B-1 Bomber* (New York: Pantheon Books, 1988). Also see U.S. Congress, Congressional Budget Office, *The B-1B Bomber and Options for Enhancements* (Washington, D.C.: Government Printing Office, August 1988).

12. The B-2 is discussed in Malcolm W. Browne, "Will the Stealth Bomber Work?" *New York Times Magazine*, July 17, 1988, pp. 25–31.

13. The C-5B and C-17 are discussed in Stubbing, *Defense Game,* pp. 31–40.

14. *AWST,* July 25, 1988, p. 22.

15. Ibid., June 27, 1988, p. 16.

16. Ibid., July 18, 1988, p. 20.

17. Ibid., November 7, 1988, p. 18. The F-111 and commonality are discussed in Coulam, *Illusions of Choice.*

18. *AWST,* August 29, 1988, p. 36.

19. Ibid., July 18, 1988, p. 20.

20. On the completion of the C-5A and its impact on Lockheed-Georgia, see ibid., March 28, 1988, pp. 36–47.

21. Ibid., November 7, 1988, p. 18.

22. Ibid.

23. Accounts of the rise in unit costs and the decline in numbers procured are given in James Fallows, *National Defense* (New York: Random House, 1981); and Burnett and Scherer, "The Weapons Industry."

24. Historical statistics for federal defense and nondefense spending as a percentage of GNP are given in "Federal Government Finances: 1983 Budget Data," compiled by U.S. Office of Management and Budget, Budget Review Division, Fiscal Analysis Branch (Washington, D.C.: Government Printing Office, February 1982), esp. table 12, pp. 71–75.

25. James R. Kurth, "The Political Consequences of the Product Cycle: Industrial History and Political Outcomes," *International Organization* 33, no. 1 (Winter 1979): 1–34; and Kurth, "Military Power and Industrial Competitiveness: The Industrial Dimension of Military Strategy," *Naval War College Review* 35, no. 5 (September–October 1982): 33–47.

26. David P. Calleo, *Beyond American Hegemony: The Future of the Atlantic Alliance* (New York: Basic Books, 1987), pt. II.

27. The current situation in regard to engineers in the United States is reviewed comprehensively in a special issue of *AWST,* December 5, 1988, pp. 36–67.

28. A comprehensive case for these reform proposals is given in Fallows, *National Defense;* also see Pierre Sprey, "The Case for Better and Cheaper Weapons," in Asa A. Clark IV et al., *The Defense Reform Debate: Issues and Analysis* (Baltimore: John Hopkins University Press, 1984), pp. 193–208.

29. One version of competitive strategies is proposed in *Discriminate Deterrence,* Report of the Commission on Integrated Long-Term Strategy (Washington, D.C.: U.S. Government Printing Office, January 1988). A comprehensive case for precision-guide munitions is given in John J. Mearsheimer, *Conventional Deterrence* (Ithaca: Cornell University Press, 1983), chap. 7.

30. *AWST,* March 21, 1988, p. 17.

Appendix A

1. Unless otherwise indicated, all quoted material in this appendix is from the FY 1990 DOD *Annual Report to the Congress* (Washington, D.C.: U.S. Government Printing Office, 1989).

2. Edward Luttwak, *The Pentagon and the Art of War* (New York: Simon and Schuster, 1984), p. 69.

3. *New York Times,* January 19, 1989, p. 23.

Index

About the
Contributors

Gordon Adams is the director of the Defense Budget Project at the Center on Budget and Policy Priorities in Washington, D.C. He has served as an adviser on defense budget and policy issues and has authored several major Defense Budget Project Reports.

Kenneth L. Adelman served as director of the U.S. Arms Control and Disarmament Agency from 1983 to 1987. Prior to that time he served as deputy permanent representative to the United Nations and as assistant to the secretary of defense. He is a nationally syndicated columnist and vice-president of the Institute for Contemporary Studies, and he teaches at the Johns Hopkins School of Advanced International Studies.

Stephen Alexis Cain is senior budget analyst for the Defense Budget Project at the Center on Budget and Policy Priorities. He has done research and analysis at the Center for Defense Information and the Center for Population Options and is the author of two major Defense Budget Project reports.

Eliot A. Cohen is Secretary of the Navy Senior Research Fellow at the U.S. Naval War College and a professor and former acting chairman of the Department of Strategy at the war college. He is a visiting professor of government at Harvard University and consultant to various government agencies. The author of two books and several dozen articles, he is completing two coauthored books on operational failure in war and net assessment.

J. Ronald Fox is Tiampo Professor of Business Administration and senior associate dean for faculty development in the Graduate School of Business Administration at Harvard University. He served with the Armed Forces Special Weapons Project as a nuclear specialist and was subsequently the project manager for the design and pilot test of the cost planning and control system on the Navy's Polaris program. Dr. Fox is the author of several books and articles, including *The Defense Management Challenge: Weapons Acquisition* and *Arming America: How the U.S. Buys Weapons.*

James L. George is an adjunct fellow at the Hudson Institute. He graduated from the U.S. Naval Academy in 1961, and is a four-time winner of the U.S. Naval Institute's Arleigh Burke essay contest. He served as an assistant director of the Arms Control and Disarmament Agency. Mr. George has published a large number of books and papers on arms control and naval affairs.

Paul F. Gorman served in the Army for forty years and retired in 1985 at the rank of general. His final assignment was commander in chief, U.S. Southern Command. He has been the director of planning for the Joint Chiefs of Staff, assistant to two chairmen of the JCS, a national intelligence officer, and a member of the U.S. delegation at the U.S.-Vietnamese talks in Paris. Since retiring, he has served with the Packard Commission on Defense Management, the Commission on Organized Crime, and the Commission on Integrated Long-Term Strategy.

James R. Kurth is professor of political science at Swarthmore College. He has taught at Harvard University and the U.S. Naval War College, where he worked on the development of the maritime strategy for which he received the Navy Medal for Meritorious Civilian Service. His professional publications have focused on American foreign and defense policies, and particularly on the political and economic sources of these policies.

James L. Lacy is a senior policy analyst for national and international security at the RAND Corporation. He spent five years as a senior strategic analyst at the Center for Naval Analyses. He was a senior research fellow at the National Defense University and a special assistant for manpower and reserve affairs in the Department of Defense. Mr. Lacy is the author of a number of publications on conventional forces, arms control, and U.S. military personnel.

Jan M. Lodal is president of Intelus, a computer systems company in Rockville, Maryland. Mr. Lodal previously served as a systems analyst in the Pentagon and as deputy of program analysis on the National Security Council staff under former Secretary of State Henry A. Kissinger. Mr. Lodal is a member of several government and private advisory panels on national security subjects and has published numerous articles on arms control and national defense topics.

Edward N. Luttwak holds the Arleigh A. Burke Chair of Strategy, Center for Strategic and International Studies, Washington, D.C. He has been a consultant to the U.S. Department of State, the U.S. Department of Defense, and allied governments. He is the author of a number of books and articles, including *The Grand Strategy of the Roman Empire, The Pentagon and the Art of War,* and *Strategy: The Logic of War and Peace.*

Allan R. Millett has been a professor of history at the Ohio State University since 1969 and is associate director of the Mershon Center. He served in the U.S. Marine Corps and is a colonel in the Marine reserves. Dr. Millett is the author of a number of books on the history of American military policy and institutions, including *For the Common Defense: A Military History of the United States of America, 1607–1983.* He also coedited the three-volume set *Military Effectiveness.*

Williamson Murray is a professor of history at the Ohio State University and a lieutenant colonel in the U.S. Air Force Reserve. Dr. Murray has taught at Yale University, West Point, the Naval War College, and the Air War College. He is the author of a number of books and articles on the history of military affairs in Europe, including *Luftwaffe,* and he coedited the three-volume set *Military Effectiveness.*

About the Editor

Joseph Kruzel is acting director of the Mershon Center and associate professor of political science at The Ohio State University. He served as a member of the U.S. delegation to SALT I and as a consultant to the U.S. Senate and the Department of Defense. Professor Kruzel taught previously at Harvard and Duke universities. He has written and lectured extensively on arms control and U.S. defense strategy.